World Order

ALSO BY Henry Kissinger

World Order

Henry Kissinger

PENGUIN PRESS | *New York* | 2014

PENGUIN PRESS
Published by the Penguin Group
Penguin Group (USA) LLC
375 Hudson Street
New York, New York 10014

USA · Canada · UK · Ireland · Australia
New Zealand · India · South Africa · China

penguin.com
A Penguin Random House Company

First published by Penguin Press,
a member of Penguin Group (USA) LLC, 2014

ISBN 978-1-59420-614-6

Printed in the United States of America
1   3   5   7   9   10   8   6   4   2

DESIGNED BY MARYSARAH QUINN
INTERIOR MAPS BY JEFFREY L. WARD

To Nancy

Contents

World Order

The Question of World Order

I N 1961, as a young academic, I called on President Harry S. Truman when I found myself in Kansas City delivering a speech. To the question of what in his presidency had made him most proud, Truman replied, "That we totally defeated our enemies and then brought them back to the community of nations. I would like to think that only America would have done this." Conscious of America's vast power, Truman took pride above all in its humane and democratic values. He wanted to be remembered not so much for America's victories as for its conciliations.

All of Truman's successors have followed some version of this narrative and have taken pride in similar attributes of the American experience. And for most of this period, the community of nations that they aimed to uphold reflected an American consensus—an inexorably expanding cooperative order of states observing common rules and norms, embracing liberal economic systems, forswearing territorial conquest, respecting national sovereignty, and adopting participatory and democratic systems of governance. American presidents of both parties have continued to urge other governments, often with great vehemence and eloquence, to embrace the preservation and enhancement of human rights. In many instances, the defense of these values by the United States and its allies has ushered in important changes in the human condition.

Yet today this "rules-based" system faces challenges. The frequent exhortations for countries to "do their fair share," play by "twenty-first-century rules," or be "responsible stakeholders" in a common system reflect the fact that there is no shared definition of the system or understanding of what a "fair" contribution would be. Outside the Western world, regions that have played a minimal role in these rules' original formulation question their validity in their present form and have made clear that they would work to modify them. Thus while "the international community" is invoked perhaps more insistently now than in any other era, it presents no clear or agreed set of goals, methods, or limits.

Our age is insistently, at times almost desperately, in pursuit of a concept of world order. Chaos threatens side by side with unprecedented interdependence: in the spread of weapons of mass destruction, the disintegration of states, the impact of environmental depredations, the persistence of genocidal practices, and the spread of new technologies threatening to drive conflict beyond human control or comprehension. New methods of accessing and communicating information unite regions as never before and project events globally—but in a manner that inhibits reflection, demanding of leaders that they register instantaneous reactions in a form expressible in slogans. Are we facing a period in which forces beyond the restraints of any order determine the future?

Varieties of World Order

No truly global "world order" has ever existed. What passes for order in our time was devised in Western Europe nearly four centuries ago, at a peace conference in the German region of Westphalia, conducted without the involvement or even the awareness of most other continents or civilizations. A century of sectarian conflict and political upheaval across Central Europe had culminated in the Thirty Years' War of 1618–48—a conflagration in which political and religious disputes commingled, combatants resorted to "total war" against population centers, and nearly a quarter of the population of Central Europe died from combat, disease, or starvation. The exhausted participants met to define a set of arrangements that would stanch the bloodletting. Religious unity had fractured with the survival and spread of Protestantism; political diversity was inherent in the number of autonomous political units that had fought to a draw. So it was that in Europe the conditions of the contemporary world were approximated: a multiplicity of political units, none powerful enough to defeat all others, many adhering to contradictory philosophies and internal practices, in search of neutral rules to regulate their conduct and mitigate conflict.

The Westphalian peace reflected a practical accommodation to reality, not a unique moral insight. It relied on a system of independent states refraining from interference in each other's domestic affairs and checking each other's ambitions through a general equilibrium of power. No single claim to truth or universal rule had prevailed in Europe's contests. Instead, each state was assigned the attribute of sovereign power over its territory. Each would acknowledge the domestic structures and religious vocations of its fellow states as realities and refrain from challenging their existence. With a balance of power now perceived as natural and desirable, the ambitions of rulers would be set in counterpoise against each other, at least in theory curtailing the scope of conflicts. Division and multiplicity, an accident of Europe's history, became the hallmarks of a new system of international order with its own distinct philosophical outlook. In this sense the European effort to end its conflagration shaped and prefigured the modern sensibility: it reserved judgment on the absolute in favor of the practical and ecumenical; it sought to distill order from multiplicity and restraint.

The seventeenth-century negotiators who crafted the Peace of Westphalia did not think they were laying the foundation for a globally applicable system. They made no attempt to include neighboring Russia, which was then reconsolidating its own order after the nightmarish "Time of Troubles" by enshrining principles distinctly at odds with Westphalian balance: a single absolute ruler, a unified religious orthodoxy, and a program of territorial expansion in all directions. Nor did the other major power centers regard the Westphalian settlement (to the extent they learned of it at all) as relevant to their own regions.

The idea of world order was applied to the geographic extent known to the statesmen of the time—a pattern repeated in other regions. This was largely because the then-prevailing technology did not encourage or even permit the operation of a single global system. With no means of interacting with each other on a sustained basis and no framework for measuring the power of one region against another, each region viewed its own order as unique and defined the others as "barbarians"—governed in a manner incomprehensible to the established system and irrelevant to its designs except as a threat. Each defined itself as a template for the legitimate organization of all humanity, imagining that in governing what lay before it, it was ordering the world.

At the opposite end of the Eurasian landmass from Europe, China was the center of its own hierarchical and theoretically universal concept of order. This system had operated for millennia—it had been in place when the Roman Empire governed Europe as a unity—basing itself not on the sovereign equality of states but on the presumed boundlessness of the Emperor's reach. In this concept, sovereignty in the European sense did not exist, because the Emperor held sway over

"All Under Heaven." He was the pinnacle of a political and cultural hierarchy, distinct and universal, radiating from the center of the world in the Chinese capital outward to all the rest of humankind. The latter were classified as various degrees of barbarians depending in part on their mastery of Chinese writing and cultural institutions (a cosmography that endured well into the modern era). China, in this view, would order the world primarily by awing other societies with its cultural magnificence and economic bounty, drawing them into relationships that could be managed to produce the aim of "harmony under heaven."

In much of the region between Europe and China, Islam's different universal concept of world order held sway, with its own vision of a single divinely sanctioned governance uniting and pacifying the world. In the seventh century, Islam had launched itself across three continents in an unprecedented wave of religious exaltation and imperial expansion. After unifying the Arab world, taking over remnants of the Roman Empire, and subsuming the Persian Empire, Islam came to govern the Middle East, North Africa, large swaths of Asia, and portions of Europe. Its version of universal order considered Islam destined to expand over the "realm of war," as it called all regions populated by unbelievers, until the whole world was a unitary system brought into harmony by the message of the Prophet Muhammad. As Europe built its multistate order, the Turkish-based Ottoman Empire revived this claim to a single legitimate governance and spread its supremacy through the Arab heartland, the Mediterranean, the Balkans, and Eastern Europe. It was aware of Europe's nascent interstate order; it considered it not a model but a source of division to be exploited for westward Ottoman expansion. As Sultan Mehmed the Conqueror admonished the Italian city-states practicing an early version of multipolarity in the fifteenth century, "You are 20 states . . . you are in disagreement among yourselves . . . There must be only one empire, one faith, and one sovereignty in the world."

Meanwhile, across the Atlantic the foundations of a distinct vision of world order were being laid in the "New World." As Europe's seventeenth-century political and sectarian conflicts raged, Puritan settlers had set out to redeem God's plan with an "errand in the wilderness" that would free them from adherence to established (and in their view corrupted) structures of authority. There they would build, as Governor John Winthrop preached in 1630 aboard a ship bound for the Massachusetts settlement, a "city upon a hill," inspiring the world through the justness of its principles and the power of its example. In the American view of world order, peace and balance would occur naturally, and ancient enmities would be set aside—once other nations were given the same principled say in their own governance that Americans had in theirs. The task of foreign policy was thus not so much the pursuit of a specifically American interest as the cultivation of shared principles. In time, the United States would become the indispensable defender of the order Europe designed. Yet even as the United States lent its weight to the effort, an ambivalence endured— for the American vision rested not on an embrace of the European balance-of-power system but on the achievement of peace through the spread of democratic principles.

Of all these concepts of order, Westphalian principles are, at this writing, the sole generally recognized basis of what exists of a world order. The Westphalian system spread around the world as the framework for a state-based international order spanning multiple civilizations and regions because, as the European nations expanded, they carried the blueprint of their international order with them. While they often neglected to apply concepts of sovereignty to the colonies and colonized peoples, when these peoples began to demand their independence, they did so in the name of Westphalian concepts. The principles of national independence, sovereign statehood, national interest, and noninterference proved effective arguments against the colonizers themselves during the struggles for independence and protection for their newly formed states afterward.

The contemporary, now global Westphalian system—what colloquially is called the world community—has striven to curtail the anarchical nature of the world with an extensive network of international legal and organizational structures designed to foster open trade and a stable international financial system, establish accepted principles of resolving international disputes, and set limits on the conduct of wars when they do occur. This system of states now encompasses every culture and region. Its institutions have provided the neutral framework for the interactions of diverse societies—to a large extent independent of their respective values.

Yet Westphalian principles are being challenged on all sides, sometimes in the name of world order itself. Europe has set out to depart from the state system it designed and to transcend it through a concept of pooled sovereignty. And ironically, though Europe invented the balance-of-power concept, it has consciously and severely limited the element of power in its new institutions. Having downgraded its military capacities, Europe has little scope to respond when universal norms are flouted.

In the Middle East, jihadists on both sides of the Sunni-Shia divide tear at societies and dismantle states in quest of visions of global revolution based on the fundamentalist version of their religion. The state itself—as well as the regional system based on it—is in jeopardy, assaulted by ideologies rejecting its constraints as illegitimate and by terrorist militias that, in several countries, are stronger than the armed forces of the government.

Asia, in some ways the most strikingly successful of the regions to adopt concepts of sovereign statehood, still recalls alternative concepts of order with nostalgia and churns with rivalries and historical claims of the kind that dashed Europe's order a century ago. Nearly every country considers itself to be "rising," driving disagreements to the edge of confrontation.

The United States has alternated between defending the Westphalian system and castigating its premises of balance of power and non-interference in domestic affairs as immoral and outmoded, and sometimes both at once. It continues to assert the universal relevance of its values in building a peaceful world order and reserves the right to support them globally. Yet after withdrawing from three wars in two generations—each begun with idealistic aspirations and widespread public support but ending in national trauma—America struggles to define the relationship between its power (still vast) and its principles.

All of the major centers of power practice elements of Westphalian order to some degree, but none considers itself the natural defender of the system. All are undergoing significant internal shifts. Can regions with such divergent cultures, histories, and traditional theories of order vindicate the legitimacy of any common system?

Success in such an effort will require an approach that respects both the multifariousness of the human condition and the ingrained human quest for freedom. Order in this sense must be cultivated; it cannot be imposed. This is particularly so in an age of instantaneous communication and revolutionary political flux. Any system of world order, to be sustainable, must be accepted as just—not only by leaders, but also by citizens. It must reflect two truths: order without freedom, even if sustained by momentary exaltation, eventually creates its own counterpoise; yet freedom cannot be secured or sustained without a framework of order to keep the peace. Order and freedom, sometimes described as opposite poles on the spectrum of experience, should instead be understood as interdependent. Can today's leaders rise above the urgency of day-to-day events to achieve this balance?

Legitimacy and Power

An answer to these questions must deal with three levels of order. World order describes the concept held by a region or civilization about the nature of just arrangements and the distribution of power thought to be applicable to the entire world. An international order is the practical application of these concepts to a substantial part of the globe—large enough to affect the global balance of power. Regional orders involve the same principles applied to a defined geographic area.

Any one of these systems of order bases itself on two components: a set of commonly accepted rules that define the limits of permissible action and a balance of power that enforces restraint where rules break down, preventing one political unit from subjugating all others. A consensus on the legitimacy of existing arrangements does not—now or in the past—foreclose competitions or confrontations, but it helps ensure that they will occur as adjustments within the existing order rather than as fundamental challenges to it. A balance of forces does not in itself secure peace, but if thoughtfully assembled and invoked, it can limit the scope and frequency of fundamental challenges and curtail their chance of succeeding when they do occur.

No book can hope to address every historic approach to international order or every country now active in shaping world affairs. This volume attempts to deal with the regions whose concepts of order have most shaped the evolution of the modern era.

The balance between legitimacy and power is extremely complex; the smaller the geographic area to which it applies and the more coherent the cultural convictions within it, the easier it is to distill a workable consensus. But in the modern world the need is for a global world order. An array of entities unrelated to each other by history or values (except at arm's length), and defining themselves essentially by the limit of their capabilities, is likely to generate conflict, not order.

During my first visit to Beijing, undertaken in 1971 to reestablish contact with China after two decades of hostility, I mentioned that to the American delegation, China was a "land of mystery." Premier Zhou Enlai responded, "You will find it not mysterious. When you have become familiar with it, it will not seem so mysterious as before." There were 900 million Chinese, he observed, and it seemed perfectly normal to them. In our time, the quest for world order will require relating the perceptions of societies whose realities have largely been self-contained. The mystery to be overcome is one all peoples share—how divergent historic experiences and values can be shaped into a common order.

CHAPTER I

Europe: The Pluralistic International Order

The Uniqueness of the European Order

The history of most civilizations is a tale of the rise and fall of empires. Order was established by their internal governance, not through an equilibrium among states: strong when the central authority was cohesive, more haphazard under weaker rulers. In imperial systems, wars generally took place at the frontiers of the empire or as civil wars. Peace was identified with the reach of imperial power.

In China and Islam, political contests were fought for control of an established framework of order. Dynasties changed, but each new ruling group portrayed itself as restoring a legitimate system that had fallen into disrepair. In Europe, no such evolution took hold. With the end of Roman rule, pluralism became the defining characteristic of the European order. The idea of Europe loomed as a geographic designation, as an expression of Christianity or of court society, or as the center of enlightenment of a community of the educated and of modernity. Yet although it was comprehensible as a single civilization, Europe never had a single governance, or a united, fixed identity. It changed the principles in the name of which its various units governed themselves at frequent intervals, experimenting with a new concept of political legitimacy or international order.

In other regions of the world, a period of competing rulers came by posterity to be regarded as a "time of troubles," a civil war, or a "warlord period"—a lamented interlude of disunity that had been transcended. Europe thrived on fragmentation and embraced its own divisions. Distinct competing dynasties and nationalities were perceived not as a form of "chaos" to be expunged but, in the idealized view of Europe's statesmen—sometimes conscious, sometimes not—as an intricate mechanism tending toward a balance that preserved each people's interests, integrity, and autonomy. For more than a thousand years, in the mainstream of modern European statecraft order has derived from equilibrium, and identity from resistance to universal rule. It is not that European monarchs were more immune to the glories of conquest than their counterparts in other civilizations or more committed to an ideal of diversity in the abstract. Rather, they lacked the strength to impose their will on each other decisively. In time, pluralism took on the characteristics of a model of world order. Has Europe in our time transcended this pluralistic tendency—or do the internal struggles of the European Union affirm it?

For five hundred years, Rome's imperial rule had ensured a single set of laws, a common defense, and an extraordinary level of civilization. With the fall of Rome, conventionally dated in 476, the empire disintegrated. In what historians have called the Dark Ages, nostalgia for the lost universality flourished. The vision of harmony and unity focused increasingly on the Church. In that worldview, Christendom was a single society administered by two complementary authorities: civil government, the "successors of Caesar" maintaining order in the temporal sphere; and the Church, the successors of Peter tending to universal and absolute principles of salvation. Augustine of Hippo, writing in North Africa as Roman rule crumbled, theologically concluded that temporal political authority was legitimate to the extent that it furthered the pursuit of a God-fearing life and with it man's salvation. "There are two systems," Pope Gelasius I wrote to the Byzantine Emperor Anastasius in A.D. 494, "under which this world is governed, the sacred authority of the priests and the royal power. Of these, the greater weight is with the priests in so far as they will answer to the Lord, even for kings, in the Last Judgment." The real world order was in this sense not in this world.

This all-encompassing concept of world order had to contend with an anomaly from the start: in the post–Roman Europe, dozens of political rulers exercised sovereignty with no clear hierarchy among them; all invoked fealty to Christ, but their link to the Church and its authority was ambiguous. Fierce debates attended the delineation of Church authority, while kingdoms with separate militaries and independent policies maneuvered for advantage in a manner that bore no apparent relationship to Augustine's *City of God*.

Aspirations to unity were briefly realized on Christmas Day 800, when Pope Leo III crowned Charlemagne, the Frankish King and conqueror of much of present-day France and Germany, as *Imperator Romanorum* (Emperor of the Romans), and awarded him theoretical title to the former eastern half of the erstwhile Roman Empire, at that point the lands of Byzantium. The Emperor pledged to the Pope "to defend on all sides the holy church of Christ from pagan incursion and infidel devastation abroad, and within to add strength to the Catholic faith by our recognition of it."

But Charlemagne's empire did not fulfill its aspirations: in fact it began to crumble almost as soon as it was inaugurated. Charlemagne, beset by tasks closer to home, never attempted to rule the lands of the erstwhile Eastern Roman Empire the Pope had allotted him. In the west, he made little progress in recapturing Spain from its Moorish conquerors. After Charlemagne's death, his successors sought to reinforce his position by appeal to tradition, by naming his possessions the

Holy Roman Empire. But debilitated by civil wars, less than a century after its founding, Charlemagne's empire passed from the scene as a coherent political entity (though its name remained in use throughout a shifting series of territories until 1806).

China had its Emperor; Islam had its Caliph—the recognized leader of the lands of Islam. Europe had the Holy Roman Emperor. But the Holy Roman Emperor operated from a much weaker base than his confreres in other civilizations. He had no imperial bureaucracy at his disposal. His authority depended on his strength in the regions he governed in his dynastic capacity, essentially his family holdings. His position was not formally hereditary and depended on election by a franchise of seven, later nine, princes; these elections were generally decided by a mixture of political maneuvering, assessments of religious piety, and vast financial payoffs. The Emperor theoretically owed his authority to his investiture by the Pope, but political and logistical considerations often excluded it, leaving him to rule for years as "Emperor-Elect." Religion and politics never merged into a single construct, leading to Voltaire's truthful jest that the Holy Roman Empire was "neither Holy, nor Roman, nor an Empire." Medieval Europe's concept of international order reflected a case-by-case accommodation between the Pope and the Emperor and a host of other feudal rulers. A universal order based on the possibility of a single reign and a single set of legitimating principles was increasingly drained of any practicality.

A full flowering of the medieval concept of world order was envisioned only briefly with the rise of the sixteenth-century Habsburg prince Charles (1500–1558); his rule also ushered in its irrevocable decay. The stern and pious Flemish-born prince was born to rule; except for a widely noted taste for spiced food, he was generally perceived to be without vices and immune to distraction. He inherited the crown of the Netherlands as a child and that of Spain—with its vast and expanding array of colonies in Asia and the Americas—at sixteen.

Shortly after, in 1519, he prevailed in the election for the post of Holy Roman Emperor, making him Charlemagne's formal successor. The coincidence of these titles meant that the medieval vision seemed poised to be fulfilled. A single, pious ruler now governed territories approximately equivalent to today's Austria, Germany, northern Italy, Czech Republic, Slovakia, Hungary, eastern France, Belgium, Netherlands, Spain, and much of the Americas. (This massive agglomeration of political power was accomplished almost entirely through strategic marriages and gave rise to the Habsburg saying "Bella gerant alii; tu, felix Austria, nube!"—"Leave the waging of wars to others; you, happy Austria, marry!") Spanish explorers and conquistadores—Magellan and Cortés sailed under Charles's auspices—were in the process of destroying the ancient empires of the Americas and carrying the sacraments together with European political power across the New World. Charles's armies and navies were engaged in the defense of Christendom against a new wave of invasions, by the Ottoman Turks and their surrogates in southeastern Europe and North Africa. Charles personally led a counterattack in Tunisia, with a fleet funded by gold from the New World. Caught up in these heady developments, Charles was hailed by his contemporaries as the "greatest emperor since the division of the empire in 843," destined to return the world to "a single shepherd."

In the tradition of Charlemagne, at his coronation Charles vowed to be "the protector and defender of the Holy Roman Church," and crowds paid him obeisance as "Caesare" and "Imperio"; Pope Clement affirmed Charles as the temporal force for "seeing peace and order reestablished" in Christendom.

A Chinese or Turkish visitor to Europe at that time might well have perceived a seemingly familiar political system: a continent presided over by a single dynasty imbued with a sense of divine mandate. If Charles had been able to consolidate his authority and manage an orderly succession in the vast Habsburg territorial conglomerate,

Europe would have been shaped by a dominant central authority like the Chinese Empire or the Islamic caliphate.

It did not happen; nor did Charles try. In the end, he was satisfied to base order on equilibrium. Hegemony might be his inheritance but not his objective, as he proved when, after capturing his temporal political rival the French King Francis I in the Battle of Pavia in 1525, he released him—freeing France to resume a separate and adversarial foreign policy at the heart of Europe. The French King repudiated Charles's grand gesture by taking the remarkable step—so at odds with the medieval concept of Christian statecraft—of proposing military cooperation to the Ottoman Sultan Suleiman, who was then invading Eastern Europe and challenging Habsburg power from the east.

The universality of the Church Charles sought to vindicate was not to be had. He proved unable to prevent the new doctrine of Protestantism from spreading through the lands that were the principal base of his power. Both religious and political unity were fracturing. The effort to fulfill his aspirations inherent in his office was beyond the capabilities of a single individual. A haunting portrait by Titian from 1548 at Munich's Alte Pinakothek reveals the torment of an eminence who cannot reach spiritual fulfillment or manipulate the, to him, ultimately secondary levers of hegemonic rule. Charles resolved to abdicate his dynastic titles and divide his vast empire, and did so in a manner reflecting the pluralism that had defeated his quest for unity. To his son Philip, he bequeathed the Kingdom of Naples and Sicily, then the crown of Spain and its global empire. In an emotional 1555 ceremony in Brussels, he reviewed the record of his reign, attested to the diligence with which he had fulfilled his duties, and in the process handed the States-General of the Netherlands to Philip as well. The same year, Charles concluded a landmark treaty, the Peace of Augsburg, which recognized Protestantism within the Holy Roman Empire. Abandoning the spiritual foundation of his empire, Charles afforded princes the right to choose the confessional orientation of their territory. Shortly afterward, he resigned his title as Holy Roman Emperor, passing responsibility for the empire, its upheavals, and its external challenges to his brother Ferdinand. Charles retired to a monastery in a rural region of Spain, to a life of seclusion. He spent his last days in the company of his confessor and of an Italian clock maker, whose works lined the walls and whose trade Charles attempted to learn. When Charles died in 1558, his will expressed regret for the fracturing of doctrine that had taken place during his reign and charged his son to redouble the Inquisition.

Three events completed the disintegration of the old ideal of unity. By the time Charles V died, revolutionary changes had raised Europe's sights from a regional to a global enterprise while fragmenting the medieval political and religious order: the beginning of the age of discovery, the invention of printing, and the schism in the Church.

A map depicting the universe, as comprehended by educated Europeans in the medieval age, would have shown Northern and Southern Hemispheres stretching from India in the east to Iberia and the islands of Britain in the west, with Jerusalem in the center. In the medieval perception, this was not a map for travelers but a stage divinely ordained for the drama of human redemption. The world, it was believed on biblical authority, was six-sevenths land and one-seventh water. Because the principles of salvation were fixed and could be cultivated through efforts in the lands known to Christendom, there was no reward for venturing past the fringes of civilization. In the *Inferno,* Dante described Ulysses' sailing out through the Pillars of Hercules (the Rock of Gibraltar and the adjacent heights of North Africa, at the western edge of the Mediterranean Sea) in search of knowledge, and being punished for his transgression against God's plan by a whirlwind that dooms his ship and all its crew.

The modern era announced itself when enterprising societies sought glory and wealth by exploring the oceans and whatever lay beyond them. In the fifteenth century, Europe and China ventured forth almost contemporaneously. Chinese ships, then the world's largest and technologically most advanced, undertook journeys of exploration reaching Southeast Asia, India, and the east coast of Africa. They exchanged presents with local dignitaries, enrolled princes in China's imperial "tribute system," and brought home with them cultural and zoological curiosities. Yet following the head navigator Zheng He's death in 1433, the Chinese Emperor put an end to overseas adventures, and the fleet was abandoned. China continued to insist on the universal relevance of its principles of world order, but it would henceforth cultivate them at home and with the peoples along its borders. It never again attempted a comparable naval effort—until perhaps our own time.

Sixty years later, the European powers sailed from a continent of competing sovereign authorities; each monarch sponsored naval exploration largely in the hope of achieving a commercial or strategic edge over his rivals. Portuguese, Dutch, and English ships ventured to India; Spanish and English ships journeyed to the Western Hemisphere. Both began to displace the existing trade monopolies and political structures. The age of three centuries of preponderant European influence in world affairs had been launched. International relations, once a regional enterprise, would henceforth be geographically global, with the center of gravity in Europe, in which the concept of world order was defined and its implementation determined.

A revolution of thinking about the nature of the political universe followed. How was one to conceive of the inhabitants of regions no one had known existed? How did they fit into the medieval cosmology of empire and papacy? A council of theologians summoned by Charles V in 1550–51 in the Spanish city of Valladolid had concluded that the people living in the Western Hemisphere were human beings with souls—hence eligible for salvation. This theological conclusion was, of course, also a maxim justifying conquest and conversion. Europeans were enabled to increase their wealth and salve their consciences simultaneously. Their global competition for territorial control changed the nature of international order. Europe's perspective expanded—until successive colonial efforts by various European states covered most of the globe and concepts of world order merged with the operation of the balance of power in Europe.

The second seminal event was the invention of movable-type printing in the middle of the fifteenth century, which made it possible to share knowledge on a hitherto-unimaginable scale. Medieval society had stored knowledge by memorizing or laboriously hand-copying religious texts or by understanding history through epic poetry. In the age of exploration, what was being discovered needed to be understood, and printing permitted accounts to be disseminated. The exploration of new worlds inspired as well a quest to rediscover the ancient world and its verities, with special emphasis on the centrality of the individual. The growing embrace of reason as an objective force of illumination and explication began to shake existing institutions, including the hitherto-unassailable Catholic Church.

The third revolutionary upheaval, that of the Protestant Reformation, was initiated when Martin Luther posted ninety-five theses on the door of the Wittenberg Castle Church in 1517, insisting on the individual's direct relationship with God; hence individual conscience—not established orthodoxy—was put forward as the key to salvation. A number of feudal rulers seized the opportunity to enhance their authority by embracing Protestantism, imposing it on their populations, and enriching themselves by seizing Church lands. Each side regarded the other as heretical, and disagreements turned into life-or-death struggles as political and sectarian disputes commingled. The barrier separating domestic and foreign disputes collapsed as sovereigns backed rival factions in their neighbors' domestic, often bloody, religious struggles. The Protestant Reformation destroyed the concept of a world order sustained by the "two swords" of papacy and empire. Christianity was split and at war with itself.

The Thirty Years' War: What Is Legitimacy?

A century of intermittent wars attended the rise and spread of the Protestant critique of Church supremacy: the Habsburg Empire and the papacy both sought to stamp out the challenge to their authority, and Protestants resisted in defense of their new faith.

The period labeled by posterity as the Thirty Years' War (1618–48) brought this turmoil to a climax. With an imperial succession looming and the Catholic King of Bohemia, the Habsburg Ferdinand, emerging as the most plausible candidate, the Protestant Bohemian nobility attempted an act of "regime change," offering their crown—and its decisive electoral vote—to a Protestant German prince, an outcome in which the Holy Roman Empire would have ceased to be a Catholic institution. Imperial forces moved to crush the Bohemian rebellion and then pressed their advantage against Protestantism generally, triggering a war that devastated Central Europe. (The Protestant princes were generally located in the north of Germany, including the then relatively insignificant Prussia; the Catholic heartland was the south of Germany and Austria.)

In theory, the Emperor's fellow Catholic sovereigns were obliged to unite in opposition to the new heresies. Yet faced with a choice between spiritual unity and strategic advantage, more than a few chose the latter. Foremost among them was France.

In a period of general upheaval, a country that maintains domestic authority is in a position to exploit chaos in neighboring states for larger international objectives. A cadre of sophisticated and ruthless French ministers saw their opportunity and moved decisively. The Kingdom of France began the process by giving itself a new governance. In feudal systems, authority was personal; governance reflected the ruler's will but was also circumscribed by tradition, limiting the resources available for a country's national or international actions. France's chief minister from 1624 to 1642, Armand-Jean du Plessis, Cardinal de Richelieu, was the first statesman to overcome these limitations.

A man of the cloth steeped in court intrigue, Richelieu was well adapted to a period of religious upheaval and crumbling established structures. As the youngest of three sons from a minor noble family, he embarked on a military career but then switched to theology after his brother's unexpected resignation from the bishopric of Luçon, considered a family birthright. Lore holds that Richelieu completed his religious studies so swiftly that he was below the normal minimum age for a clerical appointment; he resolved this obstacle by traveling to Rome and personally lying to the Pope about his age. His credentials obtained, he launched himself into factional politics at the French royal court, becoming first a close aide to the queen mother, Marie de' Medici, and then a trusted advisor to her chief political rival, her minor son King Louis XIII. Both evinced a strong distrust of Richelieu, but wracked by internal conflicts with France's Huguenot Protestants, they could not bring themselves to forgo his political and administrative genius. The young cleric's mediation between these contending royals won him a recommendation to Rome for a cardinal's hat; when given it, he became the highest-ranking member of the King's privy council. Maintaining the role for nearly two decades, the "red eminence" (so called because of his flowing red cardinal's robes) became France's chief minister, the power behind the throne, and the charting genius of a new concept of centralized statecraft and foreign policy based on the balance of power.

When Richelieu conducted the policies of his country, Machiavelli's treatises on statesmanship circulated. It is not known whether Richelieu was familiar with these texts on the politics of power. He surely practiced their essential principles. Richelieu developed a radical approach to international order. He invented the idea that the state was an abstract and permanent entity existing in its own right. Its requirements were not determined by the ruler's personality, family interests, or the universal demands of religion. Its lodestar was the national interest following calculable principles—what later came to be known as *raison d'état.* Hence it should be the basic unit of international relations.

Richelieu commandeered the incipient state as an instrument of high policy. He centralized authority in Paris, created so-called intendants or professional stewards to project the government's authority into every district of the kingdom, brought efficiency to the gathering of taxes, and decisively challenged traditional local authorities of the old nobility. Royal power would continue to be exercised by the King as the symbol of the sovereign state and an expression of the national interest.

Richelieu saw the turmoil in Central Europe not as a call to arms to defend the Church but as a means to check imperial Habsburg preeminence. Though France's King had been styled as the *Rex Catholicissimus,* or the "Most Catholic King," since the fourteenth century, France moved—at first unobtrusively, then openly—to support the Protestant coalition (of Sweden, Prussia, and the North German princes) on the basis of cold national-interest calculation.

To outraged complaints that, as a cardinal, he owed a duty to the universal and eternal Catholic Church—which would imply an alignment *against* the rebellious Protestant princes of Northern and Central Europe—Richelieu cited his duties as a minister to a temporal, yet vulnerable, political entity. Salvation might be his personal objective, but as a statesman he was responsible for a political entity that did not have an eternal soul to be redeemed. "Man is immortal, his salvation is hereafter," he said. "The state has no immortality, its salvation is now or never."

The fragmentation of Central Europe was perceived by Richelieu as a political and military necessity. The basic threat to France was strategic, not metaphysical or religious: a united Central Europe would be in a position to dominate the rest of the Continent. Hence it was in France's national interest to prevent the consolidation of Central Europe: "If the [Protestant] party is entirely ruined, the brunt of the power of the House of Austria will fall on France." France, by supporting a plethora of small states in Central Europe and weakening Austria, achieved its strategic objective.

Richelieu's design would endure through vast upheavals. For two and a half centuries—from the emergence of Richelieu in 1624 to Bismarck's proclamation of the German Empire in 1871—the aim of keeping Central Europe (more or less the territory of contemporary Germany, Austria, and northern Italy) divided remained the guiding principle of French foreign policy. For as long as this concept served as the essence of the European order, France was preeminent on the Continent. When it collapsed, so did France's dominant role.

Three conclusions emerge from Richelieu's career. First, the indispensable element of a successful foreign policy is a long-term strategic concept based on a careful analysis of all relevant factors. Second, the statesman must distill that vision by analyzing and shaping an array of ambiguous, often conflicting pressures into a coherent and purposeful direction. He (or she) must know where this strategy is leading and why. And, third, he must act at the outer edge of the possible, bridging the gap between his society's experiences and its aspirations. Because repetition of the familiar leads to stagnation, no little daring is required.

The Peace of Westphalia

In our time, the Peace of Westphalia has acquired a special resonance as the path breaker of a new concept of international order that has spread around the world. The representatives meeting to negotiate it were more focused at the time on considerations of protocol and status.

By the time representatives of the Holy Roman Empire and its two main adversaries, France and Sweden, agreed in principle to convene a peace conference, the conflict had ground on for twenty-three years. Another two years of battle transpired before the delegations actually met; in the meantime, each side maneuvered to strengthen its allies and internal constituencies.

Unlike other landmark agreements such as the Congress of Vienna in 1814–15 or the Treaty of Versailles in 1919, the Peace of Westphalia did not emerge from a single conference, and the setting was not one generally associated with a gathering of statesmen pondering transcendent questions of world order. Mirroring the variety of contenders in a war that had ranged from Spain to Sweden, the peace emerged from a series of separate arrangements made in two different Westphalian towns. Catholic powers, including 178 separate participants from the different states constituting the Holy Roman Empire, gathered in the Catholic city of Münster. Protestant powers gathered in the mixed Lutheran and Catholic city of Osnabrück, roughly thirty miles away. The 235 official envoys and their staffs took up residence in whatever rooms they could find in the two small cities, neither of which had ever been considered suitable for a large-scale event, let alone a congress of all European powers. The Swiss envoy "lodged above a wool weaver's shop in a room that stank of sausage and fish oil," while the Bavarian delegation secured eighteen beds for its twenty-nine members. With no official conference head or mediator and no plenary sessions, representatives met on an ad hoc basis and traveled in a neutral zone between the two cities to coordinate positions, sometimes meeting informally in towns in the middle. Some of the major powers stationed representatives in both cities. Combat continued in various parts of Europe throughout the talks, with shifting military dynamics affecting the course of the negotiations.

Most representatives had come with eminently practical instructions based on strategic interests. While they employed almost identical high-minded phrases about achieving a "peace for Christendom," too much blood had been spilled to conceive of reaching this lofty goal through doctrinal or political unity. It was now taken for granted that peace would be built, if at all, through balancing rivalries.

The Peace of Westphalia that emerged from these convoluted discussions is probably the most frequently cited diplomatic document in European history, though in fact no single treaty exists to embody its terms. Nor did the delegates ever meet in a single plenary session to adopt it. The peace is in reality the sum of three separate complementary agreements signed at different times in different cities. In the January 1648 Peace of Münster, Spain recognized the independence of the Dutch Republic, capping an eight-decades-long Dutch revolt that had merged with the Thirty Years' War. In October 1648, separate groupings of powers signed the Treaty of Münster and the Treaty of Osnabrück, with terms mirroring each other and incorporating key provisions by reference.

Both of the main multilateral treaties proclaimed their intent as "a Christian, universal, perpetual, true, and sincere peace and friendship" for "the glory of God and the security of Christendom." The operative terms were not substantially different from other documents of the period. Yet the mechanisms through which they were to be reached were unprecedented. The war had shattered pretensions to universality or confessional solidarity. Begun as a struggle of Catholics against Protestants, particularly after France's entry against the Catholic Holy Roman Empire it had turned into a free-for-all of shifting and conflicting alliances. Much like the Middle Eastern conflagrations of our own period, sectarian alignments were invoked for solidarity and motivation in battle but were just as often discarded, trumped by clashes of geopolitical interests or simply the ambitions of outsized personalities. Every party had been abandoned at some point during the war by its "natural" allies; none signed the documents under the illusion that it was doing anything but advancing its own interests and prestige.

Paradoxically, this general exhaustion and cynicism allowed the participants to transform the practical means of ending a particular war into general concepts of world order. With dozens of battle-hardened parties meeting to secure hard-won gains, old forms of hierarchical deference were quietly discarded. The inherent equality of sovereign states, regardless of their power or domestic system, was instituted. Newly arrived powers, such as Sweden and the Dutch Republic, were granted protocol treatment equal to that of established great powers like France and Austria. All kings were referred to as "majesty" and all ambassadors "excellency." This novel concept was carried so far that the delegations, demanding absolute equality, devised a process of entering the sites of negotiations through individual doors, requiring the construction of many entrances, and advancing to their seats at equal speed so that none would suffer the ignominy of waiting for the other to arrive at his convenience.

The Peace of Westphalia became a turning point in the history of nations because the elements it set in place were as uncomplicated as they were sweeping. The state, not the empire, dynasty, or religious confession, was affirmed as the building block of European order. The concept of state sovereignty was established. The right of each signatory to choose its own domestic structure and religious orientation free from intervention was affirmed, while novel clauses ensured that minority sects could practice their faith in peace and be free from the prospect of forced conversion. Beyond the immediate demands of the moment, the principles of a system of "international relations" were taking shape, motivated by the common desire to avoid a recurrence of total war on the Continent. Diplomatic exchanges, including the stationing of resident representatives in the capitals of fellow states (a practice followed before then generally only by Venetians), were designed to regulate relations and promote the arts of peace. The parties envisioned future conferences and consultations on the Westphalian model as forums for settling disputes before they led to conflict. International law, developed by traveling scholar-advisors such as Hugo de Groot (Grotius) during the war, was treated as an expandable body of agreed doctrine aimed at the cultivation of harmony, with the Westphalian treaties themselves at its heart.

The genius of this system, and the reason it spread across the world, was that its provisions were procedural, not substantive. If a state would accept these basic requirements, it could be recognized as an international citizen able to maintain its own culture, politics, religion, and internal policies, shielded by the international system from outside intervention. The ideal of imperial or religious unity—the operating premise of Europe's and most other regions' historical orders—had implied that in theory only one center of power could be fully legitimate. The Westphalian concept took multiplicity as its starting point and drew a variety of multiple societies, each accepted as a reality, into a common search for order. By the mid-twentieth century, this international system was in place on every continent; it remains the scaffolding of international order such as it now exists.

The Peace of Westphalia did not mandate a specific arrangement of alliances or a permanent European political structure. With the end of the universal Church as the ultimate source of legitimacy, and the weakening of the Holy Roman Emperor, the ordering concept for Europe became the balance of power—which, by definition, involves ideological neutrality and adjustment to evolving circumstances. The nineteenth-century British statesman Lord Palmerston expressed its basic principle as follows: "We have no eternal allies, and we have no perpetual enemies. Our interests are eternal and perpetual, and those

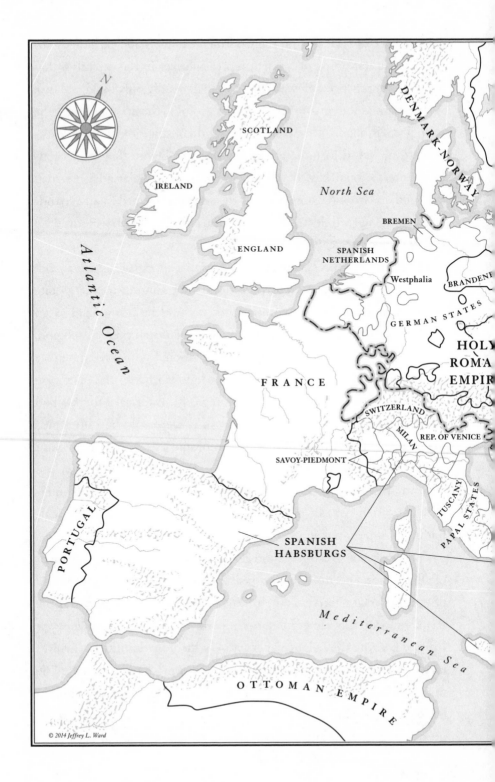

SCOTLAND

IRELAND

North Sea

DENMARK-NORWAY

BREMEN

ENGLAND

SPANISH
NETHERLANDS

Westphalia

BRANDENE

GERMAN STATES

HOLY
ROMA
EMPIR

Atlantic Ocean

FRANCE

SWITZERLAND

MILAN

REP. OF VENICE

SAVOY-PIEDMONT

TUSCANY

PAPAL STATES

PORTUGAL

SPANISH
HABSBURGS

Mediterranean Sea

OTTOMAN EMPIRE

© 2014 Jeffrey L. Ward

EUROPE AFTER THE PEACE OF WESTPHALIA, 1648

SWEDEN AND
TS POSSESSIONS

Baltic Sea

0 Miles 300

0. Kilometers 300

RUSSIA

EAST PRUSSIA

HOHENZOLLERN
POSSESSIONS (PRUSSIA)

HABSBURG
POSSESSIONS (AUSTRIA)

P O L A N D

HEMIA

RIA

HUNGARY

Black Sea

O T T O M A N

E M P I R E

APLES

KEY

━ ∙ ━ ∙ ━ Holy Roman Empire boundary

━━━━ Great power boundaries

───── State boundaries

interests it is our duty to follow." Asked to define these interests more specifically in the form of an official "foreign policy," the acclaimed steward of British power professed, "When people ask me . . . for what is called a policy, the only answer is that we mean to do what may seem to be best, upon each occasion as it arises, making the Interests of Our Country one's guiding principle." (Of course this deceptively simple concept worked for Britain in part because its ruling class was trained in a common, almost intuitive sense of what the country's enduring interests were.)

Today these Westphalian concepts are often maligned as a system of cynical power manipulation, indifferent to moral claims. Yet the structure established in the Peace of Westphalia represented the first attempt to institutionalize an international order on the basis of agreed rules and limits and to base it on a multiplicity of powers rather than the dominance of a single country. The concepts of *raison d'état* and the "national interest" made their first appearance, representing not an exaltation of power but an attempt to rationalize and limit its use. Armies had marched across Europe for generations under the banner of universal (and contradictory) moral claims; prophets and conquerors had unleashed total war in pursuit of a mixture of personal, dynastic, imperial, and religious ambitions. The theoretically logical and predictable intermeshing of state interests was intended to overcome the disorder unfolding in every corner of the Continent. Limited wars over calculable issues would replace the era of contending universalisms, with its forced expulsions and conversions and general war consuming civilian populations.

With all its ambiguities, the balancing of power was thought an improvement over the exactions of religious wars. But how was the balance of power to be established? In theory, it was based on realities; hence every participant in it should see it alike. But each society's perceptions are affected by its domestic structure, culture, and history and by the overriding reality that the elements of power—however objective—are in constant flux. Hence the balance of power needs to be recalibrated from time to time. It produces the wars whose extent it also limits.

The Operation of the Westphalian System

With the Treaty of Westphalia, the papacy had been confined to ecclesiastical functions, and the doctrine of sovereign equality reigned. What political theory could then explain the origin and justify the functions of secular political order? In his *Leviathan,* published in 1651, three years after the Peace of Westphalia, Thomas Hobbes provided such a theory. He imagined a "state of nature" in the past when the absence of authority produced a "war of all against all." To escape such intolerable insecurity, he theorized, people delivered their rights to a sovereign power in return for the sovereign's provision of security for all within the state's borders. The sovereign state's monopoly on power was established as the only way to overcome the perpetual fear of violent death and war.

This social contract in Hobbes's analysis did *not* apply beyond the borders of states, for no supranational sovereign existed to impose order. Therefore:

> Concerning the offices of one sovereign to another, which are comprehended in that law which is commonly called the law of nations, I need not say anything in this place, because the law of nations and the law of nature is the same thing. And every sovereign hath the same right, in procuring the safety of his people, that any particular man can have, in procuring the safety of his own body.

The international arena remained in the state of nature and was anarchical because there was no world sovereign available to make it secure and none could be practically constituted. Thus each state would have to place its own national interest above all in a world where power was the paramount factor. Cardinal Richelieu would have emphatically agreed.

The Peace of Westphalia in its early practice implemented a Hobbesian world. How was this new balance of power to be calibrated? A distinction must be made between the balance of power as a fact and the balance of power as a system. Any international order—to be worthy of that name—must sooner or later reach an equilibrium, or else it will be in a constant state of warfare. Because the medieval world contained dozens of principalities, a practical balance of power frequently existed in fact. After the Peace of Westphalia, the balance of power made its appearance as a system; that is to say, bringing it about was accepted as one of the key purposes of foreign policy; disturbing it would evoke a coalition on behalf of equilibrium.

The rise of Britain as a major naval power by early in the eighteenth century made it possible to turn the facts of the balance of power into a system. Control of the seas enabled Britain to choose the timing and scale of its involvement on the Continent to act as the arbiter of the balance of power, indeed the guarantor that Europe would have a balance of power at all. So long as England assessed its strategic requirements correctly, it would be able to back the weaker side on the Continent against the stronger, preventing any single country from achieving hegemony in Europe and thereby mobilizing the resources of the Continent to challenge Britain's control of the seas. Until the outbreak of World War I, England acted as the balancer of the equilibrium. It fought in European wars but with shifting alliances—not in pursuit of specific, purely national goals, but by identifying the national interest with the preservation of the balance of power. Many of these principles apply to America's role in the contemporary world, as will be discussed later.

There were in fact two balances of power being conducted in

Europe after the Westphalian settlement: The overall balance, of which England acted as a guardian, was the protector of general stability. A Central European balance essentially manipulated by France aimed to prevent the emergence of a unified Germany in a position to become the most powerful country on the Continent. For more than two hundred years, these balances kept Europe from tearing itself to pieces as it had during the Thirty Years' War; they did not prevent war, but they limited its impact because equilibrium, not total conquest, was the goal.

The balance of power can be challenged in at least two ways: The first is if a major country augments its strength to a point where it threatens to achieve hegemony. The second occurs when a heretofore-secondary state seeks to enter the ranks of the major powers and sets off a series of compensating adjustments by the other powers until a new equilibrium is established or a general conflagration takes place. The Westphalian system met both tests in the eighteenth century, first by thwarting the thrust for hegemony by France's Louis XIV, then by adjusting the system to the insistence of Prussia's Frederick the Great for equal status.

Louis XIV took full control of the French crown in 1661 and developed Richelieu's concept of governance to unprecedented levels. The French King had in the past ruled through feudal lords with their own autonomous claims to authority based on heredity. Louis governed through a royal bureaucracy dependent entirely on him. He downgraded courtiers of noble blood and ennobled bureaucrats. What counted was service to the King, not rank of birth. The brilliant Finance Minister Jean-Baptiste Colbert, son of a provincial draper, was charged with unifying the tax administration and financing constant war. The memoirs of Saint-Simon, a duke by inheritance and man of letters, bear bitter witness to the social transformation:

> He [Louis] was well aware that though he might crush a
> nobleman with the weight of his displeasure, he could not

destroy him or his line, whereas a secretary of state or other such minister could be reduced together with his whole family to those depths of nothingness from which he had been elevated. No amount of wealth or possessions would avail him then. That was one reason why he liked to give his ministers authority over the highest in the Land, even over the Princes of the Blood.

In 1680, Louis symbolized the nature of his all-embracing rule by assuming the title "the Great" to go with his earlier self-granted appellation as "the Sun King." In 1682, France's North American territories were named "Louisiana." The same year, Louis's court moved to Versailles, where the King oversaw in elaborate detail a "theater monarchy" dedicated, above all, to the performance of his own majesty.

With a unified kingdom spared the ravages of internal war, possessing a skilled bureaucracy and a military surpassing that of any neighboring state, France was for a while in a position to seek dominance in Europe. Louis's reign resolved itself into a series of almost continuous wars. In the end, as was the case with all later aspirants to European hegemony, each new conquest galvanized an opposing coalition of nations. At first, Louis's generals won battles everywhere; ultimately, they were defeated or checked everywhere, most signally in the first decade of the eighteenth century by John Churchill, later Duke of Marlborough and forebear of the great twentieth-century Prime Minister Winston Churchill. Louis's legions could not overcome the basic resilience of the Westphalian system.

Decades after Richelieu's death, the demonstrated effectiveness of a consolidated, centralized state pursuing a secular foreign policy and centralized administration inspired imitators that united to counterbalance French power. England, Holland, and Austria created the Grand Alliance, joined later by Spain, Prussia, Denmark, and several German principalities. The opposition to Louis was not ideological or religious in nature: French remained the language of diplomacy and high culture through much of Europe, and the Catholic-Protestant divide ran through the allied camp. Rather, it was inherent in the Westphalian system and indispensable to preserve the pluralism of the European order. Its character was defined in the name contemporary observers gave it: the Great Moderation. Louis sought what amounted to hegemony in the name of the glory of France. He was defeated by a Europe that sought its order in diversity.

THE FIRST HALF of the eighteenth century was dominated by the quest to contain France; the second was shaped by Prussia's effort to find a place for itself among the major powers. Where Louis had fought wars to translate power into hegemony, Prussia's Frederick II went to war to transmute latent weakness into great-power status. Situated on the harsh North German plain and extending from the Vistula across Germany, Prussia cultivated discipline and public service to substitute for the larger population and greater resources of better-endowed countries. Split into two noncontiguous pieces, it jutted precariously into the Austrian, Swedish, Russian, and Polish spheres of influence. It was relatively sparsely populated; its strength was the discipline with which it marshaled its limited resources. Its greatest assets were civic-mindedness, an efficient bureaucracy, and a well-trained army.

When Frederick II ascended the throne in 1740, he seemed an unlikely contender for the greatness history has vouchsafed him. Finding the dour discipline of the position of Crown Prince oppressive, he had attempted to flee to England accompanied by a friend, Hans Hermann von Katte. They were apprehended. The King ordered von Katte decapitated in front of Frederick, whom he submitted to a court-martial headed by himself. He cross-examined his son with 178 questions, which Frederick answered so deftly that he was reinstated.

Surviving this searing experience was possible only by adopting his father's austere sense of duty and developing a general misanthropic attitude toward his fellow man. Frederick saw his personal authority as absolute but his policies as limited rigidly by the principles of *raison d'état* Richelieu had put forward a century earlier. "Rulers are the slaves of their resources," his credo held, "the interest of the State is their law, and this law may not be infringed." Courageous and cosmopolitan (Frederick spoke and wrote French and composed sentimental French poetry even on military campaigns, subtitling one of his literary efforts "Pas trop mal pour la veille d'une grande bataille"), he embodied the new era of Enlightenment governance by benevolent despotism, which was legitimized by its effectiveness, not ideology.

Frederick concluded that great-power status required territorial contiguity for Prussia, hence expansion. There was no need for any other political or moral justification. "The superiority of our troops, the promptitude with which we can set them in motion, in a word the clear advantage we have over our neighbors" was all the justification Frederick required to seize the wealthy and traditionally Austrian province of Silesia in 1740. Treating the issue as a geopolitical, not a legal or moral, one, Frederick aligned himself with France (which saw in Prussia a counter to Austria) and retained Silesia in the peace settlement of 1742, nearly doubling Prussia's territory and population.

In the process, Frederick brought war back to the European system, which had been at peace since 1713 when the Treaty of Utrecht had put an end to the ambitions of Louis XIV. The challenge to the established balance of power caused the Westphalian system to begin to function. The price for being admitted as a new member to the European order turned out to be seven years of near-disastrous battle. Now the alliances were reversed, as Frederick's previous allies sought to quash his operations and their rivals tried to harness Prussia's disciplined fighting force for their own aims. Russia, remote and mysterious, for the first time entered a contest over the European balance of power. At the edge of defeat, with Russian armies at the gates of Berlin, Frederick was saved by the sudden death of Czarina Elizabeth. The new Czar, a longtime admirer of Frederick, withdrew from the war. (Hitler, besieged in encircled Berlin in April 1945, waited for an event comparable to the so-called Miracle of the House of Brandenburg and was told by Joseph Goebbels that it had happened when President Franklin D. Roosevelt died.)

The Holy Roman Empire had become a facade; no rival European claimant to universal authority had arisen. Almost all rulers asserted that they ruled by divine right—a claim not challenged by any major power—but they accepted that God had similarly endowed many other monarchs. Wars were therefore fought for limited territorial objectives, not to overthrow existing governments and institutions, nor to impose a new system of relations between states. Tradition prevented rulers from conscripting their subjects and severely constrained their ability to raise taxes. The impact of wars on civilian populations was in no way comparable to the horrors of the Thirty Years' War or what technology and ideology would produce two centuries later. In the eighteenth century, the balance of power operated as a theater in which "lives and values were put on display, amid splendor, polish, gallantry, and shows of utter self-assurance." The exercise of that power was constrained by the recognition that the system would not tolerate hegemonic aspirations.

International orders that have been the most stable have had the advantage of uniform perceptions. The statesmen who operated the eighteenth-century European order were aristocrats who interpreted intangibles like honor and duty in the same way and agreed on fundamentals. They represented a single elite society that spoke the same language (French), frequented the same salons, and pursued romantic liaisons in each other's capitals. National interests of course varied, but in a world where a foreign minister could serve a monarch of another nationality (every Russian foreign minister until 1820 was recruited abroad), or when a territory could change its national affiliation as the result of a marriage pact or a fortuitous inheritance, a sense of overarching common purpose was inherent. Power calculations in the eighteenth century took place against this ameliorating background of a shared sense of legitimacy and unspoken rules of international conduct.

This consensus was not only a matter of decorum; it reflected the moral convictions of a common European outlook. Europe was never more united or more spontaneous than during what came to be perceived as the age of enlightenment. New triumphs in science and philosophy began to displace the fracturing European certainties of tradition and faith. The swift advance of the mind on multiple fronts—physics, chemistry, astronomy, history, archaeology, cartography, rationality—bolstered a new spirit of secular illumination auguring that the revelation of all of nature's hidden mechanisms was only a question of time. "The true system of the world has been recognized, developed, and perfected," wrote the brilliant French polymath Jean Le Rond d'Alembert in 1759, embodying the spirit of the age:

> In short, from the earth to Saturn, from the history of the heavens to that of insects, natural philosophy has been revolutionized; and nearly all other fields of knowledge have assumed new forms . . . [T]he discovery and application of a new method of philosophizing, the kind of enthusiasm which accompanies discoveries, a certain exaltation of ideas which the spectacle of the universe produces in us—all these causes have brought about a lively fermentation of minds. Spreading through nature in all directions like a river which has burst its dams, this fermentation has swept with a sort of violence everything along with it which stood in its way.

This "fermentation" based itself on a new spirit of analysis and a rigorous testing of all premises. The exploration and systematization of all knowledge—an endeavor symbolized by the twenty-eight-volume *Encyclopédie* that d'Alembert co-edited between 1751 and 1772—proclaimed a knowable, demystified universe with man as its central actor and explicator. Prodigious learning would be combined, d'Alembert's colleague Denis Diderot wrote, with a "zeal for the best interests of the human race." Reason would confront falsehoods with "solid principles [to] serve as the foundation for diametrically opposed truths," whereby "we shall be able to throw down the whole edifice of mud and scatter the idle heap of dust" and instead "put men on the right path."

Inevitably, this new way of thinking and analysis was applied to concepts of governance, political legitimacy, and international order. The political philosopher Charles-Louis de Secondat, Baron of Montesquieu, applied the principles of the balance of power to domestic policy by describing a concept of checks and balances later institutionalized in the American Constitution. He went on from there into a philosophy of history and of the mechanisms of societal change. Surveying the histories of various societies, Montesquieu concluded that events were never caused by accident. There was always an underlying cause that reason could discover and then shape to the common good:

> It is not fortune which rules the world . . . There are general intellectual as well as physical causes active in every monarchy which bring about its rise, preservation, and fall. All [seeming] accidents are subject to these causes, and whenever an accidental battle, that is, a particular cause, has destroyed a state, a general cause also existed which led to the fall of this state as a result of a single battle. In short, it is the general pace of things which draws all particular events along with it.

The German philosopher Immanuel Kant, probably the greatest philosopher of the Enlightenment period, took Montesquieu a step further by developing a concept for a permanent peaceful world order. Pondering the world from the former Prussian capital of Königsberg, casting his gaze on the period of the Seven Years' War, the American Revolutionary War, and the French Revolution, Kant dared to see in the general upheaval the faint beginnings of a new, more peaceful international order.

Humanity, Kant reasoned, was characterized by a distinctive "*unsocial sociability*": the "tendency to come together in society, coupled, however, with a continual resistance which constantly threatens to break this society up." The problem of order, particularly international order, was "the most difficult and the last to be solved by the human race." Men formed states to constrain their passions, but like individuals in the state of nature each state sought to preserve its absolute freedom, even at the cost of "a lawless state of savagery." But the "devastations, upheavals and even complete inner exhaustion of their powers" arising from interstate clashes would in time oblige men to contemplate an alternative. Humanity faced either the peace of "the vast graveyard of the human race" or peace by reasoned design.

The answer, Kant held, was a voluntary federation of republics pledged to non-hostility and transparent domestic and international conduct. Their citizens would cultivate peace because, unlike despotic rulers, when considering hostilities, they would be deliberating about "calling down on *themselves* all the miseries of war." Over time the attractions of this compact would become apparent, opening the way toward its gradual expansion into a peaceful world order. It was Nature's purpose that humanity eventually reason its way toward "a system of united power, hence a cosmopolitan system of general political security" and "*a perfect civil union of mankind.*"

The confidence, verging on brashness, in the power of reason reflected in part a species of what the Greeks called hubris—a kind of spiritual pride that bore the seeds of its own destruction within itself. The Enlightenment philosophers ignored a key issue: Can governmental orders be invented from scratch by intelligent thinkers, or is the range of choice limited by underlying organic and cultural realities (the Burkean view)? Is there a single concept and mechanism logically uniting all things, in a way that can be discovered and explicated (as d'Alembert and Montesquieu argued), or is the world too complicated and humanity too diverse to approach these questions through logic alone, requiring a kind of intuition and an almost esoteric element of statecraft?

The Enlightenment philosophers on the Continent generally opted for the rationalist rather than the organic view of political evolution. In the process, they contributed—unintentionally, indeed contrary to their intention—to an upheaval that rent Europe for decades and whose aftereffects reach to this day.

The French Revolution and Its Aftermath

Revolutions are most unsettling when least expected. So it was with the French Revolution, which proclaimed a domestic and world order as different from the Westphalian system as it was possible to be. Abandoning the separation between domestic and foreign policy, it resurrected—and perhaps exceeded—the passions of the Thirty Years' War, substituting a secular crusade for the religious impulse of the seventeenth century. It demonstrated how internal changes within societies are able to shake the international equilibrium more profoundly than aggression from abroad—a lesson that would be driven home by the upheavals of the twentieth century, many of which drew explicitly on the concepts first advanced by the French Revolution.

Revolutions erupt when a variety of often different resentments merge to assault an unsuspecting regime. The broader the revolutionary coalition, the greater its ability to destroy existing patterns of authority. But the more sweeping the change, the more violence is needed to reconstruct authority, without which society will disintegrate. Reigns of terror are not an accident; they are inherent in the scope of revolution.

The French Revolution occurred in the richest country of Europe, even though its government was temporarily bankrupt. Its original impetus is traceable to leaders—mostly aristocrats and upper bourgeoisie—who sought to bring the governance of their country into conformity with the principles of the Enlightenment. It gained a momentum not foreseen by those who made the Revolution and inconceivable to the prevailing ruling elite.

At its heart was a reordering on a scale that had not been seen in Europe since the end of the religious wars. For the revolutionaries, human order was the reflection of neither the divine plan of the medieval world, nor the intermeshing of grand dynastic interests of the eighteenth century. Like their progeny in the totalitarian movements of the twentieth century, the philosophers of the French Revolution equated the mechanism of history with the unadulterated operation of the popular will, which by definition could accept no inherent or constitutional limitation—and which they reserved to themselves the monopoly to identify. The popular will, as conceived in that manner, was altogether distinct from the concept of majority rule prevalent in England or of checks and balances embedded in a written constitution as in the United States. The claims of the French revolutionaries far exceeded Richelieu's concept of the authority of the state by vesting sovereignty in an abstraction—not individuals but entire peoples as indivisible entities requiring uniformity of thought and action—and then designating themselves the people's spokesmen and indeed embodiment.

The Revolution's intellectual godfather, Jean-Jacques Rousseau, formulated this universal claim in a series of writings whose erudition and charm obscured their sweeping implications. Walking readers step by step through a "rational" dissection of human society, Rousseau condemned all existing institutions—property, religion, social classes, government authority, civil society—as illusory and fraudulent. Their replacement was to be a new "rule of administration in the social order." The populace was to submit totally to it—with an obedience that no ruler by divine right had ever imagined, except the Russian Czar, whose entire populace outside the nobility and the communities on the harsh frontiers beyond the Urals had the status of serfs. These theories prefigured the modern totalitarian regime, in which the popular will ratifies decisions that have already been announced by means of staged mass demonstrations.

In pursuit of this ideology, all monarchies were by definition treated as enemies; because they would not give up power without resisting, the Revolution, to prevail, had to turn itself into a crusading international movement to achieve world peace by imposing its principles. In order to propel the new dispensation across Europe, France's entire adult male population was made subject to conscription. The Revolution based itself on a proposition similar to that made by Islam a millennium before, and Communism in the twentieth century: the impossibility of permanent coexistence between countries of different religious or political conceptions of truth, and the transformation of international affairs into a global contest of ideologies to be fought by any available means and by mobilizing all elements of society. In doing so, the Revolution again merged domestic and foreign policy, legitimacy and power, whose decoupling by the Westphalian settlement had limited the scope and intensity of Europe's wars. The concept of an international order with prescribed limits of state action was overthrown in favor of a permanent revolution that knew only total victory or defeat.

In November 1792, the French National Assembly threw down the gauntlet to Europe with a pair of extraordinary decrees. The first expressed an open-ended commitment to extend French military support to popular revolution anywhere. France, it announced, having liberated itself, "will accord fraternity and assistance to all peoples who shall wish to recover their liberty." The National Assembly gave added weight to this decree and obliged itself to give it force in the proviso that the document be "translated and printed in all languages." The National Assembly made the break with the eighteenth-century order irrevocable by guillotining France's deposed King several weeks later. It also declared war on Austria and invaded the Netherlands.

In December 1792, an even more radical decree was issued with an even more universal application. Any revolutionary movement that thought the decree applied to it was invited to "fill in the blank" of a document reading, "The French People to the _____ People," which applauded in advance the next fraternal revolution and pledged support to "the suppression of all the civil and military authorities which have governed you up to this day." This process, whose scope was implicitly limitless, was also irreversible: "The French nation declares that it will treat as enemies the people who, refusing liberty and equality, or renouncing them, may wish to preserve, recall, or treat with the prince and the privileged castes." Rousseau had written that "whoever refuses to obey the general will shall be forced to do so by the whole body . . . [H]e will be forced to be free." The Revolution undertook to expand this definition of legitimacy to all humanity.

To achieve such vast and universal objectives, the leaders of the French Revolution strove to cleanse their country of all possibility of domestic opposition. "The Terror" killed thousands of the former ruling classes and all suspected domestic opponents, even those who supported the Revolution's goals while questioning some of its methods. Two centuries later, comparable motivations underlay the Russian purges of the 1930s and the Chinese Cultural Revolution in the 1960s and 1970s.

Eventually, order was restored, as it must be if a state is not to disintegrate. The model once again came from Rousseau's "great legislator." Louis XIV had appropriated the state in the service of royal power; the Revolution commandeered the people to underwrite its design. Napoleon, who proclaimed himself "First Consul for Life," later Emperor, represented a new type: the "Great Man" swaying the world by the force of his will, legitimized by charismatic magnetism and personal success in military command. The essence of the Great Man was his refusal to acknowledge traditional limits and his insistence on reordering the world by his own authority. At the climactic moment of his coronation as Emperor in 1804, Napoleon, unlike Charlemagne, refusing to be legitimized by a power other than his own, took the imperial crown from the Pope's hands and crowned himself Emperor.

The Revolution no longer made the leader; the leader defined the Revolution. As he tamed the Revolution, Napoleon also made himself its guarantor. But he also saw himself—and not without reason—as the capstone of the Enlightenment. He rationalized France's system of government, establishing the system of prefectures through which, even at this writing, the French system of administration operates. He created the Napoleonic Code, on which the laws that still prevail in France and other European countries are based. He was tolerant of religious diversity and encouraged rationalism in government, with the end of improving the lot of the French people.

It was as the simultaneous incarnation of the Revolution and expression of the Enlightenment that Napoleon set about to achieve the domination and unification of Europe. By 1809, under his brilliant military leadership, his armies crushed all opposition in Western and Central Europe, enabling him to redraw the map of the Continent as a geopolitical design. He annexed key territories to France and established satellite republics in others, many of them governed by relatives or French marshals. A uniform legal code was established throughout Europe. Thousands of instructions on matters economic and social were issued. Would Napoleon become the unifier of a continent divided since the fall of Rome?

Two obstacles remained: England and Russia. England, in command of the seas after Nelson's crushing victory at Trafalgar in 1805, was for the moment invulnerable but not strong enough to launch a significant invasion across the English Channel. As it would a century and a half later, England stood alone in Western Europe, aware that a peace with the conqueror would make it possible for a single power to organize the resources of the entire Continent and, sooner or later, overcome its rule of the oceans. England waited behind the channel for Napoleon (and a century and a half later, for Hitler) to make a mistake that would enable it to reappear on the Continent militarily as a defender of the balance of power. (In World War II, Britain was also waiting for the United States to enter the lists.)

Napoleon had grown up under the eighteenth-century dynastic system and, in a strange way, accepted its legitimacy. In it, as a Corsican of minor standing even in his hometown, he was illegitimate by definition, which meant that, at least in his own mind, the legitimacy of his rule depended on the permanence—and, indeed, the extent—of his conquests. Whenever there remained a ruler independent of his will, Napoleon felt obliged to pursue him. Incapable of restraint by concept, temperament, or experience, he launched his forces into Spain and Russia, neither of them essential to a geopolitical design. Napoleon could not live in an international order; his ambition required an empire over at least the length and breadth of Europe, and for that his power fell just barely too short.

With the Revolutionary and Napoleonic Wars, the age of total war—the mobilization of a nation's entire resources—had arrived. The scale of bloodshed and devastation harked back to the Thirty Years' War. Napoleon's Grande Armée—now manned through conscription, including even in annexed territories—supplied and maintained itself on the assets of the conquered enemy and population, including gigantic financial "tributes." The results were an enormous increase in the size of the army and the subjection of entire regions. Not until Napoleon succumbed to the temptation to enter territories where local resources were insufficient for the support of a huge army—Spain and Russia—would he face defeat, first by overreaching himself, above all in Russia in 1812, and then as the rest of Europe united against him in a belated vindication of Westphalian principles. At the Battle of the Nations in Leipzig in 1813, the joint armies of the surviving European states inflicted Napoleon's first major, and ultimately decisive, defeat in a battle. (The defeat in Russia was by attrition.) After the Battle of the Nations, Napoleon refused settlements that would have enabled him to keep some of his conquests. He feared that any formal acceptance of limits would destroy his only claim to legitimacy. In this way, he was overthrown as much by his own insecurity as by Westphalian principles. Europe's strongest conqueror since Charlemagne was defeated not only by an international order that rose up against him, but by himself.

The Napoleonic period marked the apotheosis of the Enlightenment. Inspired by the examples of Greece and Rome, its thinkers had equated enlightenment with the power of reason, which implied a diffusion of authority from the Church to secular elites. Now these aspirations had been distilled further and concentrated on one leader as the expression of global power. An illustration of Napoleon's impact occurred on October 13, 1806, one day before the Battle of Jena, where the Prussian army was decisively defeated. As he left to reconnoiter the battlefield with his general staff, Georg Wilhelm Friedrich Hegel, then a university lecturer (he would later write *The Philosophy of History,* which inspired Marx's doctrine), described the scene in panegyrical terms as he heard the clatter of horses' hooves on the cobblestones:

> I saw the Emperor—this world-soul—riding out of the city on reconnaissance. It is indeed a wonderful sensation to see such an individual who, concentrated here at a single point, astride a horse, reaches out over the world and masters it.

But in the end, this world spirit had drawn into Europe an immense new power—of Europe and yet with three-quarters of its vast territory in Asia: imperial Russia, whose armies pursued Napoleon's decimated force back across the Continent and were occupying Paris at war's end. Its strength raised fundamental issues for the balance of power in Europe, and its aspirations threatened to make impossible a return to the prerevolutionary equilibrium.

CHAPTER 2

The European Balance-of-Power System and Its End

The Russian Enigma

When the era of the French Revolution and Napoleon ended, Russian troops were occupying Paris in a stunning display of history's reversals. A half century earlier, Russia had for the first time entered the balance of power in Western Europe by participating in the Seven Years' War and demonstrated the arbitrary nature of czarist rule when it suddenly declared its neutrality and withdrew from the war because of a newly crowned Czar's admiration for Frederick the Great. At the end of the Napoleonic period, another Czar, Alexander, proceeded to prescribe Europe's future. The liberties of Europe and its concomitant system of order required the participation of an empire far larger than the rest of Europe together and autocratic to a degree without precedent in European history.

Since then, Russia has played a unique role in international affairs: part of the balance of power in both Europe and Asia but contributing to the equilibrium of the international order only fitfully. It has started more wars than any other contemporary major power, but it has also thwarted dominion of Europe by a single power, holding fast against Charles XII of Sweden, Napoleon, and Hitler when key continental elements of the balance had been overrun. Its policy has pursued a special rhythm of its own over the centuries, expanding over a landmass spanning nearly every climate and civilization, interrupted occasionally for a time by the need to adjust its domestic structure to the vastness of the enterprise—only to return again, like a tide crossing a beach. From Peter the Great to Vladimir Putin, circumstances have changed, but the rhythm has remained extraordinarily consistent.

Western Europeans emerging from the Napoleonic upheavals viewed with awe and apprehension a country whose territory and military forces dwarfed those of the rest of the Continent combined and whose elites' polished manners seemed barely able to conceal a primitive force from before and beyond Western civilization. Russia, the French traveler the Marquis de Custine claimed in 1843—from the perspective of a France restrained and a Europe reshaped by Russian power—was a hybrid bringing the vitality of the steppe to the heart of Europe:

> A monstrous compound of the petty refinements of Byzantium, and the ferocity of the desert horde, a struggle between the etiquette of the Lower [Byzantine] Empire, and the savage virtues of Asia, have produced the mighty state which Europe now beholds, and the influence of which she will probably feel hereafter, without being able to understand its operation.

Everything about Russia—its absolutism, its size, its globe-spanning ambitions and insecurities—stood as an implicit challenge to the traditional European concept of international order built on equilibrium and restraint.

Russia's position in and toward Europe had long been ambiguous. As Charlemagne's empire had fractured in the ninth century into what would become the modern nations of France and Germany, Slavic tribes more than a thousand miles to their east had coalesced in a confederation based around the city of Kiev (now the capital and geographic center of the state of Ukraine, though perceived almost universally by Russians as simultaneously an inextricable part of their own patrimony). This "land of the Rus" stood at the fraught intersections of civilizations and trade routes. With Vikings to its north, the expanding Arab empire to its south, and raiding Turkic tribes to its east, Russia was permanently in the grip of conflating temptations and fears. Too far to the east to have experienced the Roman Empire (though "czars" claimed the "Caesars" as their political and etymological forebears), Christian but looking to the Orthodox Church in Constantinople rather than Rome for spiritual authority, Russia was close enough to Europe to share a common cultural vocabulary yet perpetually out of phase with the Continent's historical trends. The experience would leave Russia a uniquely "Eurasian" power, sprawling across two continents but never entirely at home in either.

The most profound disjunction had come with the Mongol invasions of the thirteenth century, which subdued a politically divided Russia and razed Kiev. Two and a half centuries of Mongol suzerainty (1237–1480) and the subsequent struggle to restore a coherent state based around the Duchy of Moscow imposed on Russia an eastward orientation just as Western Europe was charting the new technological and intellectual vistas that would create the modern era. During Europe's era of seaborne discovery, Russia was laboring to reconstitute itself as an independent nation and shore up its borders against threats from all directions. As the Protestant Reformation impelled political and religious diversity in Europe, Russia translated the fall of its own religious lodestar, Constantinople and the Eastern Roman Empire, to Muslim invaders in 1453 into an almost mystical conviction that Russia's Czar was now (as the monk Filofei wrote to Ivan III around 1500) "the sole Emperor of all the Christians in the whole universe," with a messianic calling to regain the fallen Byzantine capital for Christendom.

Europe was coming to embrace its multipolarity as a mechanism tending toward balance, but Russia was learning its sense of geopolitics from the hard school of the steppe, where an array of nomadic hordes contended for resources on an open terrain with few fixed borders. There raids for plunder and the enslavement of foreign civilians were regular occurrences, for some a way of life; independence was coterminous with the territory a people could physically defend. Russia affirmed its tie to Western culture but—even as it grew exponentially in size—came to see itself as a beleaguered outpost of civilization for which security could be found only through exerting its absolute will over its neighbors.

In the Westphalian concept of order, European statesmen came to identify security with a balance of power and with restraints on its exercise. In Russia's experience of history, restraints on power spelled catastrophe: Russia's failure to dominate its surroundings, in this view, had exposed it to the Mongol invasions and plunged it into its nightmarish "Time of Troubles" (a fifteen-year dynastic interregnum before the founding of the Romanov Dynasty in 1613, in which invasions, civil wars, and famine claimed a third of Russia's population). The Peace of Westphalia saw international order as an intricate balancing mechanism; the Russian view cast it as a perpetual contest of wills, with Russia extending its domain at each phase to the absolute limit of its material resources. Thus, when asked to define Russia's foreign policy, the mid-seventeenth-century Czar Alexei's minister Nashchokin offered a straightforward description: "expanding the state in every direction, and this is the business of the Department of Foreign Affairs."

This process developed into a national outlook and propelled the onetime Duchy of Moscow across the Eurasian landmass to become the world's territorially largest empire, in a slow, seemingly irresistible expansionist urge that would remain unabated until 1917. Thus the American man of letters Henry Adams recorded the outlook of the Russian ambassador in Washington in 1903 (by which point Russia had reached Korea):

> His political philosophy, like that of all Russians, seemed fixed on the single idea that Russia must roll—must, by her irresistible inertia, crush whatever stood in her way . . . When Russia rolled over a neighboring people, she absorbed their energies in her own movement of custom and race which neither Czar nor peasant could convert, or wished to convert, into any Western equivalent.

With no natural borders save the Arctic and Pacific oceans, Russia was in a position to gratify this impulse for several centuries—marching alternately into Central Asia, then the Caucasus, then the Balkans, then Eastern Europe, Scandinavia, and the Baltic Sea, to the Pacific Ocean and the Chinese and Japanese frontiers (and for a time during the eighteenth and nineteenth centuries across the Pacific into Alaskan and Californian settlements). It expanded each year by an amount larger than the entire territory of many European states (on average, 100,000 square kilometers annually from 1552 to 1917).

When it was strong, Russia conducted itself with the domineering certainty of a superior power and insisted on formal shows of deference to its status. When it was weak, it masked its vulnerability through brooding invocations of vast inner reserves of strength. In either case, it was a special challenge for Western capitals used to dealing with a somewhat more genteel style.

At the same time, Russia's awesome feats of expansion took place from a demographic and economic base that, by Western standards, was not advanced—with many regions thinly populated and seemingly untouched by modern culture and technology. Thus the world-conquering imperialism remained paired with a paradoxical sense of vulnerability—as if marching halfway across the world had generated more potential foes than additional security. From that perspective, the Czar's empire can be said to have expanded because it proved easier to keep going than to stop.

In this context, a distinctive Russian concept of political legitimacy took hold. While Renaissance Europe rediscovered its classical humanist past and refined new concepts of individualism and freedom, Russia sought its resurgence in its undiluted faith and in the coherence of a single, divinely sanctioned authority overpowering all divisions— the Czar as "the living icon of God," whose commands were irresistible and inherently just. A common Christian faith and a shared elite language (French) underscored a commonality of perspective with the West. Yet early European visitors to czarist Russia found themselves in a land of almost surreal extremes and thought they saw, beneath the veneer of a modern Western monarchy, a despotism modeled on Mongol and Tartar practices—"European discipline supporting the tyranny of Asia," in the uncharitable phrase of the Marquis de Custine.

Russia had joined the modern European state system under Czar Peter the Great in a manner unlike any other society. On both sides, it proved a wary embrace. Peter had been born in 1672 into a still essentially medieval Russia. By then, Western Europe had evolved through the age of discovery, the Renaissance, and the Reformation; it stood at the threshold of the scientific revolution and the Enlightenment. A gigantic (at six feet eight inches), intensely energetic figure, the young Czar set out to transform his empire in a reign that expressed the extremes of Russia's many traits and aspirations.

Determined to explore the fruits of modernity and measure Russia's achievements against them, Peter was a frequent visitor in the shops and factories of Moscow's émigré German quarter. As a young ruler, he toured Western capitals, where he tested modern techniques and professional disciplines personally. Having found Russia backward compared with the West, Peter announced his aim: "to sever the people from their former Asiatic customs and instruct them how all Christian peoples in Europe comport themselves."

A series of ukases issued forth: Russia would adopt Western manners and hairstyles, seek out foreign technological expertise, build a modern army and navy, round out its borders with wars against nearly every neighboring state, break through to the Baltic Sea, and construct a new capital city of St. Petersburg. The last, Russia's "window to the West," was built by hand, by a casualty-wracked conscripted labor force, on a marshy wilderness chosen at Peter's personal command, when he put his sword into the ground and announced: "Here shall be a town." When traditionalists rebelled, Peter crushed them and, at least according to the accounts that reached the West, took personal charge of the torture and decapitation of the uprising's leaders.

Peter's tour de force transformed Russian society and vaulted his empire into the first rank of Western great powers. Yet the suddenness of the transformation left Russia with the insecurities of a parvenu. In no other empire would the absolute ruler have felt it necessary to remind her subjects in writing, as Peter's successor Catherine the Great did half a century later, that "Russia is a European State. This is clearly demonstrated by the following Observations."

Russia's reforms were invariably carried out by ruthless autocrats on a population docile in its desire to overcome its past rather than energized by confidence in its future. Nevertheless, like his successor reformers and revolutionaries, when his reign was over, his subjects and their descendants credited him for having driven them, however mercilessly, to achievements they had shown little evidence of seeking. (According to recent polls, Stalin too has acquired some of this recognition in contemporary Russian thinking.)

Catherine the Great, Russia's autocratic reformist ruler from 1762 to 1796 and overseer of a historic period of cultural achievement and territorial expansion (including Russia's conquest of the Khanate of Crimea and its laying low of the Zaporizhian Host, the onetime autonomous Cossack realm in what is today central Ukraine), justified Russia's extreme autocracy as the only system of government that could hold together such a gigantic territory:

> The Extent of the Dominion requires an absolute Power to be vested in that Person who rules over it. It is expedient so to be that the quick Dispatch of Affairs, sent from distant Parts, might make ample Amends for the Delay occasioned by the great Distance of the Places.
>
> Every other Form of Government whatsoever would not only have been prejudicial to Russia, but would even have proved its entire Ruin.

Thus what in the West was regarded as arbitrary authoritarianism was presented in Russia as an elemental necessity, the precondition for functioning governance.

The Czar, like the Chinese Emperor, was an absolute ruler endowed by tradition with mystical powers and overseeing a territory of continental expanse. Yet the position of the Czar differed from that of his Chinese counterpart in one important respect. In the Chinese view, the Emperor ruled wherever possible through the serenity of his conduct; in the Russian view, the leadership of the Czar prevailed through his ability to impose his will by unchallengeable assertions of authority and to impress on all onlookers the Russian state's overwhelmingly vast power. The Chinese Emperor was conceived of as the embodiment of the superiority of Chinese civilization, inspiring other peoples to "come and be transformed." The Czar was seen as the embodiment of the defense of Russia against enemies surrounding it on all sides. Thus while the emperors were lauded for their impartial, aloof benevolence, the nineteenth-century historian Nikolai Karamzin saw in a Czar's harshness a sign that he was fulfilling his true calling:

> In Russia, the sovereign is the living law. He favors the good and punishes the bad . . . [A] soft heart in a monarch is counted as a virtue only when it is tempered with the sense of duty to use sensible severity.

Not unlike the United States in its own drive westward, Russia had imbued its conquests with the moral justification that it was spreading order and enlightenment into heathen lands (with a lucrative trade in furs and minerals an incidental benefit). Yet where the American vision inspired boundless optimism, the Russian experience ultimately based itself on stoic endurance. Stranded "at the interface of two vast and irreconcilable worlds," Russia saw itself as endowed with a special mission to bridge them but exposed on all sides to threatening forces that failed to comprehend its calling. The great Russian novelist and passionate nationalist Fyodor Dostoevsky cited "this ceaseless longing, which has always been inherent in the Russian people, for a great universal church on earth." The exaltation over Russia's world-spanning synthesis of civilizations evoked a corresponding despair over Russia's status as (in the words of an influential nineteenth-century critique) an "orphan cut off from the human family . . . For people to notice us, we have had to stretch from the Bering Straits to the Oder."

A conviction lingered in the expansive, brooding "Russian soul" (as Russian thinkers would come to call it) that someday all of Russia's vast exertions and contradictions would come to fruition: its journey would be vindicated; its achievements would be lauded, and the disdain of the West would transform into awe and admiration; Russia would combine the power and vastness of the East with the refinements of the West and the moral force of true religion; and Moscow, the "Third Rome" inheriting fallen Byzantium's mantle, with its Czar "the successor of the caesars of Eastern Rome, of the organizers of the church and of its councils which established the very creed of the Christian faith," would play the decisive role in ushering in a new era of global justice and fraternity.

It was this Russia, in Europe but not quite of it, that had tempted Napoleon with its expanse and mystique; it was his ruin (just as it was Hitler's a century and a half later) when Russia's people, steeled to great feats of endurance, proved capable of weathering deeper privation than Napoleon's Grande Armée (or Hitler's legions). When Russians burned down four-fifths of Moscow to deny Napoleon the conquest and his troops' sustenance, Napoleon, his epic strategy thus doomed, is said to have exclaimed, "What a people! They are Scythians! What resoluteness! The barbarians!" Now with Cossack horsemen drinking champagne in Paris, this massive autocratic entity loomed over a Europe that struggled to comprehend its ambitions and its method of operation.

By the time the Congress of Vienna took place, Russia was arguably the most powerful country on the Continent. Its Czar Alexander, representing Russia personally at the Vienna peace conference, was unquestionably its most absolute ruler. A man of deep, if changing, convictions, he had recently renewed his religious faith with a course of intensive Bible readings and spiritual consultations. He was convinced, as he wrote to a confidante in 1812, that triumph over Napoleon would usher in a new and harmonious world based on religious principles, and he pledged: "It is to the cause of hastening the true reign of Jesus Christ that I devote all my earthly glory." Conceiving of himself as an instrument of divine will, the Czar arrived in Vienna in 1814 with a design for a new world order in some ways even more radical than Napoleon's in its universality: a "Holy Alliance" of princes sublimating their national interests into a common search for peace and justice, forswearing the balance of power for Christian principles of brotherhood. As Alexander told Chateaubriand, the French royalist intellectual and diplomat, "There no longer exists an English policy, a French, Russian, Prussian, or Austrian policy; there is now only one common policy, which, for the welfare of all, ought to be adopted in common by all states and all peoples." It was a forerunner of the American Wilsonian conception of the nature of world order, albeit on behalf of principles dramatically the opposite of the Wilsonian vision.

Needless to say, such a design, advanced by a victorious military power whose divisions now bestrode the Continent, posed a challenge to Europe's concept of a Westphalian equilibrium of sovereign states. For on behalf of its new vision of legitimacy, Russia brought a surfeit of power. Czar Alexander ended the Napoleonic Wars by marching to Paris at the head of his armies, and in celebration of victory he oversaw an unprecedented review of 160,000 Russian troops on the plains outside the French capital—a demonstration that could not fail to disquiet even allied nations. After consultation with his spiritual advisor, Alexander proposed a draft joint declaration in which the victorious sovereigns would proclaim their agreement that "the course, formerly adopted by the powers in their mutual relations, had to be fundamentally changed and that it was urgent to replace it with an order of things based on the exalted truths of the eternal religion of our Savior."

The task of the negotiators at Vienna would be to transform Alexander's messianic vision into something compatible with the continued independent existence of their states, to welcome Russia into the international order without being crushed by its embrace.

The Congress of Vienna

The statesmen who assembled in Vienna to discuss how to design a peaceful order had been through a whirlwind of upheavals overturning nearly every established structure of authority. In the space of twenty-five years, they had seen the rationality of the Enlightenment replaced by the passions of the Reign of Terror; the missionary spirit of the French Revolution transformed by the discipline of the conquering Bonapartist empire. French power had waxed and waned. It had spilled across France's ancient frontiers to conquer almost all of the European continent, only to be nearly extinguished in the vastness of Russia.

The French envoy at the Congress of Vienna represented in his person a metaphor of the era's seemingly boundless upheavals. Charles-Maurice de Talleyrand-Périgord (or Talleyrand, as he was known) was ubiquitous. He started his career as Bishop of Autun, left the Church to support the Revolution, abandoned the Revolution to serve as Napoleon's Foreign Minister, abandoned Napoleon to negotiate the restoration of the French monarch, and appeared in Vienna as Louis XVIII's Foreign Minister. Many called Talleyrand an opportunist. Talleyrand would have argued that his goals were stability within France and peace in Europe and that he had taken whatever opportunities were available to achieve these goals. He had surely striven for positions to study the various elements of power and legitimacy at close hand without being unduly constrained by any of them. Only a formidable personality could have projected himself into the center of so many great and conflicting events.

At Vienna, Talleyrand's contribution was to achieve for France a peace that preserved the "ancient frontiers," which existed when it had started its foreign adventures. And within less than three years—in 1818—he managed France's entry into the Quadruple Alliance. The vanquished enemy would become an ally in the preservation of the European order in an alliance originally designed to contain it—a precedent followed at the end of World War II, when Germany was admitted to the Atlantic Alliance.

The order established at the Congress of Vienna was the closest that Europe has come to universal governance since the collapse of

Charlemagne's empire. It produced a consensus that peaceful evolutions within the existing order were preferable to alternatives; that the preservation of the system was more important than any single dispute that might arise within it; that differences should be settled by consultation rather than by war.

After World War I ended this vision, it became fashionable to attack the Congress of Vienna order as being excessively based on the balance of power, which by its inherent dynamic of cynical maneuvers drove the world into war. (The British delegation asked the diplomatic historian C. K. Webster, who had written on the Congress of Vienna, to produce a treatise on how to avoid its mistakes.) But that was true, if at all, only in the decade prior to World War I. The period between 1815 and the turn of the century was modern Europe's most peaceful, and the decades immediately following the Congress of Vienna were characterized by an extraordinary balance between legitimacy and power.

The statesmen who assembled in Vienna in 1814 were in a radically different situation from their predecessors who drafted the Peace of Westphalia. A century and a half earlier, a series of settlements of the various wars that made up the Thirty Years' War was conjoined with a set of principles for the general conduct of foreign policy. The European order that emerged took as its point of departure the political entities that existed, now separated from their religious impetus. The application of Westphalian principles was then expected to produce a balance of power to prevent, or at least mitigate, conflict. Over the course of the next nearly century and a half, this system had managed to constrain challengers to the equilibrium through the more or less spontaneous alignment of countervailing coalitions.

The negotiators at the Congress of Vienna faced the wreckage of this order. The balance of power had not been able to arrest the military momentum of the Revolution or of Napoleon. The dynastic legitimacy of government had been overwhelmed by Napoleon's revolutionary élan and skilled generalship.

A new balance of power had to be constructed from the wreckage of the state system and of the Holy Roman Empire—whose remnants Napoleon had dissolved in 1806, bringing to a close a thousand years of institutional continuity—and amidst new currents of nationalism unleashed by the occupation of most of the Continent by French armies. That balance had to be capable of preventing a recurrence of the French expansionism that had produced near hegemony for France in Europe, even as the advent of Russia had brought a similar danger from the east.

Hence the Central European balance also had to be reconstructed. The Habsburgs, once the Continent's dominant dynasty, were now ruling only in their ancestral territories from Vienna. These were large and polyglot (roughly present-day Austria, Hungary, Croatia, Slovenia, and southern Poland), and now of uncertain political cohesion. Several of the smaller German states whose opportunism had provided a certain elasticity to the diplomacy of the Westphalian system in the eighteenth century had been obliterated by the Napoleonic conquests. Their territory had to be redistributed in a manner compatible with a refound equilibrium.

The conduct of diplomacy at the Congress of Vienna was fundamentally different from twenty-first-century practice. Contemporary diplomats are in immediate real-time contact with their capitals. They receive minutely detailed instructions down to the texts of their presentations; their advice is sought on local conditions, much less frequently on matters of grand strategy. The diplomats at Vienna were weeks away from their capitals. It took four days for a message from Vienna to reach Berlin (so at least eight days to receive a reply to any request for guidance), three weeks for a message to reach Paris; London took a little longer. Instructions therefore had to be drafted in language general enough to cover changes in the situation, so the diplomats were instructed primarily on general concepts and long-term interests; with respect to day-to-day tactics, they were largely on their own. Czar Alexander I was two months from his capital, but he needed no instructions; his whims were Russia's commands, and he kept the Congress of Vienna occupied with the fertility of his imagination. The Austrian Foreign Minister Klemens von Metternich, perhaps the shrewdest and most experienced statesman at Vienna, said of Alexander that he was "too weak for true ambition, but too strong for pure vanity." Napoleon said of Alexander that he had great abilities but that "something" was always missing in whatever he did. And because one could never foresee which particular piece would be missing in any given instance, he was totally unpredictable. Talleyrand was more blunt: "He was not for nothing the son of [the mad] Czar Paul."

The other participants at the Congress of Vienna agreed on the general principles of international order and on the imperative of bringing Europe back into some form of equilibrium. But they did not have congruent perceptions of what this would mean in practice. Their task was to achieve some reconciliation of perspectives shaped by substantially different historical experiences.

Britain, safe from invasion behind the English Channel and with unique domestic institutions essentially impervious to developments on the Continent, defined order in terms of threats of hegemony on the Continent. But the continental countries had a lower threshold for threats; their security could be impaired by territorial adjustments short of continental hegemony. Above all, unlike Britain, they felt vulnerable to domestic transformations in neighboring countries.

The Congress of Vienna found it relatively easy to agree on a definition of the overall balance. Already during the war—in 1804—then British Prime Minister William Pitt had put forward a plan to rectify what he considered the weaknesses of the Westphalian settlement. The Westphalian treaties had kept Central Europe divided as a way to enhance French influence. To foreclose temptations, Pitt reasoned, "great masses" had to be created in Central Europe to consolidate the region by merging some of its smaller states. ("Consolidation" was a relative term, as it still left thirty-seven states in the area covered by today's Germany.) The obvious candidate to absorb these abolished principalities was Prussia, which originally preferred to annex contiguous Saxony but yielded to the entreaties of Austria and Britain to accept the Rhineland instead. This enlargement of Prussia placed a significant power on the border of France, creating a geostrategic reality that had not existed since the Peace of Westphalia.

The remaining thirty-seven German states were grouped in an entity called the German Confederation, which would provide an answer to Europe's perennial German dilemma: when Germany was weak, it tempted foreign (mostly French) interventions; when unified, it became strong enough to defeat its neighbors single-handedly, tempting them to combine against the danger. In that sense Germany has for much of history been either too weak or too strong for the peace of Europe.

The German Confederation was too divided to take offensive action yet cohesive enough to resist foreign invasions into its territory. This arrangement provided an obstacle to the invasion of Central Europe without constituting a threat to the two major powers on its flanks, Russia to the east and France to the west.

To protect the new overall territorial settlement, the Quadruple Alliance of Britain, Prussia, Austria, and Russia was formed. A territorial guarantee—which was what the Quadruple Alliance amounted to—did not have the same significance for each of the signatories. The level of urgency with which threats were perceived varied significantly. Britain, protected by its command of the seas, felt confident in withholding definite commitments to contingencies and preferred waiting until a major threat from Europe took specific shape. The continental countries had a narrower margin of safety, assessing that their survival might be at stake from actions far less dramatic than those causing Britain to take alarm.

This was particularly the case in the face of revolution—that is, when the threat involved the issue of legitimacy. The conservative states sought to build bulwarks against a new wave of revolution; they aimed to include mechanisms for the preservation of legitimate order—by which they meant monarchical rule. The Czar's proposed Holy Alliance provided a mechanism for protecting the domestic status quo throughout Europe. His partners saw in the Holy Alliance—subtly redesigned—a way to curb Russian exuberance. The right of intervention was limited because, as the eventual terms stipulated, it could be exercised only in concert; in this manner, Austria and Prussia retained a veto over the more exalted schemes of the Czar.

Three tiers of institutions buttressed the Vienna system: the Quadruple Alliance to defeat challenges to the territorial order; the Holy Alliance to overcome threats to domestic institutions; and a concert of powers institutionalized through periodic diplomatic conferences of the heads of government of the alliances to define their common purposes or to deal with emerging crises. This concert mechanism functioned like a precursor of the United Nations Security Council. Its conferences acted on a series of crises, attempting to distill a common course: the revolutions in Naples in 1820 and in Spain in 1820–23 (quelled by the Holy Alliance and France, respectively) and the Greek revolution and war of independence of 1821–32 (ultimately supported by Britain, France, and Russia). The Concert of Powers did not guarantee a unanimity of outlook, yet in each case a potentially explosive crisis was resolved without a major-power war.

A good example of the efficacy of the Vienna system was its reaction to the Belgian revolution of 1830, which sought to separate today's Belgium from the United Kingdom of the Netherlands. For most of the eighteenth century, armies had marched across that then-province of the Netherlands, in quest of the domination of Europe. For Britain, whose global strategy was based on control of the oceans, the Scheldt River estuary, at the mouth of which lay the port of Antwerp across the channel from England, needed to be in the hands of a friendly country and under no circumstances of a major European state. In the event, a London conference of European powers developed a new approach, recognizing Belgian independence while declaring the new nation "neutral," a heretofore-unknown concept in the relations of major powers, except as a unilateral declaration of intent. The new state agreed not to join military alliances or permit the stationing of foreign troops on its territory. This pledge in turn was guaranteed by the major powers, which thereby undertook the obligation to resist violations of Belgian neutrality. The internationally guaranteed status lasted for nearly a century; it was the trigger that brought England into World War I, when German troops forced a passage to France through Belgian territory.

The vitality of an international order is reflected in the balance it strikes between legitimacy and power and the relative emphasis given to each. Neither aspect is intended to arrest change; rather, in combination they seek to ensure that it occurs as a matter of evolution, not a raw contest of wills. If the balance between power and legitimacy is properly managed, actions will acquire a degree of spontaneity. Demonstrations of power will be peripheral and largely symbolic; because the configuration of forces will be generally understood, no side will feel the need to call forth its full reserves. When that balance is destroyed, restraints disappear, and the field is open to the most expansive claims and the most implacable actors; chaos follows until a new system of order is established.

That balance was the signal achievement of the Congress of Vienna. The Quadruple Alliance deterred challenges to the territorial balance, and the memory of Napoleon kept France—suffering from revolutionary exhaustion—quiescent. At the same time, a judicious attitude toward the peace led to France's swift reincorporation into the concert of powers originally formed to thwart its ambitions. And Austria, Prussia, and Russia, which on the principles of the balance of power should have been rivals, were in fact pursuing common policies: Austria and Russia in effect postponed their looming geopolitical conflict in the name of their shared fears of domestic upheaval. It was only after the element of legitimacy in this international order was shaken by the failed revolutions of 1848 that balance was interpreted less as an equilibrium subject to common adjustments and increasingly as a condition in which to prepare for a contest over preeminence.

As the emphasis began to shift more and more to the power element of the equation, Britain's role as a balancer became increasingly important. The hallmarks of Britain's balancing role were its freedom of action and its proven determination to act. Britain's Foreign Minister (later Prime Minister) Lord Palmerston offered a classic illustration when, in 1841, he learned of a message from the Czar seeking a definitive British commitment to resist "the contingency of an attack by France on the liberties of Europe." Britain, Palmerston replied, regarded "an attempt of one Nation to seize and to appropriate to itself territory which belongs to another Nation" as a threat, because "such an attempt leads to a derangement of the existing Balance of Power, and by altering the relative strength of States, may tend to create danger to other Powers." However, Palmerston's Cabinet could enter no formal alliance against France because "it is not usual for England to enter into engagements with reference to cases which have not actually arisen, or which are not immediately in prospect." In other words, neither Russia nor France could count on British support as a certainty against the other; neither could write off the possibility of British armed opposition if it carried matters to the point of threatening the European equilibrium.

The Premises of International Order

The subtle equilibrium of the Congress of Vienna system began to fray in the middle of the nineteenth century under the impact of three events: the rise of nationalism, the revolutions of 1848, and the Crimean War.

Under the impact of Napoleon's conquests, multiple nationalities that had lived together for centuries began to treat their rulers as "foreign." The German philosopher Johann Gottfried von Herder became an apostle of this trend and argued that each people, defined by language, motherland, and folk culture, had an original genius and was therefore entitled to self-government. The historian Jacques Barzun has described it another way:

> Underlying the theory was fact: the revolutionary and Napoleonic armies had redrawn the mental map of Europe. In place of the eighteenth century horizontal world of dynasties and cosmopolite upper classes, the West now consisted of vertical unities—nations, not wholly separate but unlike.

Linguistic nationalisms made traditional empires—especially the Austro-Hungarian Empire—vulnerable to internal pressure as well as to the resentments of neighbors claiming national links with subjects of the empire.

The emergence of nationalism also subtly affected the relationship between Prussia and Austria after the creation of the "great masses" of the Congress of Vienna. The competition of the two great German powers in Central Europe for the allegiance of some thirty-five smaller states of the German Confederation was originally held in check by the need to defend Central Europe. Also, tradition generated a certain deference to the country whose ruler had been Holy Roman Emperor for half a millennium. The Assembly of the German Confederation (the combined ambassadors to the confederation of its thirty-seven members) met in the Austrian Embassy in Frankfurt, and the Austrian ambassador acted as chairman.

At the same time, Prussia was developing its own claim to eminence. Setting out to overcome the handicaps inherent in its sparse population and extended frontiers, Prussia emerged as a major European state because of its leaders' ability to operate on the margin of their state's capabilities for more than a century—what Otto von Bismarck (the Prussian leader who brought this process to its culmination) called a series of "powerful, decisive and wise regents who carefully husbanded the military and financial resources of the state and kept them together in their own hands in order to throw them with ruthless courage into the scale of European politics as soon as a favorable opportunity presented itself."

The Vienna settlement had reinforced Prussia's strong social and political structure with geographic opportunity. Stretched from the Vistula to the Rhine, Prussia became the repository of Germans' hopes for the unity of their country—for the first time in history. With the passage of decades, the relative subordination of Prussian to Austrian policy became too chafing, and Prussia began to pursue a more confrontational course.

The revolutions of 1848 were a Europe-wide conflagration affecting every major city. As a rising middle class sought to force recalcitrant governments to accept liberal reform, the old aristocratic order felt the power of accelerating nationalisms. At first, the uprisings swept all before them, stretching from Poland in the east as far west as Colombia and Brazil (an empire that had recently won its independence from Portugal, after serving as the seat of its exile government during the Napoleonic Wars). In France, history seemed to repeat itself when Napoleon's nephew achieved power as Napoleon III, first as President on the basis of a plebiscite and then as Emperor.

The Holy Alliance had been designed to deal precisely with

UNITED KINGDOMS
OF SWEDEN AND NORWAY

North Sea

KINGDOM
OF DENMARK

Copenhagen

Baltic S

UNITED KINGDOM OF
GREAT BRITAIN
AND IRELAND

UNITED KINGDOM OF
THE NETHERLANDS

Berlin

KINGDOM OF PRUSSI

London

Amsterdam

K I N G D O M

Silesia

Brussels

Prague

Atlantic Ocean

Paris

GERMAN
CONFEDERATION

Bohemia

KINGDOM
OF FRANCE

Vienna

SWITZERLAND

Austria

AUSTRIAN

Bu

KINGDOM
OF SPAIN

PAPAL STATES

KINGDOM OF
PIEDMONT-SARDINIA

Rome

Mediterranean Sea

KINGDOM OF
THE TWO SICILIES

© 2014 Jeffrey L. Ward

EUROPE AFTER THE CONGRESS OF VIENNA, 1815

Moscow

N

RUSSIAN EMPIRE

igsberg

0 Miles   300

0 Kilometers   300

Warsaw

INGDOM
POLAND

ungary

MPIRE

Black Sea

osnia

Bulgaria

OTTOMAN

Constantinople

EMPIRE

Athens

KEY

——·—·— German Confederation boundary

———— State boundaries

upheavals such as these. But the position of the rulers in Berlin and Vienna had grown too precarious—and the upheavals had been too broad and their implications too varied—to make a joint enterprise possible. Russia in its national capacity intervened against the revolution in Hungary, salvaging Austria's rule there. For the rest, the old order proved just strong enough to overcome the revolutionary challenge. But it never regained the self-confidence of the previous period.

Finally, the Crimean War of 1853–56 broke up the unity of the conservative states—Austria, Prussia, and Russia—which had been one of the two key pillars of the Vienna international order. This combination had defended the existing institutions in revolutions; it had isolated France, the previous disturber of the peace. Now another Napoleon was probing for opportunities to assert himself in multiple directions. In the Crimean War, Napoleon saw the device to end his isolation by allying himself with Britain's historic effort to prevent the Russian reach for Constantinople and access to the Mediterranean. The alignment indeed checked the Russian advance, but at the cost of increasingly brittle diplomacy.

The conflict had begun not over the Crimea—which Russia had conquered from an Ottoman vassal in the eighteenth century—but over competing French and Russian claims to advance the rights of favored Christian communities in Jerusalem, then within Ottoman jurisdiction. During a dispute over which denomination, Catholic or Orthodox, would have principal access to holy sites, Czar Nicholas I demanded recognition of his right to act as "protector" of all Orthodox subjects of the Ottoman Empire, a significant population stretching across strategic territories. The demand—which amounted to a right of intervention in the affairs of a foreign state—was couched in the terms of universal moral principles but cut to the heart of Ottoman sovereignty. Ottoman refusal prompted a Russian military advance into the Balkans and naval hostilities in the Black Sea. After six months Britain and France, fearing the collapse of the Ottoman

Empire and with it the European balance, entered the war on the Ottoman side.

The alliance systems of the Congress of Vienna were shattered as a consequence. The war received its name because a Franco-British force landed in the Crimea to seize the city of Sevastopol, home of Russia's Black Sea fleet; Russian forces held out against a siege of eleven months before sinking their ships. Prussia stayed neutral. Austria foolishly decided to take advantage of Russia's isolation to improve its position in the Balkans, mobilizing Austrian troops there. "We will astonish the world by the magnitude of our ingratitude," commented Austria's Minister-President and Foreign Minister Prince Schwarzenberg when presented with a Russian request for assistance. Instead, Austria's diplomacy supported the British and French war effort diplomatically, with measures approaching the character of an ultimatum.

The effort to isolate Russia concluded by isolating Austria. Within two years, Napoleon invaded the Austrian possessions in Italy in support of Italian unification while Russia stood by. Within Germany, Prussia gained freedom of maneuver. Within a decade Otto von Bismarck started Germany on the road to unification, excluding Austria from what had been its historical role as the standard-bearer of German statehood—again with Russian acquiescence. Austria learned too late that in international affairs a reputation for reliability is a more important asset than demonstrations of tactical cleverness.

Metternich and Bismarck

Two statesmen served as the fulcrums of these vast shifts in Germany and in Europe: the Austrian Foreign Minister Klemens von Metternich and the Prussian Minister-President—later German Chancellor—Otto von Bismarck. The contrast between the legacies of the century's two principal Central European statesmen illustrates the shift in emphasis of the European international order from legitimacy to power in the second half of the nineteenth century. Both have been viewed as archetypal conservatives. Both have been recorded as master manipulators of the balance of power, which they were. But their fundamental concepts of international order were nearly opposite, and they manipulated the balance of power to vastly different ends and with significantly contrasting implications for the peace of Europe and the world.

Metternich's very appointment had testified to the cosmopolitan nature of the eighteenth-century society. He was born in the Rhineland, near the border of France, educated in Strasbourg and Mainz. Metternich did not see Austria until his thirteenth year and did not live there until his seventeenth. He was appointed Foreign Minister in 1809 and Chancellor in 1821, serving until 1848. Fate had placed him in the top civilian position in an ancient empire at the beginning of its decline. Once considered among the strongest and best-governed countries in Europe, Austria was now vulnerable because its central location meant that every European tremor made the earth move there. Its polyglot nature made it vulnerable to the emerging wave of nationalism—a force practically unknown a generation earlier. For Metternich, steadiness and reliability became the lodestar of his policy:

> Where everything is tottering it is above all necessary that
> something, no matter what, remain steadfast so that the lost
> can find a connection and the strayed a refuge.

A product of the Enlightenment, Metternich was shaped more by philosophers of the power of reason than by the proponents of the power of arms. Metternich rejected the restless search for presumed remedies to the immediate; he considered the search for truth the most important task of the statesman. In his view, the belief that whatever was imaginable was also achievable was an illusion. Truth had to reflect an underlying reality of human nature and of the structure of society. Anything more sweeping in fact did violence to the ideals it claimed to fulfill. In this sense, "invention is the enemy of history, which knows only discoveries, and only that which exists can be discovered."

For Metternich, the national interest of Austria was a metaphor for the overall interest of Europe—how to hold together many races and peoples and languages in a structure at once respectful of diversity and of a common heritage, faith, and custom. In that perspective, Austria's historical role was to vindicate the pluralism and, hence, the peace of Europe.

Bismarck, by comparison, was a scion of the provincial Prussian aristocracy, which was far poorer than its counterparts in the west of Germany and considerably less cosmopolitan. While Metternich tried to vindicate continuity and to restore a universal idea, that of a European society, Bismarck challenged all the established wisdom of his period. Until he appeared on the scene, it had been taken for granted that German unity would come about—if at all—through a combination of nationalism and liberalism. Bismarck set about to demonstrate that these strands could be separated—that the principles of the Holy Alliance were not needed to preserve order, that a new order could be built by conservatives' appealing to nationalism, and that a concept of European order could be based entirely on an assessment of power.

The divergence in these two seminal figures' views of the nature of international order is poignantly reflected in their definitions of the national interest. To Metternich, order arose not so much from the pursuit of national interest as from the ability to connect it with that of other states:

> The great axioms of political science derive from the recognition of the true interests of *all* states; it is in the general interest that the guarantee of existence is to be found, while particular interests—the cultivation of which is considered

political wisdom by restless and short-sighted men—have only a secondary importance. Modern history demonstrates the application of the principle of solidarity and equilibrium . . . and of the united efforts of states . . . to force a return to the common law.

Bismarck rejected the proposition that power could be restrained by superior principle. His famous maxims gave voice to the conviction that security could be achieved only by the correct evaluation of the components of power:

A sentimental policy knows no reciprocity . . . Every other government seeks the criteria for its actions solely in its interests, however it may cloak them with legal deductions . . . For heaven's sake no sentimental alliances in which the consciousness of having performed a good deed furnishes the sole reward for our sacrifice . . . The only healthy basis of policy for a great power . . . is egotism and not romanticism . . . Gratitude and confidence will not bring a single man into the field on our side; only fear will do that, if we use it cautiously and skillfully . . . Policy is the art of the possible, the science of the relative.

Ultimate decisions would depend strictly on considerations of utility. The European order as seen in the eighteenth century, as a great Newtonian clockwork of interlocking parts, had been replaced by the Darwinian world of the survival of the fittest.

The Dilemmas of the Balance of Power

With his appointment as Prussian Minister-President in 1862, Bismarck set about to implement his principles and to transform the

European order. With the conservative monarchies of the East divided in the aftermath of the Crimean War, France isolated on the Continent because of the memories evoked by its ruler, and Austria wavering between its national and its European roles, Bismarck saw an opportunity to bring about a German national state for the first time in history. With a few daring strokes between 1862 and 1870, he placed Prussia at the head of a united Germany and Germany in the center of a new system of order.

Disraeli called the unification of Germany in 1871 "a greater political event than the French Revolution" and concluded that "the balance of power has been entirely destroyed." The Westphalian and the Vienna European orders had been based on a divided Central Europe whose competing pressures—between the plethora of German states in the Westphalian settlement, and Austria and Prussia in the Vienna outcome—would balance each other out. What emerged after the unification of Germany was a dominant country, strong enough to defeat each neighbor individually and perhaps all the continental countries together. The bond of legitimacy had disappeared. Everything now depended on calculations of power.

The greatest triumph of Bismarck's career had also made more difficult—perhaps impossible—the operation of a flexible balance of power. The crushing defeat of France in the Franco-Prussian War of 1870–71, which Bismarck had adroitly provoked France into declaring, was attended by the annexation of Alsace-Lorraine, a retributive indemnity, and the tactless proclamation of the German Empire in the Hall of Mirrors of Versailles in 1871. Europe's new order was reduced to five major powers, two of which (France and Germany) were irrevocably estranged from each other.

Bismarck understood that a potentially dominant power at the center of Europe faced the constant risk of inducing a coalition of all others, much like the coalition against Louis XIV in the eighteenth century and Napoleon in the early nineteenth. Only the most restrained conduct could avoid incurring the collective antagonism of its neighbors. All of Bismarck's efforts thereafter would be devoted to an elaborate series of maneuvers to forestall this "cauchemar des coalitions" (nightmare of coalitions), as he called it, using the French phrase. In a world of five, Bismarck counseled, it was always better to be in the party of three. This involved a dizzying series of partly overlapping, partly conflicting alliances (for example, an alliance with Austria and a Reinsurance Treaty with Russia) with the aim of giving the other great powers—except the irreconcilable France—a greater interest to work with Germany than to coalesce against it.

The genius of the Westphalian system as adapted by the Congress of Vienna had been its fluidity and its pragmatism; ecumenical in its calculations, it was theoretically expandable to any region and could incorporate any combination of states. With Germany unified and France a fixed adversary, the system lost its flexibility. It took a genius like Bismarck to sustain the web of counterbalancing commitments keeping the equilibrium in place by a virtuoso performance that forestalled general conflict during his tenure. But a country whose security depends on producing a genius in each generation sets itself a task no society has ever met.

After Bismarck's forced departure in 1890 (after a clash with the new Kaiser Wilhelm II over the scope of his authority), his system of overlapping alliances was maintained only tenuously. Leo von Caprivi, the next Chancellor, complained that while Bismarck had been able to keep five balls in the air simultaneously, he had difficulty controlling two. The Reinsurance Treaty with Russia was not renewed in 1891 on the ground that it was partly incompatible with the Austrian alliance—which, in Bismarck's view, had been precisely its utility. Almost inevitably, France and Russia began exploring an alliance. Such realignments had happened several times before in the European kaleidoscope of shifting orders. The novelty now was its institutionalized permanence. Diplomacy had lost its resilience; it had become a matter of life and death rather than incremental adjustment. Because a switch in alliances might spell national disaster for the abandoned side, each ally was able to extort support from its partner regardless of its best convictions, thereby escalating all crises and linking them to each other. Diplomacy became an effort to tighten the internal bonds of each camp, leading to the perpetuation and reinforcement of all grievances.

The last element of flexibility was lost when Britain abandoned its "splendid isolation" and joined the Entente Cordiale of France and Russia after 1904. It did so not formally but de facto via staff talks, creating a moral obligation to fight at the side of the counterpart countries. Britain set aside its settled policy of acting as balancer—partly because of a German diplomacy that, in a series of crises over Morocco and Bosnia, had sought to break up the Franco-Russian alliance by humiliating each of its members in turn (France over Morocco in 1905 and 1911, Russia over Bosnia in 1908) in the hopes of impressing on the other its ally's unreliability. Finally, the German military programs introduced a large and growing navy challenging Britain's command of the seas.

Military planning compounded the rigidity. Since the Congress of Vienna, there had been only one general European war—the Crimean War. (The Franco-Prussian War was confined to the two adversaries.) It had been conducted about a specific issue and served limited aims. By the turn of the twentieth century, military planners—drawing on what they took to be the lessons of mechanization and new methods of mobilization—began to aim for total victory in all-out war. A system of railways permitted the rapid movement of military forces. With large reserve forces on all sides, speed of mobilization became of the essence. German strategy, the famous Schlieffen Plan, was based on the assessment that Germany needed to defeat one of its neighbors before it could combine with others to attack from east and west. Preemption was thereby built into its military planning. Germany's neighbors were under the converse imperative; they had to accelerate their mobilization and concerted action to reduce the impact of possible German preemption. Mobilization schedules dominated diplomacy; if political leaders wanted to control military considerations, it should have been the other way around.

Diplomacy, which still worked by traditional—somewhat lei-surely—methods, lost touch with the emerging technology and its corollary warfare. Europe's diplomats continued to assume that they were engaged in a common enterprise. They were reinforced in that approach because none of the many previous diplomatic crises of the new century had brought matters to the breaking point. In two crises over Morocco and one over Bosnia, the mobilization schedules had no operational impact because, however intense the posturing, events never escalated to the point of imminent confrontation. Paradoxically, the very success in resolving these crises bred a myopic form of risk-taking unmoored from any of the interests actually at stake. It came to be taken for granted that maneuvering for tactical victories to be cheered in the nationalist press was a normal method of conducting policy—that major powers could dare each other to back down in a succession of standoffs over tangential disputes without ever producing a showdown.

But history punishes strategic frivolity sooner or later. World War I broke out because political leaders lost control over their own tactics. For nearly a month after the assassination of the Austrian Crown Prince in June 1914 by a Serbian nationalist, diplomacy was conducted on the dilatory model of many other crises surmounted in recent decades. Four weeks elapsed while Austria prepared an ultimatum. Consultations took place; because it was high summer, statesmen took vacations. But once the Austrian ultimatum was submitted in July 1914, its deadline imposed a great urgency on decision making, and within less than two weeks, Europe moved to a war from which it never recovered.

All these decisions were made when the differences between the major powers were in inverse proportion to their posturing. A new concept of legitimacy—a meld of state and empire—had emerged so that none of the powers considered the institutions of the others a basic threat to their existence. The balance of power as it existed was rigid but not oppressive. Relations between the crowned heads were cordial, even social and familial. Except for France's commitment to regain Alsace-Lorraine, no major country had claims against the territory of its neighbor. Legitimacy and power were in substantial balance. But in the Balkans among the remnants of the Ottoman possessions, there were countries, Serbia in the forefront, threatening Austria with unsatisfied claims of national self-determination. If any major country supported such a claim, a general war was probable because Austria was linked by alliance to Germany as Russia was to France. A war whose consequences had not been considered descended on Western civilization over the essentially parochial issue of the assassination of the Austrian Crown Prince by a Serb nationalist, giving Europe a blow that obliterated a century of peace and order.

In the forty years following the Vienna settlement, the European order buffered conflicts. In the forty years following the unification of Germany, the system aggravated all disputes. None of the leaders foresaw the scope of the looming catastrophe that their system of routinized confrontation backed by modern military machines was making almost certain sooner or later. And they all contributed to it, oblivious to the fact that they were dismantling an international order: France by its implacable commitment to regain Alsace-Lorraine, requiring war; Austria by its ambivalence between its national and its Central European responsibilities; Germany by attempting to overcome its fear of encirclement by serially staring down France and Russia side by side with a buildup of naval forces, seemingly blind to the lessons of history that Britain would surely oppose the largest land power on the Continent if it simultaneously acted as if it meant to threaten Britain's naval preeminence. Russia, by its constant probing in all directions, threatened Austria and the remnants of the Ottoman Empire simultaneously. And Britain, by its ambiguity obscuring the degree of its growing commitment to the Allied side, combined the disadvantage of every course. Its support made France and Russia adamant; its aloof posture confused some German leaders into believing that Britain might remain neutral in a European war.

Reflecting on what might have occurred in alternative historical scenarios is usually a futile exercise. But the war that overturned Western civilization had no inevitable necessity. It arose from a series of miscalculations made by serious leaders who did not understand the consequences of their planning, and a final maelstrom triggered by a terrorist attack occurring in a year generally believed to be a tranquil period. In the end, the military planning ran away with diplomacy. It is a lesson subsequent generations must not forget.

Legitimacy and Power Between the World Wars

World War I was welcomed by enthusiastic publics and euphoric leaders who envisioned a short, glorious war for limited aims. In the event, it killed more than twenty-five million and shipwrecked the prevailing international order. The European balance's subtle calculus of shifting interests had been abandoned for the confrontational diplomacy of two rigid alliances and was then consumed by trench warfare, producing heretofore-inconceivable casualties. In the ordeal, the Russian, Austrian, and Ottoman Empires perished entirely. In Russia, a popular uprising on behalf of modernization and liberal reform was seized by an armed elite proclaiming a universal revolutionary doctrine. After a descent into famine and civil war, Russia and its possessions emerged as the Soviet Union, and Dostoevsky's yearning for "a great universal church on earth" transmogrified into a Moscow-directed world Communist movement rejecting all existing concepts of order. "Woe to the statesman whose arguments for entering a war are not as convincing at its end as they were at the beginning," Bismarck had cautioned. None of the leaders who drifted into war in August 1914 would have done so could they have foreseen the world of 1918.

Stunned by the carnage, Europe's statesmen tried to forge a postwar period that would be as different as possible from the crisis that they thought had produced the Great War, as it was then called. They blotted from their minds nearly every lesson of previous attempts to forge an international order, especially of the Congress of Vienna. It was not a happy decision. The Treaty of Versailles in 1919 refused to accept Germany back into the European order as the Congress of Vienna had included acceptance of a defeated France. The new revolutionary Marxist-Leninist government of the Soviet Union declared itself not bound by the concepts or restraints of an international order whose overthrow it prophesied; participating at the fringes of European diplomacy, it was recognized only slowly and reluctantly by the Western powers. Of the five states that had constituted the European balance, the Austrian Empire had disappeared; Russia and Germany were excluded, or had excluded themselves; and Britain was beginning to return to its historical attitude of involving itself in European affairs primarily to resist an actual threat to the balance of power rather than to preempt a potential threat.

Traditional diplomacy had brought about a century of peace in Europe by an international order subtly balancing elements of power and of legitimacy. In the last quarter of that century, the balance had shifted to relying on the power element. The drafters of the Versailles settlement veered back to the legitimacy component by creating an international order that could be maintained, if at all, only by appeals to shared principles—because the elements of power were ignored or left in disarray. The belt of states emerging from the principle of self-determination located between Germany and the Soviet Union proved too weak to resist either, inviting collusion between them. Britain was increasingly withdrawn. The United States, having entered the war decisively in 1917 despite initial public reluctance, had grown disillusioned by the outcome and withdrawn into relative isolation. The responsibility for supplying the elements of power therefore fell largely on France, which was exhausted by the war, drained by it of human resources and psychological stamina, and increasingly aware that the disparity in strength between it and Germany threatened to become congenital.

Rarely has a diplomatic document so missed its objective as the Treaty of Versailles. Too punitive for conciliation, too lenient to keep Germany from recovering, the Treaty of Versailles condemned the exhausted democracies to constant vigilance against an irreconcilable and revanchist Germany as well as a revolutionary Soviet Union.

With Germany neither morally invested in the Versailles settlement nor confronted with a clear balance of forces preventing its challenges, the Versailles order all but dared German revisionism. Germany could be prevented from asserting its potential strategic superiority only by discriminatory clauses, which challenged the moral convictions of the United States and, to an increasing degree, Great Britain. And once Germany began to challenge the settlement, its terms were maintainable only by the ruthless application of French arms or a permanent American involvement in continental affairs. Neither was forthcoming.

France had spent three centuries keeping Central Europe at first divided and then contained—at first by itself, then in alliance with Russia. But after Versailles, it lost this option. France was too drained by the war to play the role of Europe's policeman, and Central and Eastern Europe were seized by political currents beyond France's capacity to manipulate. Left alone to balance a unified Germany, it made halting efforts to guard the settlement by force but became demoralized when its historical nightmare reappeared with the advent of Hitler.

The major powers attempted to institutionalize their revulsion to war into a new form of peaceful international order. A vague formula for international disarmament was put forward, though the implementation was deferred for later negotiations. The League of Nations and a series of arbitration treaties set out to replace power contests with legal mechanisms for the resolution of disputes. Yet while membership in these new structures was nearly universal and every form of violation of the peace formally banned, no country proved willing to enforce the terms. Powers with grievances or expansionist goals— Germany, imperial Japan, Mussolini's Italy—soon learned that there were no serious consequences for violating the terms of membership of the League of Nations or for simply withdrawing. Two overlapping and contradictory postwar orders were coming into being: the world of rules and international law, inhabited primarily by the Western democracies in their interactions with each other; and an unconstrained zone appropriated by the powers that had withdrawn from this system of limits to achieve greater freedom of action. Looming beyond both and opportunistically maneuvering between them lay the Soviet Union—with its own revolutionary concept of world order threatening to submerge them all.

In the end the Versailles order achieved neither legitimacy nor equilibrium. Its almost pathetic frailty was demonstrated by the Locarno Pact of 1925, in which Germany "accepted" the western frontiers and the demilitarization of the Rhineland to which it had already agreed at Versailles but explicitly refused to extend the same assurance to its borders with Poland and Czechoslovakia—making explicit its ambitions and underlying resentments. Amazingly, France completed the Locarno agreement even though it left France's allies in Eastern Europe formally exposed to eventual German revanchism—a hint of what it would do a decade later in the face of an actual challenge.

In the 1920s, the Germany of the Weimar Republic appealed to Western consciences by contrasting the inconsistencies and punitiveness of the Versailles settlement with the League of Nations' more idealistic principles of international order. Hitler, who came to power in 1933 by the popular vote of a resentful German people, abandoned all restraints. He rearmed in violation of the Versailles peace terms and overthrew the Locarno settlement by reoccupying the Rhineland. When his challenges failed to encounter a significant response, Hitler began to dismantle the states of Central and Eastern Europe one by one: Austria first, followed by Czechoslovakia, and finally Poland.

The nature of these challenges was not singular to the 1930s. In every era, humanity produces demonic individuals and seductive ideas of repression. The task of statesmanship is to prevent their rise to power and sustain an international order capable of deterring them if they do achieve it. The interwar years' toxic mixture of facile pacifism, geopolitical imbalance, and allied disunity allowed these forces a free hand.

Europe had constructed an international order from three hundred years of conflict. It threw it away because its leaders did not understand the consequences when they entered World War I—and though they did understand the consequences of another conflagration, they recoiled before the implications of acting on their foresight. The collapse of international order was essentially a tale of abdication, even suicide. Having abandoned the principles of the Westphalian settlement and reluctant to exercise the force required to vindicate its proclaimed moral alternative, Europe was now consumed by another war that, at its end, brought with it once more the need to recast the European order.

The Postwar European Order

As a result of two world wars, the concept of Westphalian sovereignty and the principles of the balance of power were greatly diminished in the contemporary order of the Continent that spawned them. Their residue would continue, perhaps most consequentially in some of the countries to which they were brought in the age of discovery and expansion.

By the end of World War II, Europe's world-ordering material and psychological capacity had all but vanished. Every continental European country with the exception of Switzerland and Sweden had been occupied by foreign troops at one time or another. Every country's economy was in shambles. It became obvious that no European country (including Switzerland and Sweden) was able any longer to shape its own future by itself.

That Western Europe found the moral strength to launch itself on the road to a new approach to order was the work of three great men: Konrad Adenauer in Germany, Robert Schuman in France, and Alcide de Gasperi in Italy. Born and educated before World War I, they retained some of an older Europe's philosophical certitudes about the conditions for human betterment, and this endowed them with the vision and fortitude to overcome the causes of Europe's tragedies. At a moment of greatest weakness, they preserved some of the concepts of order of their youth. Their most important conviction was that if they were to bring succor to their people and prevent a recurrence of Europe's tragedies, they needed to overcome Europe's historical divisions and on that basis create a new European order.

They had to cope first with another division of Europe. In 1949, the Western allies combined their three occupation zones to create the Federal Republic of Germany. Russia turned its occupation zone into a socialist state tied to it by the Warsaw Pact. Germany was back to its position three hundred years earlier after the Peace of Westphalia: its division had become the key element of the emerging international structure.

France and Germany, the two countries whose rivalry had been at the heart of every European war for three centuries, began the process of transcending European history by merging the key elements of their remaining economic power. In 1952, they formed the Coal and Steel Community as a first step toward an "ever closer union" of Europe's constituent peoples and a keystone of a new European order.

For decades, Germany had posed the principal challenge to Europe's stability. For the first decade of the postwar period, the course of its national leadership would be crucial. Konrad Adenauer became Chancellor of the new Federal Republic of Germany at the age of seventy-three, an age by which Bismarck's career was nearing its end. Patrician in style, suspicious of populism, he created a political party, the Christian Democratic Union, which for the first time in German parliamentary history governed as a moderate party with a majority mandate. With this mandate, Adenauer committed himself to regaining the confidence of Germany's recent victims. In 1955, he brought West Germany into the Atlantic Alliance. So committed was Adenauer to the unification of Europe that he rejected, in the 1950s, Soviet proposals hinting that Germany might be unified if the Federal Republic abandoned the Western alliance. This decision surely reflected a shrewd judgment on the reliability of Soviet offers but also a severe doubt about the capacity of his own society to repeat a solitary journey as a national state in the center of the Continent. It nevertheless took a leader of enormous moral strength to base a new international order on the partition of his own country.

The partition of Germany was not a new event in European history; it had been the basis of both the Westphalian and the Vienna settlements. What was new was that the emerging Germany explicitly cast itself as a component of the West in a contest over the nature of international political order. This was all the more important because the balance of power was largely being shaped outside the European continent. For one thousand years, the peoples of Europe had taken for granted that whatever the fluctuations in the balance of power, its constituent elements resided in Europe. The world of the emerging Cold War sought its balances in the conduct and armament of two superpowers: the United States across the Atlantic and the Soviet Union at the geographic fringes of Europe. America had helped restart the European economy with the Greek-Turkish aid program of 1947 and the Marshall Plan of 1948. In 1949, the United States for the first time in its history undertook a peacetime alliance, through the North Atlantic Treaty.

The European equilibrium, historically authored by the states of Europe, had turned into an aspect of the strategy of outside powers. The North Atlantic Alliance established a regular framework for consultation between the United States and Europe and a degree of coherence in the conduct of foreign policy. But in its essence, the European balance of power shifted from internal European arrangements to the containment of the Soviet Union globally, largely by way of the nuclear capability of the United States. After the shock of two devastating wars, the Western European countries were confronted by a change in geopolitical perspective that challenged their sense of historical identity.

The international order during the first phase of the Cold War was in effect bipolar, with the operation of the Western alliance conducted essentially by America as the principal and guiding partner. What the United States understood by alliance was not so much countries acting congruently to preserve equilibrium as America as the managing director of a joint enterprise.

The traditional European balance of power had been based on the equality of its members; each partner contributed an aspect of its power in quest of a common and basically limited goal, which was equilibrium. But the Atlantic Alliance, while it combined the military forces of the allies in a common structure, was sustained largely by unilateral American military power—especially so with respect to America's nuclear deterrent. So long as strategic nuclear weapons were the principal element of Europe's defense, the objective of European policy was primarily psychological: to oblige the United States to treat Europe as an extension of itself in case of an emergency.

The Cold War international order reflected two sets of balances, which for the first time in history were largely independent of each other: the nuclear balance between the Soviet Union and the United States, and the internal balance within the Atlantic Alliance, whose operation was, in important ways, psychological. U.S. preeminence was conceded in return for giving Europe access to American nuclear protection. European countries built up their own military forces not so much to create additional strength as to have a voice in the decisions of the ally—as an admission ticket, as it were, to discussions regarding the use of the American deterrent. France and Britain developed small nuclear forces that were irrelevant to the overall balance of power but created an additional claim to a seat at the table of major-power decisions.

The realities of the nuclear age and the geographic proximity of the Soviet Union sustained the alliance for a generation. But the underlying difference in perspective was bound to reappear with the fall of the Berlin Wall in 1989.

After four decades of Cold War, NATO had achieved the vision of the Cold War's end that its founders had proclaimed. The fall of the Berlin Wall in 1989 led rapidly to the unification of Germany, together with the collapse of the Soviet satellite orbit, the belt of states in Eastern Europe with an imposed Soviet control system. In a testament to the vision of the allied leaders who had designed the Atlantic Alliance and to the subtle performance of those who oversaw the denouement, the century's third contest over Europe ended peacefully. Germany achieved unification as an affirmation of liberal democracy; it reaffirmed its commitment to European unity as a project of common values and shared development. The nations of Eastern Europe, suppressed for forty years (some longer), began to reemerge into independence and to regain their personalities.

The collapse of the Soviet Union changed the emphasis of diplomacy. The geopolitical nature of the European order was fundamentally transformed when there no longer existed a substantial military threat from within Europe. In the exultant atmosphere that followed, traditional problems of equilibrium were dismissed as "old" diplomacy, to be replaced by the spread of shared ideals. The Atlantic Alliance, it was now professed, should be concerned less about security and more about its political reach. The expansion of NATO up to the borders of Russia—even perhaps including it—was now broached as a serious prospect. The projection of a military alliance into historically contested territory within several hundred miles of Moscow was proposed not primarily on security grounds but as a sensible method of "locking in" democratic gains.

In the face of a direct threat, international order had been conceived of as the confrontation of two adversarial blocs dominated by the United States and the Soviet Union, respectively. As Soviet power declined, the world became to some extent multipolar, and Europe strove to define an independent identity.

The Future of Europe

What a journey Europe had undertaken to reach this point. It had launched itself on global explorations and spread its practices and values around the world. It had in every century changed its internal structure and invented new ways of thinking about the nature of international order. Now at the culmination of an era, Europe, in order to participate in it, felt obliged to set aside the political mechanisms through which it had conducted its affairs for three and a half centuries. Impelled also by the desire to cushion the emergent unification of Germany, the new European Union established a common currency in 2002 and a formal political structure in 2004. It proclaimed a Europe united, whole, and free, adjusting its differences by peaceful mechanisms.

German unification altered the equilibrium of Europe because no constitutional arrangement could change the reality that Germany alone was again the strongest European state. The single currency produced a degree of unity that had not been seen in Europe since the Holy Roman Empire. Would the EU achieve the global role its charter proclaimed, or would it, like Charles V's empire, prove incapable of holding itself together?

The new structure represented in some sense a renunciation of Westphalia. Yet the EU can also be interpreted as Europe's return to the Westphalian international state system that it created, spread across the globe, defended, and exemplified through much of the modern age—this time as a regional, not a national, power, as a new unit in a now global version of the Westphalian system.

The outcome has combined aspects of both the national and the regional approaches without, as yet, securing the full benefits of either. The European Union diminishes its member states' sovereignty and traditional government functions, such as control of their currency and borders. On the other hand, European politics remains primarily national, and in many countries, objections to EU policy have become the central domestic issue. The result is a hybrid, constitutionally something between a state and a confederation, operating through ministerial meetings and a common bureaucracy—more like the Holy Roman Empire than the Europe of the nineteenth century. But unlike the Holy Roman Empire (for most of its history, at least), the EU struggles to resolve its internal tensions in the quest for the principles and goals by which it is guided. In the process, it pursues monetary union side by side with fiscal dispersion and bureaucracy at odds with democracy. In foreign policy it embraces universal ideals without the means to enforce them, and cosmopolitan identity in contention with national loyalties—with European unity accompanied by east-west and north-south divides and an ecumenical attitude toward autonomy movements (Catalan, Bavarian, Scot) challenging the integrity of states. The European "social model" is dependent upon yet discomforted by market dynamism. EU policies enshrine tolerant inclusiveness, approaching unwillingness to assert distinctive Western values, even as member states practice politics driven by fears of non-European influxes.

The result is a cycle testing the popular legitimacy of the EU itself. European states have surrendered significant portions of what was once deemed their sovereign authority. Because Europe's leaders are still validated, or rejected, by national democratic processes, they are tempted to conduct policies of national advantage and, in consequence, disputes persist between the various regions of Europe—usually over economic issues. Especially in crises such as that which began in 2009, the European structure is then driven toward increasingly intrusive emergency measures simply to survive. Yet when publics are asked to make sacrifices on behalf of "the European project," a clear understanding of its obligations may not exist. Leaders then face the choice of disregarding the will of their people or following it in opposition to Brussels.

Europe has returned to the question with which it started, except now it has a global sweep. What international order can be distilled from contending aspirations and contradictory trends? Which countries will be the components of the order, and in what manner will they relate their policies? How much unity does Europe need, and how much diversity can it endure? But the converse issue is in the long run perhaps even more fundamental: Given its history, how much diversity must Europe preserve to achieve a meaningful unity?

When it maintained a global system, Europe represented the dominant concept of world order. Its statesmen designed international structures and prescribed them to the rest of the world. Today the nature of the emergent world order is itself in dispute, and regions beyond Europe will play a major role in defining its attributes. Is the world moving toward regional blocs that perform the role of states in the Westphalian system? If so, will balance follow, or will this reduce the number of key players to so few that rigidity becomes inevitable and the perils of the early twentieth century return, with inflexibly constructed blocs attempting to face one another down? In a world where continental structures like America, China, and maybe India and Brazil have already reached critical mass, how will Europe handle its transition to a regional unit? So far the process of integration has been dealt with as an essentially bureaucratic problem of increasing the competence of various European administrative bodies, in other words an elaboration of the familiar. Where will the impetus for charting the inward commitment to these goals emerge? European history has shown that unification has never been achieved by primarily administrative procedures. It has required a unifier—Prussia in Germany, Piedmont in Italy—without whose leadership (and willingness to create faits accomplis) unification would have remained stillborn. What country or institution will play that role? Or will some new institution or inner group have to be devised for charting the road?

And if Europe should achieve unity, by whatever road, how will it define its global role? It has three choices: to foster Atlantic partnership; to adopt an ever-more-neutral position; or to move toward a tacit compact with an extra-European power or grouping of them. Does it envisage shifting coalitions, or does it see itself as a member of a North Atlantic bloc that generally adopts compatible positions? To which of its pasts will Europe relate itself: to its recent past of Atlantic cohesion or to its longer-term history of maneuvering for maximum advantage on the basis of national interest? In short, will there still be an Atlantic community, and if so, as I fervently hope, how will it define itself?

It is a question both sides of the Atlantic must ask themselves. The Atlantic community cannot remain relevant by simply projecting the familiar forward. Cooperating to shape strategic affairs globally, the European members of the Atlantic Alliance in many cases have described their policies as those of neutral administrators of rules and distributors of aid. But they have often been uncertain about what to do when this model was rejected or its implementation went awry. A more specific meaning needs to be given to the often-invoked "Atlantic partnership" by a new generation shaped by a set of experiences other than the Soviet challenge of the Cold War.

The political evolution of Europe is essentially for Europeans to decide. But its Atlantic partners have an important stake in it. Will the emerging Europe become an active participant in the construction of a new international order, or will it consume itself on its own internal issues? The pure balance-of-power strategy of the traditional European great powers is precluded by contemporary geopolitical and strategic realities. But nor will the nascent organization of "rules and norms" by a Pan-European elite prove a sufficient vehicle for global strategy unless accompanied by some accounting for geopolitical realities.

The United States has every reason from history and geopolitics to bolster the European Union and prevent its drifting off into a geopolitical vacuum; the United States, if separated from Europe in politics, economics, and defense, would become geopolitically an island off the shores of Eurasia, and Europe itself could turn into an appendage to the reaches of Asia and the Middle East.

Europe, which had a near monopoly in the design of global order less than a century ago, is in danger of cutting itself off from the contemporary quest for world order by identifying its internal construction with its ultimate geopolitical purpose. For many, the outcome represents the culmination of the dreams of generations—a continent united in peace and forswearing power contests. Yet while the values espoused in Europe's soft-power approach have often been inspiring, few of the other regions have shown such overriding dedication to this single style of policy, raising the prospects of imbalance. Europe turns inward just as the quest for a world order it significantly designed faces a fraught juncture whose outcome could engulf any region that fails to help shape it. Europe thus finds itself suspended between a past it seeks to overcome and a future it has not yet defined.

CHAPTER 3

Islamism and the Middle East:
A World in Disorder

T HE MIDDLE EAST has been the chrysalis of three of the world's great religions. From its stern landscape have issued conquerors and prophets holding aloft banners of universal aspirations. Across its seemingly limitless horizons, empires have been established and fallen; absolute rulers have proclaimed themselves the embodiment of all power, only to disappear as if they had been mirages. Here every form of domestic and international order has existed, and been rejected, at one time or another.

The world has become accustomed to calls from the Middle East urging the overthrow of regional and world order in the service of a universal vision. A profusion of prophetic absolutisms has been the hallmark of a region suspended between a dream of its former glory and its contemporary inability to unify around common principles of domestic or international legitimacy. Nowhere is the challenge of international order more complex—in terms of both organizing regional order and ensuring the compatibility of that order with peace and stability in the rest of the world.

In our own time, the Middle East seems destined to experiment with all of its historical experiences simultaneously—empire, holy war, foreign domination, a sectarian war of all against all—before it arrives (if it ever does) at a settled concept of international order. Until it does so, the region will remain pulled alternately toward joining the world community and struggling against it.

The Islamic World Order

The early organization of the Middle East and North Africa developed from a succession of empires. Each considered itself the center of civilized life; each arose around unifying geographic features and then expanded into the unincorporated zones between them. In the third millennium B.C., Egypt expanded its influence along the Nile and into present-day Sudan. Beginning in the same period, the empires of Mesopotamia, Sumer, and Babylon consolidated their rule among peoples along the Tigris and Euphrates rivers. In the sixth century B.C., the Persian Empire rose on the Iranian plateau and developed a system of rule that has been described as "the first deliberate attempt in history to unite heterogeneous African, Asian and European communities into a single, organized international society," with a ruler styling himself the *Shahanshah,* or "King of Kings."

By the end of the sixth century A.D., two great empires dominated much of the Middle East: the Byzantine (or Eastern Roman) Empire with its capital in Constantinople and professing the Christian religion (Greek Orthodox), and the Sassanid Persian Empire with its capital in Ctesiphon, near modern-day Baghdad, which practiced Zoroastrianism. Conflicts between them had occurred sporadically for centuries. In 602, not long after a plague had wracked both, a Persian invasion of Byzantine territories led to a twenty-five-year-long war in which the two empires tested what remained of their strength. After an eventual Byzantine victory, exhaustion produced the peace that statesmanship had failed to achieve. It also opened the way for the ultimate victory of Islam. For in western Arabia, in a forbidding desert outside the control of any empire, the Prophet Muhammad and his followers were gathering strength, impelled by a new vision of world order.

Few events in world history equal the drama of the early spread of Islam. The Muslim tradition relates that Muhammad, born in Mecca in the year 570, received at the age of forty a revelation that continued for approximately twenty-three years and, when written down, became known as the Quran. As the Byzantine and Persian empires disabled each other, Muhammad and his community of believers organized a polity, unified the Arabian Peninsula, and set out to replace the prevailing faiths of the region—primarily Judaism, Christianity, and Zoroastrianism—with the religion of his received vision.

An unprecedented wave of expansion turned the rise of Islam into one of the most consequential events in history. In the century following the death of Muhammad in 632, Arab armies brought the new religion as far as the Atlantic coast of Africa, to most of Spain, into central France, and as far east as northern India. Stretches of Central Asia and Russia, parts of China, and most of the East Indies followed over the subsequent centuries, where Islam, carried alternately by merchants and conquerors, established itself as the dominant religious presence.

That a small group of Arab confederates could inspire a movement that would lay low the great empires that had dominated the region for centuries would have seemed inconceivable a few decades earlier. How was it possible for so much imperial thrust and such omnidirectional, all-engulfing fervor to be assembled so unnoticed? The records of neighboring societies had not, until then, regarded the Arabian Peninsula as an imperial force. For centuries, the Arabs had lived a tribal, pastoral, seminomadic existence in the desert and its fertile fringes. Until this point, though they had made a handful of evanescent challenges to Roman rule, they had founded no great states or empires. Their historical memory was encapsulated in an oral tradition of epic poetry. They figured into the consciousness of the Greeks, Romans, and Persians mainly as occasional raiders of trade routes and settled populations. To the extent they had been brought into these cultures' visions of world order, it was through ad hoc arrangements to purchase the loyalty of a tribe and charge it with enforcing security along the imperial frontiers.

In a century of remarkable exertions, this world was overturned. Expansionist and in some respects radically egalitarian, Islam was unlike any other society in history. Its requirement of frequent daily prayers made faith a way of life; its emphasis on the identity of religious and political power transformed the expansion of Islam from an imperial enterprise into a sacred obligation. Each of the peoples the advancing Muslims encountered was offered the same choice: conversion, adoption of protectorate status, or conquest. As an Arab Muslim envoy, sent to negotiate with the besieged Persian Empire, declared on the eve of a climactic seventh-century battle, "If you embrace Islam, we will leave you alone, if you agree to pay the poll tax, we will protect you if you need our protection. Otherwise it is war." Arab cavalry, combining religious conviction, military skill, and a disdain for the luxuries they encountered in conquered lands, backed up the threat. Observing the dynamism and achievements of the Islamic enterprise and threatened with extinction, societies chose to adopt the new religion and its vision.

Islam's rapid advance across three continents provided proof to the faithful of its divine mission. Impelled by the conviction that its spread would unite and bring peace to all humanity, Islam was at once a religion, a multiethnic superstate, and a new world order.

THE AREAS ISLAM had conquered or where it held sway over tribute-paying non-Muslims were conceived as a single political unit: *dar al-Islam,* the "House of Islam," or the realm of peace. It would be governed by the caliphate, an institution defined by rightful succession to the earthly political authority that the Prophet had exercised. The

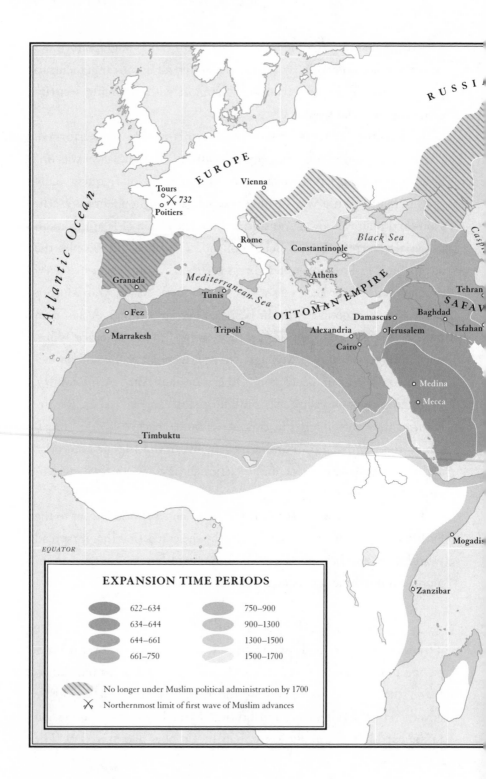

RUSSI

EUROPE

Atlantic Ocean

Tours
○ ✕ 732
Poitiers

Vienna
○

Rome
○

Constantinople
○

Black Sea

Caspi

Granada
○

Mediterranean Sea

Athens
○

OTTOMAN EMPIRE

Tehran
○

SAFAV

Tunis
○

Damascus ○

Baghdad
○

Isfahan
○

Fez
○

Tripoli
○

Alexandria
○

Jerusalem
○

Marrakesh
○

Cairo ○

Medina
○

Mecca
○

Timbuktu
○

EQUATOR

Mogadis

Zanzibar
○

EXPANSION TIME PERIODS

622–634		750–900	
634–644		900–1300	
644–661		1300–1500	
661–750		1500–1700	

No longer under Muslim political administration by 1700

✕ Northernmost limit of first wave of Muslim advances

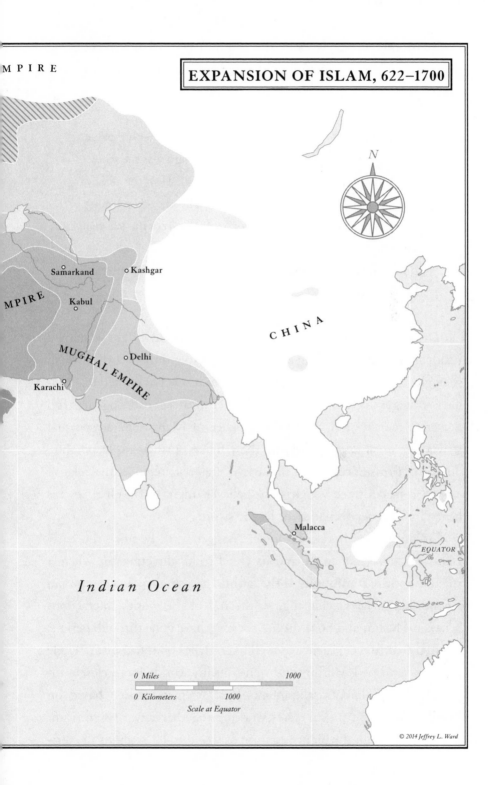

MPIRE

EXPANSION OF ISLAM, 622–1700

N

Samarkand   o Kashgar

MPIRE   Kabul
o

MUGHAL EMPIRE

o Delhi

Karachi
o

CHINA

Malacca
o

EQUATOR

Indian Ocean

0 Miles   1000

0 Kilometers   1000
Scale at Equator

© 2014 Jeffrey L. Ward

lands beyond were *dar al-harb,* the realm of war; Islam's mission was to incorporate these regions into its own world order and thereby bring universal peace:

> The dar al-Islam, in theory, was in a state of war with the dar al-harb, because the ultimate objective of Islam was the whole world. If the dar al-harb were reduced by Islam, the public order of *Pax Islamica* would supersede all others, and non-Muslim communities would either become part of the Islamic community or submit to its sovereignty as tolerated religious communities or as autonomous entities possessing treaty relations with it.

The strategy to bring about this universal system would be named jihad, an obligation binding on believers to expand their faith through struggle. "Jihad" encompassed warfare, but it was not limited to a military strategy; the term also included other means of exerting one's full power to redeem and spread the message of Islam, such as spiritual striving or great deeds glorifying the religion's principles. Depending on the circumstances—and in various eras and regions, the relative emphasis has differed widely—the believer might fulfill jihad "by his heart; his tongue; his hands; or by the sword."

Circumstances have, of course, changed greatly since the early Islamic state set out to expand its creed in all directions or when it ruled the entire community of the faithful as a single political entity in a condition of latent challenge to the rest of the world. Interactions between Muslim and non-Muslim societies have gone through periods of often fruitful coexistence as well as stretches of antagonism. Trade patterns have tied Muslim and non-Muslim worlds more closely together, and diplomatic alignments have frequently been based on Muslim and non-Muslim states working together toward significant shared aims. Still, the binary concept of world order remains the official state doctrine of Iran, embedded in its constitution; the rallying cry of armed minorities in Lebanon, Syria, Iraq, Libya, Yemen, Afghanistan, and Pakistan; and the ideology of several terrorist groups active across the world, including the Islamic State in Iraq and the Levant (ISIL).

Other religions—especially Christianity—have had their own crusading phases, at times exalting their universal mission with comparable fervor and resorting to analogous methods of conquest and forced conversions. (Spanish conquistadores abolished ancient civilizations in Central and South America in the sixteenth century in a similar spirit of world-conquering finality.) The difference is that the crusading spirit subsided in the Western world or took the form of secular concepts that proved less absolute (or less enduring) than religious imperatives. Over time, Christendom became a philosophical and historical concept, not an operational principle of strategy or international order. That process was facilitated because the Christian world had originated a distinction between "the things which are Caesar's" and "the things that are God's," permitting an eventual evolution toward pluralistic, secular-based foreign policies within a state-based international system, as we have seen in the previous two chapters. It was also driven by contingent circumstances, among them the relative unattractiveness of some of the modern crusading concepts called on to replace religious fervor—militant Soviet Communism preaching world revolution, or race-based imperialisms.

The evolution in the Muslim world has been more complex. Certain periods have inspired hopes for a convergence of approaches. On the other hand, as recently as the 1920s, a direct line of political succession from the Prophet Muhammad was still asserted as a practical reality of Middle Eastern statecraft, by the Ottoman Empire. Since this empire collapsed, the response in key Muslim countries has been divided between those who have sought to enter the new state-based, ecumenical international order as significant members—adhering to deeply felt religious beliefs but separating them from questions of foreign policy—and those who see themselves as engaged in a battle over succession to universal authority within a stringent interpretation of the traditional Islamic concept of world order.

Over the past ninety years, the exponents of each view have represented some of the outstanding figures of the era; among them are counted some of the century's most farsighted statesmen and most formidable religious absolutists. The contest between them is not concluded; under some Middle Eastern governments, believers in state-based and faith-based universal orders coexist, if occasionally uneasily. To many of its faithful, especially in a period of resurgent Islamism—the modern ideology seeking to enforce Muslim scripture as the central arbiter of personal, political, and international life—the Islamic world remains in a condition of inescapable confrontation with the outside world.

In the early Islamic system, nonaggression treaties with non-Muslim societies were permissible. According to traditional jurisprudence, these were pragmatic arrangements of limited duration, allowing the Islamic party to secure itself from threats while gathering strength and cohesion. Based on a precedent set by the early Islamic state in entering truces with foes it eventually vanquished, they were limited to terms of specific duration, up to ten years, that could be renewed as needed: in this spirit, in the early centuries of Muslim history, "Islamic legal rulings stipulate that a treaty cannot be forever, since it must be immediately void should the Muslims become capable of fighting them."

What these treaties did not imply was a permanent system in which the Islamic state would interact on equal terms with sovereign non-Muslim states: "The communities of the dar al-harb were regarded as being in a 'state of nature,' for they lacked legal competence to enter into intercourse with Islam on the basis of equality and reciprocity because they failed to conform to its ethical and legal standards." Because in this view the domestic principles of an Islamic state were divinely ordained, non-Muslim political entities were illegitimate; they could never be accepted by Muslim states as truly equal counterparts. A peaceful world order depended on the ability to forge and expand a unitary Islamic entity, not on an equilibrium of competing parts.

In the idealized version of this worldview, the spread of peace and justice under Islam was a unidirectional and irreversible process. The loss of land that had been brought into *dar al-Islam* could never be accepted as permanent, as this would effectively repudiate the legacy of the universal faith. Indeed history records no other political enterprise that spread with such inexorable results. In time, a portion of the territories reached in Islam's periods of expansion would in fact exit Muslim political control, including Spain, Portugal, Sicily, southern Italy, the Balkans (now a patchwork of Muslim and mainly Orthodox Christian enclaves), Greece, Armenia, Georgia, Israel, India, southern Russia, and parts of western China. Yet of the territories incorporated in Islam's initial wave of expansion, the significant majority remain Muslim today.

No single society has ever had the power, no leadership the resilience, and no faith the dynamism to impose its writ enduringly throughout the world. Universality has proved elusive for any conqueror, including Islam. As the early Islamic Empire expanded, it eventually fragmented into multiple centers of power. A succession crisis following Muhammad's death led to a split between Sunni and Shia branches of Islam, a defining division in the contemporary Islamic world. In any new political enterprise, the question of succession is fraught; where the founding leader is also regarded as the "Seal of the Prophets," the final messenger of God, the debate becomes at once political and theological. Following Muhammad's passing in 632, a council of tribal elders selected his father-in-law Abu Bakr as his successor, or caliph, as the figure best able to maintain consensus and harmony in the fledgling Muslim community. A minority believed that the matter should not have been put to a vote, which implied human fallibility, and that power should have passed automatically to the Prophet's closest blood relation, his cousin Ali—an instrumental early convert to Islam and heroic warrior whom Muhammad was held to have personally selected.

These factions eventually formed themselves into the two main branches of Islam. For the proponents of Abu Bakr and his immediate successors, Muhammad's relationship with God was unique and final; the caliphate's primary task was to preserve what Muhammad had revealed and built. They became the Sunnis, short for the "people of tradition and consensus." For the Party of Ali—Shiite-Ali (or Shia)— governance of the new Islamic society was also a spiritual task involving an esoteric element. In their view, Muslims could be brought into the correct relationship with Muhammad's revelation only if they were guided by spiritually gifted individuals directly descended from the Prophet and Ali, who were the "trustees" of the religion's hidden inner meanings. When Ali, eventually coming to power as the fourth caliph, was challenged by rebellion and murdered by a mob, the Sunnis treated the central task as the restoration of order in Islam and backed the faction that reestablished stability. The Shias decried the new authorities as illegitimate usurpers and lionized the martyrs who had died in resistance. These general attitudes would prevail for centuries.

Geopolitical rivalries compounded doctrinal differences. In time, separate Arab, Persian, Turkish, and Mughal spheres arose, each theoretically adhering to the same global Muslim order but increasingly conducting themselves as rival monarchies with distinct interests and distinct interpretations of their faith. In some cases, including much of the Mughal period in India, these included a relatively ecumenical and even syncretic approach stressing tolerance of other faiths and privileging practical foreign policy over sectarian imperatives. When beseeched to wage jihad against Shia Iran by fellow Sunni powers, Mughal India demurred, citing traditional amity and an absence of casus belli.

Eventually, the momentum of the world project of Islam faltered as the first wave of Muslim expansion was reversed in Europe. Battles at Poitiers and Tours in France in 732 ended an unbroken string of advances by Arab and North African Muslim forces. The Byzantine defense of Asia Minor and Eastern Europe maintained, for four centuries, a line behind which the West began developing its own post-Roman ideas of world order. Western concepts began to be projected into Muslim-administered territories as the Byzantines marched back, temporarily, into the Middle East. The Crusades—forays led by orders of Christian knights into the historic Holy Land that Islam had incorporated in the seventh century—took Jerusalem in 1099, establishing a kingdom there that endured for roughly two centuries. The Christian *reconquista* of Spain ended with the fall of Granada, the last Muslim foothold on the peninsula, in 1492, pushing Islam's western boundary back into North Africa.

In the thirteenth century, the dream of universal order reappeared. A new Muslim empire led by the Ottoman Turks, followers of the conqueror Osman, expanded their once-minor Anatolian state into a formidable power capable of challenging, and eventually displacing, the last vestiges of the Byzantine Empire. They began to construct a successor to the great Islamic caliphates of earlier centuries. Styling themselves the leaders of a unified Islamic world, they expanded in all directions by conflicts cast as holy wars, first into the Balkans. In 1453, they conquered Constantinople (Istanbul), the capital of Byzantium, geostrategically astride the Bosphorus Strait; next they moved south and west into the Arabian Peninsula, Mesopotamia, North Africa, Eastern Europe, and the Caucasus, becoming the dominant littoral power in the eastern Mediterranean. Like the early Islamic Empire, the Ottomans conceived of their political mission as universal, upholding "the order of the world"; sultans proclaimed themselves "the Shadow of God on Earth" and "the universal ruler who protects the world."

As its predecessors had a half millennium earlier, the Ottoman Empire came into contact with the states of Western Europe as it expanded westward. The divergence between what was later institutionalized as the multipolar European system and the Ottomans' concept of a single universal empire conferred a complex character on their interactions. The Ottomans refused to accept the European states as either legitimate or equal. This was not simply a matter of Islamic doctrine; it reflected as well a judgment about the reality of power relations, for the Ottoman Empire was territorially larger than all of the Western European states combined and for many decades militarily stronger than any conceivable coalition of them.

In this context, formal Ottoman documents afforded European monarchs a protocol rank below the Sultan, the ruler of the Ottoman Empire; it was equivalent to his vizier, or chief minister. By the same token, the European ambassadors permitted by the Ottomans to reside in Constantinople were cast in the status of supplicants. Compacts negotiated with these envoys were drafted not as bilateral treaties but as unilateral and freely revocable grants of privilege by a magnanimous Sultan.

When the Ottomans had reached the limits of their military capabilities, both sides occasionally found themselves drawn into alignments with each other for tactical advantage. Strategic and commercial interests occasionally circumvented religious doctrine.

In 1526, France, considering itself surrounded by Habsburg power in Spain to its south and the Habsburg-led Holy Roman Empire to its east, proposed a military alliance to the Ottoman Sultan Suleiman the Magnificent. It was the same strategic concept that caused Catholic France a hundred years later to align itself with the Protestant cause in the Thirty Years' War. Suleiman, viewing Habsburg power as the principal obstacle to Ottoman ambitions in Eastern Europe, responded favorably, though he treated France's King Francis I as an unmistakably junior partner. He did not agree to an alliance, which would have implied moral equality; instead, he bestowed his support as a unilateral act from on high:

> I who am the Sultan of Sultans, the sovereign of sovereigns, the dispenser of crowns to the monarchs on the face of the earth, the shadow of God on earth, the Sultan and sovereign lord of the White Sea and of the Black Sea, of Rumelia and of Anatolia, of Karamania . . . To thee who art Francis, king of the land of France.
>
> You have sent to my Porte, refuge of sovereigns, a letter . . . you have here asked aid and succors for your deliverance . . . Take courage then, and be not dismayed. Our glorious predecessors and our illustrious ancestors (may God light up their tombs!) have never ceased to make war to repel the foe and conquer his lands. We ourselves have followed in their footsteps, and have at all times conquered provinces and citadels of great strength and difficult of approach. Night and day our horse is saddled and our sabre is girt.

A working military cooperation emerged, including joint Ottoman-French naval operations against Spain and the Italian peninsula. Playing by the same rules, the Habsburgs leapfrogged the Ottomans to solicit an alliance with the Shia Safavid Dynasty in Persia. Geopolitical imperatives, for a time at least, overrode ideology.

The Ottoman Empire: The Sick Man of Europe

Ottoman assaults on the European order resumed, the most significant of which reached Vienna in 1683. The siege of Vienna, broken that year by a European army led by Eugene of Savoy, marked the high point of Ottoman expansion.

In the late eighteenth and, with increasing momentum, throughout the nineteenth century, European states began to reverse the process. The Ottoman Empire had gradually become sclerotic when orthodox religious factions at the court resisted modernization. Russia pressed against the empire from the north, marching toward the Black Sea and into the Caucasus. Russia and Austria moved into the Balkans from east and west, while France and Britain competed for influence in Egypt—a crown jewel of the Ottoman Empire—which in the nineteenth century achieved various degrees of national autonomy.

Convulsed by internal disturbances, the Ottoman Empire was treated by the Western powers as "the Sick Man of Europe." The fate of its vast holdings in the Balkans and the Middle East, among them significant Christian communities with historical links to the West, became "the Eastern Question," and for much of the nineteenth century the major European powers tried to divide up the Ottoman possessions without upsetting the European balance of power. On their part, the Ottomans had the recourse of the weak; they tried to manipulate the contending forces to achieve a maximum of freedom of action.

In this manner, in the late nineteenth century, the Ottoman Empire entered the European balance as a provisional member of Westphalian international order, but as a declining power not entirely in control of its fate—a "weight" to be considered in establishing the European equilibrium but not a full partner in designing it. Britain used the Ottoman Empire to block Russian advances toward the straits; Austria allied itself alternately with Russia and the Ottomans in dealing with Balkan issues.

World War I ended the wary maneuvering. Allied with Germany, the Ottomans entered the war with arguments drawn from both international systems—the Westphalian and the Islamic. The Sultan accused Russia of violating the empire's "armed neutrality" by committing an "unjustified attack, contrary to international law," and pledged to "turn to arms in order to safeguard our lawful interests" (a quintessentially Westphalian casus belli). Simultaneously, the chief Ottoman religious official declared "jihad," accusing Russia, France, and Britain of "attacks dealt against the Caliphate for the purpose of annihilating Islam" and proclaiming a religious duty for "Mohammedans of all countries" (including those under British, French, or Russian administration) to "hasten with their bodies and possessions to the Djat [jihad]" or face "the wrath of God."

Holy war occasionally moves the already powerful to even greater efforts; it is doomed, however, whenever it flouts strategic or political realities. And the impetus of the age was national identity and national interests, not global jihad. Muslims in the British Empire ignored the declaration of jihad; key Muslim leaders in British India focused instead on independence movement activities, often ecumenical in nature and in partnership with Hindu compatriots. In the Arabian Peninsula, national aspirations—inherently anti-Ottoman—awakened. German hopes for pan-Islamic backing in the war proved a chimera. Following the war's end in 1918, the former Ottoman territories were drawn into the Westphalian international system by a variety of imposed mechanisms.

The Westphalian System and the Islamic World

The 1920 Treaty of Sèvres, signed with what was left of the Ottoman Empire after World War I, reconceived the Middle East as a patchwork of states—a concept heretofore not part of its political vocabulary. Some, like Egypt and non-Arab Iran, had had earlier historical experiences as empires and cultural entities. Others were invented as British or French "mandates," variously a subterfuge of colonialism or a paternalistic attempt to define them as incipient states in need of tutelage. The Sykes-Picot Agreement of 1916 (named after its British and French negotiators) had divided the Middle East into what were in effect spheres of influence. The mandate system, as ratified by the League of Nations, put this division into effect: Syria and Lebanon were assigned to France; Mesopotamia, later Iraq, was placed under British influence; and Palestine and Transjordan became the British "mandate for Palestine," stretching from the Mediterranean coast to Iraq. Each of these entities contained multiple sectarian and ethnic groups, some of which had a history of conflict with each other. This allowed the mandating power to rule in part by manipulating tensions, in the process laying the foundation for later wars and civil wars.

With respect to burgeoning Zionism (the Jewish nationalist movement to establish a state in the Land of Israel, a cause that had predated the war but gained force in its wake), the British government's 1917 Balfour Declaration—a letter from Britain's Foreign Secretary to Lord Rothschild—announced that it favored "the establishment in Palestine of a national home for the Jewish people" while offering the reassurance that it was "clearly understood that nothing shall be done which may prejudice the civil and religious rights of existing non-Jewish communities." Britain compounded the ambiguity of this formulation by seemingly promising the same territory as well to the Sharif of Mecca.

These formal rearrangements of power propelled vast upheavals. In 1924, the secular-nationalist leaders of the newly proclaimed Republic of Turkey abolished the principal institution of pan-Islamic unity, the caliphate, and declared a secular state. Henceforth the Muslim world was stranded between the victorious Westphalian international order and the now-unrealizable concept of *dar al-Islam*. With scant experience, the societies of the Middle East set out to redefine themselves as modern states, within borders that for the most part had no historical roots.

The emergence of the European-style secular state had no precedent in Arab history. The Arabs' first response was to adapt the concepts of sovereignty and statehood to their own ends. The established commercial and political elites began to operate within the Westphalian framework of order and a global economy; what they demanded was their peoples' right to join as equal members. Their rallying cry was genuine independence for established political units, even those recently constructed, not an overthrow of the Westphalian order. In pursuit of these objectives, a secularizing current gained momentum. But it did not, as in Europe, culminate in a pluralistic order.

Two opposing trends appeared. "Pan-Arabists" accepted the premise of a state-based system. But the state they sought was a united Arab nation, a single ethnic, linguistic, and cultural entity. By contrast, "political Islam" insisted on reliance on the common religion as the best vehicle for a modern Arab identity. The Islamists—of which the Muslim Brotherhood is now the most familiar expression—were often drawn from highly educated members of the new middle class. Many considered Islamism as a way to join the postwar era without having to abandon their values, to be modern without having to become Western.

Until World War II, the European powers were sufficiently strong to maintain the regional order they had designed for the Middle East in the aftermath of World War I. Afterward the European powers' capacity to control increasingly restive populations disappeared. The United States emerged as the principal outside influence. In the 1950s and 1960s, the more or less feudal and monarchical governments in Egypt, Iraq, Syria, Yemen, and Libya were overthrown by their military leaders, who proceeded to establish secular governance.

The new rulers, generally recruited from segments of the population heretofore excluded from the political process, proceeded to broaden their popular support by appeals to nationalism. Populist, though not democratic, political cultures took root in the region: Gamal Abdel Nasser—the charismatic populist leader of Egypt from 1954 to 1970—and his successor, Anwar al-Sadat, rose through the ranks from provincial backgrounds. In Iraq, Saddam Hussein, of comparable humble origins, practiced a more extreme version of secular military governance: ruling by intimidation and brutality from the early 1970s (at first as de facto strongman, then as President beginning in 1979) to 2003, he sought to overawe the region with his bellicosity. Both Hussein and his ideological ally, Syria's shrewd and ruthless Hafez al-Assad, entrenched their sectarian minorities over far-larger majority populations (ironically, of opposite orientations—with Sunnis governing majority Shias in Iraq, and the quasi-Shia Alawites governing majority Sunnis in Syria) by avowing pan-Arab nationalism. A sense of common national destiny developed as a substitute for the Islamic vision.

But the Islamic legacy soon reasserted itself. Islamist parties merging a critique of the excesses and failures of secular rulers with scriptural arguments about the need for divinely inspired governance advocated the formation of a pan-Islamic theocracy superseding the existing states. They vilified the West and the Soviet Union alike; many backed their vision by opportunistic terrorist acts. The military rulers reacted harshly, suppressing Islamist political movements, which they charged with undermining modernization and national unity.

This era is, with reason, not idealized today. The military, monarchical, and other autocratic governments in the Middle East treated dissent as sedition, leaving little space for the development of civil society or pluralistic cultures—a lacuna that would haunt the region into the twenty-first century. Still, within the context of autocratic nationalism, a tentative accommodation with contemporary international order was taking shape. Some of the more ambitious rulers such as

Nasser and Saddam Hussein attempted to enlarge their territorial reach—either through force or by means of demagogic appeals to Arab unity. The short-lived confederation between Egypt and Syria from 1958 to 1961 reflected such an attempt. But these efforts failed because the Arab states were becoming too protective of their own patrimony to submerge it into a broader project of political amalgamation. Thus the eventual common basis of policy for the military rulers was the state and a nationalism that was, for the most part, coterminous with established borders.

Within this context, they sought to exploit the rivalry of the Cold War powers to enhance their own influence. From the late 1950s to the early 1970s, the Soviet Union was their vehicle to pressure the United States. It became the principal arms supplier and diplomatic advocate for the nationalist Arab states, which in turn generally supported Soviet international objectives. The military autocrats professed a general allegiance to "Arab socialism" and admiration of the Soviet economic model, yet in most cases economies remained traditionally patriarchal and focused on single industries run by technocrats. The overriding impetus was national interest, as the regimes conceived it, not political or religious ideology.

Cold War–era relations between the Islamic and the non-Islamic worlds, on the whole, followed this essentially Westphalian, balance-of-power-based approach. Egypt, Syria, Algeria, and Iraq generally supported Soviet policies and followed the Soviet lead. Jordan, Saudi Arabia, Iran, and Morocco were friendly to the United States and were relying on U.S. support for their security. All of these countries, with the exception of Saudi Arabia, were run as secular states—though several drew on religion-tinged traditional forms of monarchy for political legitimacy—ostensibly following principles of statecraft based on the national interest. The basic distinction was which countries saw their interests served by alignment with which particular superpower.

In 1973–74, this alignment shifted. Convinced that the Soviet

Union could supply arms but not diplomatic progress toward recovering the Sinai Peninsula from Israeli occupation (Israel had taken the peninsula during 1967's Six-Day War), Egyptian President Anwar al-Sadat switched sides. Henceforth Egypt would operate as a de facto American ally; its security would be based on American, rather than Soviet, weapons. Syria and Algeria moved to a position more equidistant between the two sides in the Cold War. The regional role of the Soviet Union was severely reduced.

The one ideological issue uniting Arab views was the emergence of Israel as a sovereign state and internationally recognized homeland for the Jewish people. Arab resistance to that prospect led to four wars: in 1948, 1956, 1967, and 1973. In each, Israeli arms prevailed.

Sadat's national-interest-based switch to, in effect, the anti-Soviet orbit inaugurated a period of intense diplomacy that led to two disengagement agreements between Egypt and Israel and a peace agreement with Israel in 1979. Egypt was expelled from the Arab League. Sadat was vilified and ultimately assassinated. Yet his courageous actions found imitators willing to reach comparable accommodations with the Jewish state. In 1974, Syria and Israel concluded a disengagement agreement to define and protect the military front lines between the two countries. This arrangement has been maintained for four decades, through wars and terrorism and even during the chaos of the Syrian civil war. Jordan and Israel practiced a mutual restraint that eventually culminated in a peace agreement. Internationally, Syria's and Iraq's authoritarian regimes continued to lean toward the Soviet Union but remained open—case by case—to supporting other policies. By the end of the 1970s, Middle East crises began to look more and more like the Balkan crises of the nineteenth century—an effort by secondary states to manipulate the rivalries of dominant powers on behalf of their own national objectives.

Diplomatic association with the United States was not, however, ultimately able to solve the conundrum faced by the nationalist military autocracies. Association with the Soviet Union had not advanced political goals; association with the United States had not defused social challenges. The authoritarian regimes had substantially achieved independence from colonial rule and provided an ability to maneuver between the major power centers of the Cold War. But their economic advance had been too slow and the access to its benefits too uneven to be responsive to their peoples' needs—problems exacerbated in many cases where their wealth of energy resources fostered a near-exclusive reliance on oil for national revenues, and an economic culture unfavorable to innovation and diversification. Above all, the abrupt end of the Cold War weakened their bargaining position and made them more politically dispensable. They had not learned how, in the absence of a foreign enemy or international crisis, to mobilize populations that increasingly regarded the state not as an end in itself but as having an obligation to improve their well-being.

As a result, these elites found themselves obliged to contend with a rising tide of domestic discontent generating challenges to their legitimacy. Radical groups promised to replace the existing system in the Middle East with a religiously based Middle East order reflecting two distinct universalist approaches to world order: the Sunni version by way of the regionally extensive Muslim Brotherhood founded in 1928, Hamas, the radical movement that gained power in Gaza in 2007, and the global terrorist movement al-Qaeda; and the Shia version through the Khomeini revolution and its offshoot, the Lebanese "state within a state" Hezbollah. In violent conflict with each other, they were united in their commitment to dismantle the existing regional order and rebuild it as a divinely inspired system.

Islamism: The Revolutionary Tide—Two Philosophical Interpretations*

In the spring of 1947, Hassan al-Banna, an Egyptian watchmaker, schoolteacher, and widely read self-taught religious activist, addressed a critique of Egyptian institutions to Egypt's King Farouk titled "Toward the Light." It offered an Islamic alternative to the secular national state. In studiedly polite yet sweeping language, al-Banna outlined the principles and aspirations of the Egyptian Society of Muslim Brothers (known colloquially as the Muslim Brotherhood), the organization he had founded in 1928 to combat what he saw as the degrading effects of foreign influence and secular ways of life.

From its early days as an informal gathering of religious Muslims repelled by British domination of Egypt's Suez Canal Zone, al-Banna's Brotherhood had grown to a nationwide network of social and political activity, with tens of thousands of members, cells in every Egyptian city, and an influential propaganda network distributing his commentaries on current events. It had won regional respect with its support for the failed 1937–39 anti-British, anti-Zionist Arab Revolt in the British mandate for Palestine. It had also attracted scrutiny from Egyptian authorities.

Barred from direct participation in Egyptian politics but nevertheless among Egypt's most influential political figures, al-Banna now

---

* Author's note: The author does not assert any standing to define the core truths of the doctrines and sects whose passionate strivings are now reordering the Muslim world. Many Muslims, in many countries the majority, have arrived at less confrontational and more pluralistic interpretations of their faith than the ones quoted in these pages. Yet the views represented here now exert a significant, often decisive influence in the direction of many of the key Middle Eastern states and almost all non-state organizations. These views represent an assertion of a separate world order by definition superior to and incompatible with the Westphalian system or the values of liberal internationalism. When one seeks to understand them, some recourse must be made to the vocabulary of religion invoked by the contending parties.

sought to vindicate the Muslim Brotherhood's vision with a public statement addressed to Egypt's monarch. Lamenting that Egypt and the region had fallen prey to foreign domination and internal moral decay, he proclaimed that the time for renewal had arrived.

The West, al-Banna asserted, "which was brilliant by virtue of its scientific perfection for a long time . . . is now bankrupt and in decline. Its foundations are crumbling, and its institutions and guiding principles are falling apart." The Western powers had lost control of their own world order: "Their congresses are failures, their treaties are broken, and their covenants torn to pieces." The League of Nations, intended to keep the peace, was "a phantasm." Though he did not use the terms, al-Banna was arguing that the Westphalian world order had lost *both* its legitimacy and its power. And he was explicitly announcing that the opportunity to create a new world order based on Islam had arrived. "The Islamic way has been tried before," he argued, and "history has testified as to its soundness." If a society were to dedicate itself to a "complete and all-encompassing" course of restoring the original principles of Islam and building the social order the Quran prescribes, the "Islamic nation in its entirety"—that is, all Muslims globally—"will support us"; "Arab unity" and eventually "Islamic unity" would result.

How would a restored Islamic world order relate to the modern international system, built around states? A true Muslim's loyalty, al-Banna argued, was to multiple, overlapping spheres, at the apex of which stood a unified Islamic system whose purview would eventually embrace the entire world. His homeland was first a "particular country"; "then it extends to the other Islamic countries, for all of them are a fatherland and an abode for the Muslim"; then it proceeds to an "Islamic Empire" on the model of that erected by the pious ancestors, for "the Muslim will be asked before God" what he had done "to restore it." The final circle was global: "Then the fatherland of the Muslim expands to encompass the entire world. Do you not hear the words of God (Blessed and Almighty is He!): 'Fight them until there is no more persecution, and worship is devoted to God'?"

Where possible, this fight would be gradualist and peaceful. Toward non-Muslims, so long as they did not oppose the movement and paid it adequate respect, the early Muslim Brotherhood counseled "protection," "moderation and deep-rooted equity." Foreigners were to be treated with "peacefulness and sympathy, so long as they behave with rectitude and sincerity." Therefore, it was "pure fantasy" to suggest that the implementation of "Islamic institutions in our modern life would create estrangement between us and the Western nations."

How much of al-Banna's counseled moderation was tactical and an attempt to find acceptance in a world still dominated by Western powers? How much of the jihadist rhetoric was designed to garner support in traditional Islamist quarters? Assassinated in 1949, al-Banna was not vouchsafed time to explain in detail how to reconcile the revolutionary ambition of his project of world transformation with the principles of tolerance and cross-civilizational amity that he espoused.

These ambiguities lingered in al-Banna's text, but the record of many Islamist thinkers and movements since then has resolved them in favor of a fundamental rejection of pluralism and secular international order. The religious scholar and Muslim Brotherhood ideologist Sayyid Qutb articulated perhaps the most learned and influential version of this view. In 1964, while imprisoned on charges of participating in a plot to assassinate Egyptian President Nasser, Qutb wrote *Milestones*, a declaration of war against the existing world order that became a foundational text of modern Islamism.

In Qutb's view, Islam was a universal system offering the only true form of freedom: freedom from governance by other men, man-made doctrines, or "low associations based on race and color, language and country, regional and national interests" (that is, all other modern forms of governance and loyalty and some of the building blocks of

Westphalian order). Islam's modern mission, in Qutb's view, was to overthrow them all and replace them with what he took to be a literal, eventually global implementation of the Quran.

The culmination of this process would be "the achievement of the freedom of man on earth—of all mankind throughout the earth." This would complete the process begun by the initial wave of Islamic expansion in the seventh and eighth centuries, "which is then to be carried throughout the earth to the whole of mankind, as the object of this religion is all humanity and its sphere of action is the whole earth." Like all utopian projects, this one would require extreme measures to implement. These Qutb assigned to an ideologically pure vanguard, who would reject the governments and societies prevailing in the region—all of which Qutb branded "unIslamic and illegal"—and seize the initiative in bringing about the new order.

Qutb, with vast learning and passionate intensity, had declared war on a state of affairs—brashly secular modernity and Muslim disunity, as ratified by the post–World War I territorial settlement in the Middle East—that many Muslims had privately lamented. While most of his contemporaries recoiled from the violent methods he advocated, a core of committed followers—like the vanguard he had envisioned—began to form.

To a globalized, largely secular world judging itself to have transcended the ideological clashes of "History," Qutb and his followers' views long appeared so extreme as to merit no serious attention. In a failure of imagination, many Western elites find revolutionaries' passions inexplicable and assume that their extreme statements must be metaphorical or advanced merely as bargaining chips. Yet for Islamic fundamentalists, these views represent truths overriding the rules and norms of the Westphalian—or indeed any other—international order. They have been the rallying cry of radicals and jihadists in the Middle East and beyond for decades—echoed by al-Qaeda, Hamas, Hezbollah, the Taliban, Iran's clerical regime, Hizb ut-Tahrir (the Party of

Liberation, active in the West and openly advocating the reestablishment of the caliphate in a world dominated by Islam), Nigeria's Boko Haram, Syria's extremist militia Jabhat al-Nusrah, and the Islamic State of Iraq and the Levant, which erupted in a major military assault in mid-2014. They were the militant doctrine of the Egyptian radicals who assassinated Anwar al-Sadat in 1981, proclaiming the "neglected duty" of jihad and branding their President an apostate for making peace with Israel. They accused him of two heresies: recognizing the legal existence of the Jewish state, and (in their view) thereby agreeing to cede land deemed historically Muslim to a non-Muslim people.

This body of thought represents an almost total inversion of Westphalian world order. In the purist version of Islamism, the state cannot be the point of departure for an international system because states are secular, hence illegitimate; at best they may achieve a kind of provisional status en route to a religious entity on a larger scale. Noninterference in other countries' domestic affairs cannot serve as a governing principle, because national loyalties represent deviations from the true faith and because jihadists have a duty to transform *dar al-harb,* the world of unbelievers. Purity, not stability, is the guiding principle of this conception of world order.

The Arab Spring and the Syrian Cataclysm

For a fleeting moment, the Arab Spring that began in late 2010 raised hopes that the region's contending forces of autocracy and jihad had been turned irrelevant by a new wave of reform. Upheavals in Tunisia and Egypt were greeted exuberantly by Western political leaders and media as a regional, youth-led revolution on behalf of liberal democratic principles. The United States officially endorsed the protesters' demands, backing them as undeniable cries for "freedom," "free and fair elections," "representative government," and "genuine democracy," which should not be permitted to fail. Yet the road to democracy was to be tortuous and anguishing, as became obvious in the aftermath of the collapse of the autocratic regimes.

Many in the West interpreted the Tahrir Square uprising in Egypt as a vindication of the argument that an alternative to autocracy should have been promoted much earlier. The real problem had been, however, that the United States found it difficult to discover elements from which pluralistic institutions could be composed or leaders committed to their practice. (This is why some drew the line as between civilian and military rule and supported the anything-but-democratic Muslim Brotherhood.)

America's democratic aspirations for the region, embraced by administrations of both parties, have led to eloquent expressions of the country's idealism. But conceptions of security necessities and of democracy promotion have often clashed. Those committed to democratization have found it difficult to discover leaders who recognize the importance of democracy other than as a means to achieve their own dominance. At the same time, the advocates of strategic necessity have not been able to show how the established regimes will ever evolve in a democratic or even reformist manner. The democratization approach could not remedy the vacuum looming in pursuit of its objectives; the strategic approach was handicapped by the rigidity of available institutions.

The Arab Spring started as a new generation's uprising for liberal democracy. It was soon shouldered aside, disrupted, or crushed. Exhilaration turned into paralysis. The existing political forces, embedded in the military and in religion in the countryside, proved stronger and better organized than the middle-class element demonstrating for democratic principles in Tahrir Square. In practice, the Arab Spring has exhibited rather than overcome the internal contradictions of the Arab-Islamic world and of the policies designed to resolve them.

The oft-repeated early slogan of the Arab Spring, "The people want the downfall of the regime," left open the question of how the people are defined and what will take the place of the supplanted authorities. The original Arab Spring demonstrators' calls for an open political and economic life have been overwhelmed by a violent contest between military-backed authoritarianism and Islamist ideology.

In Egypt, the original exultant demonstrators professing values of cosmopolitanism and democracy in Tahrir Square have not turned out to be the revolution's heirs. Electronic social media facilitate demonstrations capable of toppling regimes, but the ability to enable people to gather in a square differs from building new institutions of state. In the vacuum of authority following the demonstrations' initial success, factions from the pre-uprising period are often in a position to shape the outcome. The temptation to foster unity by merging nationalism and fundamentalism overwhelmed the original slogans of the uprising.

Mohammed Morsi, a leader of the Muslim Brotherhood backed by a coalition of even more radical fundamentalist groups, was elected in 2012 to a presidency that the Muslim Brotherhood had pledged in the heady days of the Tahrir Square demonstrations not to seek. In power, the Islamist government concentrated on institutionalizing its authority by looking the other way while its supporters mounted a campaign of intimidation and harassment of women, minorities, and dissidents. The military's decision to oust this government and declare a new start to the political process was, in the end, welcomed even among the now marginalized, secular democratic element.

This experience raises the issue of humanitarian foreign policy. It distinguishes itself from traditional foreign policy by criticizing national interest or balance-of-power concepts as lacking a moral dimension. It justifies itself not by overcoming a strategic threat but by removing conditions deemed a violation of universal principles of justice. The values and goals of this style of foreign policy reflect a vital aspect of the American tradition. If practiced as the central operating concept of American strategy, however, they raise their own dilemmas: Does America consider itself obliged to support every popular uprising against any nondemocratic government, including those heretofore considered important in sustaining the international system? Is every demonstration democratic by definition? Is Saudi Arabia an ally only until public demonstrations develop on its territory? Among America's principal contributions to the Arab Spring was to condemn, oppose, or work to remove governments it judged autocratic, including the government of Egypt, heretofore a valued ally. For some traditionally friendly governments like Saudi Arabia, however, the central message came to be seen as the threat of American abandonment, not the benefits of liberal reform.

Western tradition requires support for democratic institutions and free elections. No American president who ignores this ingrained aspect of the American moral enterprise can count on the sustained support of the American people. But applied on behalf of parties who identify democracy with a plebiscite on the implementation of religious domination that they then treat as irrevocable, the advocacy of elections may result in only one democratic exercise of them. As a military regime has again been established in Cairo, it reproduces one more time for the United States the as yet unsolved debate between security interests and the importance of promoting humane and legitimate governance. And it appears also as a question of timing: To what extent should security interests be risked for the outcome of a theoretical evolution? Both elements are important. Neglecting a democratic future—assuming we know how to shape its direction— involves long-term risks. Neglecting the present by ignoring the security element risks immediate catastrophe. The difference between traditionalists and activists hinges on that distinction. The statesman has to balance it each time the issue arises. Events can occur whose consequences—such as genocide—are so horrendous that they tilt the scale toward intervention beyond considerations of strategy. But as a general rule, the most sustainable course will involve a blend of the realism and idealism too often held out in the American debate as incompatible opposites.

The Syrian revolution at its beginning appeared like a replay of the Egyptian one at Tahrir Square. But while the Egyptian upheaval unified the underlying forces, in Syria age-old tensions broke out to reawaken the millennial conflict between Shia and Sunni. Given the demographic complexity of Syria, the civil war drew in additional ethnic or religious groups, none of which, based on historical experience, was prepared to entrust its fate to the decisions of the others. Outside powers entered the conflict; atrocities proliferated as survivors sheltered in ethnic and sectarian enclaves.

In the American public debate, the uprising against Bashar al-Assad was dealt with by analogy to the removal of Mubarak and described as a struggle for democracy. Its culmination was expected to be the removal of Assad's government and its replacement with a democratic, inclusive coalition government. President Obama articulated this position in August 2011, when he publicly called on Assad to "step aside" so that the Syrian people could vindicate their universal rights:

> The future of Syria must be determined by its people, but President Bashar al-Assad is standing in their way. His calls for dialogue and reform have rung hollow while he is imprisoning, torturing, and slaughtering his own people. We have consistently said that President Assad must lead a democratic transition or get out of the way. He has not led. For the sake of the Syrian people, the time has come for President Assad to step aside.

The statement was expected to mobilize domestic opposition to Assad and lead to international support for his removal.

This is why the United States pressed for a "political solution" through the United Nations predicated on removing Assad from power and establishing a coalition government. Consternation resulted when other veto-wielding members of the Security Council declined to endorse either this step or military measures, and when the armed opposition that ultimately appeared inside Syria had few elements that could be described as democratic, much less moderate.

By then the conflict had gone beyond the issue of Assad. For the main actors, the issues were substantially different from the focus of the American debate. The principal Syrian and regional players saw the war as not about democracy but about prevailing. They were interested in democracy only if it installed their own group; none favored a system that did not guarantee its own party's control of the political system. A war conducted solely to enforce human rights norms and without concern for the geostrategic or georeligious outcome was inconceivable to the overwhelming majority of the contestants. The conflict, as they perceived it, was not between a dictator and the forces of democracy but between Syria's contending sects and their regional backers. The war, in this view, would decide which of Syria's major sects would succeed in dominating the others and controlling what remained of the Syrian state. Regional powers poured arms, money, and logistical support into Syria on behalf of their preferred sectarian candidates: Saudi Arabia and the Gulf states for the Sunni groups; Iran supporting Assad via Hezbollah. As the combat approached a stalemate, it turned to increasingly radical groups and tactics, fighting a war of encompassing brutality, oblivious on all sides to human rights.

The contest, meanwhile, had begun to redraw the political configuration of Syria, perhaps of the region. The Syrian Kurds created an autonomous unit along the Turkish border that may in time merge with the Kurdish autonomous unit in Iraq. The Druze and Christian communities, fearing a repetition of the conduct of the Muslim Brotherhood in Egypt toward its minorities, have been reluctant to embrace regime change in Syria or have seceded into autonomous communities. The jihadist ISIL set out to build a caliphate in territory seized from Syria and western Iraq, where Damascus and Baghdad proved no longer able to impose their writ.

The main parties thought themselves in a battle for survival or, in the view of some jihadist forces, a conflict presaging the apocalypse. When the United States declined to tip the balance, they judged that it either had an ulterior motive that it was skillfully concealing—perhaps an ultimate deal with Iran—or was not attuned to the imperatives of the Middle East balance of power. This disagreement culminated in 2013 when Saudi Arabia refused a rotating seat on the UN Security Council—explaining that because the traditional arbiters of order had failed to act, it would pursue its own methods.

As America called on the world to honor aspirations to democracy and enforce the international legal ban on chemical weapons, other great powers such as Russia and China resisted by invoking the Westphalian principle of noninterference. They had viewed the uprisings in Tunisia, Egypt, Libya, Mali, Bahrain, and Syria principally through the lens of their own regional stability and the attitudes of their own restive Muslim populations. Aware that the most skilled and dedicated Sunni fighters were avowed jihadists in league with al-Qaeda (or, in the case of ISIL, disowned by it for tactics that even al-Qaeda considered too extreme), they were wary of an outright victory by Assad's opponents. China suggested it had no particular stake in the outcome in Syria, except that it be determined by "the Syrian people" and not foreign forces. Russia, a formal ally of Syria, was interested in the continuance of the Assad government and to some extent in Syria's survival as a unitary state. With an international consensus lacking and the Syrian opposition fractured, an uprising begun on behalf of democratic values degenerated into one of the major humanitarian disasters of the young twenty-first century and into an imploding regional order.

A working regional or international security system might have averted, or at least contained, the catastrophe. But the perceptions of national interest proved to be too different, and the costs of stabilization too daunting. Massive outside intervention at an early stage might have squelched the contending forces but would have required a long-term, substantial military presence to be sustained. In the wake of Iraq and Afghanistan, this was not feasible for the United States, at least not alone. An Iraqi political consensus might have halted the conflict at the Syrian border, but the sectarian impulses of the Baghdad government and its regional affiliates were in the way. Alternatively, the international community could have imposed an arms embargo on Syria and the jihadist militias. That was made impossible by the incompatible aims of the permanent members of the Security Council. If order cannot be achieved by consensus or imposed by force, it will be wrought, at disastrous and dehumanizing cost, from the experience of chaos.

The Palestinian Issue and International Order

Amidst all these upheavals in the Middle East, a peace process has been going on—sometimes fitfully, occasionally intensely—to bring about an end to the Arab-Israeli conflict, which for decades has resulted in an explosive standoff. Four conventional wars and numerous unconventional military engagements have taken place; every Islamist and jihadist group invokes the conflict as a call to arms. Israel's existence and military prowess have been felt throughout the Arab world as a humiliation. The doctrinal commitment never to give up territory has, for some, turned coexistence with Israel from an acceptance of reality into a denial of faith.

Few topics have inspired more passion than how to reconcile Israel's quest for security and identity, the Palestinians' aspirations toward self-governance, and the neighboring Arab governments' search for a policy compatible with their perception of their historic and religious imperatives. The parties involved have traveled an anguished road—from rejection and war to halting acceptance of coexistence, mostly on the basis of armistices—toward an uncertain future. Few international issues have occupied such intense concern in the United States or commanded so much of the attention of American presidents.

A series of issues are involved, each having developed its own extensive literature. The parties have elaborated them in decades of fitful negotiations. These pages deal with only one aspect of them: the conflicting concepts of peaceful order expressed by the negotiators.

Two generations of Arabs have been raised on the conviction that the State of Israel is an illegitimate usurper of Muslim patrimony. In 1947, the Arab countries rejected a UN plan for a partition of the British mandate in Palestine into separate Arab and Jewish states; they believed themselves in a position to triumph militarily and claim the entire territory. Failure of the attempt to extinguish the newly declared State of Israel did not lead to a political settlement and the opening of state-to-state relations, as happened in most other postcolonial conflicts in Asia and Africa. Instead, it ushered in a protracted period of political rejection and reluctant armistice agreement against the background of radical groups seeking to force Israel into submission through terrorist campaigns.

Great leaders have attempted to transcend the conceptual aspect of the conflict by negotiating for peace based on Westphalian principles—that is, between peoples organized as sovereign states, each driven by a realistic assessment of its national interests and capabilities, not absolutes of religious imperatives. Anwar al-Sadat of Egypt dared to look beyond this confrontation and make peace with Israel on the basis of Egypt's national interests in 1979; he paid for his statesmanship with his life, assassinated two years later by radicalized Islamists in the Egyptian military. The same fate befell Yitzhak Rabin, the first Israeli Prime Minister to sign an agreement with the Palestine

Liberation Organization, assassinated by a radical Israeli student four-teen years after Sadat's death.

Within Lebanon, Syria, and the Palestinian territories—especially in Gaza—considerable military and political power is now held by radical Islamists—Hezbollah and Hamas—proclaiming jihad as a re-ligious duty to end what is usually denounced as the "Zionist occupa-tion." The ayatollahs' regime in Iran regularly challenges the very existence of Israel; its erstwhile President Mahmoud Ahmadinejad called for its extirpation.

At least three viewpoints are identifiable in Arab attitudes: a small, dedicated, but not very vocal group accepting genuine coexistence with Israel and prepared to work for it; a much larger group seeking to destroy Israel by permanent confrontation; and those willing to negotiate with Israel but justifying negotiations, at least domestically, in part as a means to overcome the Jewish state in stages.

Israel, with a small population (compared with its neighbors) and territory and a width of just 9.3 miles at its narrowest point and some sixty miles at its widest, has hesitated to cede territory, particularly in areas adjoining major population centers, on behalf of what may turn into a revocable document. Its negotiating positions therefore tend to be legalistic, elaborating definitions of security and political assurances that have a combination of theoretical sweep and occasionally grating detail, with a tendency to reinforce the very passions a peace process is designed to overcome.

In the Arab world, the Palestinian issue has lost some of its ur-gency, though not its importance. The key participants of the peace process have diverted energies and reflection to dealing with the emer-gence of a possibly nuclear Iran and its regional proxies. This affects the peace process in two ways: in the diplomatic role major countries like Egypt and Saudi Arabia can play in shaping the peace process; and, even more important, in their ability to act as guarantors of a resulting agreement. The Palestinian leaders cannot by themselves sustain the result of the peace process unless it is endorsed not just in the toleration but in the active support of an agreement by other regional governments. At this writing, the major Arab states are either torn by civil war or preoccupied with the Sunni-Shia conflict and an increasingly powerful Iran. Nevertheless, the Palestinian issue will have to be faced sooner or later as an essential element of regional and, ultimately, world order.

Some Arab leaders have proposed to make an Arab-Israeli peace that reconciles Israel's security concerns with Arab emotions by conceding the State of Israel as a reality without formally granting it legitimate existence in the Islamic Middle East. Israel's basic demand is for binding assurance that peace will involve a kind of moral and legal recognition translated into concrete acts. Thus Israel, going beyond Westphalian practices, demands to be certified as a Jewish state, an attribute difficult for most Muslims to accept in a formal sense, for it implies a religious as well as a territorial endorsement.

Several Arab states have declared their willingness to establish diplomatic relations with Israel if it returns to the 1967 borders—a cease-fire line in a war that ended half a century ago. But the real issue is what diplomatic relations imply in terms of concrete actions. Will diplomatic recognition of Israel bring an end to the media, governmental, and educational campaign in Arab countries that presents Israel as an illegitimate, imperialist, almost criminal interloper in the region? What Arab government, wracked by pressures ignited in the Arab Spring, will be willing and able to publicly endorse and guarantee a peace that accepts Israel's existence by a precise set of operational commitments? That, rather than the label given to the State of Israel, will determine the prospects of peace.

The conflict of two concepts of world order is embedded in the Israeli-Palestinian issue. Israel is by definition a Westphalian state, founded as such in 1947; the United States, its principal ally, has been a steward and key defender of the Westphalian international order. But the core countries and factions in the Middle East view international order to a greater or lesser degree through an Islamic consciousness. Israel and its neighbors have differences inseparable from geography and history: access to water, resources, specific arrangements for security, refugees. In other regions, comparable challenges are generally solved by diplomacy. In that sense, the issue comes down to the possibility of coexistence between two concepts of world order, through two states—Israel and Palestine—in the relatively narrow space between the Jordan River and the Mediterranean Sea. Since every square mile is invested by both sides with profound significance, success may in turn require testing whether some interim arrangements can be devised that, at a minimum, enhance the possibility of a practical coexistence in which part of the West Bank is granted the attributes of sovereignty pending a final agreement.

As these negotiations have been pursued, the political and philosophical evolution of the Middle East has produced in the Western world a study in contradictions. The United States has had close associations with parties along the entire spectrum of Middle East options: an alliance with Israel, an association with Egypt, a partnership with Saudi Arabia. A regional order evolves when the principal parties take congruent approaches on issues that affect them. That degree of coherence has proved elusive in the Middle East. The principal parties differ with respect to three major issues: domestic evolution; the political future of the Palestinian Arabs; and the future of the Iranian military nuclear program. Some parties that do agree on objectives are not in a position to avow it. For example, Saudi Arabia and Israel share the same general objective with respect to Iran: to prevent the emergence of an Iranian military nuclear capability and to contain it if it becomes unavoidable. But their perception of legitimacy—and Saudi sensitivity to an Arab consensus—inhibit the promulgation of such a view or even very explicit articulation of it. This is why too much of the region remains torn between fear of jihad and fear of dealing with some of its causes.

The consequences of the religious and political conflict described in this chapter present themselves as seemingly distinct issues. In fact, they represent an underlying quest for a new definition of political and international legitimacy.

Saudi Arabia

With some historical irony, among the Western democracies' most important allies through all of these upheavals has been a country whose internal practices diverge almost completely from theirs—the Kingdom of Saudi Arabia. Saudi Arabia has been a partner, at times quietly but decisively behind the scenes, in most of the major regional security endeavors since World War II, when it aligned itself with the Allies. It has been an association demonstrating the special character of the Westphalian state system, which has permitted such distinct societies to cooperate on shared aims through formal mechanisms, generally to their significant mutual benefit. Conversely, its strains have touched on some of the main challenges of the search for contemporary world order.

The Kingdom of Saudi Arabia is a traditional Arab-Islamic realm: both a tribal monarchy and an Islamic theocracy. Two leading families, united in mutual support since the eighteenth century, form the core of its governance. The political hierarchy is headed by a monarch of the Al Saud family, who serves as the head of a complex network of tribal relationships based on ancient ties of mutual loyalty and obligation and controls the kingdom's internal and foreign affairs. The religious hierarchy is headed by the Grand Mufti and the Council of Senior Scholars, drawn largely from the Aal al-Shaykh family. The King endeavors to bridge the gap between these two branches of power by fulfilling the role of "Custodian of the Two Holy Mosques"

(Mecca and Medina), reminiscent of the Holy Roman Emperor as "Fidei defensor."

Zeal and purity of religious expression are embedded in the Saudi historical experience. Three times in as many centuries (in the 1740s, the 1820s, and the early twentieth century) the Saudi state has been founded or reunified by the same two leading families, in each case affirming their commitment to govern Islam's birthplace and holiest shrines by upholding the most austere interpretation of the religion's principles. In each case, Saudi armies fanned out to unify the deserts and mountains of the peninsula in waves of conquest strikingly similar to the original sacred exaltation and holy war that produced the first Islamic state, and in the same territory. Religious absolutism, military daring, and shrewd modern statesmanship have produced the kingdom at the heart of the Muslim world and central to its fate.

What is today Saudi Arabia emerged from Turkish rule after World War I, when Ibn Saud reunified the various feudal principalities scattered across the Arabian Peninsula and held them together by patriarchal allegiance and religious devotion. The royal family has since faced daunting tasks. It governs tribes living in the traditional nomadism and fiercely loyal to the crown, as well as urban concentrations approaching—in some cases surpassing—those of Western metropoles, though placed like mirages across otherwise barren plateaus. An emerging middle class exists in the context of an age-old, semifeudal sense of reciprocal obligation. Within the limits of an extremely conservative political culture, the ruling princes have combined a monarchy with a system of consensus by which the far-flung members of the extended royal family have some share in decisions, and ordinary citizens have gradually been granted a degree of participation in public life.

Millions of foreign workers—Palestinians, Syrians, Lebanese, Egyptians, Pakistanis, and Yemenis—combine in a mosaic held together by the bond of Islam and respect for traditional authority.

Every year several million Muslim travelers from across the world arrive in Saudi Arabia simultaneously to perform the hajj—a pilgrimage to Mecca to perform rites sanctified by the Prophet Muhammad in his own lifetime. This affirmation of faith, obligatory for able-bodied believers to perform at least once in their life, confers on Saudi Arabia a unique religious significance as well as an annual logistical challenge undertaken by no other state. Meanwhile, the discovery of vast oil reserves has made Saudi Arabia wealthy almost without parallel in the region, generating an implicit challenge to the security of a country with a sparse population, no natural land borders, and a politically detached Shia minority living in one of its key oil-producing regions.

Saudi rulers live with the awareness that the covetousness of their neighbors might translate itself into attempted conquest—or, in an era of revolution, potential sponsorship of political or sectarian agitation. Conscious of the fate of nearby nations, they are inevitably ambivalent about economic and social modernization—knowing that an absence of reform may alienate their youthful population, while reform undertaken too rapidly may develop its own momentum and ultimately endanger the cohesion of a country that has known only conservative monarchy. The dynasty has tried to lead the process of social and economic change—within the pattern of its society—precisely in order to control its pace and content. This tactic has allowed the Al Saud to produce just enough change to prevent the accumulation of potentially explosive social tensions while avoiding the destabilizing effects of overly rapid change.

Saudi foreign policy, for most of the existence of the modern Saudi state, has been characterized by a caution that has elevated indirectness into a special art form. For if the kingdom pursued a very forward policy, if it made itself the focal point of all disputes, it would be subjected to entreaties, threats, and blandishments by far more powerful countries, the cumulative impact of which could endanger either independence or coherence. Instead, its authorities achieved security and authority by remoteness; even in the midst of crises—sometimes while carrying out bold changes of course that would reverberate globally—they were almost invariably publicly withdrawn and detached. Saudi Arabia has obscured its vulnerability by opaqueness, masking uncertainty about the motivations of outsiders by a remoteness equally impervious to eloquence and to threats.

The kingdom maneuvered to keep itself out of the forefront of confrontation even when its resources sustained it, as was the case in the oil embargo in 1973, as well as the anti-Soviet jihad in Afghanistan of 1979–89. It facilitated the peace process in the Middle East but left the actual negotiations to others. In this manner, the kingdom has navigated among the fixed poles of friendship for the United States, Arab loyalty, a puritanical interpretation of Islam, and consciousness of internal and external danger. In an age of jihad, revolutionary upheavals, and a perceived American regional withdrawal, some of the obliqueness has been set aside in favor of a more direct approach, making its hostility and fear of Shiite Iran explicit.

No state in the Middle East has been more torn by the Islamist upheaval and the rise of revolutionary Iran than Saudi Arabia, divided between its formal allegiance to the Westphalian concepts that underpin its security and international recognition as a legitimate sovereign state, the religious purism that informs its history, and the appeals of radical Islamism that impair its domestic cohesion (and indeed threatened the kingdom's survival during the seizure of the Grand Mosque of Mecca by fanatic Salafis in 1979).

In 1989, one of the kingdom's disaffected sons, Osama bin Laden, returned from the anti-Soviet jihad in Afghanistan and proclaimed a new struggle. Tracking Qutb's script, he and his followers founded a vanguard organization, al-Qaeda (the Base), from which to mount an omnidirectional jihad. Its "near" targets were the Saudi government and its regional partner states; its "far" enemy was the United States, which al-Qaeda reviled for supporting non-sharia-based state governments in the Middle East and for supposedly defiling Islam by deploy-ing military personnel to Saudi Arabia during the 1990–91 Gulf War. In bin Laden's analysis, the struggle between the true faith and the infidel world was existential and already well under way. World injus-tice had reached a point where peaceful methods were useless; the re-quired tactic would be assassination and terrorism, which would strike fear into al-Qaeda's enemies both near and far and sap their will to resist.

Al-Qaeda's ambitious campaign began with attacks on American and allied facilities in the Middle East and Africa. A 1993 attack on the World Trade Center displayed the organization's global ambitions. On September 11, 2001, the offensive reached its apogee by striking New York, the hub of the world financial system, and Washington, the political hub of American power. The deadliest terrorist attack yet experienced, the 9/11 assault killed 2,977 within minutes, nearly all civilians; thousands of others were injured in the attacks or suffered severe health complications. Osama bin Laden had preceded the attack with a proclamation of al-Qaeda's aims: The West and its influence were to be expelled from the Middle East. Governments in coopera-tive partnership with America were to be overthrown and their politi-cal structures—derided as illegitimate "paper statelets" formed for the convenience of Western powers—dissolved. A new Islamic caliphate would take their place, restoring Islam to its seventh-century glory. A war of world orders was declared.

The battlefield of that conflict ran through the heart of Saudi Arabia, which eventually—after al-Qaeda mounted a failed attempt to overthrow the Al Saud dynasty in 2003—became one of the orga-nization's fiercest opponents. The attempt to find security within both the Westphalian and the Islamist orders worked for a time. Yet the great strategic error of the Saudi dynasty was to suppose, from roughly the 1960s until 2003, that it could support and even manipulate radical Islamism abroad without threatening its own position at home. The outbreak of a serious, sustained al-Qaeda insurgency in the kingdom in 2003 revealed the fatal flaw in this strategy, which the dynasty jettisoned in favor of an effective counterinsurgency campaign led by a prince of the younger generation, Prince Muhammad bin Nayif, now Saudi Interior Minister. Even so, the dynasty was at risk of being overthrown. With the surge of jihadist currents in Iraq and Syria, the acumen displayed in this campaign may again be tested.

Saudi Arabia has adopted a course as complex as the challenges facing it. The royal family has judged Saudi security and national interests to lie with constructive relations with the West and participation in the global economy. Yet as the birthplace of Islam and protector of Islam's holiest places, Saudi Arabia cannot afford deviation from Islamic orthodoxy. It has attempted to co-opt radically resurgent Islamist universalism by a tenuous amalgam of modern statehood and Westphalian international relations grafted onto the practice of Wahhabism, perhaps the most fundamentalist version of the faith, and of subsidizing it internationally. The outcome has at times been internally contradictory. Diplomatically Saudi Arabia has largely aligned itself with the United States while spiritually propagating a form of Islam at odds with modernity and implying a clash with the non-Muslim world. By financing madrassas (religious schools) preaching the austere Wahhabist creed throughout the world, the Saudis have not only carried out their Muslim duties but also taken a defensive measure by making its advocates act as missionaries abroad rather than within the kingdom. The project has had the unintended consequence of nurturing a jihadist fervor that would eventually menace the Saudi state itself and its allies.

The kingdom's strategy of principled ambiguity worked so long as the Sunni states were largely governed by military regimes. But once al-Qaeda appeared on the scene, the ayatollahs' Iran established its leadership over a militant revolutionary camp across the region, and the Muslim Brotherhood threatened to take power in Egypt and elsewhere, Saudi Arabia found itself facing two forms of civil war in the Middle East, which its own proselytizing efforts had (however inadvertently) helped to inflame: one between Muslim regimes that were members of the Westphalian state system and Islamists who considered statehood and the prevailing institutions of international order an abomination to the Quran; and another between Shias and Sunnis across the region, with Iran and Saudi Arabia seen as leaders of the two opposing sides.

This contest would unfold against the backdrop of two others, each posing its own tests for regional order: American military actions to oust the odious dictatorships in Iraq and Libya, accompanied by U.S. political pressures to bring about "the transformation of the Greater Middle East"; and the resurgence of Sunni-Shia rivalry, most devastatingly during the Iraq War and the Syrian conflict. In each of these, the parallel interests of Saudi Arabia and the United States have proved difficult to distill.

As a matter of regional leadership, balance of power, and doctrinal contention, Saudi Arabia considers itself threatened by Shia Iran, as both a religious and an imperial phenomenon. Saudi Arabia sees a Tehran-led archipelago of rising Shia power and influence running from Iran's Afghan border through Iraq, Syria, and Lebanon to the Mediterranean in confrontation with a Saudi-led Sunni order composed of Egypt, Jordan, the Gulf states, and the Arabian Peninsula, all in a wary partnership with Turkey.

The American attitude toward Iran and Saudi Arabia therefore cannot be simply a balance-of-power calculation or a democratization issue; it must be shaped in the context of what is above all a religious struggle, already lasting a millennium, between two wings of Islam. The United States and its allies have to calibrate their conduct with care. For pressures unleashed in the region will affect the delicate latticework of relationships underpinning the kingdom at its heart and administering Islam's holiest places. An upheaval in Saudi Arabia would carry profound repercussions for the world economy, the future of the Muslim world, and world peace. In light of the experience with revolutions elsewhere in the Arab world, the United States cannot assume that a democratic opposition is waiting in the wings to govern Saudi Arabia by principles more congenial to Western sensibilities. America must distill a common understanding with a country that is the central eventual prize targeted by both the Sunni and the Shia versions of jihad and whose efforts, however circuitous, will be essential in fostering a constructive regional evolution.

To Saudi Arabia, the conflict with Iran is existential. It involves the survival of the monarchy, the legitimacy of the state, and indeed the future of Islam. To the extent that Iran continues to emerge as a potentially dominant power, Saudi Arabia at a minimum will seek to enhance its own power position to maintain the balance. Given the elemental issues involved, verbal reassurances will not suffice. Depending on the outcome of the Iranian nuclear negotiations, Saudi Arabia is likely to seek access to its own nuclear capability in some form—either by acquiring warheads from an existing nuclear power, preferably Islamic (like Pakistan), or by financing their development in some other country as an insurance policy. To the extent that Saudi Arabia judges America to be withdrawing from the region, it may well seek a regional order involving another outside power, perhaps China, India, or even Russia. The tensions, turmoil, and violence wracking the Middle East in the first two decades of the twenty-first century should therefore be understood as layers of civil and religious strife carried out in a contest to determine whether and how the region will relate to any larger concept of world order. Much depends on the United States' capacity, skill, and will to help shape an outcome that fulfills American interests and that Saudi Arabia and its allies consider compatible with their security and their principles.

The Decline of the State?

Syria and Iraq—once beacons of nationalism for Arab countries—may lose their capacity to reconstitute themselves as unified Westphalian states. As their warring factions seek support from affiliated communities across the region and beyond, their strife jeopardizes the coherence of all neighboring countries. If multiple contiguous states at the heart of the Arab world are unable to establish legitimate governance and consistent control over their territories, the post–World War I Middle East territorial settlement will have reached a terminal phase.

The conflict in Syria and Iraq and the surrounding areas has thus become the symbol of an ominous new trend: the disintegration of statehood into tribal and sectarian units, some of them cutting across existing borders, in violent conflict with each other or manipulated by competing outside factions, observing no common rules other than the law of superior force—what Hobbes might have called the state of nature.

In the wake of revolution or regime change, absent the establishment of a new authority accepted as legitimate by a decisive majority of the population, a multiplicity of disparate factions will continue to engage in open conflicts with perceived rivals for power; portions of the state may drift into anarchy or permanent rebellion, or merge with parts of another disintegrating state. The existing central government may prove unwilling or unable to reestablish authority over border regions or non-state entities such as Hezbollah, al-Qaeda, ISIL, and the Taliban. This has happened in Iraq, Libya, and, to a dangerous extent, Pakistan.

Some states as presently constituted may not be governable in full except through methods of governance or social cohesion that Americans reject as illegitimate. These limitations can be overcome, in some cases, through evolutions toward a more liberal domestic system. Yet where factions within a state adhere to different concepts of world order or consider themselves in an existential struggle for survival, American demands to call off the fight and assemble a democratic coalition government tend either to paralyze the incumbent government (as in the Shah's Iran) or to fall on deaf ears (the Egyptian government led by General Sisi—now heeding the lessons of its predecessors' overthrow by tacking away from a historic American alliance in favor of greater freedom of maneuver). In such conditions, America has to make the decision on the basis of what achieves the best combination of security and morality, recognizing that both will be imperfect.

In Iraq, the dissolution of Saddam Hussein's brutal Sunni-dominated dictatorship generated pressures less for democracy than for revenge—which the various factions sought through the consolidation of their disparate forms of religion into autonomous units in effect at war with each other. In Libya, a vast country relatively thinly populated and riven by sectarian divisions and feuding tribal groups—with no common history except Italian colonialism—the overthrow of the murderous dictator Qaddafi has had the practical effect of removing any semblance of national governance. Tribes and regions have armed themselves to secure self-rule or domination via autonomous militias. A provisional government in Tripoli has gained international recognition but cannot exercise practical authority beyond city limits, if even that. Extremist groups have proliferated, propelling jihad into neighboring states—especially in Africa—armed with weapons from Qaddafi's arsenals.

When states are not governed in their entirety, the international or regional order itself begins to disintegrate. Blank spaces denoting lawlessness come to dominate parts of the map. The collapse of a state may turn its territory into a base for terrorism, arms supply, or sectarian agitation against neighbors. Zones of non-governance or jihad now stretch across the Muslim world, affecting Libya, Egypt, Yemen, Gaza, Lebanon, Syria, Iraq, Afghanistan, Pakistan, Nigeria, Mali, Sudan, and Somalia. When one also takes into account the agonies of Central Africa—where a generations-long Congolese civil war has drawn in all neighboring states, and conflicts in the Central African Republic and South Sudan threaten to metastasize similarly—a significant portion of the world's territory and population is on the verge of effectively falling out of the international state system altogether.

As this void looms, the Middle East is caught in a confrontation akin to—but broader than—Europe's pre-Westphalian wars of religion. Domestic and international conflicts reinforce each other. Political, sectarian, tribal, territorial, ideological, and traditional national-interest disputes merge. Religion is "weaponized" in the service of geopolitical objectives; civilians are marked for extermination based on their sectarian affiliation. Where states are able to preserve their authority, they consider their authority without limits, justified by the necessities of survival; where states disintegrate, they become fields for the contests of surrounding powers in which authority too often is achieved through total disregard for human well-being and dignity.

The conflict now unfolding is both religious and geopolitical. A Sunni bloc consisting of Saudi Arabia, the Gulf states, and to some extent Egypt and Turkey confronts a bloc led by Shia Iran, which backs Bashar al-Assad's portion of Syria, Nuri al-Maliki's central and southern Iraq, and the militias of Hezbollah in Lebanon and Hamas in Gaza. The Sunni bloc supports uprisings in Syria against Assad and in Iraq against Maliki; Iran aims for regional dominance by employing non-state actors tied to Tehran ideologically in order to undermine the domestic legitimacy of its regional rivals.

Participants in the contests search for outside support, particularly from Russia and the United States, in turn shaping the relations between them. Russia's goals are largely strategic, at a minimum to prevent Syrian and Iraqi jihadist groups from spreading into its Muslim territories and, on the larger global scale, to enhance its position vis-à-vis the United States (thereby reversing the results of the 1973 war described earlier in this chapter). America's quandary is that it condemns Assad on moral grounds—correctly—but the largest contingent of his opponents are al-Qaeda and more extreme groups, which the United States needs to oppose strategically. Neither Russia nor the United States has been able to decide whether to cooperate or to maneuver against each other—though events in Ukraine may resolve this ambivalence in the direction of Cold War attitudes. Iraq is contested between multiple camps—this time Iran, the West, and a variety of revanchist Sunni factions—as it has been many times in its history, with the same script played by different actors.

After America's bitter experiences and under conditions so inhospitable to pluralism, it is tempting to let these upheavals run their course and concentrate on dealing with the successor states. But several of the potential successors have declared America and the Westphalian world order as principal enemies.

In an era of suicide terrorism and proliferating weapons of mass destruction, the drift toward pan-regional sectarian confrontations must be deemed a threat to world stability warranting cooperative effort by all responsible powers, expressed in some acceptable definition of at least regional order. If order cannot be established, vast areas risk being opened to anarchy and to forms of extremism that will spread organically into other regions. From this stark pattern the world awaits the distillation of a new regional order by America and other countries in a position to take a global view.

CHAPTER **4**

The United States and Iran: Approaches to Order

I N THE SPRING OF 2013, Ayatollah Ali Khamenei, the Supreme Leader of the Islamic Republic of Iran—the figure then and now outranking all Iranian government ministers, including Iran's President and Foreign Minister—delivered a speech to an international conference of Muslim clerics, lauding the onset of a new global revolution. What elsewhere was called the "Arab Spring," he declared, was in fact an "Islamic Awakening" of world-spanning consequence. The West erred in assessing that the crowds of demonstrators represented the triumph of liberal democracy, Khamenei explained. The demonstrators would reject the "bitter and horrifying experience of following the West in politics, behavior and lifestyle" because they embodied the "miraculous fulfillment of divine promises":

> Today what lies in front of our eyes and cannot be denied by
> any informed and intelligent individual is that the world of
> Islam has now emerged out of the sidelines of social and
> political equations of the world, that it has found a promi-
> nent and outstanding position at the center of decisive global

events, and that it offers a fresh outlook on life, politics, government and social developments.

In Khamenei's analysis, this reawakening of Islamic consciousness was opening the door to a global religious revolution that would finally vanquish the overbearing influence of the United States and its allies and bring an end to three centuries of Western primacy:

> Islamic Awakening, which speakers in the arrogant and reactionary camp do not even dare to mention in words, is a truth whose signs can be witnessed in almost all parts of the world of Islam. The most obvious sign of it is the enthusiasm of public opinion, especially among young people, to revive the glory and greatness of Islam, to become aware of the nature of the international order of domination and to remove the mask from the shameless, oppressive and arrogant face of the governments and centers that have been pressuring the Islamic and non-Islamic East.

Following "the failure of communism and liberalism" and with the power and confidence of the West crumbling, the Islamic Awakening would reverberate across the world, Khamenei pledged, unifying the global Muslim *ummah* (the transnational community of believers) and restoring it to world centrality:

> This final goal cannot be anything less than creating a brilliant Islamic civilization. All parts of the Islamic Ummah—in the form of different nations and countries—should achieve the civilizational position that has been specified in the Holy Quran . . . Through religious faith, knowledge, ethics and constant struggle, Islamic civilization can gift

advanced thought and noble codes of behavior to the Islamic Ummah and to the entire humanity, and it can be the point of liberation from materialistic and oppressive outlooks and corrupt codes of behavior that form the pillars of current Western civilization.

Khamenei had expatiated upon this topic previously. As he remarked to an audience of Iranian paramilitary forces in 2011, popular protests in the West spoke to a global hunger for spirituality and legitimacy as exemplified by Iran's theocracy. A world revolution awaited:

The developments in the U.S. and Europe suggest a massive change that the world will witness in the future . . . Today the slogans of Egyptians and the Tunisians are being repeated in New York and California . . . The Islamic Republic is currently the focal point of the awakening movement of nations and this reality is what has upset the enemies.

In any other region, such declarations would have been treated as a major revolutionary challenge: a theocratic figure wielding supreme spiritual and temporal power was, in a significant country, publicly embracing a project of constructing an alternative world order in opposition to the one being practiced by the world community. The Supreme Leader of contemporary Iran was declaring that universal religious principles, not national interests or liberal internationalism, would dominate the new world he prophesied. Had such sentiments been voiced by an Asian or a European leader, they would have been interpreted as a shocking global challenge. Yet thirty-five years of repetition had all but inured the world to the radicalism of these sentiments and the actions backing them. On its part, Iran combined its challenge to modernity with a millennial tradition of a statecraft of exceptional subtlety.

The Tradition of Iranian Statecraft

The first implementation of radical Islamist principles as a doctrine of state power occurred in 1979, in a capital where it was least expected—in a country unlike the majority of Middle Eastern states, with a long and distinguished national history and a long-established reverence for its pre-Islamic past. So when Iran, an accepted state in the Westphalian system, turned itself into an advocate for radical Islam after the Ayatollah Khomeini revolution, the Middle East regional order was turned upside down.

Of all the countries of the region, Iran has perhaps the most coherent sense of nationhood and the most elaborated tradition of national-interest-based statecraft. At the same time, Iran's leaders have traditionally reached far beyond the modern borders of Iran and have rarely had occasion to adhere to Westphalian concepts of statehood and sovereign equality. Iran's founding tradition was that of the Persian Empire, which, in a series of incarnations from the seventh century B.C. to the seventh century A.D., established its rule across much of the contemporary Middle East and portions of Central Asia, Southwest Asia, and North Africa. With resplendent art and culture, a sophisticated bureaucracy experienced in administering far-flung provinces, and a vast multiethnic military steeled by successful campaigns in every direction, Persia saw itself as far more than one society among many. The Persian ideal of monarchy elevated its sovereign to quasi-divine status as a magnanimous overlord of peoples—the "King of Kings" dispensing justice and decreeing tolerance in exchange for peaceful political submission.

The Persian imperial project, like classical China's, represented a form of world ordering in which cultural and political achievements and psychological assurance played as great a role as traditional military conquests. The fifth-century B.C. Greek historian Herodotus described the self-confidence of a people that had absorbed the finest of all foreign customs—Median dress, Egyptian armor—and now regarded itself as the center of human achievement:

> Most of all they hold in honor themselves, then those who dwell next to themselves, and then those next to *them,* and so on, so that there is a progression in honor in relation to the distance. They hold least in honor those whose habitation is furthest from their own. This is because they think themselves to be the best of mankind in everything and that others have a hold on virtue in proportion to their nearness; those that live furthest away are the most base.

Roughly twenty-five hundred years later this sense of serene self-confidence had endured, as manifested in the text of an 1850 trade agreement between the United States and the Safavid Dynasty—which governed a curtailed but still expansive version of the Persian Empire consisting of Iran and significant portions of present-day Afghanistan, Iraq, Kuwait, Pakistan, Tajikistan, Turkey, and Turkmenistan. Even after the recent loss of Armenia, Azerbaijan, Dagestan, and eastern Georgia in two wars with the expanding Russian Empire, the Shah projected the assurance of the heir of Xerxes and Cyrus:

> The President of the United States of North America, and his Majesty as exalted as the Planet Saturn; the Sovereign to whom the Sun serves as a standard; whose splendor and magnificence are equal to that of the Skies; the Sublime Sovereign, the Monarch whose armies are as numerous as the Stars; whose greatness calls to mind that of Jeinshid; whose

magnificence equals that of Darius; the Heir of the Crown and Throne of the Kayanians, the Sublime Emperor of all Persia, being both equally and sincerely desirous of establishing relations of Friendship between the two Governments, which they wish to strengthen by a Treaty of Friendship and Commerce, reciprocally advantageous and useful to the Citizens and subjects of the two High contracting parties, have for this purpose named for their Plenipotentiaries . . .

At the intersection of East and West and administering provinces and dependencies stretching at their widest extent from modern-day Libya to Kyrgyzstan and India, Persia was either the starting point or the eventual target of nearly every major conqueror on the Eurasian landmass from antiquity to the Cold War. Through all these upheavals, Persia—like China under roughly comparable circumstances—retained its distinct sense of identity. Expanding across vastly diverse cultures and regions, the Persian Empire adopted and synthesized their achievements into its own distinct concept of order. Submerged in waves of conquest by Alexander the Great, the early Islamic armies, and later the Mongols—shocks that all but erased the historical memory and political autonomy of other peoples—Persia retained its confidence in its cultural superiority. It bowed to its conquerors as a temporary concession but retained its independence through its worldview, charting "great interior spaces" in poetry and mysticism and revering its connection with the heroic ancient rulers recounted in its epic *Book of Kings*. Meanwhile, Persia distilled its experience managing all manner of territories and political challenges into a sophisticated canon of diplomacy placing a premium on endurance, shrewd analysis of geopolitical realities, and the psychological manipulation of adversaries.

This sense of distinctness and adroit maneuver endured in the Islamic era, when Persia adopted the religion of its Arab conquerors but, alone among the first wave of conquered peoples, insisted on re-taining its language and infusing the new order with the cultural legacies of the empire that Islam had just overthrown. Eventually, Per-sia became the demographic and cultural center of Shiism—first as a dissenting tradition under Arab rule, later as the state religion starting in the sixteenth century (adopted partly as a way to distinguish itself from and defy the growing Ottoman Empire at its borders, which was Sunni). In contrast to the majority Sunni interpretation, this branch of Islam stressed the mystical and ineffable qualities of religious truth and authorized "prudential dissimulation" in the service of the inter-ests of the faithful. In its culture, religion, and geopolitical outlook, Iran (as it called itself officially after 1935) had preserved the distinc-tiveness of its tradition and the special character of its regional role.

The Khomeini Revolution

The revolution against Iran's twentieth-century Shah Reza Pahlavi had begun (or at least had been portrayed to the West) as an antimonar-chical movement demanding democracy and economic redistribution. Many of its grievances were real, caused by the dislocations imposed by the Shah's modernization programs and the heavy-handed and arbi-trary tactics with which the government attempted to control dissent. But when, in 1979, Ayatollah Ruhollah Khomeini returned from exile in Paris and Iraq to claim the role of the revolution's "Supreme Leader," he did so not on behalf of social programs or of democratic governance but in the name of an assault against the entire regional order and in-deed the institutional arrangements of modernity.

The doctrine that took root in Iran under Khomeini was unlike anything that had been practiced in the West since the religious wars of the pre-Westphalian era. It conceived of the state not as a legitimate entity in its own right but as a weapon of convenience in a broader religious struggle. The twentieth-century map of the Middle East,

Khomeini announced, was a false and un-Islamic creation of "imperialists" and "tyrannical self-seeking rulers" who had "separated the various segments of the Islamic *umma* [community] from each other and artificially created separate nations." All contemporary political institutions in the Middle East and beyond were "illegitimate" because they "do not base themselves on divine law." Modern international relations based on procedural Westphalian principles rested on a false foundation because "the relations between nations should be based on spiritual grounds" and not on principles of national interest.

In Khomeini's view—paralleling that of Qutb—an ideologically expansionist reading of the Quran pointed the way from these blasphemies and toward the creation of a genuinely legitimate world order. The first step would be the overthrow of all the governments in the Muslim world and their replacement by "an Islamic government." Traditional national loyalties would be overridden because "it is the duty of all of us to overthrow the *taghut;* i.e., the illegitimate political powers that now rule the entire Islamic world." The founding of a truly Islamic political system in Iran would mark, as Khomeini declared upon the founding of the Islamic Republic of Iran on April 1, 1979, "the First Day of God's Government."

This entity would not be comparable to any other modern state. As Mehdi Bazargan, Khomeini's first appointee for the post of Prime Minister, told the *New York Times,* "What was wanted . . . was a government of the type seen during the 10 years of the rule of the Prophet Mohammed and the five years under his son-in-law, Ali, the first Shiite Imam." When government is conceived of as divine, dissent will be treated as blasphemy, not political opposition. Under Khomeini, the Islamic Republic carried out those principles, beginning with a wave of trials and executions and a systematic repression of minority faiths far exceeding what had occurred under the Shah's authoritarian regime.

Amidst these upheavals a new paradox took shape, in the form of a dualistic challenge to international order. With Iran's revolution, an Islamist movement dedicated to overthrowing the Westphalian system gained control over a modern state and asserted its "Westphalian" rights and privileges—taking up its seat at the United Nations, conducting its trade, and operating its diplomatic apparatus. Iran's clerical regime thus placed itself at the intersection of two world orders, arrogating the formal protections of the Westphalian system even while repeatedly proclaiming that it did not believe in it, would not be bound by it, and intended ultimately to replace it.

This duality has been ingrained in Iran's governing doctrine. Iran styles itself as "the Islamic Republic," implying an entity whose authority transcends territorial demarcations, and the Ayatollah heading the Iranian power structure (first Khomeini, then his successor, Ali Khamenei) is conceived of not simply as an Iranian political figure but as a global authority—"the Supreme Leader of the Islamic Revolution" and "the Leader of the Islamic Ummah and Oppressed People."

The Islamic Republic announced itself on the world stage with a massive violation of a core principle of the Westphalian international system—diplomatic immunity—by storming the American Embassy in Tehran and holding its staff hostage for 444 days (an act affirmed by the current Iranian government, which in 2014 appointed the hostage takers' translator to serve as its ambassador at the United Nations). In a similar spirit, in 1989, Ayatollah Khomeini claimed global juridical authority in issuing a fatwa (religious proscription) pronouncing a death sentence on Salman Rushdie, a British citizen of Indian Muslim descent, for his publication of a book in Britain and the United States deemed offensive to Muslims.

Even while simultaneously conducting normal diplomatic relations with the countries whose territory these groups have in part arrogated, Iran in its Islamist aspect has supported organizations such as Hezbollah in Lebanon and the Mahdi Army in Iraq—non-state militias challenging established authorities and employing terror attacks as part of their strategy. Tehran's imperative of Islamic revolution has been interpreted to permit cooperation across the Sunni-Shia divide to advance broader anti-Western interests, including Iran's arming of the Sunni jihadist group Hamas against Israel and, according to some reports, the Taliban in Afghanistan; the report of the 9/11 Commission and investigations of a 2013 terrorist plot in Canada suggested that al-Qaeda operatives had found scope to operate from Iran as well.

On the subject of the need to overthrow the existing world order, Islamists on both sides—Sunni and Shia—have been in general agreement. However intense the Sunni-Shia doctrinal divide erupting across the Middle East in the early twenty-first century, Sayyid Qutb's views were essentially identical to those put forward by Iran's political ayatollahs. Qutb's premise that Islam would reorder and eventually dominate the world struck a chord with the men who recast Iran into the fount of religious revolution. Qutb's works circulate widely in Iran, some personally translated by Ayatollah Ali Khamenei. As Khamenei wrote in his 1967 introduction to Qutb's work, *The Future of This Religion*:

> This lofty and great author has tried in the course of the chapters of this book . . . to first introduce the essence of the faith as it is and then, after showing that it is a program of living . . . [to confirm] with his eloquent words and his particular world outlook that ultimately world government shall be in the hands of our school and "the future belongs to Islam."

For Iran, representing the minority Shia branch of this endeavor, victory could be envisioned through the sublimation of doctrinal differences for shared aims. Toward this end, the Iranian constitution proclaims the goal of the unification of all Muslims as a national obligation:

> In accordance with the sacred verse of the Qur'an ("This your community is a single community, and I am your Lord, so worship Me" [21:92]), all Muslims form a single nation, and the government of the Islamic Republic of Iran has the duty of formulating its general policies with a view to cultivating the friendship and unity of all Muslim peoples, and it must constantly strive to bring about the political, economic, and cultural unity of the Islamic world.

The emphasis would be not on theological disputes but on ideological conquest. As Khomeini elaborated, "We must strive to export our Revolution throughout the world, and must abandon all idea of not doing so, for not only does Islam refuse to recognize any difference between Muslim countries, it is the champion of all oppressed people." This would require an epic struggle against "America, the global plunderer," and the Communist materialist societies of Russia and Asia, as well as "Zionism, and Israel."

Khomeini and his fellow Shia revolutionaries have differed from Sunni Islamists, however—and this is the essence of their fratricidal rivalry—in proclaiming that global upheaval would be capped with the coming of the Mahdi, who would return from "occultation" (being present though not visible) to assume the sovereign powers that the Supreme Leader of the Islamic Republic temporarily exercises in the Mahdi's place. Iranian then President Mahmoud Ahmadinejad considered this principle sufficiently settled to put it before the United Nations in an address on September 27, 2007:

> Without any doubt, the Promised One who is the ultimate Savior, will come. In the company of all believers, justice-

seekers and benefactors, he will establish a bright future and
fill the world with justice and beauty. This is the promise of
God; therefore it will be fulfilled.

The peace envisaged by such a concept has as its prerequisite,
as President Ahmadinejad wrote to President George W. Bush in
2006, a global submission to correct religious doctrine. Ahmadinejad's
letter (widely interpreted in the West as an overture to negotiations)
concluded with "Vasalam Ala Man Ataba'al hoda," a phrase left
untranslated in the version released to the public: "Peace only unto
those who follow the true path." This was the identical admonition
sent in the seventh century by the Prophet Muhammad to the emperors of Byzantium and Persia, soon to be attacked by the Islamic
holy war.

For decades Western observers have sought to pinpoint the "root
causes" of such sentiments, convincing themselves that the more extreme statements are partly metaphorical and that a renunciation of
policy or of past Western conduct—such as American and British interference in Iranian domestic politics in the 1950s—might open the
door to reconciliation. Yet revolutionary Islamism has not, up to now,
manifested itself as a quest for international cooperation as the West
understands the term; nor is the Iranian clerical regime best interpreted as an aggrieved postcolonial independence movement waiting
hopefully for demonstrations of American goodwill. Under the ayatollahs' concept of policy, the dispute with the West is not a matter of
specific technical concessions or negotiating formulas but a contest
over the nature of world order.

Even at a moment hailed in the West as auguring a new spirit of
conciliation—after the completion of an interim agreement on Iran's
nuclear program with the five permanent members of the Security
Council plus Germany—the Iranian Supreme Leader, Khamenei, declared in January 2014:

By dressing up America's face, some individuals are trying to remove the ugliness, the violence and terror from this face and introduce America's government to the Iranian people as being affectionate and humanitarian . . . How can you change such an ugly and criminal face in front of the Iranian people with makeup? . . . Iran will not violate what it agreed to. But the Americans are enemies of the Islamic Revolution, they are enemies of the Islamic Republic, they are enemies of this flag that you have raised.

Or, as Khamenei put it somewhat more delicately in a speech to Iran's Guardian Council in September 2013, "When a wrestler is wrestling with an opponent and in places shows flexibility for technical reasons, let him not forget who his opponent is."

THIS STATE OF AFFAIRS is not inevitably permanent. Among the states in the Middle East, Iran has perhaps the most coherent experience of national greatness and the longest and subtlest strategic tradition. It has preserved its essential culture for three thousand years, sometimes as an expanding empire, for many centuries by the skilled manipulation of surrounding elements. Before the ayatollahs' revolution, the West's interaction with Iran had been cordial and cooperative on both sides, based on a perceived parallelism of national interests. (Ironically, the ayatollahs' ascent to power was aided in its last stages by America's dissociation from the existing regime, on the mistaken belief that the looming change would accelerate the advent of democracy and strengthen U.S.-Iranian ties.)

The United States and the Western democracies should be open to fostering cooperative relations with Iran. What they must not do is base such a policy on projecting their own domestic experience as inevitably or automatically relevant to other societies', especially Iran's.

They must allow for the possibility that the unchanged rhetoric of a generation is based on conviction rather than posturing and will have had an impact on a significant number of the Iranian people. A change of tone is not necessarily a return to normalcy, especially where definitions of normalcy differ so fundamentally. It includes as well—and more likely—the possibility of a change in tactics to reach essentially unchanged goals. The United States should be open to a genuine reconciliation and make substantial efforts to facilitate it. Yet for such an effort to succeed, a clear sense of direction is essential, especially on the key issue of Iran's nuclear program.

Nuclear Proliferation and Iran

The future of Iranian-American relations will—at least in the short run—depend on the resolution of an ostensibly technical military issue. As these pages are being written, a potentially epochal shift in the region's military balance and its psychological equilibrium may be taking place. It has been ushered in by Iran's rapid progress toward the status of a nuclear weapons state amidst a negotiation between it and the permanent members of the UN Security Council plus Germany (the P5+1). Though couched in terms of technical and scientific capabilities, the issue is at heart about international order—about the ability of the international community to enforce its demands against sophisticated forms of rejection, the permeability of the global nonproliferation regime, and the prospects for a nuclear arms race in the world's most volatile region.

The traditional balance of power emphasized military and industrial capacity. A change in it could be achieved only gradually or by conquest. The modern balance of power reflects the level of a society's scientific development and can be threatened dramatically by developments entirely within the territory of a state. No conquest could have increased Soviet military capacity as much as the breaking of the

American nuclear monopoly in 1949. Similarly, the spread of deliverable nuclear weapons is bound to affect regional balances—and the international order—dramatically and to evoke a series of escalating counteractions.

All Cold War American administrations were obliged to design their international strategies in the context of the awe-inspiring calculus of deterrence: the knowledge that nuclear war would involve casualties of a scale capable of threatening civilized life. They were haunted as well by the awareness that a demonstrated willingness to run the risk—at least up to a point—was essential if the world was not to be turned over to ruthless totalitarians. Deterrence held in the face of these parallel nightmares because only two nuclear superpowers existed. Each made comparable assessments of the perils to it from the use of nuclear weapons. But as nuclear weapons spread into more and more hands, the calculus of deterrence grows increasingly ephemeral and deterrence less and less reliable. In a widely proliferated world, it becomes ever more difficult to decide who is deterring whom and by what calculations.

Even if it is assumed that proliferating nuclear countries make the same calculus of survival as the established ones with respect to initiating hostilities against each other—an extremely dubious judgment—new nuclear weapons states may undermine international order in several ways. The complexity of protecting nuclear arsenals and installations (and building the sophisticated warning systems possessed by the advanced nuclear states) may increase the risk of preemption by tilting incentives toward a surprise attack. They can also be used as a shield to deter retaliation against the militant actions of non-state groups. Nor could nuclear powers ignore nuclear war on their doorsteps. Finally, the experience with the "private" proliferation network of technically friendly Pakistan with North Korea, Libya, and Iran demonstrates the vast consequences to international order of the spread of nuclear weapons, even when the proliferating country does not meet the formal criteria of a rogue state.

Three hurdles have to be overcome in acquiring a deployable nuclear weapons capability: the acquisition of delivery systems, the production of fissile material, and the building of warheads. For delivery systems, there exists a substantially open market in France, Russia, and to some extent China; it requires primarily financial resources. Iran has already acquired the nucleus of a delivery system and can add to it at its discretion. The knowledge of how to build warheads is not esoteric or difficult to discover, and their construction is relatively easy to hide. The best—perhaps the only—way to prevent the emergence of a nuclear weapons capability is to inhibit the development of a uranium-enrichment process. The indispensable component for this process is the device of centrifuges—the machines that produce enriched uranium. (Plutonium enrichment must also be prevented and is part of the same negotiation.)

The United States and the other permanent members of the UN Security Council have been negotiating for over ten years through two administrations of both parties to prevent the emergence of such a capability in Iran. Six UN Security Council resolutions since 2006 have insisted that Iran suspend its nuclear-enrichment program. Three American presidents of both parties, every permanent member of the UN Security Council (including China and Russia) plus Germany, and multiple International Atomic Energy Agency reports and resolutions have all declared an Iranian nuclear weapon unacceptable and demanded an unconditional halt to Iranian nuclear enrichment. No option was to be "off the table"—in the words of at least two American presidents—in pursuit of that goal.

The record shows steadily advancing Iranian nuclear capabilities taking place while the Western position has been progressively softened. As Iran has ignored UN resolutions and built centrifuges, the West has put forward a series of proposals of increasing permissiveness— from insisting that Iran terminate its uranium enrichment permanently (2004); to allowing that Iran might continue some enrichment at low-enriched uranium (LEU) levels, less than 20 percent (2005); to proposing that Iran ship the majority of its LEU out of the country so that France and Russia could turn it into fuel rods with 20 percent enriched uranium (2009); to a proposal allowing Iran to keep enough of its own 20 percent enriched uranium to run a research reactor while suspending operations at its Fordow facility of centrifuges capable of making more (2013). Fordow itself was once a secret site; when discovered, it became the subject of Western demands that it close entirely. Now Western proposals suggest that activity at it be suspended, with safeguards making it difficult to restart. When the P5+1 first formed in 2006 to coordinate the positions of the international community, its negotiators insisted that Iran halt fuel-cycle activities before negotiations could proceed; in 2009, this condition was dropped. Faced with this record, Iran has had little incentive to treat any proposal as final. With subtlety and no little daring, it has at each stage cast itself as less interested in a solution than the world's combined major powers and invited them to make new concessions.

When the negotiations started in 2003, Iran had 130 centrifuges. At this writing, it has deployed approximately 19,000 (though only half are in use). At the beginning of the negotiations, Iran was not able to produce any fissile material; in the November 2013 interim agreement, Iran acknowledged that it possessed seven tons of low-grade enriched uranium that, with the numbers of centrifuges Iran possesses, can be transformed into weapons-grade material in a number of months (enough for seven to ten Hiroshima-type bombs). In the interim agreement, Iran promised to give up about half of its 20 percent enriched uranium but through a circuitous route; it pledged to convert it into a form from which it can easily be reconverted to its original status, and it has retained the means to do so. In any event, with the number of centrifuges now in Iran's possession, the 20 percent stage is less significant because uranium enriched to 5 percent (the threshold claimed to be a negotiations achievement) can be enriched to weapons grade in a matter of months.

The attitude of the negotiators of the two sides reflected different perceptions of world order. The Iranian negotiators conveyed to their opposite numbers that they would not be deterred from pursuing their course even at the risk of an attack on Iran's nuclear facilities. The Western negotiators were convinced (and, underscoring their commitment to peace and diplomacy, periodically referred to this conviction) that the consequences of a military attack on Iran dwarfed the risks of a growth in the Iranian nuclear capability. They were reinforced in their calculations by the mantra of professionals: that every deadlock needs to be broken by a new proposal, the responsibility for which they assumed. For the West, the central question was whether a diplomatic solution could be found or whether military measures would be necessary. In Iran, the nuclear issue was treated as one aspect of a general struggle over regional order and ideological supremacy, fought in a range of arenas and territories with methods spanning the spectrum of war and peace—military and paramilitary operations, diplomacy, formal negotiation, propaganda, political subversion—in fluid and mutually reinforcing combination. In this context, the quest for an agreement must contend with the prospect that Tehran will be at least exploring a strategy of relaxing tensions just enough to break the sanctions regime but retaining a substantial nuclear infrastructure and a maximum freedom of action to turn it into a weapons program later.

The process resulted in the November 2013 interim agreement, in which Iran agreed to a qualified, temporary suspension of enrichment in return for a lifting of some of the international sanctions imposed on it for its defiance of UN Security Council demands. But because Iranian enrichment was permitted to continue for the six months of the interim agreement, its continuation as well as the implementation of more comprehensive restrictions will merge with the deadline to complete the overall agreement. The practical consequence has been the de facto acceptance of an Iranian enrichment program, leaving unresolved (but only on the Western side) its scale.

Negotiations for a permanent agreement are in process at this writing. While the terms—or whether any are achievable—are not yet known, it is clear that they will be, like so many issues in the Middle East, about "red lines." Will the Western negotiators (operating via the P5+1) insist that the red line be at the enrichment capability, as the UN resolutions have insisted? This would be a formidable task. Iran would need to reduce its centrifuges to a level consistent with the plausible requirements of a civilian nuclear program, as well as destroy or mothball the remainder. Such an outcome, whose practical effect is the abandonment of a military nuclear program by Iran, would open the prospect of a fundamental change in the West's relationship with Iran, particularly if it was linked to a consensus that the two sides would work to curtail both the Sunni and Shia waves of militant extremism now threatening the region.

In view of the Iranian Supreme Leader's repeated declarations that Iran would give up no capability it already possesses—statements reiterated by a panoply of senior Iranian officials—the Iranian emphasis seems to have shifted to moving the red line to the production of warheads, or to curtailing its centrifuges to a level that still leaves a substantial margin for a military nuclear program. Under such a scheme Iran would enshrine in an international agreement its Supreme Leader's alleged fatwa against building nuclear weapons (a ruling that has never been published or seen by anyone outside the Iranian power structure); it would pledge to the P5+1 not to build nuclear weapons, and grant inspection rights to observe compliance. The practical effect of such undertakings would depend on the amount of time it would take Iran to build a weapon after it abrogated or broke such an agreement. In view of the fact that Iran managed to build two secret enrichment plants while under international inspection, this breakout estimate would have to consider the possibility of undisclosed violations. An agreement must not leave Iran as a "virtual" nuclear power—a country that can become a military nuclear power in a time frame shorter than any non-nuclear neighbor could match or any nuclear power could reliably prevent.

Iran has brought exceptional skill and consistency to bear on its proclaimed goal of undermining the Middle East state system and ejecting Western influence from the region. Whether Iran were to build and test a nuclear weapon in the near term or "merely" retain the capability to do so within months of choosing to do so, the implications on regional and global order will be comparable. Even if Iran were to stop at a virtual nuclear weapons capability, it will be seen to have achieved this level in defiance of the most comprehensive international sanctions ever imposed on any country. The temptations of Iran's geostrategic rivals—such as Turkey, Egypt, and Saudi Arabia—to develop or purchase their own nuclear programs to match the Iranian capability will become irresistible. The risk of an Israeli preemptive attack would rise significantly. As for Iran, having withstood sanctions in developing a nuclear weapons capability, it will gain prestige, new powers of intimidation, and enhanced capacity to act with conventional weapons or non-nuclear forms of unconventional war.

It has been argued that a new approach to U.S.-Iranian relations will develop out of the nuclear negotiations, which will compensate for the abandonment of historic Western positions. The example of America's relationship with China is often cited to this effect, because it moved from hostility to mutual acceptance and even cooperation in a relatively short period of time in the 1970s. Iran may be prepared, it is sometimes said, to constrain the diplomatic use of its virtual nuclear military program in exchange for the goodwill and strategic cooperation of the United States.

The comparison is not apt. China was facing forty-two Soviet divisions on its northern border after a decade of escalating mutual hostility and Chinese internal turmoil. It had every reason to explore an alternative international system in which to anchor itself. No such incentive is self-evident in Iranian-Western relations. In the past decade,

Iran has witnessed the removal of two of its most significant adversaries, the Taliban regime in Afghanistan and Saddam Hussein's Iraq—ironically by American action—and it has deepened its influence and its military role in Lebanon, Syria, and Iraq. Two of its principal competitors for regional influence, Egypt and Saudi Arabia, have been preoccupied by internal challenges even as Iran has moved swiftly and apparently successfully to crush its internal opposition following a 2009 pro-democracy uprising. Its leaders have largely been welcomed into international respectability without committing to any major substantive change in policy and courted by Western companies for investment opportunities even while sanctions are still in place. Ironically, the rise of Sunni jihadism along Iran's frontiers may produce second thoughts in Iran. But it is equally plausible that Tehran regards the strategic landscape as shifting in its favor and its revolutionary course as being vindicated. Which option Iran chooses will be determined by its own calculations, not American preconceptions.

Until this writing, Iran and the West have attached different meanings to the concept of negotiation. While American and European negotiators were speaking with cautious optimism about prospects for a nuclear agreement and exercising utmost restraint in their public statements in hopes of fostering a favorable atmosphere, Ayatollah Khamenei described the nuclear talks as part of an eternal religious struggle in which negotiation was a form of combat and compromise was forbidden. As late as May 2014, with six weeks remaining in the interim agreement period, the Iranian Supreme Leader was reported to have described the nuclear talks as follows:

> The reason for the emphasis placed on the continuation of combat, is not because of the war-mongering of the Islamic establishment. It is only rational that for crossing a region filled with pirates, one should fully equip themselves and be motivated and capable of defending themselves.

Under such circumstances, we have no option but to continue combat and allow the idea of combat to rule all domestic and foreign affairs of the country. Those who seek to promote concession-making and surrendering to bullies and accuse the Islamic establishment of warmongering are indeed committing treason.

All the officials in the country in the field of economy, science, culture, policy-making, lawmaking and foreign negotiations should be aware that they are fighting and are continuing the combat for the establishment and survival of the Islamic system . . . Jihad is never-ending because Satan and the satanic front will exist eternally.

For nations, history plays the role that character confers on human beings. In Iran's proud and rich history, one can distinguish three different approaches to international order. There was the policy of the state preceding the Khomeini revolution: vigilant in protecting its borders, respectful of other nations' sovereignties, willing to participate in alliances—in effect, pursuing its national interests by Westphalian principles. There is also the tradition of empire, which viewed Iran as the center of the civilized world and which sought to eliminate the autonomy of its surrounding countries as far as its power could reach. Finally, there is the Iran of jihad described in the preceding pages. From which of these traditions does the changed comportment of some high-ranking Iranian officials draw its inspiration? If we assume a fundamental change, what brought it about? Is the conflict psychological or strategic? Will it be resolved by a change in attitude or a modification of policy? And if the latter, what is the modification that should be sought? Can the two countries' views of world order be reconciled? Or will the world have to wait until jihadist pressures fade, as they disappeared earlier in the Ottoman Empire as a result of a change in power dynamics and domestic priorities? On the answer to these questions depends the future of U.S.-Iranian relations and perhaps the peace of the world.

In principle, the United States should be prepared to reach a geopolitical understanding with Iran on the basis of Westphalian principles of nonintervention and develop a compatible concept of regional order. Until the Khomeini revolution, Iran and the United States had been de facto allies based on a hard-nosed assessment of the national interest by American presidents from both parties. Iranian and American national interests were treated by both sides as parallel. Both opposed the domination of the region by a superpower, which during that period was the Soviet Union. Both were prepared to rely on principles of respect for other sovereignties in their policy toward the region. Both favored the economic development of the region—even when it did not proceed on an adequately broad front. From the American point of view, there is every reason to reestablish such a relationship. The tension in Iranian-American relations has resulted from Tehran's adoption of jihadist principles and rhetoric together with direct assaults on American interests and views of international order.

How Iran synthesizes its complex legacies will be driven in large part by internal dynamics; in a country of such cultural and political intricacy, these may be unpredictable to outside observers and not subject to direct influence by foreign threats or blandishments. But whatever face Iran presents to the outside world, it does not alter the reality that Iran needs to make a choice. It must decide whether it is a country or a cause. The United States should be open to a cooperative course and encourage it. Yet the ingenuity and determination of Western negotiators, while a necessary component of this evolution, will not be sufficient to secure it. Abandonment by Iran of support for such groups as Hezbollah would be an important and necessary step in reestablishing a constructive pattern of bilateral relations. The test will be whether

Iran interprets the chaos along its frontiers as a threat or as an opportunity to fulfill millennial hopes.

The United States needs to develop a strategic view of the process in which it is engaged. Administration spokesmen explaining the reduced American role in the Middle East have described a vision of an equilibrium of Sunni states (and perhaps Israel) balancing Iran. Even were such a constellation to come to pass, it could only be sustained by an active American foreign policy. For the balance of power is never static; its components are in constant flux. The United States would be needed as a balancer for the foreseeable future. The role of balancer is best carried out if America is closer to each of the contending forces than they are to each other, and does not let itself be lured into underwriting either side's strategy, particularly at the extremes. Pursuing its own strategic objectives, the United States can be a crucial factor— perhaps *the* crucial factor—in determining whether Iran pursues the path of revolutionary Islam or that of a great nation legitimately and importantly lodged in the Westphalian system of states. But America can fulfill that role only on the basis of involvement, not of withdrawal.

Vision and Reality

The issue of peace in the Middle East has, in recent years, focused on the highly technical subject of nuclear weapons in Iran. There is no shortcut around the imperative of preventing their appearance. But it is well to recall periods when other seemingly intractable crises in the Middle East were given a new dimension by fortitude and vision.

Between 1967 and 1973, there had been two Arab-Israeli wars, two American military alerts, an invasion of Jordan by Syria, a massive American airlift into a war zone, multiple hijackings of airliners, and the breaking of diplomatic relations with the United States by most Arab countries. Yet it was followed by a peace process that yielded three Egyptian-Israeli agreements (culminating in a peace treaty in 1979); a disengagement agreement with Syria in 1974 (which has lasted four decades, despite the Syrian civil war); the Madrid Conference in 1991, which restarted the peace process; the Oslo agreement between the PLO and Israel in 1993; and a peace treaty between Jordan and Israel in 1994.

These goals were reached because three conditions were met: an active American policy; the thwarting of designs seeking to establish a regional order by imposing universalist principles through violence; and the emergence of leaders with a vision of peace.

Two events in my experience symbolize that vision. In 1981, during his last visit to Washington, President Sadat invited me to come to Egypt the following spring for the celebration when the Sinai Peninsula would be returned to Egypt by Israel. Then he paused for a moment and said, "Don't come for the celebration—it would be too hurtful to Israel. Come six months later, and you and I will drive to the top of Mount Sinai together, where I plan to build a mosque, a church, and a synagogue, to symbolize the need for peace."

Yitzhak Rabin, once chief of staff of the Israeli army, was Prime Minister during the first political agreement ever between Israel and Egypt in 1975, and then again when he and former Defense Minister, now Foreign Minister, Shimon Peres negotiated a peace agreement with Jordan in 1994. On the occasion of the Israeli-Jordanian peace agreement, in July 1994 Rabin spoke at a joint session of the U.S. Congress together with King Hussein of Jordan:

> Today we are embarking on a battle which has no dead and no wounded, no blood and no anguish. This is the only battle which is a pleasure to wage: the battle of peace . . .
>
> In the Bible, our Book of Books, peace is mentioned in its various idioms, two hundred and thirty-seven times. In the

Bible, from which we draw our values and our strength, in the Book of Jeremiah, we find a lamentation for Rachel the Matriarch. It reads:

> "Refrain your voice from weeping, and your eyes from
> tears: for their work shall be rewarded, says the Lord."

I will not refrain from weeping for those who are gone. But on this summer day in Washington, far from home, we sense that our work will be rewarded, as the Prophet foretold.

Both Sadat and Rabin were assassinated. But their achievements and inspiration are inextinguishable.

Once again, doctrines of violent intimidation challenge the hopes for world order. But when they are thwarted—and nothing less will do—there may come a moment similar to what led to the breakthroughs recounted here, when vision overcame reality.

CHAPTER 5

The Multiplicity of Asia

Asia and Europe: Different
Concepts of Balance of Power

The term "Asia" ascribes a deceptive coherence to a disparate region. Until the arrival of modern Western powers, no Asian language had a word for "Asia"; none of the peoples of what are now Asia's nearly fifty sovereign states conceived of themselves as inhabiting a single "continent" or region requiring solidarity with all the others. As "the East," it has never been clearly parallel to "the West." There has been no common religion, not even one splintered into different branches as is Christianity in the West. Buddhism, Hinduism, Islam, and Christianity all thrive in different parts of Asia. There is no memory of a common empire comparable to that of Rome. Across Northeast, East, Southeast, South, and Central Asia, prevailing major ethnic, linguistic, religious, social, and cultural differences have been deepened, often bitterly, by the wars of modern history.

The political and economic map of Asia illustrates the region's complex tapestry. It comprises industrially and technologically advanced countries in Japan, the Republic of Korea, and Singapore, with economies and standards of living rivaling those of Europe; three countries of continental scale in China, India, and Russia; two large archipelagoes (in addition to Japan), the Philippines and Indonesia, composed of thousands of islands and standing astride the main sea-lanes; three ancient nations with populations approximating those of France or Italy in Thailand, Vietnam, and Myanmar; huge Australia and pastoral New Zealand, with largely European-descended populations; and North Korea, a Stalinist family dictatorship bereft of industry and technology except for a nuclear weapons program. A large Muslim-majority population prevails across Central Asia, Afghanistan, Pakistan, Bangladesh, Malaysia, and Indonesia, and sizeable Muslim minorities exist in India, China, Myanmar, Thailand, and the Philippines.

The global order during the nineteenth century and the first half of the twentieth century was predominantly European, designed to maintain a rough balance of power between the major European countries. Outside their own continent, the European states built colonies and justified their actions under various versions of their so-called civilizing mission. From the perspective of the twenty-first century, in which Asian nations are rising in wealth, power, and confidence, it may seem improbable that colonialism gained such force or that its institutions were treated as a normal mechanism of international life. Material factors alone cannot explain it; a sense of mission and intangible psychological momentum also played a role.

The pamphlets and treatises of the colonial powers from the dawn of the twentieth century reveal a remarkable arrogance, to the effect that they were entitled to shape a world order by their maxims. Accounts of China or India condescendingly defined a European mission to educate traditional cultures to higher levels of civilization. European

administrators with relatively small staffs redrew the borders of ancient nations, oblivious that this might be an abnormal, unwelcome, or
illegitimate development.

At the dawn of what is now called the modern age in the fifteenth
century, a confident, fractious, territorially divided West had set sail to
reconnoiter the globe and to improve, exploit, and "civilize" the lands
it came upon. It impressed upon the peoples it encountered views
of religion, science, commerce, governance, and diplomacy shaped
by the Western historical experience, which it took to be the capstone
of human achievement.

The West expanded with the familiar hallmarks of colonialism—
avariciousness, cultural chauvinism, lust for glory. But it is also true
that its better elements tried to lead a kind of global tutorial in an intellectual method that encouraged skepticism and a body of political
and diplomatic practices ultimately including democracy. It all but ensured that, after long periods of subjugation, the colonized peoples
would eventually demand—and achieve—self-determination. Even
during their most brutal depredations, the expansionist powers put
forth, especially in Britain, a vision that at some point conquered peoples would begin to participate in the fruits of a common global system. Finally recoiling from the sordid practice of slavery, the West
produced what no other slaveholding civilization had: a global abolition movement based on a conviction of common humanity and the
inherent dignity of the individual. Britain, rejecting its previous
embrace of the despicable trade, took the lead in enforcing a new norm
of human dignity, abolishing slavery in its empire and interdicting
slave-trading ships on the high seas. The distinctive combination of
overbearing conduct, technological prowess, idealistic humanitarian-
ism, and revolutionary intellectual ferment proved one of the shaping
factors of the modern world.

With the exception of Japan, Asia was a victim of the international
order imposed by colonialism, not an actor in it. Thailand sustained its

independence but, unlike Japan, was too weak to participate in the balance of power as a system of regional order. China's size prevented it from full colonization, but it lost control over key aspects of its domestic affairs. Until the end of World War II, most of Asia conducted its policies as an adjunct of European powers or, in the case of the Philippines, of the United States. The conditions for Westphalian-style diplomacy only began to emerge with the decolonization that followed the devastation of the European order by two world wars.

The process of emancipation from the prevalent regional order was violent and bloody: the Chinese civil war (1927–49), the Korean War (1950–53), a Sino-Soviet confrontation (roughly 1955–80), revolutionary guerrilla insurgencies all across Southeast Asia, the Vietnam War (1961–75), four India-Pakistan wars (1947, 1965, 1971, and 1999), a Chinese-Indian war (1962), a Chinese-Vietnamese war (1979), and the depredations of the genocidal Khmer Rouge (1975–79).

After decades of war and revolutionary turmoil, Asia has transformed itself dramatically. The rise of the "Asian Tigers," evident from 1970, involving Hong Kong, the Republic of Korea, Singapore, Taiwan, and Thailand, brought prosperity and economic dynamism into view. Japan adopted democratic institutions and built an economy rivaling and in some cases surpassing those of Western nations. In 1979, China changed course and, under Deng Xiaoping, proclaimed a nonideological foreign policy and a policy of economic reforms that, continued and accelerated under his successors, have had a profound transformative effect on China and the world.

As these changes unfolded, national-interest-based foreign policy premised on Westphalian principles seemed to have prevailed in Asia. Unlike in the Middle East, where almost all the states are threatened by militant challenges to their legitimacy, in Asia the state is treated as the basic unit of international and domestic politics. The various nations emerging from the colonial period generally affirmed one another's sovereignty and committed to noninterference in one another's

RUSSIA

KAZAKHSTAN

MONGOLIA

Ulaanbaatar o

Vladivostok o

KYRGYZSTAN

Beijing o

NORTH KOREA
o Pyongyang

TAJIKISTAN

AFGHANISTAN

CHINA

o Seoul

SOUTH KOREA   Toky

Kabul o

o Islamabad

JAPA

PAKISTAN

NEPAL

BHUTAN

New Delhi
o

Kathmandu

Thimphu

Taiwan

BANGLADESH

Dhaka o

INDIA

MYANMAR

Hanoi o

LAOS

o Vientiane

Rangoon o

THAILAND

Bangkok o

VIETNAM

Manila o

PHILIPPINES

SRI LANKA

CAMBODIA

Phnom Penh

PALAU

BRUNEI

Kuala Lumpur o

MALAYSIA

SINGAPORE

Jakarta
o

INDONESIA

EAST TIMOR
Dili

EQUATOR

INDIAN OCEAN

AUSTRALIA

© 2014 Jeffrey L. Ward

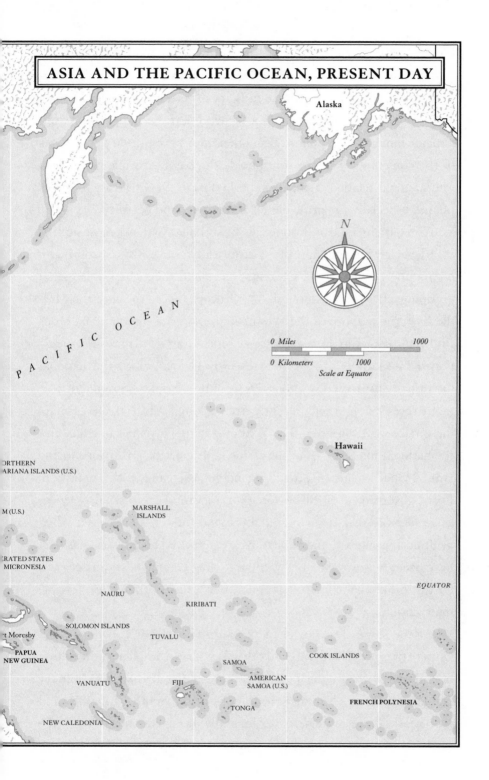

ASIA AND THE PACIFIC OCEAN, PRESENT DAY

Alaska

N

PACIFIC OCEAN

0 Miles   1000

0 Kilometers   1000
Scale at Equator

Hawaii

NORTHERN
MARIANA ISLANDS (U.S.)

GUAM (U.S.)

MARSHALL
ISLANDS

FEDERATED STATES
OF MICRONESIA

EQUATOR

NAURU

KIRIBATI

Port Moresby   SOLOMON ISLANDS

TUVALU

PAPUA
NEW GUINEA

SAMOA

COOK ISLANDS

VANUATU   FIJI   AMERICAN
SAMOA (U.S.)

TONGA   FRENCH POLYNESIA

NEW CALEDONIA

domestic affairs; they followed the norms of international organizations and built regional or interregional economic and social organizations. In this vein a top Chinese military official, the Chinese People's Liberation Army Deputy Chief of General Staff Qi Jianguo, wrote in a major January 2013 policy review that one of the primary challenges of the contemporary era is to uphold "the basic principle of modern international relations firmly established in the 1648 'Treaty of Westphalia,' especially the principles of sovereignty and equality."

Asia has emerged as among the Westphalian system's most significant legacies: historic, and often historically antagonistic, peoples are organizing themselves as sovereign states and their states as regional groupings. In Asia, far more than in Europe, not to speak of the Middle East, the maxims of the Westphalian model of international order find their contemporary expression—including doctrines since questioned by many in the West as excessively focused on the national interest or insufficiently protective of human rights. Sovereignty, in many cases wrought only recently from colonial rule, is treated as having an absolute character. The goal of state policy is not to transcend the national interest—as in the fashionable concepts in Europe or the United States—but to pursue it energetically and with conviction. Every government dismisses foreign criticism of its internal practices as a symptom of just-surmounted colonial tutelage. Thus even when neighboring states' domestic actions are perceived as excesses—as they have been, for example, in Myanmar—they are treated as an occasion for quiet diplomatic intercession, not overt pressure, much less forcible intervention.

At the same time, an element of implicit threat is ever present. China affirms explicitly, and all other key players implicitly, the option of military force in the pursuit of core national interests. Military budgets are rising. National rivalries, as in the South China Sea and Northeast Asian waters, have generally been conducted with the methods of nineteenth-century European diplomacy; force has not been excluded, though its application has been restrained, if tenuously, as the years go by.

Hierarchy, not sovereign equality, was the organizing principle of Asia's historical international systems. Power was demonstrated by the deference shown to a ruler and the structures of authority that recognized his overlordship, not the delineation of specific borders on a map. Empires spread their trade and their political writ, soliciting the alignment of smaller political units. For the peoples who existed at the intersection of two or more imperial orders, the path to independence was often to enroll as a nominal subordinate in more than one sphere (an art still remembered and practiced today in some quarters).

In Asia's historical diplomatic systems, whether based on Chinese or Hindu models, monarchy was considered an expression of divinity or, at the very least, a kind of paternal authority; tangible expressions of tribute were thought to be owed to superior countries by their inferiors. This theoretically left no room for ambiguity as to the nature of regional power relationships, leading to a series of rigid alignments. In practice, however, these principles were applied with remarkable creativity and fluidity. In Northeast Asia, the Ryukyu Kingdom for a time paid tribute to both Japan and China. In the northern hills of Burma, tribes secured a form of de facto autonomy by pledging their loyalty simultaneously to the Burmese royal court and the Chinese Emperor (and generally not straining to follow the dictates of either). For centuries, Nepal skillfully balanced its diplomatic posture between the ruling dynasties in China and those in India—offering letters and gifts that were interpreted as tribute in China but recorded as evidence of equal exchanges in Nepal, then holding out a special tie with China as a guarantee of Nepal's independence vis-à-vis India. Thailand, eyed as a strategic target by expanding Western empires in the nineteenth century, avoided colonization altogether through an even more elaborate strategy of affirming cordial ties with all foreign powers at once—welcoming foreign advisors from multiple competing Western states into its court even while sending tribute missions to China and retaining Hindu priests of Indian descent for the royal household. (The intellectual suppleness and emotional forbearance demanded by this balancing strategy were all the more remarkable given that the Thai King was himself regarded as a divine figure.) Any concept of a regional order was considered too inhibiting of the flexibility demanded from diplomacy.

Against this backdrop of subtle and diverse legacies, the grid of Westphalian sovereign states on a map of Asia presents an oversimplified picture of regional realities. It cannot capture the diversity of aspirations that leaders bring to their tasks or the combination of punctilious attention to hierarchy and protocol with adroit maneuver that characterizes much of Asian diplomacy. It is the fundamental framework of international life in Asia. But statehood there is also infused with a set of cultural legacies of a greater diversity and immediacy than perhaps any other region. This is underscored by the experiences of two of Asia's major nations, Japan and India.

Japan

Of all of Asia's historical political and cultural entities, Japan reacted the earliest and by far the most decisively to the Western irruption across the world. Situated on an archipelago some one hundred miles off the Asian mainland at the closest crossing, Japan long cultivated its traditions and distinctive culture in isolation. Possessed of ethnic and linguistic near homogeneity and an official ideology that stressed the Japanese people's divine ancestry, Japan turned conviction of its unique identity into a kind of near-religious commitment. This sense of distinctness gave it great flexibility in adjusting its policies to its conception of national strategic necessity. Within the space of little more than a century after 1868, Japan moved from total isolation to extensive borrowing from the apparently most modern states in the

West (for the army from Germany, for parliamentary institutions and for the navy from Britain); from audacious attempts at empire building to pacifism and thence to a reemergence of a new kind of major-power stance; from feudalism to varieties of Western authoritarianism and from that to embracing democracy; and in and out of world orders (first Western, then Asian, now global). Throughout, it was convinced that its national mission could not be diluted by adjusting to the techniques and institutions of other societies; it would only be enhanced by successful adaptation.

Japan for centuries existed at the fringe of the Chinese world, borrowing heavily from Sinic religion and culture. But unlike most societies in the Chinese cultural sphere, it transformed the borrowed forms into Japanese patterns and never conflated them with a hierarchical obligation to China. Japan's resilient position was at times a source of consternation for the Chinese court. Other Asian peoples accepted the premises and protocol of the tribute system—a symbolic subordination to the Chinese Emperor by which Chinese protocol ordered the universe—labeling their trade as "tribute" to gain access to Chinese markets. They respected (at least in their exchanges with the Chinese court) the Confucian concept of international order as a familial hierarchy with China as the patriarch. Japan was geographically close enough to understand this vocabulary intimately and generally made tacit allowance for the Chinese world order as a regional reality. In quest of trade or cultural exchange, Japanese missions followed etiquette close enough to established forms that Chinese officials could interpret it as evidence of Japan's aspiration to membership in a common hierarchy. Yet in a region carefully attuned to the gradations of status implied in minute protocol decisions—such as the single word used to refer to a ruler, the mode in which a formal letter was delivered, or the style of calendar date on a formal document—Japan consistently refused to take up a formal role in the Sinocentric tribute system. It hovered at the edge of a hierarchical Chinese world order, periodically insisting on its equality and, at some points, its own superiority.

At the apex of Japan's society and its own view of world order stood the Japanese Emperor, a figure conceived, like the Chinese Emperor, as the Son of Heaven, an intermediary between the human and the divine. This title—insistently displayed on Japanese diplomatic dispatches to the Chinese court—was a direct challenge to the cosmology of the Chinese world order, which posited China's Emperor as the single pinnacle of human hierarchy. In addition to this status (which carried a transcendent import above and beyond what would have been claimed by any Holy Roman Emperor in Europe), Japan's traditional political philosophy posited another distinction, that Japanese emperors were deities descended from the Sun Goddess, who gave birth to the first Emperor and endowed his successors with an eternal right to rule. According to the fourteenth-century "Records of the Legitimate Succession of the Divine Sovereigns,"

> Japan is the divine country. The heavenly ancestor it was who first laid its foundations, and the Sun Goddess left her descendants to reign over it forever and ever. This is true only of our country, and nothing similar may be found in foreign lands. That is why it is called the divine country.

Japan's insular position allowed it wide latitude about whether to participate in international affairs at all. For many centuries, it remained on the outer boundaries of Asian affairs, cultivating its military traditions through internal contests and admitting foreign trade and culture at its discretion. At the close of the sixteenth century, Japan attempted to recast its role with an abruptness and sweep of ambition that its neighbors at first dismissed as implausible. The result was one of Asia's major military conflicts—whose regional legacies remain the subject of vivid remembrance and dispute and whose lessons, if heeded, might have changed America's conduct in the twentieth-century Korean War.

In 1590, the warrior Toyotomi Hideyoshi—having bested his rivals, unified Japan, and brought more than a century of civil conflict to a close—announced a grander vision: he would raise the world's largest army, march it up the Korean Peninsula, conquer China, and subdue the world. He dispatched a letter to the Korean King announcing his intent to "proceed to the country of the Great Ming and compel the people there to adopt our customs and manners" and inviting his assistance. After the King demurred and warned him against the endeavor (citing an "inseparable relationship between the Middle Kingdom and our kingdom" and the Confucian principle that "to invade another state is an act of which men of culture and intellectual attainments should feel ashamed"), Hideyoshi launched an invasion of 160,000 men and roughly seven hundred ships. This massive force overwhelmed initial defenses and at first marched swiftly up the peninsula. Its progress slowed as Korea's Admiral Yi Sun-sin organized a determined naval resistance, harrying Hideyoshi's supply lines and deflecting the invading armies to battles along the coast. When Japanese forces reached Pyongyang, near the narrow northern neck of the peninsula (and now North Korea's capital), China intervened in force, unwilling to allow its tribute state to be overrun. A Chinese expeditionary army estimated between 40,000 and 100,000 strong crossed the Yalu River and pushed Japanese forces back as far as Seoul. After five years of inconclusive negotiations and devastating combat, Hideyoshi died, the invasion force withdrew, and the status quo ante was restored. Those who argue that history never repeats itself should ponder the comparability of China's resistance to Hideyoshi's enterprise with that encountered by America in the Korean War nearly four hundred years later.

On the failure of this venture, Japan changed course, turning to ever-increasing seclusion. Under the "locked country" policy lasting over two centuries, Japan all but absented itself from participating in any world order. Comprehensive state-to-state relations on conditions of strict diplomatic equality existed only with Korea. Chinese traders were permitted to operate in select locations, though no official Sino-Japanese relations existed because no protocol could be worked out that satisfied both sides' amour propre. Foreign trade with European countries was restricted to a few specified coastal cities; by 1673, all but the Dutch had been expelled, and they were confined to a single artificial island off the port of Nagasaki. By 1825, suspicion of the seafaring Western powers had become so great that Japan's ruling military authorities promulgated an "edict to expel foreigners at all cost"—declaring that any foreign vessel approaching Japanese shores was to be driven away unconditionally, by force if necessary.

All this was, however, prelude to another dramatic shift, under which Japan ultimately vaulted itself into the global order—for two centuries largely Western—and became a modern great power on Westphalian principles. The decisive catalyst came when Japan was confronted, in 1853, by four American naval vessels dispatched from Norfolk, Virginia, on an expedition to flout deliberately the seclusion edicts by entering Tokyo Bay. Their commanding officer, Commodore Matthew Perry, bore a letter from President Millard Fillmore to the Emperor of Japan, which he insisted on delivering directly to imperial representatives in the Japanese capital (a breach of two centuries of Japanese law and diplomatic protocol). Japan, which held foreign trade in as little esteem as China, cannot have been particularly reassured by the President's letter, which informed the Emperor (whom Fillmore addressed as his "Great and Good Friend!") that the American people "think that if your imperial majesty were so far to change the ancient laws as to allow a free trade between the two countries it would be extremely beneficial to both." Fillmore clothed the de facto ultimatum into a classically American pragmatic proposal to the effect that the established seclusion laws, heretofore described as immutable, might be loosened on a trial basis:

> If your imperial majesty is not satisfied that it would be safe altogether to abrogate the ancient laws which forbid foreign trade, they might be suspended for five or ten years, so as to try the experiment. If it does not prove as beneficial as was hoped, the ancient laws can be restored. The United States often limit their treaties with foreign States to a few years, and then renew them or not, as they please.

The Japanese recipients of the message recognized it as a challenge to their concept of political and international order. Yet they reacted with the reserved composure of a society that had experienced and studied the transitoriness of human endeavors for centuries while retaining its essential nature. Surveying Perry's far superior firepower (Japanese cannons and firearms had barely advanced in two centuries, while Perry's vessels were equipped with state-of-the-art naval gunnery capable, as he demonstrated along the Japanese coast, of firing explosive shells), Japan's leaders concluded that direct resistance to the "black ships" would be futile. They relied on the cohesion of their society to absorb the shock and maintain their independence by that cohesion. They prepared an exquisitely courteous reply explaining that although the changes America sought were "most positively forbidden by the laws of our Imperial ancestors," nonetheless, "for us to continue attached to ancient laws, seems to misunderstand the spirit of the age." Allowing that "we are governed now by imperative necessity," Japanese representatives assured Perry that they were prepared to satisfy nearly all of the American demands, including constructing a new harbor capable of accommodating American ships.

Japan drew from the Western challenge a conclusion contrary to

186 | World Order

that of China after the appearance of a British envoy in 1793 (discussed in the next chapter). China reaffirmed its traditional stance of dismissing the intruder with aloof indifference while cultivating China's distinctive virtues, confident that the vast extent of its population and territory and the refinement of its culture would in the end prevail. Japan set out, with studious attention to detail and subtle analysis of the balance of material and psychological forces, to enter the international order based on Western concepts of sovereignty, free trade, international law, technology, and military power—albeit for the purpose of expelling the foreign domination. After a new faction came to power in 1868 promising to "revere the Emperor, expel the barbarians," they announced that they would do so by mastering the barbarians' concepts and technologies and joining the Westphalian world order as an equal member. The new Meiji Emperor's coronation was marked with the Charter Oath signed by the nobility, promising a sweeping program of reform, which included provisions that all social classes should be encouraged to participate. It provided for deliberative assemblies in all provinces, an affirmation of due process, and a commitment to fulfill the aspirations of the population. It relied on the national consensus, which has been one of the principal strengths—perhaps the most distinctive feature—of Japanese society:

1. By this oath, we set up as our aim the establishment of the national wealth on a broad basis and the framing of a constitution and laws.
2. Deliberative assemblies shall be widely established and all matters decided by open discussion.
3. All classes, high and low, shall be united in vigorously carrying out the administration of affairs of state.
4. The common people, no less than the civil and military officials, shall all be allowed to pursue their own calling so that there may be no discontent.

5. Evil customs of the past shall be broken off and everything based upon the just laws of Nature.

6. Knowledge shall be sought throughout the world so as to strengthen the foundation of imperial rule.

Japan would henceforth embark on the systematic construction of railways, modern industry, an export-oriented economy, and a modern military. Amidst all these transformations, the uniqueness of Japanese culture and society would preserve Japanese identity.

The results of this dramatic change of course would, within a few decades, vault Japan into the ranks of global powers. In 1886, after a brawl between Chinese sailors and Nagasaki police, a modern German-built Chinese warship sailed toward Japan, compelling a resolution. By the next decade, intensive naval construction and training had given Japan the upper hand. When an 1894 dispute over relative Japanese and Chinese influence in Korea culminated in war, Japan prevailed decisively. The peace terms included an end of Chinese suzerainty over Korea (giving way to new contests between Japan and Russia) and the cession of Taiwan, which Japan governed as a colony.

Japan's reforms were pursued with such vigor that the Western powers were soon obliged to abandon the model of "extraterritoriality"—their "right" to try their own citizens in Japan by their own, not local, laws—which they had first applied in China. In a landmark trade treaty Britain, the preeminent Western power, committed British subjects in Japan to abide by Japanese jurisdiction. In 1902, the British treaty was transformed into a military alliance, the first formal strategic alignment between an Asian and a Western power. Britain sought the alliance to balance Russian pressures on India. Japan's goal was to defeat Russian aspirations to dominate Korea and Manchuria and to establish its own freedom of maneuver for later designs there. Three years later, Japan stunned the world by defeating the Russian Empire in a war, the first defeat of a Western country by an Asian country in the modern period. In World War I, Japan joined the Entente powers and seized German bases in China and the South Pacific.

Japan had "arrived" as the first non-Western great power in the contemporary age, accepted as a military, economic, and diplomatic equal by the countries that had heretofore shaped the international order. There was one important difference: on the Japanese side, the alliances with Western countries were not based on common strategic objectives but to expel its European allies from Asia.

After the exhaustion of Europe in World War I, Japan's leaders concluded that a world beset by conflict, financial crisis, and American isolationism favored imperial expansion aimed at imposing hegemony on Asia. Imperial Japan detached Manchuria from China in 1931 and established it as a Japanese satellite state under the exiled Chinese Emperor. In 1937, Japan declared war on China in order to subjugate additional Chinese territory. In the name of a "New Order in Asia" and then an "East Asian Co-prosperity Sphere," Japan strove to organize its own anti-Westphalian sphere of influence—a "bloc of Asian nations led by the Japanese and free of Western powers," arranged hierarchically to "thereby enable all nations to find each its proper place in the world." In this new order, other Asian states' sovereignty would be elided into a form of Japanese tutelage.

The members of the established international order were too exhausted by World War I and too preoccupied with the mounting European crisis to resist. Only one Western country remained in the way of this design: the United States, the country that had forcibly opened up Japan less than a century earlier. As though history contained a narrative, the first bombs of a war between the two countries fell on American territory in 1941, when the Japanese launched a surprise attack on Pearl Harbor. American mobilization in the Pacific eventually culminated in the use of two nuclear weapons (the sole military use of these weapons to date), bringing about Japan's unconditional surrender.

Japan adjusted to the debacle by methods similar to its response to Commodore Perry: resilience sustained by an indomitable national spirit based on a distinctive national culture. To restore the Japanese nation, Japan's postwar leaders (almost all of whom had been in the public service in the 1930s and 1940s) portrayed surrender as adaptation to American priorities; indeed, Japan used the authority of the American occupation regime to modernize more fully and to recover more rapidly than it could have by purely national efforts. It renounced war as an instrument of national policy, affirmed principles of constitutional democracy, and reentered the international state system as an American ally—though a low-key one more visibly concerned with economic revival than with participation in grand strategy. For nearly seven decades, this new orientation has proved an important anchor of Asian stability and global peace and prosperity.

Japan's postwar posture was frequently described as a new pacifism; in fact it was considerably more complex. Above all, it reflected an acquiescence in American predominance and an assessment of the strategic landscape and the imperatives of Japan's survival and long-term success. Japan's postwar governing class accepted the constitution drafted by American occupying authorities—with its stringent prohibitions on military action—as a necessity of their immediate circumstances. They avowed its liberal-democratic orientation as their own; they affirmed principles of democracy and international community akin to those embraced in Western capitals.

At the same time, Japan's leaders adapted their country's unique demilitarized role to Japanese long-term strategic purposes. They transformed the pacifist aspects of the postwar order from a prohibition against military action to an imperative to focus on other key elements of national strategy, including economic revitalization. American forces were invited to remain deployed in Japan in substantial numbers, and the defense commitment was solidified into a mutual security treaty, deterring potentially antagonistic powers (including a Soviet Union expanding its Pacific presence) from viewing Japan as a target for strategic action. Having established the framework of the relationship, Japan's Cold War leaders proceeded to reinforce their country's capacities by developing an independent military capability.

The effect of the first stage of Japan's postwar evolution was to take its strategic orientation out of Cold War contests, freeing it to focus on a transformative program of economic development. Japan placed itself legally in the camp of the developed democracies but—citing its pacifist orientation and commitment to world community—declined to join the ideological struggles of the age. The result of this subtle strategy was a period of concerted economic growth paralleled only by that following the 1868 Meiji Revolution. Within two decades of its wartime devastation, Japan had rebuilt itself as a major global economic power. The Japanese miracle was soon after invoked as a potential challenge to American economic preeminence, though it began to level off in the last decade of the twentieth century.

The social cohesion and sense of national commitment that enabled this remarkable transformation has been called forth in response to contemporary challenges. It enabled the Japanese people to respond to a devastating 2011 earthquake, tsunami, and nuclear crisis in Japan's northeast—by World Bank estimates, the costliest natural disaster in world history—with an astonishing display of mutual assistance and national solidarity. Financial and demographic challenges have been the subject of searching internal assessment and, in some aspects, equally bold measures. In each endeavor, Japan has called forth its resources with its traditional confidence that its national essence and culture could be maintained through almost any adjustments.

Dramatic changes in the balance of power will inevitably be translated by Japan's establishment into a new adaptation of Japanese foreign policy. The return of strong national leadership under Prime Minister Shinzo Abe gives Tokyo new latitude to act on its assessments. A December 2013 Japanese government white paper concluded that "as Japan's security environment becomes ever more severe . . . it has become indispensable for Japan to make more proactive efforts in line with the principle of international cooperation," including strengthening Japan's capacity to "deter" and, if needed, "defeat" threats. Surveying a changing Asian landscape, Japan increasingly articulates a desire to become a "normal country" with a military not constitutionally barred from war and an active alliance policy. The issue for Asian regional order will be the definition of "normality."

As at other pivotal moments in its history, Japan is moving toward a redefinition of its broader role in international order, sure to have far-reaching consequences in its region and beyond. Searching for a new role, it will assess once again, carefully, unsentimentally, and unobtrusively, the balance of material and psychological forces in light of the rise of China, Korean developments, and their impact on Japan's security. It will examine the utility and record of the American alliance and its considerable success in serving wide-ranging mutual interests; it will also consider America's withdrawal from three military conflicts. Japan will conduct this analysis in terms of three broad options: continued emphasis on the American alliance; adaptation to China's rise; and reliance on an increasingly national foreign policy. Which of them will emerge as dominant, or whether the choice is for a mix of them, depends on Japan's calculations of the global balance of power—not formal American assurances—and how it perceives underlying trends. Should Japan perceive a new configuration of power unfolding in its region or the world, it will base its security on its judgment of reality, not on traditional alignments. The outcome therefore depends on how credible the Japanese establishment judges American policy in Asia to be and how they assess the overall balance of forces. The long-term direction of U.S. foreign policy is as much at issue as Japan's analysis.

India

In Japan, the impetus of Western intrusion changed the course of a historic nation; in India it reshaped a great civilization into a modern state. India has long developed its qualities at the intersection of world orders, shaping and being shaped by their rhythms. It has been defined less by its political borders than by a shared spectrum of cultural traditions. No mythic founder has been credited with promulgating the Hindu tradition, India's majority faith and the wellspring of several others. History has traced its evolution, dimly and incompletely, through a synthesis of traditional hymns, legends, and rituals from cultures along the Indus and Ganges rivers and plateaus and uplands north and west. In the Hindu tradition, however, these specific forms were the diverse articulations of underlying principles that predated any written text. In its diversity and resistance to definition—encompassing distinct gods and philosophical traditions, the analogues of which would likely have been defined as separate religions in Europe—Hinduism was said to approximate and prove the ultimate oneness of manifold creation, reflecting "the long and diversified history of man's quest for reality . . . at once all-embracing and infinite."

When united—as during the fourth through second centuries B.C. and the fourth through seventh centuries A.D.—India generated currents of vast cultural influence: Buddhism spread from India to Burma, Ceylon, China, and Indonesia, and Hindu art and statecraft influenced Thailand, Indochina, and beyond. When divided—as it often was—into competing kingdoms, India was a lure for invaders, traders, and spiritual seekers (some fulfilling multiple roles at once, such as the Portuguese, who arrived in 1498 "in search of Christians and spices"), whose depredations it endured and whose cultures it eventually absorbed and mixed with its own.

China, until the modern age, imposed its own matrix of customs and culture on invaders so successfully that they grew indistinguishable from the Chinese people. By contrast, India transcended foreigners not by converting them to Indian religion or culture but by treating their ambitions with supreme equanimity; it integrated their achievements and their diverse doctrines into the fabric of Indian life without ever professing to be especially awed by any of them. Invaders might raise extraordinary monuments to their own importance, as if to reassure themselves of their greatness in the face of so much aloofness, but the Indian peoples endured by a core culture defiantly impervious to alien influence. India's foundational religions are inspired not by prophetic visions of messianic fulfillment; rather, they bear witness to the fragility of human existence. They offer not personal salvation but the solace of an inextricable destiny.

World order in Hindu cosmology was governed by immutable cycles of an almost inconceivably vast scale—millions of years long. Kingdoms would fall, and the universe would be destroyed, but it would be re-created, and new kingdoms would rise again. When each wave of invaders arrived (Persians in the sixth century B.C.; Alexander and his Bactrian Greeks in the fourth century B.C.; Arabs in the eighth century; Turks and Afghans in the eleventh and twelfth centuries; Mongols in the thirteenth and fourteenth centuries; Mughals in the sixteenth century; and various European nations following shortly after), they were fitted into this timeless matrix. Their efforts might disrupt, but measured against the perspective of the infinite, they were irrelevant. The true nature of human experience was known only to those who endured and transcended these temporal upheavals.

The Hindu classic the Bhagavad Gita framed these spirited tests in terms of the relationship between morality and power. The work, an episode within the Mahabharata (the ancient Sanskrit epic poem sometimes likened in its influence to the Bible or the Homeric epics), takes the form of a dialogue between the warrior-prince Arjuna and his charioteer, a manifestation of the god Lord Krishna. Arjuna, "overwhelmed by sorrow" on the eve of battle at the horrors he is about to unleash, wonders what can justify the terrible consequences of war. This is the wrong question, Krishna rejoins. Because life is eternal and cyclical and the essence of the universe is indestructible, "the wise grieve neither for the living nor for the dead. There has never been a time when you and I and the kings gathered here have not existed, nor will there be a time when we will cease to exist." Redemption will come through the fulfillment of a preassigned duty, paired with a recognition that its outward manifestations are illusory because "the impermanent has no reality; reality lies in the eternal." Arjuna, a warrior, has been presented with a war he did not seek. He should accept the circumstances with equanimity and fulfill his role with honor, and must strive to kill and prevail and "should not grieve."

While Lord Krishna's appeal to duty prevails and Arjuna professes himself freed from doubt, the cataclysms of the war—described in detail in the rest of the epic—add resonance to his earlier qualms. This central work of Hindu thought embodied both an exhortation to war and the importance not so much of avoiding but of transcending it. Morality was not rejected, but in any given situation the immediate considerations were dominant, while eternity provided a curative perspective. What some readers lauded as a call to fearlessness in battle, Gandhi would praise as his "spiritual dictionary."

Against the background of the eternal verities of a religion preaching the elusiveness of any single earthly endeavor, the temporal ruler was in fact afforded a wide berth for practical necessities. The pioneering exemplar of this school was the fourth-century B.C. minister Kautilya, credited with engineering the rise of India's Maurya Dynasty, which expelled Alexander the Great's successors from northern India and unified the subcontinent for the first time under a single rule.

Kautilya wrote about an India comparable in structure to Europe before the Peace of Westphalia. He describes a collection of states potentially in permanent conflict with each other. Like Machiavelli's, his is an analysis of the world as he found it; it offers a practical, not a normative, guide to action. And its moral basis is identical with that of Richelieu, who lived nearly two thousand years later: the state is a fragile organization, and the statesman does not have the moral right to risk its survival on ethical restraint.

Tradition holds that at some point during or after completing his endeavors, Kautilya recorded the strategic and foreign policy practices he had observed in a comprehensive manual of statecraft, the *Arthashastra*. This work sets out, with dispassionate clarity, a vision of how to establish and guard a state while neutralizing, subverting, and (when opportune conditions have been established) conquering its neighbors. The *Arthashastra* encompasses a world of practical statecraft, not philosophical disputation. For Kautilya, power was the dominant reality. It was multidimensional, and its factors were interdependent. All elements in a given situation were relevant, calculable, and amenable to manipulation toward a leader's strategic aims. Geography, finance, military strength, diplomacy, espionage, law, agriculture, cultural traditions, morale and popular opinion, rumors and legends, and men's vices and weaknesses needed to be shaped as a unit by a wise king to strengthen and expand his realm—much as a modern orchestra conductor shapes the instruments in his charge into a coherent tune. It was a combination of Machiavelli and Clausewitz.

Millennia before European thinkers translated their facts on the ground into a theory of balance of power, the *Arthashastra* set out an analogous, if more elaborate, system termed the "circle of states." Contiguous polities, in Kautilya's analysis, existed in a state of latent hostility. Whatever professions of amity he might make, any ruler whose power grew significantly would eventually find that it was in his interest to subvert his neighbor's realm. This was an inherent dynamic of self-preservation to which morality was irrelevant. Much like Frederick the Great two thousand years later, Kautilya concluded that the ruthless logic of competition allowed no deviation: "The conqueror shall [always] endeavor to add to his own power and increase his own happiness." The imperative was clear: "If . . . the conqueror is superior, the campaign shall be undertaken; otherwise not."

European theorists proclaimed the balance of power as a goal of foreign policy and envisaged a world order based on the equilibrium of states. In the *Arthashastra,* the purpose of strategy was to conquer all other states and to overcome such equilibrium as existed on the road to victory. In that respect, Kautilya was more comparable to Napoleon and Qin Shi Huang (the Emperor who unified China) than to Machiavelli.

In Kautilya's view, states had an obligation to pursue self-interest even more than glory. The wise ruler would seek his allies from among his neighbors' *neighbors.* The goal would be an alliance system with the conqueror at the center: "The Conqueror shall think of the circle of states as a wheel—himself at the hub and his allies, drawn to him by the spokes though separated by intervening territory, as its rim. The enemy, however strong he may be, becomes vulnerable when he is squeezed between the conqueror and his allies." No alliance is conceived as permanent, however. Even within his own alliance system, the King should "undertake such works as would increase his own power" and maneuver to strengthen his state's position and prevent neighboring states from aligning against it.

Like the Chinese strategist Sun Tzu, Kautilya held that the least direct course was often the wisest: to foment dissension between neighbors or potential allies, to "make one neighboring king fight another neighbor and having thus prevented the neighbors from getting together, proceed to overrun the territory of his own enemy." The strategic effort is unending. When the strategy prevails, the King's territory expands, and the borders are redrawn, the circle of states would need to be recalibrated. New calculations of power would have to be undertaken; some allies would now become enemies and vice versa.

What our time has labeled covert intelligence operations were described in the *Arthashastra* as an important tool. Operating in "all states of the circle" (that is, friends and adversaries alike) and drawn from the ranks of "holy ascetics, wandering monks, cart-drivers, wandering minstrels, jugglers, tramps, [and] fortune-tellers," these agents would spread rumors to foment discord within and between other states, subvert enemy armies, and "destroy" the King's opponents at opportune moments.

To be sure, Kautilya insisted that the purpose of the ruthlessness was to build a harmonious universal empire and uphold the dharma—the timeless moral order whose principles were handed down by the gods. But the appeal to morality and religion was more in the name of practical operational purposes than of principle in its own right—as elements of a conqueror's strategy and tactics, not imperatives of a unifying concept of order. The *Arthashastra* advised that restrained and humanitarian conduct was under most circumstances strategically useful: a king who abused his subjects would forfeit their support and would be vulnerable to rebellion or invasion; a conqueror who needlessly violated a subdued people's customs or moral sensibilities risked catalyzing resistance.

The *Arthashastra*'s exhaustive and matter-of-fact catalogue of the imperatives of success led the distinguished twentieth-century political theorist Max Weber to conclude that the *Arthashastra* exemplified "truly radical 'Machiavellianism' . . . compared to it, Machiavelli's *The Prince* is harmless." Unlike Machiavelli, Kautilya exhibits no nostalgia for the virtues of a better age. The only criterion of virtue he would accept was whether his analysis of the road to victory was accurate or not. Did he describe the way policy was, in fact, being conducted? In Kautilya's counsel, equilibrium, if it ever came about, was the temporary result of an interaction of self-serving motives; it was not, as in European concepts after Westphalia, the strategic aim of foreign policy. The *Arthashastra* was a guide to conquest, not to the construction of an international order.

Whether following the *Arthashastra*'s prescriptions or not, India reached its high-water mark of territorial extent in the third century B.C., when its revered Emperor Asoka governed a territory comprising all of today's India, Bangladesh, Pakistan, and part of Afghanistan and Iran. Then, about the time when China was being unified by its founding Emperor, Qin Shi Huang, in 221 B.C., India split into competing kingdoms. Reunified several centuries later, India fractured again in the seventh century, as Islam was beginning to mount its challenge to the empires of Europe and Asia.

For nearly a millennium, India—with its fertile soil, wealthy cities, and resplendent intellectual and technological achievements—became a target for conquest and conversion. Waves of conquerors and adventurers—Turks, Afghans, Parthians, Mongols—descended each century from Central and Southwest Asia into the Indian plains, establishing a patchwork of smaller principalities. The subcontinent was thus "grafted to the Greater Middle East," with ties of religion and ethnicity and strategic sensitivities that endure to this day. For most of this period, the conquerors were too hostile toward each other to permit any one to control the entire region or to extinguish the power of Hindu dynasties in the south. Then, in the sixteenth century, the most skillful of these invaders from the northwest, the Mughals, succeeded in uniting most of the subcontinent under a single rule. The Mughal Empire embodied India's diverse influences: Muslim in faith, Turkic and Mongol in ethnicity, Persian in elite culture, the Mughals ruled over a Hindu majority fragmented by regional identities.

In this vortex of languages, cultures, and creeds, the appearance of yet another wave of foreign adventurers in the sixteenth century did not at first seem to be an epochal event. Setting out to profit from an expanding trade with the wealthy Mughal Empire, private British, French, Dutch, and Portuguese companies vied with one another to establish footholds on land in friendly princely states. Britain's Indian realm grew the most, if initially without a fixed design (prompting the Regius Professor of Modern History at Cambridge to say, "We seem, as it were, to have conquered and peopled half the world in a fit of absence of mind"). Once a base of British power and commerce was established in the eastern region of Bengal, it found itself surrounded by competitors, European and Asian. With each war in Europe and the Americas, the British in India clashed with rivals' colonies and allies; with each victory, they acquired the adversary's Indian assets. As Britain's possessions—technically the holdings of the East India Company, not the British state itself—expanded, it considered itself threatened by Russia looming to the north, by Burma by turns militant and fragmented, and by ambitious and increasingly autonomous Mughal rulers, thus justifying (in British eyes) further annexations.

Ultimately, Britain found itself conceiving of an Indian entity whose unity was based on the security of a continental swath of territories encompassing the contemporary states of Pakistan, India, Bangladesh, and Myanmar. Something akin to an Indian national interest was defined, ascribed to a geographic unit that was, in fact, run as a state even in the absence (it was assumed) of an Indian nation. That policy based the security of India on British naval supremacy in the Indian Ocean; on friendly, or at least nonthreatening, regimes as far-flung as Singapore and Aden; and on a nonhostile regime at the Khyber Pass and the Himalayas. In the north, Britain fended off czarist Russia's advances through the complex forays of spies, explorers, and indigenous surrogates backed up by small contingents of British forces, in what came to be known as the "Great Game" of Himalayan geostrategy. It also edged India's borders with China north toward Tibet—an issue that arose again in China's war with India in 1962. Contemporary analogues to these policies have been taken over as key elements of the foreign policy of postindependence India. They amount to a regional order for South Asia, whose linchpin would be India, and the opposition of any country's attempts, regardless of its domestic structure, to achieve a threatening concentration of power in the neighboring territories.

When London responded to the 1857 mutiny of Muslim and Hindu soldiers in the East India Company's army by declaring direct British rule, it did not conceive of this act as establishing British governance over a foreign nation. Rather, it saw itself as a neutral overseer and civilizing uplifter of multifarious peoples and states. As late as 1888, a leading British administrator could declare,

> There is not, and never was an India, or even any country of India possessing, according to any European ideas, any sort of unity, physical, political, social or religious . . . You might with as much reason and probability look forward to a time when a single nation will have taken the place of the various nations of Europe.

By deciding after the mutiny to administer India as a single imperial unit, Britain did much to bring such an India into being. The diverse regions were connected by rail lines and a common language, English. The glories of India's ancient civilization were researched and catalogued and India's elite trained in British thought and institutions. In the process, Britain reawakened in India the consciousness that it was a single entity under foreign rule and inspired a sentiment that to defeat the foreign influence it had to constitute itself as a nation. Britain's impact on India was thus similar to Napoleon's on a Germany whose multiple states had been treated previously only as a geographic, not a national, entity.

The manner in which India achieved its independence and charted its world role reflected these diverse legacies. India had survived through the centuries by combining cultural imperviousness with extraordinary psychological skill in dealing with occupiers. Mohandas Gandhi's passive resistance to British rule was made possible in the first instance by the spiritual uplift of the Mahatma, but it also proved to be the most effective way to fight the imperial power because of its appeal to the core values of freedom of liberal British society. Like

Americans two centuries earlier, Indians vindicated their independence by invoking against their colonial rulers concepts of liberty they had studied in British schools (including at the London School of Economics, where India's future leaders absorbed many of their quasi-socialist ideas).

Modern India conceived of its independence as a triumph not only of a nation but of universal moral principles. And like America's Founding Fathers, India's early leaders equated the national interest with moral rectitude. But India's leaders have acted on Westphalian principles with respect to spreading their domestic institutions, with little interest in promoting democracy and human rights practices internationally.

As Prime Minister of a newly independent state, Jawaharlal Nehru argued that the basis of India's foreign policy would be India's national interests, not international amity per se or the cultivation of compatible domestic systems. In a speech in 1947, shortly after independence, he explained,

> Whatever policy you may lay down, the art of conducting the
> foreign affairs of a country lies in finding out what is most
> advantageous to the country. We may talk about international
> goodwill and mean what we say. But in the ultimate analysis,
> a government functions for the good of the country it governs
> and no government dare do anything which in the short or
> long run is manifestly to the disadvantage of that country.

Kautilya (and Machiavelli) could not have said it better.

Nehru and subsequent prime ministers, including his daughter, the formidable Indira Gandhi, proceeded to buttress India's position as part of the global equilibrium by elevating their foreign policy into an expression of India's superior moral authority. India presented the vindication of its own national interest as a uniquely enlightened enterprise—much as America had nearly two centuries earlier. And Nehru and later Indira Gandhi, Prime Minister from 1966 to 1977 and 1980 to 1984, succeeded in establishing their fledgling nation as one of the principal elements of the post–World War II international order.

The content of nonalignment was different from the policy undertaken by a "balancer" in a balance-of-power system. India was not prepared to move toward the weaker side—as a balancer would. It was not interested in operating an international system. Its overriding impulse was not to be found formally in either camp, and it measured its success by not being drawn into conflicts that did not affect its national interests.

Emerging into a world of established powers and the Cold War, independent India subtly elevated freedom of maneuver from a bargaining tactic into an ethical principle. Blending righteous moralism with a shrewd assessment of the balance of forces and the major powers' psychologies, Nehru announced India to be a global power that would chart a course maneuvering between the major blocs. In 1947, he stated in a message to the *New Republic*,

> We propose to avoid entanglement in any blocs or groups of Powers realizing that only thus can we serve not only [the] cause of India but of world peace. This policy sometimes leads partisans of one group to imagine that we are supporting the other group. Every nation places its own interests first in developing foreign policy. Fortunately India's interests coincide with peaceful foreign policy and co-operation with all progressive nations. Inevitably India will be drawn closer to those countries which are friendly and cooperative to her.

In other words, India was neutral and above power politics, partly as a matter of principle in the interest of world peace, but equally on the grounds of national interest. During the Soviet ultimatums on Berlin between 1957 and 1962, two American administrations, especially John F. Kennedy's, had sought Indian support on behalf of an isolated city seeking to maintain its free status. But India took the position that any attempt to impose on it the norms of a Cold War bloc would deprive it of its freedom of action and therefore of its bargaining position. Short-term moral neutrality would be the means toward long-term moral influence. As Nehru told his aides,

> It would have been absurd and impolitic for the Indian delegation to avoid the Soviet bloc for fear of irritating the Americans. A time may come when we may say clearly and definitely to the Americans or others that if their attitude continues to be unfriendly we shall necessarily seek friends elsewhere.

The essence of this strategy was that it allowed India to draw support from both Cold War camps—securing the military aid and diplomatic cooperation of the Soviet bloc, even while courting American development assistance and the moral support of the U.S. intellectual establishment. However irritating to Cold War America, it was a wise course for an emerging nation. With a then-nascent military establishment and underdeveloped economy, India would have been a respected but secondary ally. As a free agent, it could exercise a much-wider-reaching influence.

In pursuit of such a role, India set out to build a bloc of like-minded states—in effect, an alignment of the nonaligned. As Nehru told the delegates of the 1955 Afro-Asian Conference in Bandung, Indonesia,

> Are we, the countries of Asia and Africa, devoid of any positive position except being pro-communist or anti-communist? Has it come to this, that the leaders of thought who have given religions and all kinds of things to the world have to tag

on to this kind of group or that and be hangers-on of this party or the other carrying out their wishes and occasionally giving an idea? It is most degrading and humiliating to any self-respecting people or nation. It is an intolerable thought to me that the great countries of Asia and Africa should come out of bondage into freedom only to degrade themselves or humiliate themselves in this way.

The ultimate rationale for India's rejection of what it described as the power politics of the Cold War was that it saw no national interest in the disputes at issue. For the sake of disputes along the dividing lines in Europe, India would not challenge the Soviet Union only a few hundred miles away, which it wished to give no incentive to join up with Pakistan. Nor would it risk Muslim hostility on behalf of Middle East controversies. India refrained from judgment of North Korea's invasion of South Korea and North Vietnam's subversion of South Vietnam. India's leaders were determined not to isolate themselves from what they identified as the progressive trends in the developing world or risk the hostility of the Soviet superpower.

Nevertheless, India found itself involved in a war with China in 1962 and four wars with Pakistan (one of which, in 1971, was carried out under the protection of a freshly signed Soviet defense treaty and ended with the division of India's principal adversary into two separate states, Pakistan and Bangladesh—greatly improving India's overall strategic position).

In quest of a leading role among the nonaligned, India was adhering to a concept of international order compatible with the inherited one on both the global and regional level. Its formal articulation was classically Westphalian and congruent with historical European analyses of the balance of power. Nehru defined India's approach in terms of "five principles of peaceful coexistence." Though given the name of an Indian philosophical concept, *Pancha Shila* (Five Principles of

Coexistence), these were in effect a more high-minded recapitulation of the Westphalian model for a multipolar order of sovereign states:

(1) mutual respect for each other's territorial integrity and sovereignty,
(2) mutual non-aggression,
(3) mutual non-interference in each other's internal affairs,
(4) equality and mutual benefit, and
(5) peaceful co-existence.

India's advocacy of abstract principles of world order was accompanied by a doctrine for Indian security on the regional level. Just as the early American leaders developed in the Monroe Doctrine a concept for America's special role in the Western Hemisphere, so India has established in practice a special position in the Indian Ocean region between the East Indies and the Horn of Africa. Like Britain with respect to Europe in the eighteenth and nineteenth centuries, India strives to prevent the emergence of a dominant power in this vast portion of the globe. Just as early American leaders did not seek the approval of the countries of the Western Hemisphere with respect to the Monroe Doctrine, so India in the region of its special strategic interests conducts its policy on the basis of its own definition of a South Asian order. And while American and Indian views often clashed on the conduct of the Cold War, they have, after the collapse of the Soviet Union, been largely parallel for the Indian Ocean region and its peripheries.

With the end of the Cold War, India was freed from many conflicting pressures and some of its socialist infatuations. It engaged in economic reform, triggered by a balance-of-payments crisis in 1991 and assisted by an IMF program. Indian companies now lead some of the world's major industries. This new direction is reflected in India's diplomatic posture, with new partnerships globally and in particular throughout Africa and Asia and with a heightened regard around the world for India's role in multilateral economic and financial institutions. In addition to its growing economic and diplomatic influence, India has considerably enhanced its military power, including its navy and stockpile of nuclear weapons. And in a few decades, it will surpass China as Asia's most populous country.

India's role in world order is complicated by structural factors related to its founding. Among the most complex will be its relations with its closest neighbors, particularly Pakistan, Bangladesh, Afghanistan, and China. Their ambivalent ties and antagonisms reflect a legacy of a millennium of competing invasions and migrations into the subcontinent, of Britain's forays on the fringes of its Indian realm, and of the rapid end of British colonial rule in the immediate aftermath of World War II. No successor state has accepted the boundaries of the 1947 partition of the subcontinent in full. Treated as provisional by one party or another, the disputed borders have ever since been the cause of sporadic communal violence, military clashes, and terrorist infiltration.

The borders with Pakistan, which roughly traced the concentrations of Islam on the subcontinent, cut across ethnic boundaries. They brought into being a state based on the Muslim religion in two non-contiguous parts of what had been British India divided by thousands of miles of Indian territory, setting the stage for multiple subsequent wars. Borders with Afghanistan and China were proclaimed based on lines drawn by nineteenth-century British colonial administrators, later disclaimed by the opposite parties and to this day disputed. India and Pakistan have each invested heavily in a nuclear weapons arsenal and regional military postures. Pakistan also tolerates, when it does not abet, violent extremism, including terrorism in Afghanistan and in India itself.

A particular complicating factor will be India's relations with the larger Muslim world, of which it forms an integral part. India is often classified as an East Asian or South Asian country. But it has deeper historical links with the Middle East and a larger Muslim population than Pakistan itself, indeed than any Muslim country except Indonesia. India has thus far been able to wall itself off from the harshest currents of political turmoil and sectarian violence, partly through enlightened treatment of its minorities and a fostering of common Indian domestic principles—including democracy and nationalism—transcending communal differences. Yet this outcome is not foreordained, and maintaining it will require concerted efforts. A further radicalization of the Arab world or heightened civil conflict in Pakistan could expose India to significant internal pressures.

Today India pursues a foreign policy in many ways similar to the quest of the former British Raj as it seeks to base a regional order on a balance of power in an arc stretching halfway across the world, from the Middle East to Singapore, and then north to Afghanistan. Its relations with China, Japan, and Southeast Asia follow a pattern akin to the nineteenth-century European equilibrium. Like China, it does not hesitate to use distant "barbarians" like the United States to help achieve its regional aims—though in describing their policies, both countries would use more elegant terms. In the administration of George W. Bush, a strategic coordination between India and America on a global scale was occasionally discussed. It remained confined to the South Asia region because India's traditional nonalignment stood in the way of a global arrangement and because neither country was willing to adopt confrontation with China as a permanent principle of national policy.

Like the nineteenth-century British who were driven to deepen their global involvement to protect strategic routes to India, over the course of the twenty-first century India has felt obliged to play a growing strategic role in Asia and the Muslim world to prevent these regions' domination by countries or ideologies it considers hostile. In pursuing this course, India has had natural ties to the countries of the

English-speaking "Anglosphere." Yet it will likely continue to honor the legacy of Nehru by preserving freedom of maneuver in its Asian and Middle Eastern relations and in its policies toward key autocratic countries, access to whose resources India will require to maintain its expansive economic plans. These priorities will create their own imperatives transcending historical attitudes. With the reconfiguration of the American position in the Middle East, the various regional countries will seek new partners to buttress their positions and to develop some kind of regional order. And India's own strategic analysis will not permit a vacuum in Afghanistan or the hegemony in Asia of another power.

Under a Hindu nationalist-led government elected by decisive margins in May 2014 on a platform of reform and economic growth, India can be expected to pursue its traditional foreign policy goals with added vigor. With a firm mandate and charismatic leadership, the administration of Narendra Modi may consider itself in a position to chart new directions on historic issues like the conflict with Pakistan or the relationship with China. With India, Japan, and China all led by strong and strategically oriented administrations, the scope both for intensified rivalries and for potential bold resolutions will expand.

In any of these evolutions, India will be a fulcrum of twenty-first-century order: an indispensable element, based on its geography, resources, and tradition of sophisticated leadership, in the strategic and ideological evolution of the regions and the concepts of order at whose intersection it stands.

What Is an Asian Regional Order?

The historical European order had been self-contained. England was, until the early twentieth century, able to preserve the balance through its insular position and naval supremacy. Occasionally, European powers enlisted outside countries to strengthen their positions temporarily—for example, France courting the Ottoman Empire in the sixteenth century or Britain's early-twentieth-century alliance with Japan—but non-Western powers, other than occasional surges from the Middle East or North Africa, had few interests in Europe and were not called on to intervene in European conflicts.

By contrast, the contemporary Asian order includes outside powers as an integral feature: the United States, whose role as an Asia-Pacific power was explicitly affirmed in joint statements by U.S. President Barack Obama and Chinese President Hu Jintao in January 2011, and Chinese President Xi Jinping in June 2013; and Russia, geographically an Asian power and participant in Asian groupings such as the Shanghai Cooperation Organisation, even if over three-quarters of its population lives in the European portion of Russian territory.

The United States in modern times has occasionally been invited to act as a balancer of power. In the Treaty of Portsmouth of 1905, it mediated the war between Russia and Japan; in World War II, it defeated Japan's quest for Asian hegemony. The United States played a comparable Asian role during the Cold War when it sought to balance the Soviet Union through a network of alliances stretching from Pakistan to the Philippines.

The evolving Asian structure will have to take into account a plethora of states not dealt with in the preceding pages. Indonesia, anchoring Southeast Asia while affirming an Islamic orientation, plays an increasingly influential role and has thus far managed a delicate balancing act between China, the United States, and the Muslim world. With Japan, Russia, and China as neighbors, the Republic of Korea has achieved a vibrant democracy bolstered by a globally competitive economy, including leadership in strategic industries such as telecommunications and shipbuilding. Many Asian countries—including China—view North Korea's policies as destabilizing but regard a collapse of North Korea as a greater danger. South Korea on its part will have to deal with increasing domestic pressures for unification.

In the face of Asia's vast scale and the scope of its diversity, its nations have fashioned a dazzling array of multilateral groupings and bilateral mechanisms. In contrast to the European Union, NATO, and the Commission on Security and Cooperation in Europe, these institutions deal with security and economic issues on a case-by-case basis, not as an expression of formal rules of regional order. Some of the key groupings include the United States, and some, including economic ones, are Asian only, of which the most elaborated and significant is ASEAN, the Association of Southeast Asian Nations. The core principle is to welcome those nations most directly involved with the issues at hand.

But does all this amount to an Asian system of order? In Europe's equilibrium, the interests of the main parties were comparable, if not congruent. A balance of power could be developed not only in practice—as is inevitable in the absence of hegemony—but as a system of legitimacy that facilitated decisions and moderated policies. Such a congruence does not exist in Asia, as is shown by the priorities the major countries have assigned to themselves. While India appears mostly concerned with China as a peer competitor, in large measure a legacy of the 1962 border war, China sees its peer rivals in Japan and the United States. India has devoted fewer military resources to China than to Pakistan, which, if not a peer competitor, has been a strategic preoccupation for New Delhi.

The amorphous nature of Asian groupings is partly because geography has dictated a sharp dividing line between East Asia and South Asia throughout history. Cultural, philosophical, and religious influences have transcended the geographic dividing lines, and Hindu and Confucian concepts of governance have coexisted in Southeast Asia. But the mountain and jungle barriers were too impenetrable to permit military interaction between the great empires of East Asia and South Asia until the twentieth century. The Mongols and their successors entered the Indian subcontinent from Central Asia, not through the

Himalayan high passes, and they failed to reach the southern parts of India. The various regions of Asia have geopolitically and historically pursued distinct courses.

The regional orders constructed during these periods included none based on Westphalian premises. Where the European order embraced an equilibrium of territorially defined "sovereign states" recognizing each other's legal equality, traditional Asian political powers operated by more ambiguous criteria. Until well into the modern era, an "inner Asian" world influenced by the Mongol Empire, Russia, and Islam coexisted with a Chinese imperial tribute system; the latter reached outward to the kingdoms of Southeast Asia, which entertained China's claims of universality even as they practiced a form of statecraft deeply influenced by Hindu principles received from India that posited a form of divinity for monarchs.

Now these legacies are meeting, and there is far from a consensus among the various countries about the meaning of the journey they have taken or its lessons for twenty-first-century world order. Under contemporary conditions, essentially two balances of power are emerging: one in South Asia, the other in East Asia. Neither possesses the characteristic integral to the European balance of power: a balancer, a country capable of establishing an equilibrium by shifting its weight to the weaker side. The United States (after its withdrawal from Afghanistan) has refrained from treating the contemporary internal South Asian balance primarily as a military problem. But it will have to be active in the diplomacy over reestablishing a regional order lest a vacuum is created, which would inevitably draw all surrounding countries into a regional confrontation.

CHAPTER **6**

Toward an Asian Order:
Confrontation or Partnership?

T HE MOST COMMON FEATURE of Asian states is their sense of
representing "emerging" or "postcolonial" countries. All have
sought to overcome the legacy of colonial rule by asserting a strong
national identity. They share a conviction that world order is now re-
balancing after an unnatural Western irruption over the past several
centuries, but they have drawn vastly different lessons from their historical journeys. When top officials seek to evoke core interests, many
of them look to a different cultural tradition and idealize a different
golden age.

In Europe's eighteenth- and nineteenth-century systems, the preservation of the equilibrium—and by implication the status quo—was
seen as a positive virtue. In Asia, almost every state is impelled by its
own dynamism. Convinced that it is "rising," it operates with the conviction that the world has yet to affirm its full deserved role. Even
while no state questions the others' sovereignty and dignity and all
affirm a dedication to "non-zero-sum" diplomacy, the simultaneous
pursuit of so many programs of national prestige building introduces
a measure of volatility to the regional order. With the evolution of
modern technology, the major powers of Asia have armed themselves

with far more destructive military arsenals than even the strongest nineteenth-century European state possessed, compounding the risks of miscalculation.

The organization of Asia is thus an inherent challenge for world order. Major countries' perception and pursuit of their national interests, rather than the balance of power as a system, have shaped the mechanisms of order that have developed. Their test will be whether a transpacific partnership, providing a peaceful framework for the interplay of many established interests, will be possible.

Asia's International Order and China

Of all conceptions of world order in Asia, China operated the longest lasting, the most clearly defined, and the one furthest from Westphalian ideas. China has also taken the most complex journey, from ancient civilization through classical empire, to Communist revolution, to modern great-power status—a course which will have a profound impact on mankind.

From its unification as a single political entity in 221 B.C. through the early twentieth century, China's position at the center of world order was so ingrained in its elite thinking that in the Chinese language there was no word for it. Only retrospectively did scholars define the "Sinocentric" tribute system. In this traditional concept, China considered itself, in a sense, the sole sovereign government of the world. Its Emperor was treated as a figure of cosmic dimensions and the linchpin between the human and the divine. His purview was not a sovereign state of "China"—that is, the territories immediately under his rule—but "All Under Heaven," of which China formed the central, civilized part: "the Middle Kingdom," inspiring and uplifting the rest of humanity.

In this view, world order reflected a universal hierarchy, not an equilibrium of competing sovereign states. Every known society was conceived of as being in some kind of tributary relationship with China, based in part on its approximation of Chinese culture; none could reach equality with it. Other monarchs were not fellow sovereigns but earnest pupils in the art of governance, striving toward civilization. Diplomacy was not a bargaining process between multiple sovereign interests but a series of carefully contrived ceremonies in which foreign societies were given the opportunity to affirm their assigned place in the global hierarchy. In keeping with this perspective, in classical China what would now be called "foreign policy" was the province of the Ministry of Rituals, which determined the shades of the tributary relationship, and the Office of Border Affairs, charged with managing relations with nomadic tribes. A Chinese foreign ministry was not established until the mid-nineteenth century, and then perforce to deal with intruders from the West. Even then, officials considered their task the traditional practice of barbarian management, not anything that might be regarded as Westphalian diplomacy. The new ministry carried the telling title of the "Office for the Management of the Affairs of All Nations," implying that China was not engaging in interstate diplomacy at all.

The goal of the tribute system was to foster deference, not to extract economic benefit or to dominate foreign societies militarily. China's most imposing architectural achievement, the Great Wall eventually extending over roughly five thousand miles, was begun by the Emperor Qin Shi Huang, who had just defeated all rivals militarily, ending the period of Warring States and unifying China. It was a grandiose testimony to military victory but also to its inherent limits, denoting vast power coupled with a consciousness of vulnerability. For millennia, China sought to beguile and entice its adversaries more often than it attempted to defeat them by force of arms. Thus a minister in the Han Dynasty (206 B.C.–A.D. 220) described the "five baits" with which he proposed to manage the mounted Xiongnu tribes to

China's northwestern frontier, though by conventional analysis China was the superior military power:

> To give them . . . elaborate clothes and carriages in order to corrupt their eyes; to give them fine food in order to corrupt their mouth; to give them music and women in order to corrupt their ears; to provide them with lofty buildings, granaries and slaves in order to corrupt their stomach . . . and, as for those who come to surrender, the emperor [should] show them favor by honoring them with an imperial reception party in which the emperor should personally serve them wine and food so as to corrupt their mind. These are what may be called the five baits.

The hallmark of China's diplomatic rituals, the kowtow—kneeling and touching one's head to the ground to acknowledge the Emperor's superior authority—was an abasement, to be sure, and proved a stumbling block to relations with modern Western states. But the kowtow was symbolically voluntary: it was the representative deference of a people that had been not so much conquered as awed. The tribute presented to China on such occasions was often exceeded in value by the Emperor's return gifts.

Traditionally, China sought to dominate psychologically by its achievements and its conduct—interspersed with occasional military excursions to teach recalcitrant barbarians a "lesson" and to induce respect. Both these strategic goals and this fundamentally psychological approach to armed conflict were in evidence as recently as China's wars with India in 1962 and Vietnam in 1979, as well as in the manner in which core interests vis-à-vis other neighbors are affirmed.

Still, China was not a missionary society in the Western sense of the term. It sought to induce respect, not conversion; that subtle line could never be crossed. Its mission was its performance, which foreign societies were expected to recognize and acknowledge. It was possible for another country to become a friend, even an old friend, but it could never be treated as China's peer. Ironically, the only foreigners who achieved something akin to this status were conquerors. In one of history's most amazing feats of cultural imperialism, two peoples that conquered China—the Mongols in the thirteenth century and the Manchus in the seventeenth—were induced to adopt core elements of Chinese culture to facilitate the administration of a people so numerous and so obdurate in its assumption of cultural superiority. The conquerors were significantly assimilated by the defeated Chinese society, to a point where substantial parts of their home territory came to be treated as traditionally Chinese. China had not sought to export its political system; rather, it had seen others come to it. In that sense, it has expanded not by conquest but by osmosis.

In the modern era, Western representatives with their own sense of cultural superiority set out to enroll China in the European world system, which was becoming the basic structure of international order. They pressured China to cultivate ties with the rest of the world through exchanges of ambassadors and free trade and to uplift its people through a modernizing economy and a society open to Christian proselytizing.

What the West conceived of as a process of enlightenment and engagement was treated in China as an assault. China tried at first to parry it and then to resist outright. When the first British envoy, George Macartney, arrived in the late eighteenth century, bringing with him some early products of the Industrial Revolution and a letter from King George III proposing free trade and the establishment of reciprocal resident embassies in Beijing and London, the Chinese boat that carried him from Guangzhou to Beijing was festooned with a banner that identified him as "The English ambassador bringing tribute to the Emperor of China." He was dismissed with a letter to the

King of England explaining that no ambassador could be permitted to reside in Beijing because "Europe consists of many other nations besides your own: if each and all demanded to be represented at our Court, how could we possibly consent? The thing is utterly impracticable." The Emperor saw no need for trade beyond what was already occurring in limited, tightly regulated amounts, because Britain had no goods China desired:

> Swaying the wide world, I have but one aim in view, namely, to maintain a perfect governance and to fulfil the duties of the State; strange and costly objects do not interest me. If I have commanded that the tribute offerings sent by you, O King, are to be accepted, this was solely in consideration for the spirit which prompted you to dispatch them from afar . . . As your Ambassador can see for himself, we possess all things.

After the defeat of Napoleon, as its mercantile expansion gathered pace, Britain attempted another overture, dispatching a second envoy with a similar proposal. Britain's display of naval power during the Napoleonic Wars had done little to change China's estimate of the desirability of diplomatic relations. When William Amherst, the envoy, declined to attend the kowtow ceremony, offering the excuse that his dress uniform had been delayed, his mission was dismissed, and any further attempt at diplomacy was explicitly discouraged. The Emperor dispatched a message to England's Prince Regent, explaining that as "overlord of all under Heaven," China could not be troubled to walk each barbarian envoy through the correct protocol. The imperial records would duly acknowledge that "thy kingdom far away across the oceans proffers its loyalty and yearns for civilization," but (as a nineteenth-century Western missionary publication translated the edict):

henceforward no more envoys need be sent over this distant route, as the result is but a vain waste of travelling energy. If thou canst but incline thine heart to submissive service, thou mayest dispense with sending missions to court at certain periods; that is the true way to turn toward civilization. That thou mayest for ever obey We now issue this mandate.

Though such admonitions seem presumptuous by today's standards—and were deeply offensive to the country that had just maintained the European equilibrium and could count itself Europe's most advanced naval, economic, and industrial power—the Emperor was expressing himself in a manner consistent with the ideas about his place in the world that had prevailed for millennia, and that many neighboring peoples had been induced to at least indulge.

The Western powers, to their shame, eventually brought matters to a head over the issue of free trade in the most self-evidently harmful product they sold, insisting on the right to the unrestricted importation of—from all the fruits of Western progress—opium. China in the late Qing Dynasty had neglected its military technology partly because it had been unchallenged for so long but largely because of the low status of the military in China's Confucian social hierarchy, expressed in the saying "Good iron is not used for nails. Good men do not become soldiers." Even when under assault by Western forces, the Qing Dynasty diverted military funds in 1893 to restore a resplendent marble boat in the imperial Summer Palace.

Temporarily overwhelmed by military pressure in 1842, China signed treaties conceding Western demands. But it did not abandon its sense of uniqueness and fought a tenacious rearguard action. After scoring a decisive victory in an 1856–58 war (fought over an alleged improper impoundment of a British-registered ship in Guangzhou), Britain insisted on a treaty enshrining its long-sought right to station a resident minister in Beijing. Arriving the next year to take up his post with a triumphal retinue, the British envoy found the main river route to the capital blocked with chains and spikes. When he ordered a contingent of British marines to clear the obstacles, Chinese forces opened fire; 519 British troops died and another 456 were wounded in the ensuing battle. Britain then dispatched a military force under Lord Elgin that stormed Beijing and burned the Summer Palace as the Qing court fled. This brutal intervention compelled the ruling dynasty's grudging acceptance of a "legation quarter" to house the diplomatic representatives. China's acquiescence in the concept of reciprocal diplomacy within a Westphalian system of sovereign states was reluctant and resentful.

At the heart of these disputes was a larger question: Was China a world order entire unto itself or a state like others that was part of a wider international system? China clung to the traditional premise. As late as 1863, after two military defeats by "barbarian" powers and a massive domestic uprising (the Taiping Rebellion) quelled only by calling in foreign troops, the Emperor dispatched a letter to Abraham Lincoln assuring him of China's benign favor: "Having, with reverence, received the commission from Heaven to rule the universe, we regard both the middle empire [China] and the outside countries as constituting one family, without any distinction."

In 1872, the eminent Scottish Sinologist James Legge phrased the issue pointedly and with his era's characteristic confidence in the self-evident superiority of the Western concept of world order:

> During the past forty years her [China's] position with regard
> to the more advanced nations of the world has been entirely
> changed. She has entered into treaties with them upon equal
> terms; but I do not think her ministers and people have yet
> looked this truth fairly in the face, so as to realize the fact that
> China is only one of many independent nations in the world,
> and that the "beneath the sky," over which her emperor has

> rule, is not *all* beneath the sky, but only a certain portion of it
> which is defined on the earth's surface and can be pointed out
> upon the map.

With technology and trade impelling contradictory systems into closer contact, which world order's norms would prevail?

In Europe, the Westphalian system was an outgrowth of a plethora of de facto independent states at the end of the Thirty Years' War. Asia entered the modern era without such a distinct apparatus of national and international organization. It possessed several civilizational centers surrounded by smaller kingdoms, with a subtle and shifting set of mechanisms for interactions between them.

The rich fertility of China's plains and a culture of uncommon resilience and political acumen had enabled China to remain unified over much of a two-millennia period and to exercise considerable political, economic, and cultural influence—even when it was militarily weak by conventional standards. Its comparative advantage resided in the wealth of its economy, which produced goods that all of its neighbors desired. Shaped by these elements, the Chinese idea of world order differed markedly from the European experience based on a multiplicity of co-equal states.

The drama of China's encounter with the developed West and Japan was the impact of great powers, organized as expansionist states, on a civilization that initially saw the trappings of modern statehood as an abasement. The "rise" of China to eminence in the twenty-first century is not new, but reestablishes historic patterns. What is distinctive is that China has returned as both the inheritor of an ancient civilization and as a contemporary great power on the Westphalian model. It combines the legacies of "All Under Heaven," technocratic modernization, and an unusually turbulent twentieth-century national quest for a synthesis between the two.

China and World Order

The imperial dynasty collapsed in 1911, and the foundation of a Chinese republic under Sun Yat-sen in 1912 left China with a weak central government and ushered in a decade of warlordism. A stronger central government under Chiang Kai-shek emerged in 1928 and sought to enable China to assume a place in the Westphalian concept of world order and in the global economic system. Seeking to be both modern and traditionally Chinese, it attempted to fit into an international system that was itself in upheaval. Yet at that point, Japan, which had launched its modernization drive half a century earlier, began a bid for Asian hegemony. The occupation of Manchuria in 1931 was followed by Japan's invasion of large stretches of central and eastern China in 1937. The Nationalist government was prevented from consolidating its position, and the Communist insurgency was given breathing space. Though emerging as one of the victorious Allied powers with the end of World War II in 1945, China was torn apart by civil war and revolutionary turmoil that challenged all relationships and legacies.

On October 1, 1949, in Beijing, the victorious Communist Party leader Mao Zedong proclaimed the establishment of the People's Republic of China with the words "The Chinese people have stood up." Mao elaborated this slogan as a China purifying and strengthening itself through a doctrine of "continuous revolution" and proceeded to dismantle established concepts of domestic and international order. The entire institutional spectrum came under attack: Western democracy, Soviet leadership of the Communist world, and the legacy of the Chinese past. Art and monuments, holidays and traditions, vocabulary and dress, fell under various forms of interdict—blamed for bringing about the passivity that had rendered China unprepared in the face of foreign intrusions. In Mao's concept of order—which he called the "great harmony," echoing classical Chinese philosophy—a new China would emerge out of the destruction of traditional Confucian culture emphasizing harmony. Each wave of revolutionary exertion, he proclaimed, would serve as a precursor to the next. The process of revolution must be ever accelerated, Mao held, lest the revolutionaries become complacent and indolent. "Disequilibrium is a general, objective rule," wrote Mao:

> The cycle, which is endless, evolves from disequilibrium to equilibrium and then to disequilibrium again. Each cycle, however, brings us to a higher level of development. Disequilibrium is normal and absolute whereas equilibrium is temporary and relative.

In the end, this upheaval was designed to produce a kind of traditional Chinese outcome: a form of Communism intrinsic to China, setting itself apart by a distinctive form of conduct that swayed by its achievements, with China's unique and now revolutionary moral authority again swaying "All Under Heaven."

Mao conducted international affairs by the same reliance on the unique nature of China. Though China was objectively weak by the way the rest of the world measured strength, Mao insisted on its central role via psychological and ideological superiority, to be demonstrated by defying rather than conciliating a world emphasizing superior physical power. When speaking in Moscow to an international conference of Communist Party leaders in 1957, Mao shocked fellow delegates by predicting that in the event of nuclear war China's more numerous population and hardier culture would be the ultimate victor, and that even casualties of hundreds of millions would not deflect China from its revolutionary course. While this might have been partly bluff to discourage countries with vastly superior nuclear arsenals, Mao wanted the world to believe that he contemplated nuclear war with equanimity. In July 1971—during my secret visit to Beijing—

Zhou Enlai summed up Mao's conception of world order by invoking the Chairman's claimed purview of Chinese emperors with a sardonic twist: "All under heaven is in chaos, the situation is excellent." From a world of chaos, the People's Republic, hardened by years of struggle, would ultimately emerge triumphant not just in China but everywhere "under heaven." The Communist world order would merge with the traditional view of the Imperial Court.

Like the founder of China's first all-powerful dynasty (221–207 B.C.), the Emperor Qin Shi Huang, Mao sought to unify China while also striving to destroy the ancient culture that he blamed for China's weakness and humiliation. He governed in a style as remote as that of any Emperor (though the emperors would not have convened mass rallies), and he combined it with the practices of Lenin and Stalin. Mao's rule embodied the revolutionary's dilemma. The more sweeping the changes the revolutionary seeks to bring about, the more he encounters resistance, not necessarily from ideological and political opponents but from the inertia of the familiar. The revolutionary prophet is ever tempted to defy his mortality by speeding up his timetable and multiplying the means of enforcing his vision. Mao launched his disastrous Great Leap Forward in 1958 to compel breakneck industrialization and the Cultural Revolution in 1966 to purge the ruling group to prevent its institutionalization in a decade-long ideological campaign that exiled a generation of educated youth to the countryside. Tens of millions died in pursuit of Mao's goals—most eliminated without love or hatred, mobilized to foreshorten into one lifetime what had heretofore been considered a historical process.

Revolutionaries prevail when their achievements come to be taken for granted and the price paid for them is treated as inevitable. Some of China's contemporary leaders suffered grievously during the Cultural Revolution, but they now present that suffering as having given them the strength and self-discovery to steel themselves for the daunting tasks of leading another period of vast transformation. And the

Chinese public, especially those too young to have experienced the travail directly, seems to accept the depiction of Mao as primarily a unifier on behalf of Chinese dignity. Which aspect of this legacy prevails—the taunting Maoist challenge to the world or the quiet resolve gained through weathering Mao's upheavals—will do much to determine China's relationship with twenty-first-century world order.

In the early stages of the Cultural Revolution, China by its own choice had only four ambassadors around the world and was in confrontation with both nuclear superpowers, the United States and the Soviet Union. By the end of the 1960s, Mao recognized that the Cultural Revolution had exhausted even the Chinese people's millennially tested capacity for endurance and that China's isolation might tempt the foreign interventions he had sought to overcome by ideological rigor and defiance. In 1969, the Soviet Union seemed on the verge of attacking China to a point that caused Mao to disperse all ministries to the provinces, with only Premier Zhou Enlai remaining in Beijing. To this crisis, Mao reacted with a characteristically unexpected reversal of direction. He ended the most anarchical aspects of the Cultural Revolution by using the armed forces to put an end to the Red Guards, who had been his shock troops—sending them to the countryside, where they joined their erstwhile victims at, in effect, forced labor. And he strove to checkmate the Soviet Union by moving toward the heretofore-vilified adversary: the United States.

Mao calculated that the opening with the United States would end China's isolation and provide other countries that were holding back with a justification for recognizing the People's Republic of China. (Interestingly, a CIA analysis, written as I was preparing for my first trip, held that Sino-Soviet tensions were so great as to make a U.S.-China rapprochement possible but that Mao's ideological fervor would prevent it in his lifetime.)

Revolutions, no matter how sweeping, need to be consolidated and, in the end, adapted from a moment of exaltation to what is sustainable over a period of time. That was the historic role played by Deng Xiao-ping. Although he had been twice purged by Mao, he became the effective ruler two years after Mao's death in 1976. He quickly undertook to reform the economy and open up the society. Pursuing what he defined as "socialism with Chinese characteristics," he liberated the latent energies of the Chinese people. Within less than a generation, China advanced to become the second-largest economy in the world. To speed up this dramatic transformation—if not necessarily by conviction—China entered international institutions and accepted the established rules of world order.

Yet China's participation in aspects of the Westphalian structure carried with it an ambivalence born of the history that brought it to enter into the international state system. China has not forgotten that it was originally forced to engage with the existing international order in a manner utterly at odds with its historical image of itself or, for that matter, with the avowed principles of the Westphalian system. When urged to adhere to the international system's "rules of the game" and "responsibilities," the visceral reaction of many Chinese—including senior leaders—has been profoundly affected by the awareness that China has not participated in making the rules of the system. They are asked—and, as a matter of prudence, have agreed—to adhere to rules they had had no part in making. But they expect—and sooner or later will act on this expectation—the international order to evolve in a way that enables China to become centrally involved in further international rule making, even to the point of revising some of the rules that prevail.

While waiting for this to transpire, Beijing has become much more active on the world scene. With China's emergence as potentially the world's largest economy, its views and support are now sought in every international forum. China has participated in many of the prestige aspects of the nineteenth- and twentieth-century Western orders: hosting the Olympics; addresses by its presidents before the United Nations;

reciprocal visits with heads of state and governments from leading countries around the world. By any standard, China has regained the stature by which it was known in the centuries of its most far-reaching influence. The question now is how it will relate to the contemporary search for world order, particularly in its relations with the United States.

THE UNITED STATES AND CHINA are both indispensable pillars of world order. Remarkably, both have historically exhibited an ambivalent attitude toward the international system they now anchor, affirming their commitment to it even as they reserve judgment on aspects of its design. China has no precedent for the role it is asked to play in twenty-first-century order, as one major state among others. Nor does the United States have experience interacting on a sustained basis with a country of comparable size, reach, and economic performance embracing a distinctly different model of domestic order.

The cultural and political backgrounds of the two sides diverge in important aspects. The American approach to policy is pragmatic; China's is conceptual. America has never had a powerful threatening neighbor; China has never been without a powerful adversary on its borders. Americans hold that every problem has a solution; Chinese think that each solution is an admission ticket to a new set of problems. Americans seek an outcome responding to immediate circumstances; Chinese concentrate on evolutionary change. Americans outline an agenda of practical "deliverable" items; Chinese set out general principles and analyze where they will lead. Chinese thinking is shaped in part by Communism but embraces a traditionally Chinese way of thought to an increasing extent; neither is intuitively familiar to Americans.

China and the United States have, in their histories, only recently fully participated in an international system of sovereign states. China has believed that it was unique and largely contained within its own reality. America also considers itself unique—that is, "exceptional"—but with a moral obligation to support its values around the world for reasons beyond *raison d'état*. Two great societies of different cultures and different premises are both undergoing fundamental domestic adjustments; whether this translates into rivalry or into a new form of partnership will importantly shape prospects for twenty-first-century world order.

China is now governed by the fifth generation of leaders since the revolution. Each previous leader distilled his generation's particular vision of China's needs. Mao Zedong was determined to uproot established institutions, even those he had built in the original phase of his victory, lest they stagnate under China's bureaucratic propensities. Deng Xiaoping understood that China could not maintain its historic role unless it became internationally engaged. Deng's style was sharply focused: not to boast—lest foreign countries become disquieted—not to claim to lead but to extend China's influence by modernizing both the society and the economy. On that basis, starting in 1989, Jiang Zemin, appointed during the Tiananmen Square crisis, overcame its aftermath with his personal diplomacy internationally and by broadening the base of the Communist Party domestically. He led the PRC into the international state and trading system as a full member. Hu Jintao, selected by Deng, skillfully assuaged concerns about China's growing power and laid the basis for the concept of the new type of major-power relationship enunciated by Xi Jinping.

The Xi Jinping leadership has sought to build on these legacies by undertaking a massive reform program of the Deng scale. It has projected a system that, while eschewing democracy, would be made more transparent and in which outcomes would be determined more by legal procedures than by the established pattern of personal and family relationships. It has announced challenges to many established institutions and practices—state-run enterprises, fiefdoms of regional officials, and large-scale corruption—in a manner that combines vision with courage but is certain to bring in its train a period of flux and some uncertainty.

The composition of the Chinese leadership reflects China's evolution toward participating in—and even shaping—global affairs. In 1982, not a single member of the Politburo had a college degree. At this writing, almost all of them are college educated, and a significant number have advanced degrees. A college degree in China is based on a Western-style curriculum, not a legacy of the old mandarin system (or the subsequent Communist Party curriculum, which imposed its own form of intellectual inbreeding). This represents a sharp break with China's past, when the Chinese were intensely and proudly parochial in their perception of the world outside their immediate sphere. Contemporary Chinese leaders are influenced by their knowledge of China's history but are not captured by it.

A Longer Perspective

Potential tensions between an established and a rising power are not new. Inevitably, the rising power impinges on some spheres heretofore treated as the exclusive preserve of the established power. By the same token, the rising power suspects that its rival may seek to quash its growth before it is too late. A Harvard study has shown that in fifteen cases in history where a rising and an established power interacted, ten ended in war.

It is therefore not surprising that significant strategic thinkers on both sides invoke patterns of behavior and historical experience to predict the inevitability of conflict between the two societies. On the Chinese side, many American actions are interpreted as a design to thwart

China's rise, and the American promotion of human rights is seen as a project to undermine China's domestic political structure. Some major figures describe America's so-called pivot policy as the forerunner of an ultimate showdown designed to keep China permanently in a secondary position—an attitude all the more remarkable because it has not involved any significant military redeployments at this writing.

On the American side, the fear is that a growing China will systematically undermine American preeminence and thus American security. Significant groups view China, by analogy to the Soviet Union in the Cold War, as determined to achieve military as well as economic dominance in all surrounding regions and hence, ultimately, hegemony.

Both sides are reinforced in their suspicions by the military maneuvers and defense programs of the other. Even when they are "normal"—that is, composed of measures a country would reasonably take in defense of national interest as it is generally understood—they are interpreted in terms of worst-case scenarios. Each side has a responsibility for taking care lest its unilateral deployments and conduct escalate into an arms race.

The two sides need to absorb the history of the decade before World War I, when the gradual emergence of an atmosphere of suspicion and latent confrontation escalated into catastrophe. The leaders of Europe trapped themselves by their military planning and inability to separate the tactical from the strategic.

Two other issues are contributing to tension in Sino-American relations. China rejects the proposition that international order is fostered by the spread of liberal democracy and that the international community has an obligation to bring this about, and especially to achieve its perception of human rights by international action. The United States may be able to adjust the application of its views on human rights in relation to strategic priorities. But in light of its history and the convictions of its people, America can never abandon these principles altogether. On the Chinese side, the dominant elite view on this subject was expressed by Deng Xiaoping:

> Actually, national sovereignty is far more important than human rights, but the Group of Seven (or Eight) often infringe upon the sovereignty of poor, weak countries of the Third World. Their talk about human rights, freedom and democracy is designed only to safeguard the interests of the strong, rich countries, which take advantage of their strength to bully weak countries, and which pursue hegemony and practice power politics.

No formal compromise is possible between these views; to keep the disagreement from spiraling into conflict is one of the principal obligations of the leaders of both sides.

A more immediate issue concerns North Korea, to which Bismarck's nineteenth-century aphorism surely applies: "We live in a wondrous time, in which the strong is weak because of his scruples and the weak grows strong because of his audacity." North Korea is ruled under no accepted principle of legitimacy, not even its claimed Communist one. Its principal achievement has been to build a few nuclear devices. It has no military capability to engage in war with the United States. But the existence of these weapons has a political impact far exceeding their military utility. They provide an incentive for Japan and South Korea to create a nuclear military capability. They embolden Pyongyang into risk-taking disproportionate to its capabilities, raising the danger of another war on the Korean Peninsula.

For China, North Korea embodies complex legacies. In many Chinese eyes, the Korean War is seen as a symbol of China's determination to end its "century of humiliation" and "stand up" on the world stage, but also as a warning against becoming involved in wars whose origins China does not control and whose repercussions may have serious long-range, unintended consequences. This is why China and the United States have taken parallel positions in the UN Security Council in demanding that North Korea abandon—not curtail—its nuclear program.

For the Pyongyang regime, abandoning nuclear weapons may well involve political disintegration. But abandonment is precisely what the United States and China have publicly demanded in the UN resolutions that they have fostered. The two countries need to coordinate their policies for the contingency that their stated objectives are realized. Will it be possible to merge the concerns and goals of the two sides over Korea? Are China and the United States able to work out a collaborative strategy for a denuclearized, unified Korea that leaves all parties more secure and more free? It would be a big step toward the "new type of great-power relations" so often invoked and so slow in emerging.

China's new leaders will recognize that the reaction of the Chinese population to their vast agenda cannot be known; they are sailing into uncharted waters. They cannot want to seek foreign adventures, but they will resist intrusions on what they define as their core interests with perhaps greater insistence than their predecessors, precisely because they feel obliged to explain the adjustments inseparable from reform by a reinforced emphasis on the national interest. Any international order comprising both the United States and China must involve a balance of power, but the traditional management of the balance needs to be mitigated by agreement on norms and reinforced by elements of cooperation.

The leaders of China and the United States have publicly recognized the two countries' common interest in charting a constructive outcome. Two American presidents (Barack Obama and George W. Bush) have agreed with their Chinese counterparts (Xi Jinping and Hu Jintao) to create a strategic partnership in the Pacific region, which is a way to preserve a balance of power while reducing the military threat inherent in it. So far the proclamations of intent have not been matched by specific steps in the agreed direction.

Partnership cannot be achieved by proclamation. No agreement can guarantee a specific international status for the United States. If the United States comes to be perceived as a declining power—a matter of choice, not destiny—China and other countries will succeed to much of the world leadership that America exercised for most of the period following World War II, after an interlude of turmoil and upheaval.

Many Chinese may see the United States as a superpower past its peak. Yet among China's leadership, there is also a demonstrated recognition that the United States will sustain a significant leadership capacity for the foreseeable future. The essence of building a constructive world order is that no single country, neither China nor the United States, is in a position to fill by itself the world leadership role of the sort that the United States occupied in the immediate post–Cold War period, when it was materially and psychologically preeminent.

In East Asia, the United States is not so much a balancer as an integral part of the balance. Previous chapters have shown the precariousness of the balance when the number of players is small and a shift of allegiance can become decisive. A purely military approach to the East Asian balance is likely to lead to alignments even more rigid than those that produced World War I.

In East Asia, something approaching a balance of power exists between China, Korea, Japan, and the United States, with Russia and Vietnam peripheral participants. But it differs from the historical balances of power in that one of the key participants, the United States, has its center of gravity located far from the geographic center of East Asia—and, above all, because the leaders of both countries whose military forces conceive themselves as adversaries in their military journals and pronouncements also proclaim partnership as a goal on political and economic issues. So it comes about that the United States is an ally of Japan and a proclaimed partner of China—a situation comparable to Bismarck's when he made an alliance with Austria balanced by a treaty with Russia. Paradoxically, it was precisely that ambiguity which preserved the flexibility of the European equilibrium. And its abandonment—in the name of transparency—started a sequence of increasing confrontations, culminating in World War I.

For over a century—since the Open Door policy and Theodore Roosevelt's mediation of the Russo-Japanese War—it has been a fixed American policy to prevent hegemony in Asia. Under contemporary conditions, it is an inevitable policy in China to keep potentially adversarial forces as far from its borders as possible. The two countries navigate in that space. The preservation of peace depends on the restraint with which they pursue their objectives and on their ability to ensure that competition remains political and diplomatic.

In the Cold War, the dividing lines were defined by military forces. In the contemporary period, the lines should not be defined primarily by military deployment. The military component should not be conceived as the only, or even the principal, definition of the equilibrium. Concepts of partnership need to become, paradoxically, elements of the modern balance of power, especially in Asia—an approach that, if implemented as an overarching principle, would be as unprecedented as it is important. The combination of balance-of-power strategy with partnership diplomacy will not be able to remove all adversarial aspects, but it can mitigate their impact. Above all, it can give Chinese and American leaders experiences in constructive cooperation, and convey to their two societies a way of building toward a more peaceful future.

Order always requires a subtle balance of restraint, force, and legitimacy. In Asia, it must combine a balance of power with a concept of partnership. A purely military definition of the balance will shade into confrontation. A purely psychological approach to partnership will raise fears of hegemony. Wise statesmanship must try to find that balance. For outside it, disaster beckons.

CHAPTER 7

"Acting for All Mankind": The United States and Its Concept of Order

No country has played such a decisive role in shaping contemporary world order as the United States, nor professed such ambivalence about participation in it. Imbued with the conviction that its course would shape the destiny of mankind, America has, over its history, played a paradoxical role in world order: it expanded across a continent in the name of Manifest Destiny while abjuring any imperial designs; exerted a decisive influence on momentous events while disclaiming any motivation of national interest; and became a superpower while disavowing any intention to conduct power politics. America's foreign policy has reflected the conviction that its domestic principles were self-evidently universal and their application at all times salutary; that the real challenge of American engagement abroad was not foreign policy in the traditional sense but a project of spreading values that it believed all other peoples aspired to replicate.

Inherent in this doctrine was a vision of extraordinary originality and allure. While the Old World considered the New an arena for conquest to amass wealth and power, in America a new nation arose affirming freedom of belief, expression, and action as the essence of its national experience and character.

In Europe, a system of order had been founded on the careful sequestration of moral absolutes from political endeavors—if only because attempts to impose one faith or system of morality on the Continent's diverse peoples had ended so disastrously. In America, the proselytizing spirit was infused with an ingrained distrust of established institutions and hierarchies. Thus the British philosopher and Member of Parliament Edmund Burke would recall to his colleagues that the colonists had exported "liberty according to English ideas" along with diverse dissenting religious sects constrained in Europe ("the protestantism of the protestant religion") and "agreeing in nothing but in the communion of the spirit of liberty." These forces, intermingling across an ocean, had produced a distinct national outlook: "In this character of the Americans, a love of freedom is the predominating feature which marks and distinguishes the whole."

Alexis de Tocqueville, the French aristocrat who came to the United States in 1831 and wrote what remains one of the most perceptive books about the spirit and attitudes of its people, traced the American character similarly to what he called its "point of departure." In New England, "we see the birth and growth of that local independence which is still the mainspring and life blood of American freedom." Puritanism, he wrote, "was not just a religious doctrine; in many respects it shared the most absolute democratic and republican theories." This, he concluded, was the product "of two perfectly distinct elements which elsewhere have often been at war with one another but which in America it was somehow possible to incorporate with each other, forming a marvelous combination. I mean the *Spirit of Religion* and the *Spirit of Freedom*."

The openness of American culture and its democratic principles made the United States a model and a refuge for millions. At the same time, the conviction that American principles are universal has introduced a challenging element into the international system because it implies that governments not practicing them are less than fully legitimate. This tenet—so ingrained in American thinking that it is only occasionally put forward as official policy—suggests that a significant portion of the world lives under a kind of unsatisfactory, probationary arrangement, and will one day be redeemed; in the meantime, their relations with the world's strongest power must have some latent adversarial element to them.

These tensions have been inherent since the beginning of the American experience. For Thomas Jefferson, America was not only a great power in the making but an "empire for liberty"—an ever-expanding force acting on behalf of all humanity to vindicate principles of good governance. As Jefferson wrote during his presidency:

> We feel that we are acting under obligations not confined to the limits of our own society. It is impossible not to be sensible that we are acting for all mankind; that circumstances denied to others, but indulged to us, have imposed on us the duty of proving what is the degree of freedom and self-government in which a society may venture to leave its individual members.

So defined, the spread of the United States and the success of its endeavors was coterminous with the interests of humanity. Having doubled the size of the new country through his shrewd engineering of the Louisiana Purchase in 1803, in retirement Jefferson "candidly confess[ed]" to President Monroe, "I have ever looked on Cuba as the most interesting addition which could ever be made to our system of States." And to James Madison, Jefferson wrote, "We should then have only to include the North [Canada] in our confederacy . . . and we should have such an empire for liberty as she has never surveyed since the creation: & I am persuaded no constitution was ever before so well calculated as ours for extensive empire & self government." The empire envisaged by Jefferson and his colleagues differed, in their minds, from the European empires, which they considered based on the subjugation and oppression of foreign peoples. The empire imagined by Jefferson was in essence North American and conceived as the extension of liberty. (And, in fact, whatever may be said about the contradictions in this project or of the personal lives of its Founders, as the United States expanded and thrived, so too did democracy, and the aspiration toward it spread and took root across the hemisphere and the world.)

Despite such soaring ambitions, America's favorable geography and vast resources facilitated a perception that foreign policy was an optional activity. Secure behind two great oceans, the United States was in a position to treat foreign policy as a series of episodic challenges rather than as a permanent enterprise. Diplomacy and force, in this conception, were distinct stages of activity, each following its own autonomous rules. A doctrine of universal sweep was paired with an ambivalent attitude toward countries—necessarily less fortunate than the United States—that felt the compulsion to conduct foreign policy as a permanent exercise based on the elaboration of the national interest and the balance of power.

Even after the United States assumed great-power status in the course of the nineteenth century, these habits endured. Three times in as many generations, in the two world wars and the Cold War, the United States took decisive action to shore up international order against hostile and potentially terminal threats. In each case, America preserved the Westphalian state system and the balance of power while blaming the very institutions of that system for the outbreak of hostilities and proclaiming a desire to construct an entirely new world. For much of this period, the implicit goal of American strategy beyond the Western Hemisphere was to transform the world in a manner that would make an American strategic role unnecessary.

From the beginning, America's intrusion into European consciousness had forced a reexamination of received wisdom; its settlement would open new vistas for individuals promising to fundamentally reinvent world order. For the early settlers of the New World, the Americas were a frontier of a Western civilization whose unity was fracturing, a new stage on which to dramatize the possibility of a moral order. These settlers left Europe not because they no longer believed in its centrality but because they thought it had fallen short of its calling. As religious disputes and bloody wars drove Europe in the Peace of Westphalia to the painful conclusion that its ideal of a continent unified by a single divine governance would never be achieved, America provided a place to do so on distant shores. Where Europe reconciled itself to achieving security through equilibrium, Americans (as they began to think of themselves) entertained dreams of unity and governance enabling a redeemed purpose. The early Puritans spoke of demonstrating their virtue on the new continent as the way to transform the lands of which they had taken leave. As John Winthrop, a Puritan lawyer who left East Anglia to escape religious suppression, preached aboard the *Arbella* in 1630, bound for New England, God intended America as an example for "all people":

> We shall find that the God of Israel is among us, when ten of us shall be able to resist a thousand of our enemies; when He shall make us a praise and glory that men shall say of succeeding plantations, "may the Lord make it like that of New England." For we must consider that we shall be as a city upon a hill. The eyes of all people are upon us.

None doubted that humanity and its purpose would in some way be revealed and fulfilled in America.

America on the World Stage

Setting out to affirm its independence, the United States defined itself as a new kind of power. The Declaration of Independence put forth its principles and assumed as its audience "the opinions of mankind." In the opening essay of *The Federalist Papers,* published in 1787, Alexander Hamilton described the new republic as "an empire in many respects the most interesting in the world" whose success or failure would prove the viability of self-governance anywhere. He treated this proposition not as a novel interpretation but as a matter of common knowledge that "has been frequently remarked"—an assertion all the more notable considering that the United States at the time comprised only the Eastern Seaboard from Maine to Georgia.

Even while propounding these doctrines, the Founders were sophisticated men who understood the European balance of power and manipulated it to the new country's advantage. An alliance with France was enlisted in the war for independence from Britain, then loosened in the aftermath, as France undertook revolution and embarked on a European crusade in which the United States had no direct interest. When President Washington, in his 1796 Farewell Address—delivered in the midst of the French revolutionary wars—counseled that the United States "steer clear of permanent alliances with any portion of the foreign world" and instead "safely trust to temporary alliances for extraordinary emergencies," he was issuing not so much a moral pronouncement as a canny judgment about how to exploit America's comparative advantage: the United States, a fledgling power safe behind oceans, did not have the need or the resources to embroil itself in continental controversies over the balance of power. It joined alliances not to protect a concept of international order but simply to serve its national interests strictly defined. As long as the European balance held, America was better served by a strategy of preserving its freedom of maneuver and consolidating at home—a course of conduct substantially followed by former colonial countries (for example, India) after their independence a century and a half later.

This strategy prevailed for a century, following the last short war with Britain in 1812, allowing the United States to accomplish what no other country was in a position to conceive: it became a great power and a nation of continental scope through the sheer accumulation of domestic power, with a foreign policy focused almost entirely on the negative goal of keeping foreign developments as far at bay as possible.

The United States soon set out to expand this maxim to all of the Americas. A tacit accommodation with Britain, the premier naval power, allowed the United States to declare in the Monroe Doctrine of 1823 its entire hemisphere off-limits for foreign colonization, decades before it had anything close to the power to enforce so sweeping a pronouncement. In the United States, the Monroe Doctrine was interpreted as the extension of the War of Independence, sheltering the Western Hemisphere from the operation of the European balance of power. No Latin American countries were consulted (not least because few existed at the time). As the frontiers of the nation crept across the continent, the expansion of America was seen as the operation of a kind of law of nature. When the United States practiced what elsewhere was defined as imperialism, Americans gave it another name: "the fulfillment of our manifest destiny to overspread the continent allotted by Providence for the free development of our yearly multiplying millions." The acquisition of vast tracts of territory was treated as a commercial transaction in the purchase of the Louisiana Territory from France and as the inevitable consequence of this Manifest Destiny in the case of Mexico. It was not until the close of the nineteenth century, in the Spanish-American War of 1898, that the United States engaged in full-scale hostilities overseas with another major power.

Throughout the nineteenth century, the United States had the good fortune of being able to address its challenges sequentially, and frequently to the point of definitive resolution. The drive to the Pacific and the establishment of favorable northern and southern borders; the vindication of the Union in the Civil War; the projection of power against the Spanish Empire and the inheritance of many of its possessions: each took place as a discrete phase of activity, after which Americans returned to the task of building prosperity and refining democracy. The American experience supported the assumption that peace was the natural condition of humanity, prevented only by other countries' unreasonableness or ill will. The European style of state-craft, with its shifting alliances and elastic maneuvers on the spectrum between peace and hostility, seemed to the American mind a perverse departure from common sense. In this view, the Old World's entire system of foreign policy and international order was an outgrowth of despotic caprice or a malignant cultural penchant for aristocratic cer-emony and secretive maneuver. America would forgo these practices, disclaiming colonial interests, remaining warily at arm's length from the European-designed international system, and relating to other countries on the basis of mutual interests and fair dealing.

John Quincy Adams summed up these sentiments in 1821, in a tone verging on exasperation at other countries' determination to pursue more complicated and devious courses:

> America, in the assembly of nations, since her admission among them, has invariably, though often fruitlessly, held forth to them the hand of honest friendship, of equal free-dom, of generous reciprocity. She has uniformly spoken among them, though often to heedless and often to disdainful ears, the language of equal liberty, of equal justice, and of equal rights. She has, in the lapse of nearly half a century, without a single exception, respected the independence of other nations while asserting and maintaining her own. She has abstained from interference in the concerns of others,

even when conflict has been for principles to which she clings,
as to the last vital drop that visits the heart.

Because America sought "not *dominion,* but *liberty,*" it should avoid, Adams argued, involvement in all the contests of the European world. America would maintain its uniquely reasonable and disinterested stance, seeking freedom and human dignity by offering moral sympathy from afar. The assertion of the universality of American principles was coupled with the refusal to vindicate them outside the Western (that is, American) Hemisphere:

[America] goes not abroad, in search of monsters to destroy.
She is the well-wisher to the freedom and independence of
all. She is the champion and vindicator only of her own.

In the Western Hemisphere, no such restraint prevailed. As early as 1792, the Massachusetts minister and geographer Jedidiah Morse argued that the United States—whose existence had been internationally recognized for less than a decade and whose Constitution was only four years old—marked the apogee of history. The new country, he predicted, would expand westward, spread principles of liberty throughout the Americas, and become the crowning achievement of human civilization:

Besides, it is well known that empire has been travelling
from east to west. Probably her last and broadest feat will be
America . . . [W]e cannot but anticipate the period, as not far
distant, when the AMERICAN EMPIRE will comprehend millions of souls, west of the Mississippi.

All the while America ardently maintained that the endeavor was not territorial expansion in the traditional sense but the divinely ordained spread of principles of liberty. In 1839, as the official United States Exploring Expedition reconnoitered the far reaches of the hemisphere and the South Pacific, the *United States Magazine and Democratic Review* published an article heralding the United States as "the great nation of futurity," disconnected from and superior to everything in history that had preceded it:

> The American people having derived their origin from many other nations, and the Declaration of National Independence being entirely based on the great principle of human equality, these facts demonstrate at once our disconnected position as regards any other nation; that we have, in reality, but little connection with the past history of any of them, and still less with all antiquity, its glories, or its crimes. On the contrary, our national birth was the beginning of a new history.

The success of the United States, the author confidently predicted, would serve as a standing rebuke to all other forms of government, ushering in a future democratic age. A great, free union, divinely sanctioned and towering above all other states, would spread its principles throughout the Western Hemisphere—a power destined to become greater in scope and in moral purpose than any previous human endeavor:

> We are the nation of human progress, and who will, what can, set limits to our onward march? Providence is with us, and no earthly power can.

The United States was thus not simply a country but an engine of God's plan and the epitome of world order.

In 1845, when American westward expansion embroiled the country in a dispute with Britain over the Oregon Territory and with

Mexico over the Republic of Texas (which had seceded from Mexico and declared its intent to join the United States), the magazine concluded that the annexation of Texas was a defensive measure against the foes of liberty. The author reasoned that "California will probably, next fall away" from Mexico, and an American sweep north into Canada would likely follow. The continental force of America, he reasoned, would eventually render Europe's balance of power inconsequential by its sheer countervailing weight. Indeed the author of the *Democratic Review* article foresaw a day, one hundred years hence—that is, 1945—when the United States would outweigh even a unified, hostile Europe:

> Though they should cast into the opposite scale all the bayonets and cannon, not only of France and England, but of Europe entire, how would it kick the beam against the simple, solid weight of the two hundred and fifty, or three hundred millions—and American millions—destined to gather beneath the flutter of the stripes and stars, in the fast hastening year of the Lord 1945!

This is, in fact, what transpired (except that the Canadian border was peacefully demarcated, and England was not part of a hostile Europe in 1945, but rather an ally). Bombastic and prophetic, the vision of America transcending and counterbalancing the harsh doctrines of the Old World would inspire a nation—often while being largely ignored elsewhere or prompting consternation—and reshape the course of history.

As the United States experienced total war—unseen in Europe for half a century—in the Civil War, with stakes so desperate that both North and South breached the principle of hemispheric isolation to involve especially France and Britain in their war efforts, Americans interpreted their conflict as a singular event of transcendent moral significance. Reflecting the view of that conflict as a terminal endeavor, the vindication of "the last best hope of earth," the United States built up by far the world's largest and most formidable army and used it to wage total war, then, within a year and a half of the end of the war, all but disbanded it, reducing a force of more than one million men to roughly 65,000. In 1890, the American army ranked fourteenth in the world, after Bulgaria's, and the American navy was smaller than Italy's, a country with one-thirteenth of America's industrial strength. As late as the presidential inaugural of 1885, President Grover Cleveland described American foreign policy in terms of detached neutrality and as entirely different from the self-interested policies pursued by older, less enlightened states. He rejected

> any departure from that foreign policy commended by the history, the traditions, and the prosperity of our Republic. It is the policy of independence, favored by our position and defended by our known love of justice and by our power. It is the policy of peace suitable to our interests. It is the policy of neutrality, rejecting any share in foreign broils and ambitions upon other continents and repelling their intrusion here.

A decade later, America's world role having expanded, the tone had become more insistent and considerations of power loomed larger. In a border dispute in 1895 between Venezuela and British Guiana, Secretary of State Richard Olney warned Great Britain—then still considered the premier world power—of the inequality of military strength in the Western Hemisphere: "To-day the United States is practically sovereign on this continent, and its fiat is law." America's "infinite resources combined with its isolated position render it master of the situation and practically invulnerable as against any or all other powers."

America was now a major power, no longer a fledgling republic on the fringes of world affairs. American policy no longer limited itself to neutrality; it felt obliged to translate its long-proclaimed universal moral relevance into a broader geopolitical role. When, later that year, the Spanish Empire's colonial subjects in Cuba rose in revolt, a reluctance to see an anti-imperial rebellion crushed on America's doorstep mingled with the conviction that the time had come for the United States to demonstrate its ability and will to act as a great power, at a time when the importance of European nations was in part judged by the extent of their overseas empires. When the battleship USS *Maine* exploded in Havana harbor in 1898 under unexplained circumstances, widespread popular demand for military intervention led President McKinley to declare war on Spain, the first military engagement by the United States with another major power overseas.

Few Americans imagined how different the world order would be after this "splendid little war," as John Hay, then the American ambassador in London, described it in a letter to Theodore Roosevelt, at that time a rising political reformer in New York City. After just three and a half months of military conflict, the United States had ejected the Spanish Empire from the Caribbean, occupied Cuba, and annexed Puerto Rico, Hawaii, Guam, and the Philippines. President McKinley stuck to established verities in justifying the enterprise. With no trace of self-consciousness, he presented the war that had established America as a great power in two oceans as a uniquely unselfish mission. "The American flag has not been planted in foreign soil to acquire more territory," he explained in a remark emblazoned on his reelection poster of 1900, "but for humanity's sake."

The Spanish-American War marked America's entry into great-power politics and into the contests it had so long disdained. The American presence was intercontinental in extent, stretching from the Caribbean to the maritime waters of Southeast Asia. By virtue of its size, its location, and its resources, the United States would be among the most consequential global players. Its actions would now be scrutinized, tested, and, on occasion, resisted by the more traditional powers already sparring over the territories and sea-lanes into which American interests now protruded.

Theodore Roosevelt: America as a World Power

The first President to grapple systematically with the implications of America's world role was Theodore Roosevelt, who succeeded in 1901 upon McKinley's assassination, after a remarkably rapid political ascent culminating in the vice presidency. Hard-driving, ferociously ambitious, highly educated, and widely read, a brilliant cosmopolitan cultivating the air of a ranch hand and subtle far beyond the estimation of his contemporaries, Roosevelt saw the United States as potentially the greatest power—called by its fortuitous political, geographic, and cultural inheritance to an essential world role. He pursued a foreign policy concept that, unprecedentedly for America, based itself largely on geopolitical considerations. According to it, America as the twentieth century progressed would play a global version of the role Britain had performed in Europe in the nineteenth century: maintaining peace by guaranteeing equilibrium, hovering offshore of Eurasia, and tilting the balance against any power threatening to dominate a strategic region. As he declared in his 1905 inaugural address,

> To us as a people it has been granted to lay the foundations of our national life in a new continent . . . Much has been given us, and much will rightfully be expected from us. We have duties to others and duties to ourselves; and we can shirk neither. We have become a great nation, forced by the fact of its greatness into relations with the other nations of the earth, and we must behave as beseems a people with such responsibilities.

Educated partly in Europe and knowledgeable about its history (he wrote a definitive account of the naval component of the War of 1812 while still in his twenties), Roosevelt was on cordial terms with prominent "Old World" elites and was well versed in traditional principles of strategy, including the balance of power. Roosevelt shared his compatriots' assessment of America's special character. Yet he was convinced that to fulfill its calling, the United States would need to enter a world in which power, and not only principle, shared in governing the course of events.

In Roosevelt's view, the international system was in constant flux. Ambition, self-interest, and war were not simply the products of foolish misconceptions of which Americans could disabuse traditional rulers; they were a natural human condition that required purposeful American engagement in international affairs. International society was like a frontier settlement without an effective police force:

> In new and wild communities where there is violence, an honest man must protect himself; and until other means of securing his safety are devised, it is both foolish and wicked to persuade him to surrender his arms while the men who are dangerous to the community retain theirs.

This essentially Hobbesian analysis delivered in, of all occasions, a Nobel Peace Prize lecture, marked America's departure from the proposition that neutrality and pacific intent were adequate to serve the peace. For Roosevelt, if a nation was unable or unwilling to act to defend its own interests, it could not expect others to respect them.

Inevitably, Roosevelt was impatient with many of the pieties that dominated American thinking on foreign policy. The newly emerging extension of international law could not be efficacious unless backed by force, he concluded, and disarmament, emerging as an international topic, was an illusion:

> As yet there is no likelihood of establishing any kind of inter-
> national power . . . which can effectively check wrong-doing,
> and in these circumstances it would be both foolish and an
> evil thing for a great and free nation to deprive itself of the
> power to protect its own rights and even in exceptional cases
> to stand up for the rights of others. Nothing would more pro-
> mote iniquity . . . than for the free and enlightened peoples . . .
> deliberately to render themselves powerless while leaving
> every despotism and barbarism armed.

Liberal societies, Roosevelt believed, tended to underestimate the
elements of antagonism and strife in international affairs. Implying a
Darwinian concept of the survival of the fittest, Roosevelt wrote to the
British diplomat Cecil Spring Rice,

> It is . . . a melancholy fact that the countries which are most
> humanitarian, which are most interested in internal improve-
> ment, tend to grow weaker compared with the other coun-
> tries which possess a less altruistic civilization . . .
> I abhor and despise that pseudo-humanitarianism which
> treats advance of civilization as necessarily and rightfully im-
> plying a weakening of the fighting spirit and which therefore
> invites destruction of the advanced civilization by some less-
> advanced type.

If America disclaimed strategic interests, this only meant that more
aggressive powers would overrun the world, eventually undermining
the foundations of American prosperity. Therefore, "we need a large
navy, composed not merely of cruisers, but containing also a full
proportion of powerful battle-ships, able to meet those of any other
nation," as well as a demonstrated willingness to use it.

In Roosevelt's view, foreign policy was the art of adapting American policy to balance global power discreetly and resolutely, tilting events in the direction of the national interest. He saw the United States—economically vibrant, the only country without threatening regional competitors, and distinctively both an Atlantic and a Pacific power—as in a unique position to "grasp the points of vantage which will enable us to have our say in deciding the destiny of the oceans of the East and the West." Shielding the Western Hemisphere from outside powers and intervening to preserve an equilibrium of forces in every other strategic region, America would emerge as the decisive guardian of the global balance and, through this, international peace.

This was an astonishingly ambitious vision for a country that had heretofore viewed its isolation as its defining characteristic and that had conceived of its navy as primarily an instrument of coastal defense. But through a remarkable foreign policy performance, Roosevelt succeeded—at least temporarily—in redefining America's international role. In the Americas, he went beyond the Monroe Doctrine's well-established opposition to foreign intervention. He pledged the United States not only to repel foreign colonial designs in the Western Hemisphere—personally threatening war to deter an impending German encroachment on Venezuela—but also, in effect, to preempt them. Thus he proclaimed the "Roosevelt Corollary" to the Monroe Doctrine, to the effect that the United States had the right to intervene preemptively in the domestic affairs of other Western Hemisphere nations to remedy flagrant cases of "wrongdoing or impotence." Roosevelt described the principle as follows:

> All that this country desires is to see the neighboring countries stable, orderly, and prosperous. Any country whose people conduct themselves well can count upon our hearty friendship. If a nation shows that it knows how to act with reasonable efficiency and decency in social and political matters, if it keeps order and pays its obligations, it need fear no

> interference from the United States. Chronic wrongdoing, or
> an impotence which results in a general loosening of the ties
> of civilized society, may in America, as elsewhere, ultimately
> require intervention by some civilized nation, and in the
> Western Hemisphere the adherence of the United States to
> the Monroe Doctrine may force the United States, however
> reluctantly, in flagrant cases of such wrongdoing or impo-
> tence, to the exercise of an international police power.

As in the original Monroe Doctrine, no Latin American countries
were consulted. The corollary also amounted to a U.S. security umbrella for the Western Hemisphere. Henceforth no outside power
would be able to use force to redress its grievances in the Americas;
it would be obliged to work through the United States, which assigned
itself the task of maintaining order.

Backing up this ambitious concept was the new Panama Canal,
which enabled the United States to shift its navy between the Atlantic
and the Pacific oceans without the long circumnavigations of Cape
Horn at the southern tip of South America. Begun in 1904 with
American funds and engineering expertise on territory seized from
Colombia by means of a local rebellion supported by the United States,
and controlled by a long-term American lease of the Canal Zone, the
Panama Canal, officially opened in 1914, would stimulate trade while
affording the United States a decisive advantage in any military conflict in the region. (It would also bar any foreign navy from using a
similar route except with U.S. permission.) Hemispheric security was
to be the linchpin of an American world role based on the muscular
assertion of America's national interest.

So long as Britain's naval power remained dominant, it would see
to the equilibrium in Europe. During the Russo-Japanese conflict of
1904–5, Roosevelt demonstrated how he would apply his concept of
diplomacy to the Asian equilibrium and, if necessary, globally. For

Roosevelt, the issue was the balance of power in the Pacific, not flaws in Russia's czarist autocracy (though he had no illusions about these). Because the unchecked eastward advance into Manchuria and Korea of Russia—a country that, in Roosevelt's words, "pursued a policy of consistent opposition to us in the East, and of literally fathomless mendacity"—was inimical to American interests, Roosevelt at first welcomed the Japanese military victories. He described the total destruction of the Russian fleet, which had sailed around the world to its demise in the Battle of Tsushima, as Japan "playing our game." But when the scale of Japan's victories threatened to overwhelm the Russian position in Asia entirely, Roosevelt had second thoughts. Though he admired Japan's modernization—and perhaps because of it—he began to treat an expansionist Japanese Empire as a potential threat to the American position in Southeast Asia and concluded that it might someday "make demands on [the] Hawaiian Islands."

Roosevelt, though in essence a partisan of Russia, undertook a mediation of a conflict in distant Asia underlining America's role as an Asian power. The Treaty of Portsmouth in 1905 was a quintessential expression of Roosevelt's balance-of-power diplomacy. It limited Japanese expansion, prevented a Russian collapse, and achieved an outcome in which Russia, as he described it, "should be left face to face with Japan so that each may have a moderative action on the other." For his mediation, Roosevelt was awarded the Nobel Peace Prize, the first American to be so honored.

Roosevelt treated the achievement not as ushering in a static condition of peace but as the *beginning* of an American role in managing the Asia-Pacific equilibrium. When Roosevelt began to receive threatening intelligence about Japan's "war party," he set out to bring America's resolve to its attention, but with exquisite subtlety. He dispatched sixteen battleships painted white to signify a peaceful mission—called the Great White Fleet—on a "practice cruise around the world," paying friendly visits to foreign ports and serving as a reminder that the United States could now deploy overwhelming naval power to any region. As he wrote to his son, the show of force was intended to warn the aggressive faction in Japan, thus achieving peace through strength: "I do not believe there will be war with Japan, but I do believe that there is enough chance of war to make it eminently wise to insure against it by building such a navy as to forbid Japan's hoping for success."

Japan, while afforded a massive display of American naval power, was at the same time to be treated with utmost courtesy. Roosevelt cautioned the Admiral leading the fleet that he was to go to the limit to avoid offending the sensibilities of the country he was deterring:

> I wish to impress upon you, what I do not suppose is necessary, to see to it that none of our men does anything out of the way while in Japan. If you give the enlisted men leave while at Tokyo or anywhere else in Japan be careful to choose only those upon whom you can absolutely depend. There must be no suspicion of insolence or rudeness on our part . . . Aside from the loss of a ship I had far rather that we were insulted than that we insult anybody under these peculiar conditions.

America would, in the words of Roosevelt's favorite proverb, "speak softly and carry a big stick."

In the Atlantic, Roosevelt's apprehensions were primarily directed at Germany's increasing power and ambitions, especially its large naval building program. If British command of the seas was upset, so would be Britain's ability to maintain the European equilibrium. He saw Germany as gradually overwhelming its neighbors' countervailing force. At the outbreak of World War I, Roosevelt from his retirement called on America to increase its military spending and enter the conflict early on the side of the Triple Entente—Britain, France, and Russia—lest the threat spread to the Western Hemisphere. As he wrote in 1914 to an American German sympathizer:

> Do you not believe that if Germany won in this war, smashed the English Fleet and destroyed the British Empire, within a year or two she would insist upon taking a dominant position in South America . . . ? I believe so. Indeed I know so. For the Germans with whom I have talked, when once we could talk intimately, accepted this view with a frankness that bordered on the cynical.

It was through the contending ambitions of major powers, Roosevelt believed, that the ultimate nature of world order would be decided. Humane values would be best preserved by the geopolitical success of liberal countries in pursuing their interests and maintaining the credibility of their threats. Where they prevailed in the strife of international competition, civilization would spread and be strengthened, with salutary effects.

Roosevelt adopted a generally skeptical view of abstract invocations of international goodwill. He averred that it did no good, and often active harm, for America to make grand pronouncements of principle if it was not in a position to enforce them against determined opposition. "Our words must be judged by our deeds." When the industrialist Andrew Carnegie urged Roosevelt to commit the United States more fully to disarmament and international human rights, Roosevelt replied, invoking some principles of which Kautilya would have approved,

> We must always remember that it would be a fatal thing for the great free peoples to reduce themselves to impotence and leave the despotisms and barbarisms armed. It would be safe

to do so if there was some system of international police; but
there is now no such system . . . The one thing I won't do is to
bluff when I cannot make good; to bluster and threaten and
then fail to take the action if my words need to be backed up.

Had Roosevelt been succeeded by a disciple—or perhaps had he
won the election of 1912—he might have introduced America into
the Westphalian system of world order or an adaptation of it. In this
course of events, America almost certainly would have sought an earlier conclusion to World War I compatible with the European balance
of power—along the lines of the Russo-Japanese Treaty—that left
Germany defeated but indebted to American restraint and surrounded
by sufficient force to deter future adventurism. Such an outcome,
before the bloodletting had assumed nihilistic dimensions, would have
changed the course of history and forestalled the devastation of
Europe's culture and political self-confidence.

In the event, Roosevelt died a respected statesman and conserva-
tionist but founded no foreign policy school of thought. He had no
major disciple, among either the public or his successors as President.
And Roosevelt did not win the 1912 election, because he split the conservative vote with William Howard Taft, the incumbent President.

It was probably inevitable that Roosevelt's attempt to preserve his
legacy by running for a third term would destroy any chance for it.
Tradition matters because it is not given to societies to proceed through
history as if they had no past and as if every course of action were
available to them. They may deviate from the previous trajectory only
within a finite margin. The great statesmen act at the outer limit of
that margin. If they fall short, the society stagnates. If they exceed it,
they lose the capacity to shape posterity. Theodore Roosevelt was
operating at the absolute margin of his society's capabilities. Without
him, American foreign policy returned to the vision of the shining city
on a hill—not participation in, much less domination of, a geopolitical

equilibrium. Nevertheless, America paradoxically fulfilled the leading role Roosevelt had envisioned for it, and within his lifetime. But it did so on behalf of principles Roosevelt derided and under the guidance of a president whom Roosevelt despised.

Woodrow Wilson: America as the World's Conscience

Emerging victorious in the 1912 election with just 42 percent of the popular vote and only two years after his transition from academia to national politics, Woodrow Wilson turned the vision America had asserted largely for itself into an operational program applicable to the entire world. The world was sometimes inspired, occasionally puzzled, yet always obliged to pay attention, both by the power of America and by the scope of his vision.

When America entered World War I, a conflict which started a process that would destroy the European state system, it did so not on the basis of Roosevelt's geopolitical vision but under a banner of moral universality not seen in Europe since the religious wars three centuries before. This new universality proclaimed by the American President sought to universalize a system of governance that existed only in the North Atlantic countries and, in the form heralded by Wilson, only in the United States. Imbued by America's historic sense of moral mission, Wilson proclaimed that America had intervened not to restore the European balance of power but to "make the world safe for democracy"—in other words, to base world order on the compatibility of domestic institutions reflecting the American example. Though this concept ran counter to their tradition, Europe's leaders accepted it as the price of America's entry into the war.

Setting out his vision of the peace, Wilson denounced the balance of power for the preservation of which his new allies had originally entered the war. He rejected established diplomatic methods (decried as "secret diplomacy") as having been a major contributing cause of the conflict. In their place he put forward, in a series of visionary speeches, a new concept of international peace based on a mixture of traditional American assumptions and a new insistence on pushing them toward a definitive and global implementation. This has been, with minor variations, the American program for world order ever since.

Like many American leaders before him, Wilson asserted that a divine dispensation had made the United States a different kind of nation. "It was as if," Wilson told the graduating class at West Point in 1916, "in the Providence of God a continent had been kept unused and waiting for a peaceful people who loved liberty and the rights of men more than they loved anything else, to come and set up an unselfish commonwealth."

Nearly all of Wilson's predecessors in the presidency would have subscribed to such a belief. Where Wilson differed was in his assertion that an international order based on it could be achieved within a single lifetime, even a single administration. John Quincy Adams had lauded the special American commitment to self-government and international fair play but warned his countrymen against seeking to impose these virtues outside the Western Hemisphere among other powers not similarly inclined. Wilson was playing for higher stakes and set a more urgent objective. The Great War, he told Congress, would be "the culminating and final war for human liberty."

When Wilson took the oath of office, he had sought for America to remain neutral in international affairs, offering its services as disinterested mediator and promoting a system of international arbitration meant to forestall war. On assuming the presidency in 1913, Woodrow Wilson had launched a "new diplomacy," authorizing his Secretary of State, William Jennings Bryan, to negotiate an array of international arbitration treaties. Bryan's efforts produced thirty-some such treaties in 1913 and 1914. In general, they provided that every otherwise insoluble dispute should be submitted to a disinterested commission for investigation; there would be no resort to arms until a recommendation had been submitted to the parties. A "cooling off" period was to be established in which diplomatic solutions could prevail over nationalist passions. There is no record that any such treaty was ever applied to a concrete issue. By July 1914, Europe and much of the rest of the world were at war.

When, in 1917, Wilson declared that the grave outrages of one party, Germany, had obliged the United States to join the war in "association" with the belligerents of the other side (Wilson declined to contemplate an "alliance"), he maintained that America's purposes were not self-interested but universal:

> We have no selfish ends to serve. We desire no conquest, no dominion. We seek no indemnities for ourselves, no material compensation for the sacrifices we shall freely make. We are but one of the champions of the rights of mankind.

The premise of Wilson's grand strategy was that all peoples around the world were motivated by the same values as America:

> These are American principles, American policies. We could stand for no others. And they are also the principles and policies of forward looking men and women everywhere, of every modern nation, of every enlightened community.

It was the scheming of autocracies, not any inherent contradiction between differing national interests or aspirations, that caused conflict. If all facts were made openly available and publics were offered a choice, ordinary people would opt for peace—a view also held by the Enlightenment philosopher Kant (described earlier) and by the contemporary advocates of an open Internet. As Wilson told Congress in April 1917, in his request for a declaration of war against Germany:

> Self-governed nations do not fill their neighbor states with spies or set the course of intrigue to bring about some critical posture of affairs which will give them an opportunity to strike and make conquest. Such designs can be successfully worked only under cover and where no one has the right to ask questions. Cunningly contrived plans of deception or aggression, carried, it may be, from generation to generation, can be worked out and kept from the light only within the privacy of courts or behind the carefully guarded confidences of a narrow and privileged class. They are happily impossible where public opinion commands and insists upon full information concerning all the nation's affairs.

The procedural aspect of the balance of power, its neutrality as to the moral merit of contending parties, was therefore immoral as well as dangerous. Not only was democracy the best form of governance; it was also the sole guarantee for permanent peace. As such, American intervention was intended not simply to thwart Germany's war aims but, Wilson explained in a subsequent speech, to alter Germany's system of government. The goal was not primarily strategic, for strategy was an expression of governance:

> The worst that can happen to the detriment of the German people is this, that if they should still, after the war is over, continue to be obliged to live under ambitious and intriguing masters interested to disturb the peace of the world, men or classes of men whom the other peoples of the world could not trust, it might be impossible to admit them to the partnership

of nations which must henceforth guarantee the world's peace.

In keeping with this view, when Germany declared itself ready to discuss an armistice, Wilson refused to negotiate until the Kaiser abdicated. International peace required "the destruction of every arbitrary power anywhere that can separately, secretly and of its single choice disturb the peace of the world; or, if it cannot be presently destroyed, at the least its reduction to virtual impotence." A rules-based, peaceful international order was achievable, but because "no autocratic government could be trusted to keep faith within it or observe its covenants," peace required "that autocracy must first be shown the utter futility of its claims to power or leadership in the modern world."

The spread of democracy, in Wilson's view, would be an automatic consequence of implementing the principle of self-determination. Since the Congress of Vienna, wars had ended with an agreement on the restoration of the balance of power by territorial adjustments. Wilson's concept of world order called instead for "self-determination"—for each nation, defined by ethnic and linguistic unity, to be given a state. Only through self-government, he assessed, could peoples express their underlying will toward international harmony. And once they had achieved independence and national unity, Wilson argued, they would no longer have an incentive to practice aggressive or self-interested policies. Statesmen following the principle of self-determination would not "dare . . . attempting any such covenants of selfishness and compromise as were entered into at the Congress of Vienna," where elite representatives of the great powers had redrawn international borders in secret, favoring equilibrium over popular aspirations. The world would thus enter

> an age . . . which rejects the standards of national selfishness
> that once governed the counsels of nations and demands that

they shall give way to a new order of things in which the only
questions will be: "Is it right?" "Is it just?" "Is it in the interest
of mankind?"

Scant evidence supported the Wilsonian premise that public opinion was more attuned to the overall "interest of mankind" than the
traditional statesmen whom Wilson castigated. The European countries that entered the war in 1914 all had representative institutions of
various influence. (The German parliament was elected by universal
suffrage.) In every country, the war was greeted by universal enthusiasm with nary even token opposition in any of the elected bodies.
After the war, the publics of democratic France and Britain demanded
a punitive peace, ignoring their own historical experience that a stable
European order had never come about except through an ultimate reconciliation of victor and defeated. Restraint was much more the attribute of the aristocrats who negotiated at the Congress of Vienna, if
only because they shared common values and experiences. Leaders
who had been shaped by a domestic policy of balancing a multitude of
pressure groups were arguably more attuned to the moods of the moment or to the dictates of national dignity than to abstract principles of
the benefit of humanity.

The concept of transcending war by giving each nation a state, similarly admirable as a general concept, faced analogous difficulties in
practice. Ironically, the redrawing of Europe's map on the new principle
of linguistically based national self-determination, largely at Wilson's
behest, enhanced Germany's geopolitical prospects. Before the war,
Germany was surrounded by three major powers (France, Russia, and
Austria-Hungary), constraining any territorial expansion. Now it faced
a collection of small states built on the principle of self-determination—
only partially applied, because in Eastern Europe and the Balkans the
nationalities were so jumbled that each new state included other
nationalities, compounding their strategic weakness with ideological

vulnerability. On the eastern flank of Europe's disaffected central power were no longer great masses—which at the Congress of Vienna had been deemed essential to restrain the then-aggressor France—but, as Britain's Prime Minister Lloyd George ruefully assessed, "a number of small states, many of them consisting of people who have never previously set up a stable government for themselves, but each of them containing large masses of Germans clamoring for reunion with their native land."

The implementation of Wilson's vision was to be fostered by the construction of new international institutions and practices allowing for the peaceful resolution of disputes. The League of Nations would replace the previous concert of powers. Forswearing the traditional concept of an equilibrium of competing interests, League members would implement "not a balance of power, but a community of power; not organized rivalries, but an organized common peace." It was understandable that after a war that had been caused by the confrontation of two rigid alliance systems, statesmen might seek a better alternative. But the "community of power" of which Wilson was speaking replaced rigidity with unpredictability.

What Wilson meant by community of power was a new concept that later became known as "collective security." In traditional international policy, states with congruent interests or similar apprehensions might assign themselves a special role in guaranteeing the peace and form an alliance—as they had, for example, after the defeat of Napoleon. Such arrangements were always designed to deal with specific strategic threats, either named or implied: for example, a revanchist France after the Congress of Vienna. The League of Nations, by contrast, would be founded on a moral principle, the universal opposition to military aggression as such, whatever its source, its target, or its proclaimed justification. It was aimed not at a specific issue but at the violation of norms. Because the definition of norms has proved to be subject to divergent interpretations, the operation of collective security is, in that sense, unpredictable.

All states, in the League of Nations concept, would pledge themselves to the peaceful resolution of disputes and would subordinate themselves to the neutral application of a shared set of rules of fair conduct. If states differed in their view as to their rights or duties, they would submit their claims to arbitration by a panel of disinterested parties. If a country violated this principle and used force to press its claims, it would be labeled an aggressor. League members would then unite to resist the belligerent party as a violator of the general peace. No alliances, "separate interests," secret agreements, or "plottings of inner circles" would be permitted within the League, because this would obstruct the neutral application of the system's rules. International order would be refounded instead on "open covenants of peace, openly arrived at."

The distinction Wilson made between alliances and collective security—the key element of the League of Nations system—was central to dilemmas that have followed ever since. An alliance comes about as an agreement on specific facts or expectations. It creates a formal obligation to act in a precise way in defined contingencies. It brings about a strategic obligation fulfillable in an agreed manner. It arises out of a consciousness of shared interests, and the more parallel those interests are, the more cohesive the alliance will be. Collective security, by contrast, is a legal construct addressed to no specific contingency. It defines no particular obligations except joint action of some kind when the rules of peaceful international order are violated. In practice, action must be negotiated from case to case.

Alliances grow out of a consciousness of a defined common interest identified in advance. Collective security declares itself opposed to any aggressive conduct anywhere within the purview of the participating states that, in the proposed League of Nations, involved every recognized state. In the event of a violation, such a collective security system must distill its common purpose after the fact, out of variegated national interests. Yet the idea that in such situations countries will identify violations of peace identically and be prepared to act in common against them is belied by the experience of history. From Wilson to the present, in the League of Nations or its successor, the United Nations, the military actions that can be classed as collective security in the conceptual sense were the Korean War and the first Iraq War, and came about in both cases because the United States had made clear that it would act unilaterally if necessary (in fact, it had in both cases started deployments before there was a formal UN decision). Rather than inspire an American decision, the United Nations decision ratified it. The commitment to support the United States was more a means to gain influence over American actions—already in train—than the expression of a moral consensus.

The balance-of-power system collapsed with the outbreak of World War I because the alliances it spawned had no flexibility, and it was indiscriminately applied to peripheral issues, thereby exacerbating all conflicts. The system of collective security demonstrated the opposite failing when confronted by the initial steps toward World War II. The League of Nations was impotent in the face of the dismemberment of Czechoslovakia, the Italian attack on Abyssinia, the German derogation of the Locarno Treaty, and the Japanese invasion of China. Its definition of aggression was so vague, the reluctance to undertake common action so deep, that it proved inoperative even against flagrant threats to peace. Collective security has repeatedly revealed itself to be unworkable in situations that most seriously threaten international peace and security. (For example, during the Middle East war of 1973, the UN Security Council did not meet, by collusion among the permanent members, until a ceasefire had been negotiated between Washington and Moscow.)

Nevertheless, Wilson's legacy has so shaped American thinking that

American leaders have conflated collective security with alliances. When explaining the nascent Atlantic Alliance system after World War II to a wary Congress, administration spokesmen insisted on describing the NATO alliance as the pure implementation of the doctrine of collective security. They submitted an analysis to the Senate Foreign Relations Committee tracing the difference between historic alliances and the NATO treaty, which held that NATO was not concerned with the defense of territory (surely news to America's European allies). Its conclusion was that the North Atlantic Treaty "is directed against no one; it is directed solely against aggression. It seeks not to influence any shifting 'balance of power' but to strengthen the 'balance of principle.'" (One can imagine the gleam in Secretary of State Dean Acheson's eyes—an astute student of history, he knew far better—when he presented a treaty designed to get around the weaknesses of the doctrine of collective security to Congress as a measure to implement them.)

In retirement, Theodore Roosevelt deplored Wilson's attempts at the beginning of World War I to remain aloof from the unfolding conflict in Europe. He then, at its end, questioned the claims made on behalf of the League of Nations. After armistice was declared in November 1918, Roosevelt wrote,

> I am for such a League provided we don't expect too much from it . . . I am not willing to play the part which even Aesop held up to derision when he wrote of how the wolves and the sheep agreed to disarm, and how the sheep as a guarantee of good faith sent away the watchdogs, and were then forthwith eaten by the wolves.

The test of Wilsonianism has never been whether the world has managed to enshrine peace through sufficiently detailed rules with a broad enough base of signatories. The essential question has been what to do when these rules were violated or, more challengingly, manipulated to ends contrary to their spirit. If international order was a legal system operating before the jury of public opinion, what if an aggressor chose conflict on an issue that the democratic publics regarded as too obscure to warrant involvement—for example, a border dispute between Italy's colonies in East Africa and the independent Empire of Abyssinia? If two sides violated the proscription against force and the international community cut off arms shipments to both parties as a result, this would often allow the stronger party to prevail. If a party "legally" withdrew from the mechanism of peaceful international order and declared itself no longer bound by its strictures—as with Germany's, Japan's, and Italy's eventual withdrawal from the League of Nations, the Washington Naval Treaty in 1922, and the Kellogg-Briand Pact in 1928, or in our own day the defiance of the Nuclear Non-proliferation Treaty by proliferating countries—were the status quo powers authorized to use force to punish this defiance, or should they attempt to coax the renegade power back into the system? Or simply ignore the challenge? And would a course of appeasement not then provide rewards for defiance? Above all, were there "legal" outcomes that should nonetheless be resisted because they violated other principles of military or political equilibrium—for example, the popularly ratified "self-determination" of Austria and the German-speaking communities of the Czechoslovak Republic to merge with Nazi Germany in 1938, or Japan's concoction of a supposedly self-determining Manchukuo ("Manchu Country") in 1932 carved from northeastern China? Were the rules and principles *themselves* the international order, or were they a scaffolding on top of a geopolitical structure capable of—indeed requiring—more sophisticated management?

THE "OLD DIPLOMACY" had sought to counterbalance the interests of rival states and the passions of antagonistic nationalisms in an equilibrium of contending forces. In that spirit, it had brought France back into the European order after the defeat of Napoleon, inviting it to participate in the Congress of Vienna even while ensuring that it would be surrounded by great masses to contain any future temptations to aggrandizement. For the new diplomacy, which promised to reorder international affairs on moral and not strategic principles, no such calculations were permissible.

This placed the statesmen of 1919 in a precarious position. Germany was not invited to the peace conference and in the resulting treaty was labeled the war's sole aggressor and assigned the entire financial and moral burden of the conflict. To Germany's east, however, the statesmen at Versailles struggled to mediate between the multiple peoples who claimed a right to determine themselves on the same territories. This placed a score of weak, ethnically fragmented states between two potentially great powers, Germany and Russia. In any event, there were too many nations to make independence for all realistic or secure; instead, a wavering effort to draft minority rights was begun. The nascent Soviet Union, also not represented at Versailles, was antagonized but not destroyed by an abortive Allied intervention in northern Russia and afterward isolated. And to cap these shortcomings, the U.S. Senate rejected America's accession to the League of Nations, to Wilson's shattering disappointment.

In the years since Wilson's presidency, his failures have generally been ascribed not to shortcomings in his conception of international relations but to contingent circumstances—an isolationist Congress (whose reservations Wilson made little attempt to address or assuage)—or to the stroke that debilitated him during his nationwide speaking tour in support of the League.

As humanly tragic as these events were, it must be said that the failure of Wilson's vision was not due to America's insufficient commitment to Wilsonianism. Wilson's successors tried to implement his visionary program through other complementary and essentially Wilsonian means. In the 1920s and 1930s, America and its democratic partners made a major commitment to a diplomacy of disarmament and peaceful arbitration. At the Washington Naval Conference of 1921–22, the United States attempted to forestall an arms race by offering to scrap thirty naval vessels in order to achieve proportionate limitations of the American, British, French, Italian, and Japanese fleets. In 1928, Calvin Coolidge's Secretary of State Frank Kellogg pioneered the Kellogg-Briand Pact, which purported to outlaw war entirely as "an instrument of national policy"; signatories, who included the vast majority of the world's independent states, all of the belligerents of World War I, and all of the eventual Axis powers, promised to peacefully arbitrate "all disputes or conflicts of whatever nature or of whatever origin they may be, which may arise among them." No significant element of these initiatives survived.

And yet Woodrow Wilson, whose career would appear more the stuff of Shakespearean tragedy than of foreign policy textbooks, had touched an essential chord in the American soul. Though far from being the most geopolitically astute or diplomatically skillful American foreign policy figure of the twentieth century, he consistently ranks among the "greatest" presidents in contemporary polls. It is the measure of Wilson's intellectual triumph that even Richard Nixon, whose foreign policy in fact embodied most of Theodore Roosevelt's precepts, considered himself a disciple of Wilson's internationalism and hung a portrait of the wartime President in the Cabinet room.

Woodrow Wilson's ultimate greatness must be measured by the degree to which he rallied the tradition of American exceptionalism behind a vision that outlasted these shortcomings. He has been revered as a prophet toward whose vision America has judged itself obliged to aspire. Whenever America has been tested by crisis or conflict—in World War II, the Cold War, and our own era's upheavals in the Islamic world—it has returned in one way or another to Woodrow Wilson's vision of a world order that secures peace through democracy, open diplomacy, and the cultivation of shared rules and standards.

The genius of this vision has been its ability to harness American idealism in the service of great foreign policy undertakings in peacemaking, human rights, and cooperative problem-solving, and to imbue the exercise of American power with the hope for a better and more peaceful world. Its influence has been in no small way responsible for the spread of participatory governance throughout the world in the past century and for the extraordinary conviction and optimism that America has brought to its engagement with world affairs. The tragedy of Wilsonianism is that it bequeathed to the twentieth century's decisive power an elevated foreign policy doctrine unmoored from a sense of history or geopolitics.

Franklin Roosevelt and the New World Order

Wilson's principles were so pervasive, so deeply related to the American perception of itself, that when two decades later the issue of world order came up again, the failure of the interwar period did not obstruct their triumphal return. Amidst another world war, America turned once more to the challenge of building a new world order essentially on Wilsonian principles.

When Franklin Delano Roosevelt (a cousin of Theodore Roosevelt's and by now a historic third-term President) and Winston Churchill met for the first time as leaders in Newfoundland aboard HMS *Prince of Wales* in August 1941, they expressed what they described as their common vision in the Atlantic Charter of eight "common principles"—all of which Wilson would have endorsed, while no previous British Prime Minister would have been comfortable with all of them. They included "the right of all peoples to choose the form of government under which they will live"; the end of territorial acquisitions against the will of subject populations; "freedom from fear and want"; and a program of international disarmament, to precede the eventual "abandonment of the use of force" and "establishment of a wider and permanent system of general security." Not all of this—especially the point on decolonization—would have been initiated by Winston Churchill, nor would he have accepted it had he not thought it essential to win an American partnership that was Britain's best, perhaps only, hope to avoid defeat.

Roosevelt even went beyond Wilson in spelling out his ideas of the foundation of international peace. Coming from the academy, Wilson had relied on building an international order on essentially philosophical principles. Having emerged from the manipulatory maelstrom of American politics, Roosevelt placed great reliance on the management of personalities.

Thus Roosevelt expressed the conviction that the new international order would be built on the basis of personal trust:

> The kind of world order which we the peace-loving Nations must achieve, must depend essentially on friendly human relations, on acquaintance, on tolerance, on unassailable sincerity and good will and good faith.

Roosevelt returned to this theme in his fourth inaugural address in 1945:

> We have learned the simple truth, as Emerson said, that "The only way to have a friend is to be one." We can gain no lasting peace if we approach it with suspicion and mistrust or with fear.

When Roosevelt dealt with Stalin during the war, he implemented these convictions. Confronted with evidence of the Soviet Union's record of broken agreements and anti-Western hostility, Roosevelt is reported to have assured the former U.S. ambassador in Moscow William C. Bullitt:

> Bill, I don't dispute your facts; they are accurate. I don't dispute the logic of your reasoning. I just have a hunch that Stalin is not that kind of man . . . I think if I give him everything that I possibly can and ask nothing from him in return, *noblesse oblige,* he won't try to annex anything and will work for a world of democracy and peace.

During the first encounter of the two leaders at Tehran for a summit in 1943, Roosevelt's conduct was in keeping with his pronouncements. Upon arrival, the Soviet leader warned Roosevelt that Soviet intelligence had discovered a Nazi plot threatening the President's safety and offered him hospitality in the heavily fortified Soviet compound, arguing that the American Embassy was less secure and too distant from the projected meeting place. Roosevelt accepted the Soviet offer and rejected the nearby British Embassy to avoid the impression that the Anglo-Saxon leaders were ganging up against Stalin. Going further at joint meetings with Stalin, Roosevelt ostentatiously teased Churchill and generally sought to create the impression of dissociation from Britain's wartime leader.

The immediate challenge was to define a concept of peace. What principles would guide the relations of the world's powers? What contribution was required from the United States in designing and securing an international order? Should the Soviet Union be conciliated or confronted? And if these tasks were carried out successfully, what type of world would result? Would peace be a document or a process?

The geopolitical challenge in 1945 was as complex as any confronted by an American president. Even in its war-ravaged condition, the Soviet Union posed two obstacles to the construction of a postwar international order. Its size and the scope of its conquests overthrew the balance of power in Europe. And its ideological thrust challenged the legitimacy of any Western institutional structure: rejecting all existing institutions as forms of illegitimate exploitation, Communism had called for a world revolution to overthrow the ruling classes and restore power to what Karl Marx had called the "workers of the world."

When in the 1920s the majority of the first wave of European Communist uprisings were crushed or withered for lack of support among the anointed proletariat, Joseph Stalin, implacable and ruthless, promulgated the doctrine of consolidating "socialism in one country." He eliminated all of the other original revolutionary leaders in a decade of purges, and deployed a largely conscripted labor force to build up Russia's industrial capacity. Seeking to deflect the Nazi storm to the west, in 1939 he entered a neutrality pact with Hitler, dividing northern and eastern Europe into Soviet and German spheres of influence. When in June 1941 Hitler invaded Russia anyway, Stalin recalled Russian nationalism from its ideological internment and declared the "Great Patriotic War," imbuing Communist ideology with an opportunistic appeal to Russian imperial feeling. For the first time in Communist rule, Stalin evoked the Russian psyche that had called the Russian state into being and defended it over the centuries through domestic tyrannies and foreign invasions and depredations.

Victory in the war confronted the world with a Russian challenge analogous to that at the end of the Napoleonic Wars, only more acute. How would this wounded giant—having lost at least twenty million lives and with the western third of its vast territory devastated—react to the vacuum opening before it? Attention to Stalin's pronouncements could have provided the answer but for the conventional wartime illusion, which Stalin had carefully cultivated, that he was moderating Communist ideologues rather than instigating them.

Stalin's global strategy was complex. He was convinced that the capitalist system inevitably produced wars; hence the end of World War II would at best be an armistice. He considered Hitler a sui generis representative of the capitalist system, not an aberration from it. The capitalist states remained adversaries after Hitler's defeat, no matter what their leaders said or even thought. As he had said with scorn of the British and French leaders of the 1920s,

> They talk about pacifism; they speak about peace among European states. Briand and Chamberlain are embracing each other . . . All this is nonsense. From European history we know that every time treaties envisaging a new arrangement of forces for new wars have been signed, these treaties have been called treaties of peace . . . [although] they were signed for the purpose of depicting new elements of the coming war.

In Stalin's worldview, decisions were determined by objective factors, not personal relationships. Thus the goodwill of wartime alliance was "subjective" and superseded by the new circumstances of victory. The goal of Soviet strategy would be to achieve the maximum security for the inevitable showdown. This meant pushing the security borders of Russia as far west as possible and weakening the countries beyond these security borders through Communist parties and covert operations.

While the war was going on, Western leaders resisted acknowledging assessments of this kind: Churchill because of his need to stay in step with America; Roosevelt because he was advocating a "master plan" to secure a just and lasting peace, which was in effect a reversal of what had been the European international order—he would countenance neither a balance of power nor a restoration of empires. His public progam called for rules for the peaceful resolution of disputes and parallel efforts of the major powers, the so-called Four Policemen:

the United States, the Soviet Union, Britain, and China. The United States and the Soviet Union especially were expected to take the lead in checking violations of peace.

Charles Bohlen, then a young Foreign Service officer working as Roosevelt's Russian-language translator and later an architect of the Cold War U.S. policy relationship, faulted Roosevelt's "American conviction that the other fellow is a 'good guy' who will respond properly and decently if you treat him right":

> He [Roosevelt] felt that Stalin viewed the world somewhat in the same light as he did, and that Stalin's hostility and distrust . . . were due to the neglect that Soviet Russia had suffered at the hands of other countries for years after the Revolution. What he did not understand was that Stalin's enmity was based on profound ideological convictions.

Another view holds that Roosevelt, who had demonstrated his subtlety in the often ruthless way in which he maneuvered the essentially neutralist American people toward a war that few contemporaries considered necessary, was beyond being deceived by a leader even as wily as Stalin. According to this interpretation, Roosevelt was biding his time and humoring the Soviet leader to keep him from making a separate deal with Hitler. He must have known—or would soon discover—that the Soviet view of world order was antithetical to the American one; invocations of democracy and self-determination would serve to rally the American public but must eventually prove unacceptable to Moscow. Once Germany's unconditional surrender had been achieved and Soviet intransigence had been demonstrated, according to this view, Roosevelt would have rallied the democracies with the same determination he had shown in opposition to Hitler.

Great leaders often embody great ambiguities. When he was assassinated, was President John F. Kennedy on the verge of expanding

America's commitment to Vietnam or withdrawing from it? Naïveté was not, generally speaking, a charge Roosevelt's critics made against him. Probably the answer is that Roosevelt, like his people, was ambivalent about the two sides of international order. He hoped for a peace based on legitimacy, that is, trust between individuals, respect for international law, humanitarian objectives, and goodwill. But confronted with the Soviet Union's insistently power-based approach, he would likely have reverted to the Machiavellian side that had brought him to leadership and made him the dominant figure of his period. The question of what balance he would have struck was preempted by his death in the fourth month of his fourth presidential term, before his design for dealing with the Soviet Union could be completed. Harry S. Truman, excluded by Roosevelt from any decision making, was suddenly catapulted into that role.

CHAPTER 8

The United States: Ambivalent Superpower

ALL TWELVE POSTWAR presidents have passionately affirmed an exceptional role for America in the world. Each has treated it as axiomatic that the United States was embarked on an unselfish quest for the resolution of conflicts and the equality of all nations, in which the ultimate benchmark for success would be world peace and universal harmony.

All presidents from both political parties have proclaimed the applicability of American principles to the entire world, of which perhaps the most eloquent articulation (though in no sense unique) was President John F. Kennedy's inaugural address on January 20, 1961. Kennedy called on his country to "pay any price, bear any burden, meet any hardship, support any friend, oppose any foe, in order to assure the survival and the success of liberty." He made no distinction between threats; he established no priorities for American engagement. He specifically rejected the shifting calculations of the traditional balance of power. What he called for was a "new endeavor"—"not a balance of power, but a new world of law." It would be a "grand and global alliance" against the "common enemies of mankind." What in other countries would have been treated as a rhetorical flourish has, in

American discourse, been presented as a specific blueprint for global action. Speaking to the UN General Assembly one month after President Kennedy's assassination, Lyndon Johnson affirmed the same unconditional global commitment:

> Any man and any nation that seeks peace, and hates war, and is willing to fight the good fight against hunger and disease and misery, will find the United States of America by their side, willing to walk with them, walk with them every step of the way.

That sense of responsibility for world order and of the indispensability of American power, buttressed by a consensus that based the moral universalism of the leaders on the American people's dedication to freedom and democracy, led to the extraordinary achievements of the Cold War period and beyond. America helped rebuild the devastated European economies, created the Atlantic Alliance, and formed a global network of security and economic partnerships. It moved from the isolation of China to a policy of cooperation with it. It designed a system of open world trade that has fueled productivity and prosperity, and was (as it has been over the past century) at the cutting edge of almost all of the technological revolutions of the period. It supported participatory governance in both friendly and adversarial countries; it played a leading role in articulating new humanitarian principles, and since 1945 it has, in five wars and on several other occasions, spent American blood to redeem them in distant corners of the world. No other country would have had the idealism and the resources to take on such a range of challenges or the capacity to succeed in so many of them. American idealism and exceptionalism were the driving forces behind the building of a new international order.

For a few decades, there was an extraordinary correspondence between America's traditional beliefs and historical experience and the world in which it found itself. For the generation of leaders who assumed the responsibility for constructing the postwar order, the two great experiences had been surmounting the recession of the 1930s and victory over aggression in the 1940s. Both tasks lent themselves to definite solutions: in the economic field, the restoration of growth and the inauguration of new social-welfare programs; in the war, unconditional surrender of the enemy.

At the end of the war, the United States, as the only major country to emerge essentially undamaged, produced about 60 percent of the world's GNP. It was thereby able to define leadership as essentially practical progress along lines modeled on the American domestic experience; alliances as Wilsonian concepts of collective security; and governance as programs of economic recovery and democratic reform. America's Cold War undertaking began as a defense of countries that shared the American view of world order. The adversary, the Soviet Union, was conceived as having strayed from the international community to which it would eventually return.

On the journey toward that vision, America began to encounter other historic views of world order. New nations with different histories and cultures appeared on the scene as colonialism ended. The nature of Communism became more complex and its impact more ambiguous. Governments and armed doctrines rejecting American concepts of domestic and international order mounted tenacious challenges. Limits to American capabilities, however vast, became apparent. Priorities needed to be set.

America's encounters with these realities raised a new question that had not heretofore been put to the United States: Is American foreign policy a story with a beginning and an end, in which final victories are possible? Or is it a process of managing and tempering ever-recurring challenges? Does foreign policy have a destination, or is it a process of never-completed fulfillment?

In answering these questions, America put itself through anguishing debates and domestic divisions about the nature of its world role. They were the reverse side of its historic idealism. By framing the issue of America's world role as a test of moral perfection, it castigated itself—sometimes to profound effect—for falling short. In expectation of a final culmination to its efforts—the peaceful, democratic, rules-based world that Wilson prophesied—it was often uncomfortable with the prospect of foreign policy as a permanent endeavor for contingent aims. With nearly every president insisting that America had universal *principles* while other countries merely had national interests, the United States has risked extremes of overextension and disillusioned withdrawal.

Since the end of World War II, in quest of its vision of world order, America has embarked on five wars on behalf of expansive goals initially embraced with near-universal public support, which then turned into public discord—often on the brink of violence. In three of these wars, the Establishment consensus shifted abruptly to embrace a program of effectively unconditional unilateral withdrawal. Three times in two generations, the United States abandoned wars midstream as inadequately transformative or as misconceived—in Vietnam as a result of congressional decisions, in Iraq and Afghanistan by choice of the President.

Victory in the Cold War has been accompanied by congenital ambivalence. America has been searching its soul about the moral worth of its efforts to a degree for which it is difficult to find historical parallels. Either American objectives had been unfulfillable, or America did not pursue a strategy compatible with reaching these objectives. Critics will ascribe these setbacks to the deficiencies, moral and intellectual, of America's leaders. Historians will probably conclude that they derived from the inability to resolve an ambivalence about force and diplomacy, realism and idealism, power and legitimacy, cutting across the entire society.

The Beginning of the Cold War

Nothing in Harry S. Truman's career would have suggested that he would become President, even less that he would preside over the creation of a structure of international order that would last through the Cold War and help decide it. Yet this quintessentially American "common man" would emerge as one of the seminal American presidents.

No president has faced a more daunting task. The war had ended without any attempt by the powers to redefine international order as in the Westphalian settlement of 1648 and at the Congress of Vienna in 1815. Therefore, Truman's first task was to make concrete Roosevelt's vision of a realistically conceived international organization, named the United Nations. Signed in San Francisco in 1945, its charter merged two forms of international decision making. The General Assembly would be universal in membership and based upon the doctrine of the equality of states—"one state, one vote." At the same time, the United Nations would implement collective security via a global concert, the Security Council, designating five major powers (the United States, Britain, France, the U.S.S.R., and China) as "permanent members" wielding veto power. (Britain, France, and China were included as much in homage to their record of great achievements as in reflection of their current capacities.) Together with a rotating group of nine additional countries, the Security Council was vested with special responsibility "to maintain international peace and security."

The United Nations could achieve its designated purpose only if the permanent members shared a conception of world order. On issues where they disagreed, the world organization might enshrine, rather than assuage, their differences. The last summit meeting of the wartime allies at Potsdam in July and August 1945 of Truman, Winston Churchill, and Stalin established the zones of occupation of Germany. (Churchill was replaced as the result of electoral defeat halfway through by Clement Attlee, his wartime deputy.) It also put Berlin under joint administration by the four victorious powers, with guaranteed access to the Western zones of occupation through Soviet-occupied territory. It turned out to be the last significant agreement between the wartime allies.

In the negotiations to implement the accords, the Western allies and the Soviet Union found themselves in mounting deadlock. The Soviet Union insisted on shaping a new international, social, and political structure of Eastern Europe on a principle laid down by Stalin in 1945: "Whoever occupies a territory also imposes on it his own social system. Everyone imposes his own system as far as his army can reach. It cannot be otherwise." Abandoning any notion of Westphalian principles in favor of "objective factors," Stalin now imposed Moscow's Marxist-Leninist system ruthlessly, though gradually, across Eastern Europe.

The first direct military confrontation between the wartime allies occurred over access routes to the capital of the erstwhile enemy, Berlin. In 1948, Stalin, in response to the merging of the three occupation zones of the Western allies, cut the access routes to Berlin, which until the end of the blockade was sustained by a largely American airlift.

How Stalin analyzed "objective" factors is illustrated by a conversation in 1989 I had with Andrei Gromyko, Soviet Foreign Minister for twenty-eight years until he was kicked upstairs by the newly installed Mikhail Gorbachev into the largely ceremonial office of President. He therefore had much time for discussions about what he had observed of Russian history and no future to protect by discretion. I raised a question of how, in light of the vast casualties and devastation it had suffered in the war, the Soviet Union could have dealt with an American military response to the Berlin blockade. Gromyko replied that Stalin had answered similar questions from subordinates to this effect: he doubted the United States would use nuclear weapons on so local an issue. If the Western allies undertook a conventional ground force probe along the access routes to Berlin, Soviet forces were ordered to resist without referring the decision to Stalin. If American forces were mobilizing along the entire front, Stalin said, "Come to me." In other words, Stalin felt strong enough for a local war but would not risk general war with the United States.

Henceforth two power blocs were seeking to stare each other down, without resolving the causes of the underlying crisis. Europe, liberated from Nazism, stood in danger of falling under the sway of a new hegemonic power. The newly independent states in Asia, with fragile institutions and deep domestic and often ethnic divisions, might be delivered to self-government only to be confronted by a doctrine hostile to the West and inimical to pluralism domestically or internationally.

At this juncture, Truman made a strategic choice fundamental for American history and the evolution of the international order. He put an end to the historical temptation of "going it alone" by committing America to the permanent shaping of a new international order. He advanced a series of crucial initiatives. The Greek-Turkish aid program of 1947 replaced the subsidies with which Britain had sustained these pivotal Mediterranean countries and which Britain could no longer afford; the Marshall Plan in 1948 put forward a recovery plan that in time restored Europe's economic health. In 1949, Truman's Secretary of State, Dean Acheson, presided over a ceremony marking the creation of NATO (the North Atlantic Treaty Organization) as the capstone of the American-sponsored new international order.

NATO was a new departure in the establishment of European security. The international order no longer was characterized by the traditional European balance of power distilled from shifting coalitions of multiple states. Rather, whatever equilibrium prevailed had been reduced to that existing between the two nuclear superpowers. If either disappeared or failed to engage, the equilibrium would be lost, and its opponent would become dominant. The first was what happened in 1990 with the collapse of the Soviet Union; the second was the perennial fear of America's allies during the Cold War that America might lose interest in the defense of Europe. The nations joining the North Atlantic Treaty Organization provided some military forces but more in the nature of an admission ticket for a shelter under America's nuclear umbrella than as an instrument of local defense. What America was constructing in the Truman era was a unilateral guarantee in the form of a traditional alliance.

With the structure in place, the historical debates about the ultimate purpose of American foreign policy reemerged. Were the goals of the new alliance moral or strategic? Coexistence or the adversary's collapse? Did America seek conversion of the adversary or evolution? Conversion entails inducing an adversary to break with its past in one comprehensive act or gesture. Evolution involves a gradual process, a willingness to pursue ultimate foreign policy goals in imperfect stages and to deal with the adversary as a reality while this process is going on. What course would America choose? Exhibiting its historical ambivalence on the subject, America chose both.

Strategies of a Cold War Order

The most comprehensive American strategic design in the Cold War was put forward by a then-obscure Foreign Service officer, George Kennan, serving as head of the Political Section of the American Embassy in Moscow. No Foreign Service officer has ever shaped the U.S. debate over America's world role to such an extent. While Washington was still basking in the wartime euphoria based on belief in Stalin's goodwill, Kennan predicted a looming confrontation. The United States, he asserted in a personal letter to a colleague in 1945, needed to face the fact that its Soviet ally would, at the conclusion of the war, turn into an adversary:

> A basic conflict is thus arising over Europe between the inter-
> ests of Atlantic sea-power, which demand the preservation of
> vigorous and independent political life on the European pen-
> insula, and the interests of the jealous Eurasian land power,
> which must always seek to extend itself to the west and will
> never find a place, short of the Atlantic Ocean, where it can
> from its own standpoint safely stop.

Kennan proposed an explicitly strategic response: to "gather together at once into our hands all the cards we hold and begin to play
them for their full value." Eastern Europe, Kennan concluded, would
be dominated by Moscow: it stood closer to Russian centers of power
than it did to Washington and, however regrettably, Soviet troops had
reached it first. Hence the United States should consolidate a sphere in
Western Europe under American protection—with the dividing line
running through Germany—and endow its sphere with sufficient
strength and cohesion to maintain the geopolitical balance.

This prescient prediction of the postwar outcome was rejected by
Kennan's colleague Charles "Chip" Bohlen on Wilsonian grounds that
"foreign policy of that kind cannot be made in a democracy. Only totalitarian states can make and carry out such policies." Washington
might accept a balance of power as a fact; it could not adopt it as a
policy.

In February 1946, the American Embassy in Moscow received a
query from Washington as to whether a doctrinaire speech by Stalin
inaugurated a change in the Soviet commitment to a harmonious international order. Kennan, at that time deputy chief of mission, was
given an opportunity many Foreign Service officers dream of: to present their views directly to high levels without requiring ambassadorial approval. Kennan replied in a five-part telegram of nineteen
single-spaced pages. The essence of the so-called Long Telegram was
that the entire American debate over Soviet intentions needed to be

reconceived. Soviet leaders saw East-West relations as a contest between antithetical concepts of world order. They had taken a "traditional and instinctive Russian sense of insecurity" and grafted onto it a revolutionary doctrine of global sweep. The Kremlin would interpret every aspect of international affairs in light of Soviet doctrine about a battle for advantage between what Stalin had called the "two centers of world significance," capitalism and Communism, whose global contest was inevitable and could end with only one winner. They thought the battle was inevitable, and thus made it so.

The next year, Kennan, now head of the Policy Planning Staff in the State Department, went public in an article in *Foreign Affairs* published anonymously by "X." On the surface, the article made the same point as the Long Telegram: Soviet pressure on the West was real and inherent, but it could be "contained by the adroit and vigilant application of counter-force at a series of constantly shifting geographical and political points."

Theodore Roosevelt would have had no difficulty endorsing this analysis. But when outlining his idea of how the conflict might end, Kennan reentered Wilsonian territory. At some point in Moscow's futile confrontations with the outside world, he predicted, some Soviet leader would feel the need to achieve additional support by reaching out beyond the Party apparatus to the general public, which was immature and inexperienced, having never been permitted to develop an independent political sense. But if "the unity and efficacy of the Party as a political instrument" was ever so disrupted, "Soviet Russia might be changed overnight from one of the strongest to one of the weakest and most pitiable of national societies." This prediction—essentially correct—was Wilsonian in the belief that at the end of the process democratic principles would prevail, that legitimacy would trump power.

This belief is what Dean Acheson, the model and seminal Secretary of State to many of his successors (including me), practiced. From

1949 to 1953 he concentrated on building what he called "situations of strength" via NATO; East-West diplomacy would more or less automatically reflect the balance of power. During the Eisenhower administration, his successor, John Foster Dulles, extended the alliance system through SEATO for Southeast Asia (1954) and the Baghdad Pact for the Middle East (1955). In effect, containment came to be equated with the construction of military alliances around the entire Soviet periphery over two continents. World order would consist of the confrontation of two incongruent superpowers—each of which organized an international order within its sphere.

Both secretaries of state viewed power and diplomacy as successive stages: America would first consolidate and demonstrate its power; then the Soviet Union would be obliged to cease its challenges and arrive at a reasonable accommodation with the non-Communist world. Yet if diplomacy was to be based on positions of military strength, why was it necessary to suspend it in the formative stages of the Atlantic relationship? And how was the strength of the free world to be conveyed to the other side? For in fact, America's nuclear monopoly coupled with the war's devastating impact on the Soviet Union ensured that the actual balance of power was uniquely favorable to the West at the beginning of the Cold War. A situation of strength did not need to be built; it already existed.

Winston Churchill recognized this in a speech in October 1948, when he argued that the West's bargaining position would never be stronger than it was at that moment. Negotiations should be pressed, not suspended:

> The question is asked: What will happen when they get the atomic bomb themselves and have accumulated a large store? You can judge yourselves what will happen then by what is happening now. If these things are done in the green wood, what will be done in the dry? . . . No one in his senses can

believe that we have a limitless period of time before us.
We ought to bring matters to a head and make a final
settlement . . . The Western Nations will be far more likely to
reach a lasting settlement, without bloodshed, if they formu-
late their just demands while they have the atomic power and
before the Russian Communists have got it too.

Truman and Acheson undoubtedly considered the risk too great
and resisted a grand negotiation for fear that it might undermine Allied cohesion. Above all, Churchill was leader of the opposition, not
Prime Minister, when he urged an at least diplomatic showdown, and
the incumbent Clement Attlee and his Foreign Secretary, Ernest
Bevin, would surely have resisted a design invoking the threat of war.

In this context, the United States assumed leadership of the global
effort to contain Soviet expansionism—but as a primarily moral, not
geopolitical, endeavor. Valid interests existed in both spheres, yet the
manner in which they were described tended to obscure attempts to
define strategic priorities. Even NSC-68, which codified Truman's national security policy as a classified document and was largely written
by the hard-line Paul Nitze, avoided the concept of national interest
and placed the conflict into traditional moral, almost lyrical, categories. The struggle was between the forces of "freedom under a government of laws" (which entailed "marvelous diversity, the deep tolerance,
the lawfulness of the free society . . . in which every individual has the
opportunity to realize his creative powers") and forces of "slavery
under the grim oligarchy of the Kremlin." By its own lights, America
was joining the Cold War struggle not as a geopolitical contest over
the limits of Russian power but as a moral crusade for the free world.

In such an endeavor, American policies were presented as a disinterested effort to advance the general interests of humanity. John Foster Dulles, a shrewd operator in crises and tough exponent of American
power, nonetheless described American foreign policy as a kind of

global volunteer effort guided by principles totally different from any other historic state's approach. He observed that though it was "difficult for many to understand," the United States was "really . . . motivated by considerations other than short-range expediency." America's influence would not restore the geopolitical balance, in this view, but transcend it: "It has been customary, for so many centuries, for nations to act merely to promote their own immediate self-interest, to hurt their rivals, that it is not readily accepted that there can be a new era when nations will be guided by principle."

The implication that other nations had "selfish interests" while America had "principles" and "destiny" was as old as the Republic. What was new was that a global geopolitical contest in which the United States was the leader, not a bystander, was justified primarily on moral grounds, and the American national interest was disavowed. This call to universal responsibility underpinned the decisive American commitment to restoring a devastated postwar world holding the line against Soviet expansion. Yet when it came time to fighting "hot" wars on the periphery of the Communist world, it proved a less certain guide.

The Korean War

The Korean War ended inconclusively. But the debates it generated foreshadowed issues that tore the country apart a decade later.

In 1945, Korea, until then a Japanese colony, had been liberated by the victorious Allies. The northern half of the Korean Peninsula was occupied by the Soviet Union, the southern half by the United States. Each established its form of government in its zone before it withdrew, in 1948 and 1949, respectively. In June 1950, the North Korean army invaded South Korea. The Truman administration considered it a classic case of Soviet-Chinese aggression on the model of the German and Japanese challenges preceding World War II. Although U.S. armed forces had been drastically reduced in the previous years, Truman took the courageous decision to resist, largely with American forces based in Japan.

Contemporary research has shown that the motivation on the Communist side was complex. When the North Korean leader Kim Il-sung asked Stalin's approval for the invasion in April 1950, the Soviet dictator encouraged him. He had learned from the defection of Tito two years earlier that first-generation Communist leaders were especially difficult to fit into the Soviet satellite system that he thought imperative for Russia's national interest. Starting with Mao's visit to Moscow in late 1949—less than three months after the People's Republic of China was proclaimed—Stalin had been uneasy about the looming potential of China led by a man of Mao's dominating attributes. An invasion of South Korea might divert China into a crisis on its borders, deflect America's attention from Europe to Asia, and, in any event, absorb some of America's resources in that effort. If achieved with Soviet support, Pyongyang's unification project might give the Soviet Union a dominant position in Korea and, in view of the historical suspicions of these countries for each other, create a kind of counterbalance to China in Asia. Mao followed Stalin's lead—conveyed to him by Kim Il-sung in almost certainly exaggerated terms—for the converse reason; he feared encirclement by the Soviet Union, whose acquisitive interest in Korea had been demonstrated over the centuries and was even then displayed in the demands for ideological subservience Stalin was making as a price for the Sino-Soviet alliance.

On one occasion, an eminent Chinese told me that letting Stalin lead Mao into authorizing the Korean War was the only strategic mistake Mao ever made because, in the end, the Korean War delayed Chinese unification by a century in that it led to America's commitment to Taiwan. Be that as it may, the origin of the Korean War was less a

Sino-Soviet conspiracy against America than a three-cornered maneuver for dominance within the Communist international order, with Kim Il-sung driving up the bidding to gain support for a program of conquest whose global consequences in the end surprised all of the main participants.

The complex strategic considerations of the Communist world were not matched on the American side. In effect, the United States was fighting for a principle, defeating aggression, and a method of implementing it, via the United Nations. America could gain UN approval because the Soviet ambassador to the UN, in a continuing protest over the exclusion of Communist China from the UN, had absented himself from the crucial vote of the Security Council. There was less clarity about what was meant by the phrase "defeating aggression." Was it total victory? If less, what was it? How, in short, was the war supposed to end?

As it happened, experience outran theory. General Douglas MacArthur's surprise landing at Inchon in September 1950 trapped the North Korean army in the South and brought about its substantial defeat. Should the victorious army cross the previous dividing line along the 38th parallel into North Korea and achieve unification? If it did so, it would exceed the literal interpretation of collective security principles because the legal concept of defeating aggression had been achieved. But from a geopolitical point of view, what would have been the lesson? If an aggressor need fear no consequence other than a return to the status quo ante, would a recurrence somewhere else not be likely?

Several alternatives presented themselves—for example, holding the advance at the narrow neck of the peninsula on a line from the cities of Pyongyang to Wonsan, a line roughly 150 miles short of the Chinese frontier. This would have destroyed most of the North's war-making capacity and brought nine-tenths of the North Korean population into a unified Korea while staying well clear of the Chinese border.

We now know that even before American planners had broached the topic of where to arrest their advance, China was preparing for a possible intervention. As early as July 1950, China had concentrated 250,000 troops on its border with Korea. By August, top Chinese planners were operating on the premise that their still-advancing North Korean ally would collapse once superior American forces were fully deployed to the theater (indeed, they accurately predicted MacArthur's surprise landing at Inchon). On August 4—while the front was still deep in South Korea, along the so-called Pusan perimeter—Mao told the Politburo, "If the American imperialists are victorious, they will become dizzy with success, and then be in a position to threaten us. We have to help Korea; we have to assist them. This can be in the form of a volunteer force, and be at a time of our choosing, but we must start to prepare." However, he had told Zhou Enlai that if the United States remained along the Pyongyang to Wonsan line, Chinese forces did not need to attack immediately and should pause for intensified training. What would have happened during or after such a pause must be left to speculation.

But the American forces did not pause; Washington ratified MacArthur's crossing of the 38th parallel and set no limit to his advance other than the Chinese border.

For Mao, the American movement to the Chinese border involved more than Korean stakes. Truman had, on the outbreak of the Korean War, placed the Seventh Fleet between the combatants in the Taiwan Strait on the argument that protecting both sides of the Chinese civil war from each other demonstrated American commitment to peace in Asia. It was less than nine months since Mao had proclaimed the People's Republic of China. If the final outcome of the Korean War was the presence of largely American military forces along the

Chinese border, and an American fleet interposed between Taiwan and the mainland, approving the North Korean invasion of South Korea would have turned into a strategic disaster.

In an encounter between two different conceptions of world order, America sought to protect the status quo following Westphalian and international legal principles. Nothing ran more counter to Mao's perceptions of his revolutionary mission than the protection of the status quo. Chinese history taught him the many times Korea had been used as an invasion route into China. His own revolutionary experience had been based on the proposition that civil wars ended with victory or defeat, not stalemate. And he convinced himself that America, once ensconced along the Yalu River separating China from Korea, would as a next step complete the encirclement of China by moving into Vietnam. (This was four years before America's actual involvement in Indochina.) Zhou Enlai gave voice to this analysis, and demonstrated the outsized role Korea plays in Chinese strategic thinking, when he told an August 26, 1950, meeting of the Central Military Commission that Korea was "indeed the focus of the struggles in the world . . . After conquering Korea, the United States will certainly turn to Vietnam and other colonial countries. Therefore the Korean problem is at least the key to the East."

Considerations such as these induced Mao to repeat the strategy pursued by Chinese leaders in 1593 against the Japanese invasion led by Toyotomi Hideyoshi. Fighting a war with a superpower was a daunting proposition; at least two Chinese field marshals refused to command the units destined for battle with American forces. Mao insisted, and the Chinese surprise attack drove back the American deployments from the Yalu River.

But after the Chinese intervention, what was now the purpose of the war, and which strategy would implement it? These questions produced an intense American debate foreshadowing far more bitter controversies in later American wars. (The difference was that, in contrast to the opponents of the Vietnam War, the critics of the Korean War accused the Truman administration of using not enough force; they sought victory, not withdrawal.)

The public controversy took place between the theater commander Douglas MacArthur and the Truman administration backed by the Joint Chiefs of Staff. MacArthur argued the traditional case that had been the basis of every previous American military involvement: the purpose of war was victory to be achieved by whatever means required, including aerial attacks on China itself; stalemate was a strategic setback; Communist aggression had to be defeated where it was occurring, which was in Asia; American military capacity needed to be used to the extent necessary, not conserved for hypothetical contingencies in distant geographic regions, meaning Western Europe.

The Truman administration responded in two ways: In a demonstration of civilian control over the American military, on April 11, 1951, President Truman relieved MacArthur of his military command for making statements contradicting the administration's policy. On substance, Truman stressed the containment concept: the major threat was the Soviet Union, whose strategic goal was the domination of Europe. Hence fighting the Korean War to a military conclusion, even more extending it into China, was, in the words of the Chairman of the Joint Chiefs of Staff, General Omar Bradley, a combat leader in the war against Germany, "the wrong war, at the wrong place, at the wrong time, and with the wrong enemy."

After some months, the battlefront settled near the 38th parallel in June 1951, where the war had started—just as it had half a millennium earlier. At that point, the Chinese offered negotiations, which the United States accepted. A settlement was reached two years later that has, with some intense but short interruptions, lasted more than sixty years to this writing.

In the negotiations, as in the origins of the war, two different approaches to strategy confronted each other. The Truman administration expressed the American view about the relationship of power and legitimacy. According to it, war and peace were distinct phases of policy; when negotiations started, the application of force ceased, and diplomacy took over. Each activity was thought to operate by its own rules. Force was needed to produce the negotiation, then it had to stand aside; the outcome of the negotiation would depend on an atmosphere of goodwill, which would be destroyed by military pressure. In that spirit, American forces were ordered to confine themselves to essentially defensive measures during the talks and avoid initiating large-scale offensive measures.

The Chinese view was the exact opposite. War and peace were two sides of the same coin. Negotiations were an extension of the battlefield. In accordance with China's ancient strategist Sun Tzu in his *Art of War,* the essential contest would be psychological—to affect the adversary's calculations and degrade his confidence in success. De-escalation by the adversary was a sign of weakness to be exploited by pressing one's own military advantage. The Communist side used the stalemate to enhance the discomfort of the American public with an inconclusive war. In fact, during the negotiations, America suffered as many casualties as it had during the offensive phase of the war.

In the end, each side achieved its objective: America had upheld the doctrine of containment and preserved the territorial integrity of an ally that has since evolved into one of the key countries of Asia; China vindicated its determination to defend the approaches to its borders, and demonstrated its disdain of international rules it had had no voice in creating. The outcome was a draw. But it revealed a potential vulnerability in America's ability to relate strategy to diplomacy, power to legitimacy, and to define its essential aims. Korea, in the end, drew a line across the century. It was the first war in which America specifically renounced victory as an objective, and in that was an augur of things to come.

The biggest loser, as it turned out, was the Soviet Union. It had

encouraged the original decision to invade and sustained its consequences by providing large stores of supplies to its allies. But it lost
their trust. The seeds of the Sino-Soviet split were sown in the Korean
War because the Soviets insisted on payment for their assistance and
refused to give combat support. The war also triggered a rapid and
vast American rearmament, which restored the imbalance in Western
Europe in a big step toward the situation of strength that the American containment doctrine demanded.

Each side suffered setbacks. Some Chinese historians hold that
China lost an opportunity to unify Taiwan with the mainland in order
to sustain an unreliable ally; the United States lost its aura of invincibility that had attached to it since World War II and some of its sense
of direction. Other Asian revolutionaries learned the lesson of drawing America into an inconclusive war that might outrun the American public's willingness to support it. America was left with the gap
in its thinking on strategy and international order that was to haunt
it in the jungles of Vietnam.

Vietnam and the Breakdown of the National Consensus

Even amidst the hardships of the Korean War, a combination of
Wilsonian principles and Rooseveltian geostrategy produced an extraordinary momentum behind the first decade and a half of Cold
War policy. Despite the incipient domestic debate, it saw America
through the 1948–49 American airlift to thwart Soviet ultimatums on
access to Berlin, the Korean War, and the defeat of the Soviet effort to
place intermediate-range nuclear ballistic missiles in Cuba in 1962.
This was followed by the 1963 treaty with the Soviet Union renouncing nuclear testing in the atmosphere—a symbol of the need for the
superpowers to discuss and limit their capability to destroy humanity.
The containment policy was supported by an essentially bipartisan

consensus in Congress. Relations between the policymaking and the intellectual communities were professional, assumed to be based on shared long-term goals.

But roughly coincident with the assassination of President John F. Kennedy, the national consensus began to break down. Part of the reason was the shock of the assassination of a young President who had called on America to fulfill its idealistic traditions. Though the assailant was a Communist who had sojourned in the Soviet Union, among many of the younger generation the loss raised questions about the moral validity of the American enterprise.

The Cold War had begun with a call to support democracy and liberty across the world, reinforced by Kennedy at his inauguration. Yet over a period of time, the military doctrines that sustained the strategy of containment began to have a blighting effect on public perceptions. The gap between the destructiveness of the weapons and the purposes for which they might be used proved unbridgeable. All theories for the limited use of military nuclear technology proved infeasible. The reigning strategy was based on the ability to inflict a level of civilian casualties judged unbearable but surely involving tens of millions on both sides in a matter of days. This calculus constrained the self-confidence of national leaders and the public's faith in their leadership.

Besides this, as the containment policy migrated into the fringes of Asia, it encountered conditions quite opposite of those in Europe. The Marshall Plan and NATO succeeded because a political tradition of government remained in Europe, even if impaired. Economic recovery could restore political vitality. But in much of the underdeveloped world, the political framework was fragile or new, and economic aid led to corruption as frequently as to stability.

These dilemmas came to a head in the Vietnam War. Truman had sent civilian advisors to South Vietnam to resist a guerrilla war in 1951; Eisenhower had added military advisors in 1954; Kennedy authorized combat troops as auxiliaries in 1962; Johnson deployed an expeditionary force in 1965 that eventually rose to more than half a million. The Kennedy administration had gone to the edge of participating in the war, and the Johnson administration made it its own because it was convinced that the North Vietnamese assault into South Vietnam was the spearhead of a Sino-Soviet drive for global domination and that it needed to be resisted by American forces lest all of Southeast Asia fall under Communist control.

In defending Asia, America proposed to proceed as it had in Western Europe. In accord with President Eisenhower's "domino theory," in which the fall of one country to Communism would cause others to fall, it applied the doctrine of containment to thwart the aggressor (on the model of NATO) and economic and political rehabilitation (as in the Marshall Plan). At the same time, to avoid "widening the war," the United States refrained from targeting sanctuaries in Cambodia and Laos from which Hanoi's forces launched attacks to inflict thousands of casualties and to which they withdrew to thwart pursuit.

None of these administrations had vouchsafed a plan for ending the war other than preserving the independence of South Vietnam, destroying the forces armed and deployed by Hanoi to subvert it, and bombing North Vietnam with sufficient force to cause Hanoi to reconsider its policy of conquest and begin negotiations. This had not been treated as a remarkable or controversial program until the middle of the Johnson administration. Then a wave of protests and media critiques—culminating after the 1968 Tet Offensive, in conventional military terms a devastating defeat for North Vietnam but treated in the Western press as a stunning victory and evidence of American failure—struck a chord with administration officials.

Lee Kuan Yew, the founder of the Singapore state and perhaps the wisest Asian leader of his period, was vocal in his firm belief, maintained to this writing, that American intervention was indispensable to preserve the possibility of an independent Southeast Asia. The analysis of the consequences for the region of a Communist victory in

Vietnam was largely correct. But by the time of America's full-scale participation in Vietnam, Sino-Soviet unity no longer existed, having been in perceptible crisis throughout the 1960s. China, wracked by the Great Leap Forward and the Cultural Revolution, increasingly regarded the Soviet Union as a dangerous and threatening adversary.

The containment principles employed in Europe proved much less applicable in Asia. European instability came about when the economic crisis caused by the war threatened to undermine traditional domestic political institutions. In Southeast Asia, after a century of colonization, these institutions had yet to be created—especially in South Vietnam, which had never existed as a state in history.

America attempted to close the gap through a campaign of political construction side by side with the military effort. While simultaneously fighting a conventional war against North Vietnamese divisions and a jungle war against Vietcong guerrillas, America threw itself into political engineering in a region that had not known self-government for centuries or democracy ever.

After a series of coups (the first of which, in November 1963, was actually encouraged by the American Embassy and acquiesced in by the White House in the expectation that military rule would produce more liberal institutions), General Nguyen Van Thieu emerged as the South Vietnamese President. At the outset of the Cold War, the non-Communist orientation of a government had been taken—perhaps overly expansively—as proof that it was worth preserving against Soviet designs. Now, in the emerging atmosphere of recrimination, the inability of South Vietnam to emerge as a fully operational democracy (amidst a bloody civil war) led to bitter denunciation. A war initially supported by a considerable majority and raised to its existing dimensions by a president citing universal principles of liberty and human rights was now decried as evidence of a unique American moral obtuseness. Charges of immorality and deception were used with abandon; "barbaric" was a favorite adjective. American military involvement was described as a form of "insanity" revealing profound flaws in the American way of life; accusations of wanton slaughter of civilians became routine.

The domestic debate over the Vietnam War proved to be one of the most scarring in American history. The administrations that had involved America in Indochina were staffed by individuals of substantial intelligence and probity who suddenly found themselves accused of near-criminal folly and deliberate deception. What had started as a reasonable debate about feasibility and strategy turned into street demonstrations, invective, and violence.

The critics were right in pointing out that American strategy, particularly in the opening phases of the war, was ill suited to the realities of asymmetric conflict. Bombing campaigns alternating with "pauses" to test Hanoi's readiness for negotiation tended to produce stalemate— bringing to bear enough power to incur denunciation and resistance, but not enough to secure the adversary's readiness for serious negotiations. The dilemmas of Vietnam were very much the consequence of academic theories regarding graduated escalation that had sustained the Cold War; while conceptually coherent in terms of a standoff between nuclear superpowers, they were less applicable to an asymmetric conflict fought against an adversary pursuing a guerrilla strategy. Some of the expectations for the relationship of economic reform to political evolution proved unfeasible in Asia. But these were subjects appropriate for serious debate, not vilification and, at the fringes of the protest movement, assaults on university and government buildings.

The collapse of high aspirations shattered the self-confidence without which establishments flounder. The leaders who had previously sustained American foreign policy were particularly anguished by the rage of the students. The insecurity of their elders turned the normal grievances of maturing youth into an institutionalized rage and a national trauma. Public demonstrations reached dimensions obliging President Johnson—who continued to describe the war in traditional terms of defending a free people against the advance of totalitarianism—to confine his public appearances in his last year in office largely to military bases.

In the months following the end of Johnson's presidency in 1969, a number of the war's key architects renounced their positions publicly and called for an end to military operations and an American withdrawal. These themes were elaborated until the Establishment view settled on a program to "end the war" by means of a unilateral American withdrawal in exchange only for the return of prisoners.

Richard Nixon became President at a time when 500,000 American troops were in combat—and the number was still increasing, on a schedule established by the Johnson administration—in Vietnam, as far from the U.S. borders as the globe allows. From the beginning, Nixon was committed to ending the war. But he also thought it his responsibility to do so in the context of America's global commitments for sustaining the postwar international order. Nixon took office five months after the Soviet military occupation of Czechoslovakia, while the Soviet Union was building intercontinental missiles at a rate threatening—and, some argued, surpassing—America's deterrent forces, and China remained adamantly and truculently hostile. America could not jettison its security commitments in one part of the world without provoking challenges to its resolve in others. The preservation of American credibility in defense of allies and the global system of order—a role the United States had performed for two decades—remained an integral part of Nixon's calculations.

Nixon withdrew American forces at the rate of 150,000 per year and ended participation in ground combat in 1971. He authorized negotiations subject to one irreducible condition: he never accepted Hanoi's demand that the peace process begin with the replacement of the government of South Vietnam—America's ally—by a so-called coalition government in effect staffed by figures put forward by Hanoi. This was adamantly rejected for four years until after a failed North Vietnamese offensive (defeated without American ground forces) in 1972 finally induced Hanoi to agree to a cease-fire and political settlement it had consistently rejected over the years.

In the United States debate focused on a widespread desire to end the trauma wrought by the war on the populations of Indochina, as if America was the cause of their travail. Yet Hanoi had insisted on continued battle—not because it was unconvinced of the American commitment to peace, but because it counted on it to exhaust American willingness to sustain the sacrifices. Fighting a psychological war, it ruthlessly exploited America's quest for compromise on behalf of a program of domination with which, it turned out, there was no splitting the difference.

The military actions that President Nixon ordered, and that as his National Security Advisor I supported, together with the policy of diplomatic flexibility, brought about a settlement in 1973. The Nixon administration was convinced that Saigon would be able to overcome ordinary violations of the agreement with its own forces; that the United States would assist with air and naval power against an all-out attack; and that over time the South Vietnamese government would be able, with American economic assistance, to build a functioning society and undergo an evolution toward more transparent institutions (as would in fact occur in South Korea).

Whether this process could have been accelerated and whether another definition could have been given to American credibility will remain the subject of heated debate. The chief obstacle was the difficulty Americans had understanding Hanoi's way of thinking. The Johnson administration overestimated the impact of American military power. Contrary to conventional wisdom, the Nixon administration overestimated the scope for negotiation. For the battle-hardened leadership in Hanoi, having spent their lives fighting for victory, compromise was the same as defeat, and a pluralistic society near inconceivable.

A resolution of this debate is beyond the scope of this volume; it was a painful process for all involved. Nixon managed a complete withdrawal and a settlement he was convinced gave the South Vietnamese a decent opportunity to shape their own fate. However, having traversed a decade of controversy and in the highly charged aftermath of the Watergate crisis, Congress severely restricted aid in 1973 and cut off all aid in 1975. North Vietnam conquered South Vietnam by sending almost its entire army across the international border. The international community remained silent, and Congress had proscribed American military intervention. The governments of Laos and Cambodia fell shortly after to Communist insurgencies, and in the latter the Khmer Rouge imposed a reckoning of almost unimaginable brutality.

America had lost its first war and also the thread to its concept of world order.

Richard Nixon and International Order

After the carnage of the 1960s with its assassinations, civil riots, and inconclusive wars, Richard Nixon inherited in 1969 the task of restoring cohesion to the American body politic and coherence to American foreign policy. Highly intelligent, with a level of personal insecurity unexpected in such an experienced public figure, Nixon was not the ideal leader for the restoration of domestic peace. But it must also be remembered that the tactics of mass demonstrations, intimidation, and civil disobedience at the outer limit of peaceful protests had been well established by the time Nixon took his oath of office on January 20, 1969.

Nevertheless, for the task of redefining the substance of American foreign policy, Nixon was extraordinarily well prepared. As Senator from California, Vice President under Dwight D. Eisenhower, and perennial presidential candidate, he had traveled widely. The foreign leaders Nixon encountered would spare him the personal confrontations that made him uncomfortable and engage him in substantive dialogue at which he excelled. Because his solitary nature gave him more free time than ordinary political aspirants, he found extensive reading congenial. This combination made him the best prepared incoming president on foreign policy since Theodore Roosevelt.

No president since Theodore Roosevelt had addressed international order as a global concept in such a systematic and conceptual manner. In speaking with the editors of *Time* in 1971, Nixon articulated such a concept. In his vision, five major centers of political and economic power would operate on the basis of an informal commitment by each to pursue its interests with restraint. The outcome of their interlocking ambitions and inhibitions would be equilibrium:

> We must remember the only time in the history of the world that we have had any extended period of peace is when there has been balance of power. It is when one nation becomes infinitely more powerful in relation to its potential competitor that the danger of war arises. So I believe in a world in which the United States is powerful. I think it will be a safer world and a better world if we have a strong, healthy United States, Europe, Soviet Union, China, Japan, each balancing the other, not playing one against the other, an even balance.

What was remarkable in this presentation was that two of the countries listed as part of a concert of powers were in fact adversaries: the U.S.S.R., with which America was engaged in a cold war, and China, with which it had just resumed diplomatic contact after a hiatus of over two decades and where the United States had no embassy or formal diplomatic relations. Theodore Roosevelt had articulated an idea of world order in which the United States was the guardian of the global equilibrium. Nixon went further in arguing that the United States should be an integral part of an ever-changing, fluid balance, not as the balancer, but as a component.

The passage also displayed Nixon's tactical skill, as when he renounced any intention of playing off one of the components of the balance against another. A subtle way of warning a potential adversary is to renounce a capability he knows one possesses and that will not be altered by the renunciation. Nixon made these remarks as he was about to leave for Beijing, marking a dramatic improvement in relations and the first time a sitting American president had visited China. Balancing China against the Soviet Union from a position in which America was closer to each Communist giant than they were to each other was, of course, exactly the design of the evolving strategy. In February 1971, Nixon's annual foreign policy report referred to China as the People's Republic of China—the first time an official American document had accorded it that degree of recognition—and stated that the United States was "prepared to establish a dialogue with Peking" on the basis of national interest.

Nixon made a related point regarding Chinese domestic policies while I was on the way to China on the so-called secret trip in July 1971. Addressing an audience in Kansas City, Nixon argued that "Chinese domestic travail"—that is, the Cultural Revolution—should not confer

> any sense of satisfaction that it will always be that way. Because when we see the Chinese as people—and I have seen them all over the world . . .—they are creative, they are productive, they are one of the most capable people in the world. And 800 million Chinese are going to be, inevitably, an enormous economic power, with all that that means

in terms of what they could be in other areas if they move in
that direction.

These phrases, commonplace today, were revolutionary at that
time. Because they were delivered extemporaneously—and I was out
of communication with Washington—it was Zhou Enlai who brought
them to my attention as I started the first dialogue with Beijing in
more than twenty years. Nixon, inveterate anti-Communist, had decided that the imperatives of geopolitical equilibrium overrode the
demands of ideological purity—as, fortuitously, had his counterparts
in China.

In the presidential election campaign of 1972, Nixon's opponent,
George McGovern, had taunted, "Come home, America!" Nixon replied in effect that if America shirked its international responsibility, it
would surely fail at home. He declared that "only if we act greatly in
meeting our responsibilities abroad will we remain a great nation, and
only if we remain a great nation will we act greatly in meeting our
challenges at home." At the same time, he sought to temper "our instinct that we knew what was best for others," which in turn brought
on "their temptation to lean on our prescriptions."

To this end, Nixon established a practice of annual reports on the
state of the world. Like all presidential documents, these were drafted
by White House associates, in this case the National Security Council
staff under my direction. But Nixon set the general strategic tone of
the documents and reviewed them as they were being completed.
They were used as guidance to the governmental agencies dealing
with foreign policy and, more important, as an indication to foreign
countries of the direction of American strategy.

Nixon was enough of a realist to stress that the United States
could not entrust its destiny entirely or even largely to the goodwill of
others. As his 1970 report underscored, peace required a willingness to

negotiate and seek new forms of partnership, but these alone would not suffice: "The second element of a durable peace must be America's strength. Peace, we have learned, cannot be gained by goodwill alone." Peace would be strengthened, not obstructed, he assessed, by continued demonstrations of American power and a proven willingness to act globally—which evoked shades of Theodore Roosevelt sending the Great White Fleet to circumnavigate the globe in 1907–9. Neither could the United States expect other countries to mortgage their future by basing their foreign policy primarily on the goodwill of others. The guiding principle was the effort to build an international order that related power to legitimacy—in the sense that all its key members considered the arrangement just:

> All nations, adversaries and friends alike, must have a stake in preserving the international system. They must feel that their principles are being respected and their national interests secured . . . If the international environment meets their vital concerns, they will work to maintain it.

It was the vision of such an international order that provided the first impetus for the opening to China, which Nixon considered an indispensable component of it. One facet of the opening to China was the attempt to transcend the domestic strife of the past decade. Nixon became President of a nation shaken by a decade of domestic and international upheaval and an inconclusive war. It was important to convey to it a vision of peace and international comity to lift it toward visions worthy of its history and its values. Equally significant was a redefinition of America's concept of world order. An improved relationship with China would gradually isolate the Soviet Union or impel it to seek better relations with the United States. As long as the United States took care to remain closer to each of the Communist superpowers than they were to each other, the specter of the Sino-Soviet cooperative quest for world hegemony that had haunted American foreign policy for two decades would be stifled. (In time, the Soviet Union found itself unable to sustain this insoluble, largely self-created dilemma of facing adversaries in both Europe and Asia, including within its own ostensible ideological camp.)

Nixon's attempt to make American idealism practical and American pragmatism long-range was attacked by both sides, reflecting the American ambivalence between power and principle. Idealists criticized Nixon for conducting foreign policy by geopolitical principles. Conservatives challenged him on the ground that a relaxation of tensions with the Soviet Union was a form of abdication vis-à-vis the Communist challenge to Western civilization. Both types of critics overlooked that Nixon undertook a tenacious defense along the Soviet periphery, that he was the first American President to visit Eastern Europe (Yugoslavia, Poland, and Romania), symbolically challenging Soviet control, and that he saw the United States through several crises with the Soviet Union, during two of which (in October 1970 and October 1973) he did not flinch from putting American military forces on alert.

Nixon had shown unusual skill in the geopolitical aspect of building a world order. He patiently linked the various components of strategy to each other, and he showed extraordinary courage in withstanding crises and great persistence in pursuing long-range aims in foreign policy. One of his oft-repeated operating principles was as follows: "You pay the same price for doing something halfway as for doing it completely. So you might as well do it completely." As a result, in one eighteen-month period, during 1972–73, he brought about the end of the Vietnam War, an opening to China, a summit with the Soviet Union even while escalating the military effort in response to a North Vietnamese offensive, the switch of Egypt from a Soviet ally to close cooperation with the United States, two disengagement agreements in the Middle East—one between Israel and Egypt, the other

with Syria (lasting to this writing, even amidst a brutal civil war)—
and the start of the European Security Conference, whose outcome
over the long term severely weakened Soviet control of Eastern Europe.

But at the juncture when tactical achievement might have been
translated into a permanent concept of world order linking inspira-
tional vision to a workable equilibrium, tragedy supervened. The Vietnam War had exhausted energies on all sides. The Watergate debacle,
foolishly self-inflicted and ruthlessly exploited by Nixon's longtime
critics, paralyzed executive authority. In a normal period, the various
strands of Nixon's policy would have been consolidated into a new
long-term American strategy. Nixon had a glimpse of the promised
land, where hope and reality conjoined—the end of the Cold War, a
redefinition of the Atlantic Alliance, a genuine partnership with
China, a major step toward Middle East peace, the beginning of Russia's reintegration into an international order—but he did not have
time to merge his geopolitical vision with the occasion. It was left to
others to undertake that journey.

The Beginning of Renewal

After the anguish of the 1960s and the collapse of a presidency,
America needed above all to restore its cohesion. It was fortunate that
the man called to this unprecedented task was Gerald Ford.

Propelled into an office he had not sought, Ford had never been
involved in the complex gyrations of presidential politics. For that reason, freed from obsession with focus groups and public relations, he
could practice in the presidency the values of goodwill and faith in his
country on which he had been brought up. His long service in the
House, where he sat on key defense and intelligence subcommittees,
gave him an overview of foreign policy challenges.

Ford's historic service was to overcome America's divisions. In his
foreign policy, he strove—and largely succeeded—to relate power to

principle. His administration witnessed the completion of the first agreement between Israel and an Arab state—in this case, Egypt—whose provisions were largely political. The second Sinai disengagement agreement marked Egypt's irrevocable turning toward a peace agreement. Ford initiated an active diplomacy to bring about majority rule in southern Africa—the first American President to do so explicitly. In the face of strong domestic opposition, he supervised the conclusion of the European Security Conference. Among its many provisions were clauses that enshrined human rights as one of the European security principles. These terms were used by heroic individuals such as Lech Walesa in Poland and Václav Havel in Czechoslovakia to bring democracy to their countries and start the downfall of Communism.

I introduced my eulogy at President Ford's funeral with the following sentences:

> According to an ancient tradition, God preserves humanity despite its many transgressions because, at any one period, there exist ten just individuals who, without being aware of their role, redeem mankind. Gerald Ford was such a man.

Jimmy Carter became President when the impact of America's defeat in Indochina began to be translated into challenges inconceivable while America still had the aura of invincibility. Iran, heretofore a pillar of the regional Middle East order, was taken over by a group of ayatollahs, who in effect declared political and ideological war on the United States, overturning the prevailing balance of power in the Middle East. A symbol of it was the incarceration of the American diplomatic mission in Tehran for more than four hundred days. Nearly concurrently, the Soviet Union felt itself in a position to invade and occupy Afghanistan.

Amidst all this turmoil, Carter had the fortitude to move the Middle East peace process toward a signing ceremony at the White House. The peace treaty between Israel and Egypt was a historic event. Though its origin lay in the elimination of Soviet influence and the start of a peace process by previous administrations, its conclusion under Carter was the culmination of persistent and determined diplomacy. Carter solidified the opening to China by establishing full diplomatic relations with it, cementing a bipartisan consensus behind the new direction. And he reacted strongly to the Soviet invasion of Afghanistan by supporting those who resisted the Soviet takeover. In an anguished period, Carter reaffirmed values of human dignity essential to America's image of itself even while he hesitated before the new strategic challenges—to find the appropriate balance between power and legitimacy—toward the end of his term.

Ronald Reagan and the End of the Cold War

Rarely has America produced a president so suited to his time and so attuned to it as Ronald Reagan. A decade earlier, Reagan had seemed too militant to be realistic; a decade later, his convictions might have appeared too one-dimensional. But faced with a Soviet Union whose economy was stagnating and whose gerontocratic leadership was quite literally perishing serially, and supported by an American public opinion eager to shed a period of disillusionments, Reagan combined America's latent, sometimes seemingly discordant strengths: its idealism, its resilience, its creativity, and its economic vitality.

Sensing potential Soviet weakness and deeply confident in the superiority of the American system (he had read more deeply in American political philosophy than his domestic critics credited), Reagan blended the two elements—power and legitimacy—that had in the previous decade produced American ambivalence. He challenged the Soviet Union to a race in arms and technology that it could not win, based on programs long stymied in Congress. What came to be known as the Strategic Defense Initiative—a defensive shield against missile attack—was largely derided in Congress and the media when Reagan put it forward. Today it is widely credited with convincing the Soviet leadership of the futility of its arms race with the United States.

At the same time, Reagan generated psychological momentum with pronouncements at the outer edge of Wilsonian moralism. Perhaps the most poignant example is his farewell address as he left office in 1989, in which he described his vision of America as the shining city on a hill:

> I've spoken of the shining city all my political life, but I don't know if I ever quite communicated what I saw when I said it. But in my mind, it was a tall proud city built on rocks stronger than oceans, wind swept, God blessed, and teeming with people of all kinds living in harmony and peace—a city with free ports that hummed with commerce and creativity, and if there had to be city walls, the walls had doors, and the doors were open to anyone with the will and the heart to get here. That's how I saw it, and see it still.

America as a shining city on a hill was not a metaphor for Reagan; it actually existed for him because he willed it to exist.

This was the important difference between Ronald Reagan and Richard Nixon, whose actual policies were quite parallel and not rarely identical. Nixon treated foreign policy as an endeavor with no end, as a set of rhythms to be managed. He dealt with its intricacies and contradictions like school assignments by an especially demanding teacher. He expected America to prevail but in a long, joyless enterprise, perhaps after he left office. Reagan, by contrast, summed up his Cold War strategy to an aide in 1977 in a characteristically optimistic epigram:

"We win, they lose." The Nixon style of policymaking was important to restore fluidity to the diplomacy of the Cold War; the Reagan style was indispensable for the diplomacy of ending it.

On one level, Reagan's rhetoric—including his March 1983 speech referring to the Soviet Union as the Evil Empire—might have spelled the end of any prospect of East-West diplomacy. On a deeper level, it symbolized a period of transition, as the Soviet Union became aware of the futility of an arms race while its aging leadership was facing issues of succession. Hiding complexity behind a veneer of simplicity, Reagan also put forward a vision of reconciliation with the Soviet Union beyond what Nixon would ever have been willing to articulate.

Reagan was convinced that Communist intransigence was based more on ignorance than on ill will, more on misunderstanding than on hostility. Unlike Nixon, who thought that a calculation of self-interest could bring about accommodation between the United States and the Soviet Union, Reagan believed the conflict was likely to end with the realization by the adversary of the superiority of American principles. In 1984, on the appointment of the Communist Party veteran Konstantin Chernenko as top Soviet leader, Reagan confided to his diary, "I have a gut feeling I'd like to talk to him about our problems man to man and see if I could convince him there would be a material benefit to the Soviets if they'd join the family of nations, etc."

When Mikhail Gorbachev succeeded Chernenko one year later, Reagan's optimism mounted. He told associates of his dream to escort the new Soviet leader on a tour of a working-class American neighborhood. As a biographer recounted, Reagan envisioned that "the helicopter would descend, and Reagan would invite Gorbachev to knock on doors and ask the residents 'what they think of our system.' The workers would tell him how wonderful it was to live in America." All this would persuade the Soviet Union to join the global move toward democracy, and this in turn would produce peace—because "governments which rest upon the consent of the governed do not wage war on their neighbors"—a core principle of Wilson's view of international order.

Applying his vision to the control of nuclear weapons, Reagan, at the Reykjavík summit with Gorbachev in 1986, proposed to eliminate all nuclear delivery systems while retaining and building up antimissile systems. Such an outcome would achieve one of Reagan's oftproclaimed goals to eliminate the prospect of nuclear war by doing away with the offensive capability for it and containing violators of the agreement by missile defense systems. The idea went beyond the scope of Gorbachev's imagination, which is why he bargained strenuously over a niggling reservation about confining missile defense system tests "to the laboratory." (The proposal to eliminate nuclear delivery systems was in any event beyond practicality in that it would have been bitterly opposed by British Prime Minister Margaret Thatcher and French President François Mitterrand, who were convinced that Europe could not be defended without nuclear weapons and who treated their independent deterrents as an ultimate insurance policy.) Years later, I asked the Soviet ambassador Anatoly Dobrynin why the Soviets had not offered a compromise on the testing issue. He replied, "Because it never occurred to us that Reagan would simply walk out."

Gorbachev sought to counter Reagan's vision with a concept of Soviet reform. But by the 1980s, the "balance of forces," which Soviet leaders had never tired of invoking over the decades of their rule, had turned against them. Four decades of imperial expansion in all directions could not be sustained on the basis of an unworkable economic model. The United States, despite its divisions and vacillations, had preserved the essential elements of a situation of strength; over two generations it had built an informal anti-Soviet coalition of every other major industrial center and most of the developing world. Gorbachev realized that the Soviet Union could not sustain its prevailing course, but he underestimated the fragility of the Soviet system. His calls for reform—

glasnost (publicity) and *perestroika* (restructuring)—unleashed forces too disorganized for genuine reform and too demoralized to continue totalitarian leadership, much as Kennan had predicted half a century earlier.

Reagan's idealistic commitment to democracy alone could not have produced such an outcome; strong defense and economic policies, a shrewd analysis of Soviet weaknesses, and an unusually favorable alignment of external circumstances all played a role in the success of his policies. Yet without Reagan's idealism—bordering sometimes on a repudiation of history—the end of the Soviet challenge could not have occurred amidst such a global affirmation of a democratic future.

Forty years earlier and for the decades since, it was thought that the principal obstacle to a peaceful world order was the Soviet Union. The corollary was that the collapse of Communism—imagined, if at all, in some distant future—would bring with it an era of stability and goodwill. It soon became apparent that history generally operates in longer cycles. Before a new international order could be constructed, it was necessary to deal with the debris of the Cold War.

THIS TASK FELL TO GEORGE H. W. BUSH, who managed America's predominance with moderation and wisdom. Patrician in upbringing in Connecticut, yet choosing to make his fortune in Texas, the more elemental, entrepreneurial part of the United States, and with wide experience in all levels of government, Bush dealt with great skill with a stunning succession of crises testing both the application of America's values and the reach of its vast power. Within months of his taking office, the Tiananmen upheaval in China challenged America's basic values but also the importance for the global equilibrium of preserving the U.S.-China relationship. Having been head of the American liaison office in Beijing (before the establishment of formal relations), Bush navigated in a manner that maintained America's principles while retaining the prospect of ultimate cooperation. He managed the unification of Germany—heretofore considered a probable cause of war—by a skillful diplomacy facilitated by his decision not to exploit Soviet embarrassment at the collapse of its empire. In that spirit, when the Berlin Wall fell in 1989, Bush rejected all proposals to fly to Berlin to celebrate this demonstration of the collapse of Soviet policy.

The adroit manner in which Bush brought the Cold War to a close obscured the domestic disputes through which the U.S. effort had been sustained and which would characterize the challenges of the next stage. As the Cold War receded, the American consensus held that the main work of conversion had been achieved. A peaceful world order would now unfold, so long as the democracies took care to assist in the final wave of democratic transformations in countries still under authoritarian rule. The ultimate Wilsonian vision would be fulfilled. Free political and economic institutions would spread and eventually submerge outdated antagonisms in a broader harmony.

In that spirit, Bush defeated Iraqi aggression in Kuwait during the first Gulf War by forging a coalition of the willing through the UN, the first joint action involving great powers since the Korean War; he stopped military operations when the limit that had been authorized by UN resolutions had been reached (perhaps, as former ambassador to the UN, he sought to apply the lesson of General MacArthur's decision to cross the dividing line between the two Koreas after his victory at Inchon).

For a brief period, the global consensus behind the American-led defeat of Saddam Hussein's military conquest of Kuwait in 1991 seemed to vindicate the perennial American hope for a rules-based international order. In Prague in November 1990, Bush invoked a "commonwealth of freedom," which would be governed by the rule of law; it would be "a moral community united in its dedication to free ideals." Membership in this commonwealth would be open to all; it might someday become universal. As such the "great and growing strength of the commonwealth of freedom" would "forge for all nations a new world order far more stable and secure than any we have known." The United States and its allies would move "beyond containment and to a policy of active engagement."

Bush's term was cut short by electoral defeat in 1992, in some sense because he ran as a foreign policy president while his opponent, Bill Clinton, appealed to a war-weary public, promising to focus on America's domestic agenda. Nonetheless, the newly elected President rapidly reasserted a foreign policy vocation comparable to that of Bush. Clinton expressed the confidence of the era when, in a 1993 address to the UN General Assembly, he described his foreign policy concept as not containment but "enlargement." "Our overriding purpose," he announced, "must be to expand and strengthen the world's community of market-based democracies." In this view, because the principles of political and economic liberty were universal "from Poland to Eritrea, from Guatemala to South Korea," their spread would require no force. Describing an enterprise consisting of enabling an inevitable historical evolution, Clinton pledged that American policy would aspire to "a world of thriving democracies that cooperate with each other and live in peace."

When Secretary of State Warren Christopher attempted to apply the enlargement theory to the People's Republic of China by making economic ties conditional on modifications within the Chinese system, he encountered a sharp rebuff. The Chinese leaders insisted that relations with the United States could only be conducted on a geostrategic basis, not (as had been proposed) on the basis of China's progress toward political liberalization. By the third year of his presidency, the Clinton approach to world order reverted to less insistent practice.

Meanwhile, the enlargement concept encountered a much more militant adversary. Jihadism sought to spread its message and assaulted Western values and institutions, particularly those of the United States, as the principal obstacle. A few months before Clinton's General Assembly speech, an international group of extremists, including one

American citizen, bombed the World Trade Center in New York City. Their secondary target, had the first been thwarted, was the United Nations Secretariat building. The Westphalian concept of the state and international law, because it was based on rules not explicitly pre-scribed in the Quran, was an abomination to this movement. Similarly objectionable was democracy for its capacity to legislate separately from sharia law. America, in the view of the jihadist forces, was an op-pressor of Muslims seeking to implement their own universal mission. The challenge broke into the open with the attacks on New York and Washington on September 11, 2001. In the Middle East, at least, the end of the Cold War ushered in not a hoped-for time of democratic consensus but a new age of ideological and military confrontation.

The Afghanistan and Iraq Wars

After an anguishing discussion of the "lessons of Vietnam," equally intense dilemmas recapitulated themselves three decades later with wars in Afghanistan and Iraq. Both conflicts had their origins in a breakdown of international order. For America, both ended in withdrawal.

Afghanistan

Al-Qaeda, having issued a fatwa in 1998 calling for the indiscrimi-nate killing of Americans and Jews everywhere, enjoyed a sanctuary in Afghanistan, whose governing authorities, the Taliban, refused to expel the group's leadership and fighters. An American response to the attack on American territory was inevitable and widely so under-stood around the world.

A new challenge opened up almost immediately: how to establish international order when the principal adversaries are non-state orga-nizations that defend no specific territory and reject established prin-ciples of legitimacy.

The Afghan war began on a note of national unanimity and international consensus. Prospects for a rules-based international order seemed vindicated when NATO, for the first time in its history, applied Article 5 of the North Atlantic Treaty—stipulating that "an armed attack against one or more [NATO ally] in Europe or North America shall be considered an attack against them all." Nine days after the September 11 attacks, President George W. Bush dispatched an ultimatum to the Taliban authorities of Afghanistan, then harboring al-Qaeda: "Deliver to United States authorities all the leaders of al Qaeda who hide in your land . . . Give the United States full access to terrorist training camps, so we can make sure they are no longer operating." When the Taliban failed to comply, the United States and its allies launched a war whose aims Bush described, on October 7, in similarly limited terms: "These carefully targeted actions are designed to disrupt the use of Afghanistan as a terrorist base of operations, and to attack the military capability of the Taliban regime."

Initial warnings about Afghanistan's history as the "graveyard of empires" appeared unfounded. After a rapid effort led by American, British, and allied Afghan forces, the Taliban were deposed from power. In December 2001, an international conference in Bonn, Germany, proclaimed a provisional Afghan government with Hamid Karzai as its head and set up a process for convening a *loya jirga* (a traditional tribal council) to design and ratify postwar Afghan institutions. The allied war aims seemed achieved.

The participants in the Bonn negotiations optimistically asserted a vast vision: "the establishment of a broad-based, gender-sensitive, multi-ethnic and fully representative government." In 2003, a UN Security Council resolution authorized the expansion of the NATO International Security Assistance Force

> to support the Afghan Transitional Authority and its successors in the maintenance of security in areas of Afghanistan

> outside of Kabul and its environs, so that the Afghan Au-
> thorities as well as the personnel of the United Nations . . .
> can operate in a secure environment.

The central premise of the American and allied effort became "rebuilding Afghanistan" by means of a democratic, pluralistic, transparent Afghan government whose writ ran across the entire country and an Afghan national army capable of assuming responsibility for security on a national basis. With a striking idealism, these efforts were imagined to be comparable to the construction of democracy in Germany and Japan after World War II.

No institutions in the history of Afghanistan or of any part of it provided a precedent for such a broad-based effort. Traditionally, Afghanistan has been less a state in the conventional sense than a geographic expression for an area never brought under the consistent administration of any single authority. For most of recorded history, Afghan tribes and sects have been at war with each other, briefly uniting to resist invasion or to launch marauding raids against their neighbors. Elites in Kabul might undertake periodic experiments with parliamentary institutions, but outside the capital an ancient tribal code of honor predominated. Unification of Afghanistan has been achieved by foreigners only unintentionally, when the tribes and sects coalesce in opposition to an invader.

Thus what American and NATO forces met in the early twenty-first century was not radically different from the scene encountered by a young Winston Churchill in 1897:

> Except at harvest-time, when self-preservation enjoins a tem-
> porary truce, the Pathan [Pashtun] tribes are always engaged
> in private or public war. Every man is a warrior, a politician,
> and a theologian. Every large house is a real feudal fortress . . .
> Every village has its defence. Every family cultivates its ven-

detta; every clan, its feud. The numerous tribes and combina-
tions of tribes all have their accounts to settle with one another.
Nothing is ever forgotten, and very few debts are left unpaid.

In this context, the proclaimed coalition and UN goals of a transparent, democratic Afghan central government operating in a secure
environment amounted to a radical reinvention of Afghan history. It
effectively elevated one clan above all others—Hamid Karzai's Pashtun Popalzai tribe—and required it to establish itself across the country either through force (its own or that of the international coalition)
or through distribution of the spoils of foreign aid, or both. Inevitably,
the efforts required to impose such institutions trampled on age-old
prerogatives, reshuffling the kaleidoscope of tribal alliances in ways
that were difficult for any outside force to understand or control.

The American election of 2008 compounded complexity with ambivalence. The new President, Barack Obama, had campaigned on the
proposition that he would restore to the "necessary" war in Afghanistan the forces drained by the "dumb" war in Iraq, which he intended
to end. But in office, he was determined to bring about a peacetime
focus on transformational domestic priorities. The outcome was a
reemergence of the ambivalence that has accompanied American
military campaigns in the post–World War II period: the dispatch of
thirty thousand additional troops for a "surge" in Afghanistan coupled,
in the same announcement, with a public deadline of eighteen months
for the beginning of their withdrawal. The purpose of the deadline, it
was argued, was to provide an incentive to the Karzai government to
accelerate its effort to build a modern central government and army to
replace Americans. Yet, in essence, the objective of a guerrilla strategy
like the Taliban's is to outlast the defending forces. For the Kabul leadership, the announcement of a fixed date for losing its outside support
set off a process of factional maneuvering, including with the Taliban.

The strides made by Afghanistan during this period have been significant and hard-won. The population has adopted electoral institutions with no little daring—because the Taliban continues to threaten death to those participating in democratic structures. The United States also succeeded in its objective of locating and eliminating Osama bin Laden, sending a powerful message about the country's global reach and determination to avenge atrocities.

Nevertheless, the regional prospects remain challenging. In the period following the American withdrawal (imminent as of this writing), the writ of the Afghan government is likely to run in Kabul and its environs but not uniformly in the rest of the country. There a confederation of semiautonomous, feudal regions is likely to prevail on an ethnic basis, influenced substantially by competing foreign powers. The challenge will return to where it began—the compatibility of an independent Afghanistan with a regional political order.

Afghanistan's neighbors should have at least as much of a national interest as the United States—and, in the long run, a far greater one—in defining and bringing about a coherent, non-jihadist outcome in Afghanistan. Each of Afghanistan's neighbors would risk turmoil within its own borders if Afghanistan returns to its prewar status as a base for jihadist non-state organizations or as a state dedicated to jihadist policies: Pakistan above all in its entire domestic structure, Russia in its partly Muslim south and west, China with a significantly Muslim Xinjiang, and even Shiite Iran from fundamentalist Sunni trends. All of them, from a strategic point of view, are more threatened by an Afghanistan hospitable to terrorism than the United States is (except perhaps Iran, which may calculate, as it has in Syria, Lebanon, and Iraq, that a chaotic situation beyond its borders enables it to manipulate the contending factions).

The ultimate irony may be that Afghanistan, torn by war, may be a test case of whether a regional order can be distilled from divergent security interests and historical perspectives. Without a sustainable international program regarding Afghanistan's security, each major neighbor will support rival factions across ancient ethnic and sectarian lines. The likely outcome would be a de facto partition, with Pakistan controlling the Pashtun south, and India, Russia, and perhaps China favoring the ethnically mixed north. To avoid a vacuum, a major diplomatic effort is needed to define a regional order to deal with the possible reemergence of Afghanistan as a jihadist center. In the nineteenth century, the major powers guaranteed Belgian neutrality, a guarantee that, in the event, lasted nearly one hundred years. Is an equivalent, with appropriate redefinitions, possible? If such a concept—or a comparable one—is evaded, Afghanistan is likely to drag the world back into its perennial warfare.

IRAQ

In the wake of the 9/11 attacks, President George W. Bush articulated a global strategy to counter jihadist extremism and to shore up the established international order by infusing it with a commitment to democratic transformation. The "great struggles of the twentieth century," the White House's *National Security Strategy* of 2002 argued, had demonstrated that there was "a single sustainable model for national success: freedom, democracy, and free enterprise."

The present moment, the *National Security Strategy* document stressed, saw a world shocked by an unprecedented terrorist atrocity and the great powers "on the same side—united by common dangers of terrorist violence and chaos." The encouragement of free institutions and cooperative major-power relations offered "the best chance since the rise of the nation-state in the seventeenth century to build a world where great powers compete in peace instead of continually prepare for war." The centerpiece of what came to be called the Freedom Agenda was to be a transformation of Iraq from among the Middle East's most repressive states to a multiparty democracy, which would in turn inspire a regional democratic transformation: "Iraqi democracy will succeed—and that success will send forth the news, from Damascus to Teheran—that freedom can be the future of every nation."

The Freedom Agenda was not, as was later alleged, the arbitrary invention of a single president and his entourage. Its basic premise was an elaboration of quintessentially American themes. The 2002 *National Security Strategy* document—which first announced the policy—repeated the arguments of NSC-68 that, in 1950, had defined America's mission in the Cold War, albeit with one decisive difference. The 1950 document had enlisted America's values in defense of the free world. The 2002 document argued for the ending of tyranny everywhere on behalf of universal values of freedom.

UN Security Council Resolution 687 of 1991 had required Iraq to destroy all stockpiles of its weapons of mass destruction and commit never to develop such weapons again. Ten Security Council resolutions since then had held Iraq in substantial violation.

What was distinctive—and traditionally American—about the military effort in Iraq was the decision to cast this, in effect, enforcement action as an aspect of a project to spread freedom and democracy. America reacted to the mounting tide of radical Islamist universalism by reaffirming the universality of its own values and concept of world order.

The basic premise began with significant public support, especially extending to the removal of Saddam Hussein. In 1998, the U.S. Congress passed the Iraq Liberation Act with overwhelming bipartisan support (360–38 in the House and unanimously in the Senate), declaring that "it should be the policy of the United States to support efforts to remove the regime headed by Saddam Hussein from power in Iraq and to promote the emergence of a democratic government to replace that regime." Signing the bill into law on October 31, the same day as its passage in the Senate, President Clinton expressed the consensus of both parties:

> The United States wants Iraq to rejoin the family of nations
> as a freedom-loving and law-abiding member. This is in our
> interest and that of our allies within the region . . . The United
> States is providing support to opposition groups from all sec-
> tors of the Iraqi community that could lead to a popularly
> supported government.

Because no political parties were permitted in Iraq except the governing Baath Party, which Saddam Hussein ran with an iron fist, and
therefore no formal opposition parties existed, the President's phrase
had to mean that the United States would generate a covert program
to overthrow the Iraqi dictator.

After the military intervention in Iraq, Bush elaborated broader
implications in a November 2003 speech marking the twentieth anniversary of the National Endowment for Democracy. Bush condemned
past U.S. policies in the region for having sought stability at the price
of liberty:

> Sixty years of Western nations excusing and accommodating
> the lack of freedom in the Middle East did nothing to make
> us safe—because in the long run, stability cannot be pur-
> chased at the expense of liberty.

In the changed circumstances of the twenty-first century, traditional
policy approaches posed unacceptable risks. The administration was
therefore shifting from a policy of stability to "a forward strategy of
freedom in the Middle East." American experience in Europe and
Asia demonstrated that "the advance of freedom leads to peace."

I supported the decision to undertake regime change in Iraq. I
had doubts, expressed in public and governmental forums, about expanding it to nation building and giving it such universal scope. But
before recording my reservations, I want to express here my continu-

ing respect and personal affection for President George W. Bush, who guided America with courage, dignity, and conviction in an unsteady time. His objectives and dedication honored his country even when in some cases they proved unattainable within the American political cycle. It is a symbol of his devotion to the Freedom Agenda that Bush is now pursuing it in his postpresidential life and made it the key theme of his presidential library in Dallas.

Having spent my childhood as a member of a discriminated minority in a totalitarian system and then as an immigrant to the United States, I have experienced the liberating aspects of American values. Spreading them by example and civil assistance as in the Marshall Plan and economic aid programs is an honored and important part of the American tradition. But to seek to achieve them by military occupation in a part of the world where they had no historical roots, and to expect fundamental change in a politically relevant period of time— the standard set by many supporters and critics of the Iraq effort alike—proved beyond what the American public would support and what Iraqi society could accommodate.

Given the ethnic divisions in Iraq and the millennial conflict between Sunni and Shia, the dividing line of which ran through the center of Baghdad, the attempt to reverse historical legacies under combat conditions, amidst divisive American domestic debates, imbued the American endeavor in Iraq with a Sisyphean quality. The determined opposition of neighboring regimes compounded the difficulties. It became an endless effort always just short of success.

Implementing a pluralist democracy in place of Saddam Hussein's brutal rule proved infinitely more difficult than the overthrow of the dictator. The Shias, long disenfranchised and hardened by decades of oppression under Hussein, tended to equate democracy with a ratification of their numeric dominance. The Sunnis treated democracy as a foreign plot to repress them; on this basis, most Sunnis boycotted the 2004 elections, instrumental in defining the postwar constitutional order. The Kurds in the north, with memories of murderous onslaughts by Baghdad, enhanced their separate military capabilities and strove for control of oil fields to provide themselves with revenue not dependent on the national treasury. They defined autonomy in terms minutely different, if at all, from national independence.

Passions, already high in an atmosphere of revolution and foreign occupation, were ruthlessly inflamed and exploited after 2003 by outside forces: Iran, which backed Shia groups subverting the nascent government's independence; Syria, which abetted the transfer of arms and jihadists through its territory (ultimately with devastating consequences for its own cohesion); and al-Qaeda, which began a campaign of systematic slaughter against the Shias. Each community increasingly treated the postwar order as a zero-sum battle for power, territory, and oil revenues.

In this atmosphere, Bush's courageous January 2007 decision to deploy a "surge" of additional troops to quell violence was met with a nonbinding resolution of disapproval supported by 246 members of the House; though it failed on procedural grounds in the Senate, 56 Senators joined in opposition to the surge. The Senate majority leader soon declared that "this war is lost and the surge is not accomplishing anything." The same month, the House and the Senate passed bills, vetoed by the President, mandating that American withdrawal start within a year.

Bush, it has been reported, closed a 2007 planning session with the question "If we're not there to win, why are we there?" The remark embodied the resoluteness of the President's character as well as the tragedy of a country whose people have been prepared for more than half a century to send its sons and daughters to remote corners of the world in defense of freedom but whose political system has not been able to muster the same unified and persistent purpose. For while the surge, daringly ordered by Bush and brilliantly executed by General

David Petraeus, succeeded in wresting an honorable outcome from looming collapse, the American mood had shifted by this point. Barack Obama won the Democratic nomination in part on the strength of his opposition to the Iraq War. On taking office, he continued his public critiques of his predecessor, and undertook an "exit strategy" with greater emphasis on exit than on strategy. As of this writing, Iraq functions as a central battlefield in an unfolding regional sectarian contest—its government leaning toward Iran, elements of its Sunni population in military opposition to the government, members of both sides of its sectarian divide supporting the contending jihadist efforts in Syria, and the terrorist group ISIL attempting to build a caliphate across half of its territory.

The issue transcends political debates about its antecedents. The consolidation of a jihadist entity at the heart of the Arab world, equipped with substantial captured weaponry and a transnational fighting force, engaged in religious war with radical Iranian and Iraqi Shia groups, calls for a concerted and forceful international response or it will metastasize. A sustained strategic effort by America, the other permanent members of the Security Council, and potentially its regional adversaries will be needed.

The Purpose and the Possible

The nature of the international order was at issue when the Soviet Union emerged as a challenge to the Westphalian state system. With decades of hindsight, one can debate whether the balance sought by America was always the optimum. But it is hard to gainsay that the United States, in a world of weapons of mass destruction and political and social upheaval, preserved the peace, helped restore Europe's vitality, and provided crucial economic aid to emerging countries.

It was in the conduct of its "hot" wars that America found it difficult to relate purpose to possibility. In only one of the five wars America fought after World War II (Korea, Vietnam, the first Gulf War, Iraq, and Afghanistan), the first Gulf War under President George H. W. Bush, did America achieve the goals it had put forward for entering it without intense domestic division. When the outcomes of the other conflicts—ranging from stalemate to unilateral withdrawal—became foreordained is a subject for another debate. For present purposes, it is sufficient to state that a country that has to play an indispensable role in the search for world order needs to begin that task by coming to terms with that role and with itself.

The essence of historical events is rarely fully apparent to those living through them. The Iraq War may be seen as a catalyzing event in a larger transformation of the region—the fundamental character of which is as yet unknown and awaits the long-term outcome of the Arab Spring, the Iranian nuclear and geopolitical challenge, and the jihadist assault on Iraq and Syria. The advent of electoral politics in Iraq in 2004 almost certainly inspired demands for participatory institutions elsewhere in the region; what is yet to be seen is whether they can be combined with a spirit of tolerance and peaceful compromise.

As America examines the lessons of its twenty-first-century wars, it is important to remember that no other major power has brought to its strategic efforts such deeply felt aspirations for human betterment. There is a special character to a nation that proclaims as war aims not only to punish its enemies but to improve the lives of their people—that has sought victory not in domination but in sharing the fruits of liberty. America would not be true to itself if it abandoned this essential idealism. Nor would it reassure friends (or win over adversaries) by setting aside such a core aspect of its national experience. But to be effective, these aspirational aspects of policy must be paired with an unsentimental analysis of underlying factors, including the cultural and geopolitical configuration of other regions and the dedication and resourcefulness of adversaries opposing American interests and values.

America's moral aspirations need to be combined with an approach that takes into account the strategic element of policy in terms the American people can support and sustain through multiple political cycles.

Former Secretary of State George Shultz has articulated the American ambivalence wisely:

> Americans, being a moral people, want their foreign policy to reflect the values we espouse as a nation. But Americans, being a practical people, also want their foreign policy to be effective.

The American domestic debate is frequently described as a contest between idealism and realism. It may turn out—for America and the rest of the world—that if America cannot act in both modes, it will not be able to fulfill either.

CHAPTER 9

Technology, Equilibrium, and Human Consciousness

E VERY AGE HAS ITS LEITMOTIF, a set of beliefs that explains the universe, that inspires or consoles the individual by providing an explanation for the multiplicity of events impinging on him. In the medieval period, it was religion; in the Enlightenment, it was Reason; in the nineteenth and twentieth centuries, it was nationalism combined with a view of history as a motivating force. Science and technology are the governing concepts of our age. They have brought about advances in human well-being unprecedented in history. Their evolution transcends traditional cultural constraints. Yet they have also produced weapons capable of destroying mankind. Technology has brought about a means of communication permitting instantaneous contact between individuals or institutions in every part of the globe as well as the storage and retrieval of vast quantities of information at the touch of a button. Yet by what purposes is this technology informed? What happens to international order if technology has become such a part of everyday life that it defines its own universe as the sole relevant one? Is the destructiveness of modern weapons technology so vast that a common fear may unite mankind in order to eliminate the scourge of war? Or will possession of these weapons create a permanent foreboding?

Will the rapidity and scope of communication break down barriers between societies and individuals and provide transparency of such magnitude that the age-old dreams of a human community will come into being? Or will the opposite happen: Will mankind, amidst weapons of mass destruction, networked transparency, and the absence of privacy, propel itself into a world without limits or order, careening through crises without comprehending them?

The author claims no competence in the more advanced forms of technology; his concern is with its implications.

World Order in the Nuclear Age

Since history began to be recorded, political units—whether described as states or not—had at their disposal war as the ultimate recourse. Yet the technology that made war possible also limited its scope. The most powerful and well-equipped states could only project force over limited distances, in certain quantities, and against so many targets. Ambitious leaders were constrained, both by convention and by the state of communications technology. Radical courses of action were inhibited by the pace at which they unfolded. Diplomatic instructions were obliged to take into account contingencies that might occur in the time in which a message could make a round trip. This imposed a built-in pause for reflection and acknowledged a distinction between what leaders could and could not control.

Whether a balance of power between states operated as a formal principle or was simply practiced without theoretical elaboration, equilibrium of some kind was an essential component of any international order—either at the periphery, as with the Roman and Chinese empires, or as a core operating principle, as in Europe.

With the Industrial Revolution, the pace of change quickened, and the power projected by modern militaries grew more devastating. When the technological gap was great, even rudimentary technology—

by present standards—could be genocidal in effect. European technology and European diseases did much to wipe out existing civilizations in the Americas. With the promise of new efficiencies came new potentials for destruction, as the impact of mass conscription multiplied the compounding effect of technology.

The advent of nuclear weapons brought this process to a culmination. In World War II, scientists from the major powers labored to achieve mastery of the atom and with it the ability to release its energy. The American effort, known as the Manhattan Project and drawing on the best minds from the United States, Britain, and the European diaspora, prevailed. After the first successful atomic test in July 1945 in the deserts of New Mexico, J. Robert Oppenheimer, the theoretical physicist who headed the secret weapons-development effort, awed by his triumph, recalled a verse from the Bhagavad Gita: "Now I am become Death, the destroyer of worlds."

In earlier periods, wars had an implicit calculus: the benefits of victory outweighed its cost, and the weaker fought to impose such costs on the stronger as to disturb this equation. Alliances were formed to augment power, to leave no doubt about the alignment of forces, to define the casus belli (insofar as the removal of doubt about ultimate intentions is possible in a society of sovereign states). The penalties of military conflict were considered less than the penalties of defeat. By contrast, the nuclear age based itself on a weapon whose use would impose costs out of proportion to any conceivable benefit.

The nuclear age posed the dilemma of how to bring the destructiveness of modern weapons into some moral or political relationship with the objectives that were being pursued. Prospects for any kind of international order—indeed, for human survival—now urgently required the amelioration, if not elimination, of major-power conflict. A theoretical limit was sought—short of the point of either superpower using the entirety of its military capabilities.

Strategic stability was defined as a balance in which neither side would use its weapons of mass destruction because the adversary was always able to inflict an unacceptable level of destruction in retaliation. In a series of seminars at Harvard, Caltech, MIT, and the Rand Corporation among others in the 1950s and 1960s, a doctrine of "limited use" explored confining nuclear weapons to the battlefield or to military targets. All such theoretical efforts failed; whatever limits were imagined, once the threshold to nuclear warfare was crossed, modern technology overrode observable limits and always enabled the adversary to escalate. Ultimately, strategists on both sides coalesced, at least tacitly, on the concept of a mutual assured destruction as the mechanism of nuclear peace. Based on the premise that both sides possessed a nuclear arsenal capable of surviving an initial assault, the objective was to counterbalance threats sufficiently terrifying that neither side would conceive of actually invoking them.

By the end of the 1960s, the prevailing strategic doctrine of each superpower relied on the ability to inflict an "unacceptable" level of damage on the presumed adversary. What the adversary would consider unacceptable was, of course, unknowable; nor was this judgment communicated.

A surreal quality haunted this calculus of deterrence, which relied on "logical" equations of scenarios positing a level of the casualties exceeding that suffered in four years of world wars and occurring in a matter of days or hours. Because there was no prior experience with the weapons underpinning these threats, deterrence depended in large part on the ability to affect the adversary psychologically. When, in the 1950s, Mao spoke of China's willingness to accept sacrifices of hundreds of millions in a nuclear war, it was widely treated in the West as a symptom of emotional or ideological derangement. It was, in fact, probably the consequence of a sober calculation that to withstand military capacities beyond previous human experience, a country needed to demonstrate a willingness to sacrifice beyond human comprehension. In any case, the shock in Western and Warsaw Pact capitals at these statements ignored that the superpowers' own concepts of deterrence rested on apocalyptic risks. Even if more urbanely expressed, the doctrine of mutual assured destruction relied on the proposition that leaders were acting in the interest of peace by deliberately exposing their civilian populations to the threat of annihilation.

Many efforts were undertaken to avoid the dilemma of possessing a huge arsenal that could not be used and whose use could not even plausibly be threatened. Complicated war scenarios were devised. But neither side, to the best of my knowledge—and for some of this period I was in a position to know—ever approached the point of actually using nuclear weapons in a specific crisis between the two superpowers. Except for the Cuban missile crisis of 1962, when a Soviet combat division was initially authorized to use its nuclear weapons to defend itself, neither side approached their use, either against each other or in wars against non-nuclear third countries.

In this manner, the most fearsome weapons, commanding large shares of each superpower's defense budget, lost their relevance to the actual crises facing leaders. Mutual suicide became the mechanism of international order. When, during the Cold War, the two sides, Washington and Moscow, challenged each other, it was through proxy wars. At the pinnacle of the nuclear era, it was conventional forces that assumed pivotal importance. The military struggles of the time were taking place on the far-flung periphery—Inchon, the Mekong River delta, Luanda, Iraq, and Afghanistan. The measure of success was effectiveness in supporting local allies in the developing world. In short, the strategic arsenals of the major powers, incommensurable with conceivable political objectives, created an illusion of omnipotence belied by the actual evolution of events.

It was in this context that in 1969 President Nixon started formal talks with the Soviets on the limitation of strategic arms (with the acronym SALT). They resulted in a 1972 agreement that established a ceiling for the offensive buildup and limited each superpower's anti-ballistic missile sites to one (in effect turning them into training sites because a full ABM deployment for the United States under an original Nixon proposal in 1969 would have required twelve sites). The reasoning was that since the U.S. Congress refused to approbate missile defense beyond two sites, deterrence needed to be based on mutual assured destruction. For that strategy, the offensive nuclear weapons on each side were sufficient—in fact, more than sufficient—to produce an unacceptable level of casualties. The absence of missile defense would remove any uncertainty from that calculation, guaranteeing mutual deterrence—but also the destruction of the society, should deterrence fail.

At the Reykjavík summit in 1986, Reagan reversed the mutual assured destruction approach. He proposed the abolition of all offensive weapons by both sides and the scrapping of the Anti-Ballistic Missile Treaty, thereby allowing a defensive system. His intent was to do away with the concept of mutual assured destruction by proscribing offensive systems and keeping defense systems as a hedge against violations. But Gorbachev, believing—mistakenly—that the U.S. missile defense program was well under way while the Soviet Union, lacking an equivalent technological-economic base, could not keep up, insisted on maintaining the ABM Treaty. The Soviets in effect gave up the race in strategic weapons three years later, ending the Cold War.

Since then, the number of strategic nuclear offensive warheads has been reduced, first under President George W. Bush and then under President Obama, by agreement with Russia to about fifteen hundred warheads for each side—approximately 10 percent of the number of warheads that existed at the high point of the mutual assured destruction strategy. (The reduced number is more than enough to implement a mutual assured destruction strategy.)

The nuclear balance has produced a paradoxical impact on the international order. The historic balance of power had facilitated the Western domination of the then-colonial world; by contrast, the nuclear order—the West's own creation—had the opposite effect. The margin of military superiority of advanced countries over the developing countries has been incomparably larger than at any previous period in history. But because so much of their military effort has been devoted to nuclear weapons, whose use in anything but the gravest crisis was implicitly discounted, regional powers could redress the overall military balance by a strategy geared to prolonging any war beyond the willingness of the "advanced" country's public to sustain it—as France experienced in Algeria and Vietnam; the United States in Korea, Vietnam, Iraq, and Afghanistan; and the Soviet Union in Afghanistan. (All except Korea resulted in, in effect, a unilateral withdrawal by the formally much stronger power after protracted conflict with conventional forces.) Asymmetric warfare operated in the interstices of traditional doctrines of linear operations against an enemy's territory. Guerrilla forces, which defend no territory, could concentrate on inflicting casualties and eroding the public's political will to continue the conflict. In this sense, technological supremacy turned into geopolitical impotence.

The Challenge of Nuclear Proliferation

With the end of the Cold War, the threat of nuclear war between the existing nuclear superpowers has essentially disappeared. But the spread of technology—especially the technology to produce peaceful nuclear energy—has vastly increased the feasibility of acquiring a nuclear-weapons capability. The sharpening of ideological dividing lines and the persistence of unresolved regional conflicts have magnified the incentives to acquire nuclear weapons, including for rogue states or non-state actors. The calculations of mutual insecurity that produced restraint during the Cold War do not apply with anything like the same degree—if at all—to the new entrants in the nuclear field, and even less so to the non-state actors. Proliferation of nuclear weapons has become an overarching strategic problem for the contemporary international order.

In response to these perils, the United States, the Soviet Union, and the United Kingdom negotiated a Nuclear Non-proliferation Treaty (NPT) and opened it for signature in 1968. It proposed to prevent any further spread of nuclear weapons (the United States, the U.S.S.R., and the U.K. signed in 1968, and France and China signed in 1992). Non-nuclear-weapons states were to be given assistance by the nuclear states in the peaceful utilization of nuclear technology provided they accepted safeguards to guarantee their nuclear programs remained purely nonmilitary endeavors. At this writing, there are 189 signatories of the nonproliferation agreement.

Yet the global nonproliferation regime has had difficulty embedding itself as a true international norm. Assailed by some as a form of "nuclear apartheid" and treated by many states as a rich-country fixation, the NPT's restrictions have often functioned as a set of aspirations that countries must be cajoled to implement rather than as a binding legal obligation. Illicit progress toward nuclear weapons has proved difficult to discover and resist, for its initial steps are identical with the development of peaceful uses of nuclear energy specifically authorized by the NPT. The treaty proscribed but did not prevent signatories such as Libya, Syria, Iraq, and Iran from maintaining covert nuclear programs in violation of NPT safeguards or, in the case of North Korea, withdrawing from the NPT in 2003 and testing and proliferating nuclear technology without international control.

Where a state has violated or repudiated the terms of the NPT, hovered on the edge of compliance, or simply declined to recognize the legitimacy of nonproliferation as an international norm, there exists no defined international mechanism for enforcing it. So far preemptive action has been taken by the United States only against Iraq—a contributing motive for the war against Saddam Hussein—and by Israel against Iraq and Syria; the Soviet Union considered it against China in the 1960s, though ultimately refrained.

The nonproliferation regime has scored a few significant successes in bringing about the negotiated dismantlement of nuclear programs. South Africa, Brazil, Argentina, and several "post-Soviet" republics have abandoned nuclear weapons programs that had either come to fruition or made significant technical progress. At the same time, since the end of the American monopoly in 1949, nuclear weapons have been acquired by the Soviet Union/Russia, Britain, France, Israel, China, India, Pakistan, North Korea, and at a threshold level by Iran. Moreover, Pakistan and North Korea have proliferated their nuclear know-how widely.

Proliferation has had an impact on the nuclear equilibrium in a differential way, depending on the perceived willingness of the new nuclear country to use its weapons. British and French nuclear capabilities add to the NATO arsenal only marginally. They are conceived primarily as a last resort, as a safety net in case of abandonment by the United States, if some major power were to threaten British and French perceptions of their basic national interest, or as a means to stay apart from a nuclear war between superpowers—all essentially remote contingencies. The Indian and Pakistani nuclear establishments are, in the first instance, directed against each other, affecting the strategic equilibrium in two ways. The risks of escalation may reduce the likelihood of full-scale conventional war on the subcontinent. But because the weapon systems are so vulnerable and technically so difficult to protect against short-range attack, the temptation for preemption is inherent in the technology, especially in situations when emotions are already running high. In short, proliferation generates the classic nuclear dilemma: even when nuclear weapons reduce the likelihood of war, they would gigantically magnify its ferocity were war to occur.

India's nuclear relations with China are likely to approximate the deterrent posture that existed between the adversaries in the Cold War; that is, they will tend toward preventing their use. Pakistan's nuclear establishment impinges on wider regional and global issues. Abutting the Middle East and with a significant domestic Islamist presence at home, Pakistan has occasionally hinted at the role of nuclear protector or of nuclear armorer. The impact of the proliferation of nuclear weapons to Iran would compound all these issues—as discussed in Chapter 4.

Over time, the continued proliferation of nuclear weapons will affect even the overall nuclear balance between the nuclear superpowers. Leaders of the established nuclear powers are obliged to prepare for the worst contingency. This involves the possibility of nuclear threats posed not only by the other superpower but also by proliferating countries. Their arsenals will reflect the conviction that they need, beyond deterrence of the principal potential adversary, a residual force to cope with the proliferated part of the rest of the world. If each major nuclear power calculates in this manner, proliferation will impel a proportional increase in these residual forces, straining or exceeding existing limits. Further, these overlapping nuclear balances will grow more complicated as proliferation proceeds. The relatively stable nuclear order of the Cold War will be superseded by an international order in which projection by a state possessing nuclear weapons of an image of a willingness to take apocalyptic decisions may offer it a perverse advantage over rivals.

To provide themselves a safety net against nuclear superpowers, even countries with nuclear capabilities have an incentive to nestle under the tacit or overt support of a superpower (examples are Israel, the European nuclear forces, Japan with its threshold nuclear capability, other proliferating or near-proliferating states in the Middle East). So it may transpire that the proliferation of weapons will lead to alliance systems comparable in their rigidity to the alliances that led to World War I, though far exceeding them in global reach and destructive power.

A particularly serious imbalance may arise if a proliferated country approaches the military offensive capability of the two nuclear superpowers (a task which for both China and India seems attainable). Any major nuclear country, if it succeeds in staying out of a nuclear conflict between the others, would emerge as potentially dominant. In a multipolar nuclear world, that too could occur if such a country aligns with one of the superpowers because the combined forces might then have a strategic advantage. The rough nuclear balance that exists between current superpowers may then tilt away from strategic stability; the lower the agreed level of offensive forces between Russia and the United States, the more this will be true.

Any further spread of nuclear weapons multiplies the possibilities of nuclear confrontation; it magnifies the danger of diversion, deliberate or unauthorized. It will eventually affect the balance between nuclear superpowers. And as the development of nuclear weapons spreads into Iran and continues in North Korea—in defiance of all ongoing negotiations—the incentives for other countries to follow the same path could become overwhelming.

In the face of these trends, the United States needs to constantly review its own technology. During the Cold War, nuclear technology was broadly recognized as the forefront of American scientific achievements—a frontier of knowledge then posing the most important and strategic challenges. Now the best technical minds are encouraged to devote efforts instead to projects seen as more publicly relevant. Perhaps partly as a result, inhibitions on the elaboration of nuclear technology are treated as inexorable even as proliferating countries arm and other countries enhance their technology. The United States must remain at the frontier of nuclear technology, even while it negotiates about restraint in its use.

From the perspective of the past half century's absence of a major-power conflict, it could be argued that nuclear weapons have made the world less prone to war. But the decrease in the number of wars has been accompanied by a vast increase in violence carried out by non-state groups or by states under some label other than war. A combination of extraordinary risk and ideological radicalism has opened up the possibilities for asymmetric war and for challenges by non-state groups that undermine long-term restraint.

Perhaps the most important challenge to the established nuclear powers is for them to determine their reaction if nuclear weapons were actually used by proliferating countries against each other. First, what must be done to prevent the use of nuclear weapons beyond existing agreements? If they should nonetheless be used, what immediate steps must be taken to stop such a war? How can the human and social damage be addressed? What can be done to prevent retaliatory escalation while still upholding the validity of deterrence and imposing appropriate consequences should deterrence fail? The march of technological progress must not obscure the fearsomeness of the capabilities humanity has invented and the relative fragility of the balances restraining their use. Nuclear weapons must not be permitted to turn into conventional arms. At that juncture, international order will require an understanding between the existing major nuclear countries to insist on nonproliferation, or order will be imposed by the calamities of nuclear war.

Cyber Technology and World Order

For most of history, technological change unfolded over decades and centuries of incremental advances that refined and combined existing technologies. Even radical innovations could over time be fitted within previous tactical and strategic doctrines: tanks were considered in terms of precedents drawn from centuries of cavalry warfare; airplanes could be conceptualized as another form of artillery, battleships as mobile forts, and aircraft carriers as airstrips. For all their magnification of destructive power, even nuclear weapons are in some respects an extrapolation from previous experience.

What is new in the present era is the rate of change of computing power and the expansion of information technology into every sphere of existence. Reflecting in the 1960s on his experiences as an engineer at the Intel Corporation, Gordon Moore concluded that the trend he had observed would continue at regular intervals to double the capacity of computer processing units every two years. "Moore's Law" has proved astoundingly prophetic. Computers have shrunk in size, declined in cost, and grown exponentially faster to the point where advanced computer processing units can now be embedded in almost any object—phones, watches, cars, home appliances, weapons systems, unmanned aircraft, and the human body itself.

The revolution in computing is the first to bring so many individuals and processes into the same medium of communication and to translate and track their actions in a single technological language. Cyberspace—a word coined, at that point as an essentially hypothetical concept, only in the 1980s—has colonized physical space and, at least in major urban centers, is beginning to merge with it. Communication across it, and between its exponentially proliferating nodes, is near instantaneous. As tasks that were primarily manual or paper based a generation ago—reading, shopping, education, friendship, industrial and scientific research, political campaigns, finance, government record keeping, surveillance, military strategy—are filtered through the computing realm, human activity becomes increasingly "datafied" and part of a single "quantifiable, analyzable" system.

This is all the more so as, with the number of devices connected to the Internet now roughly ten billion and projected to rise to fifty billion by 2020, an "Internet of Things" or an "Internet of Everything" looms. Innovators now forecast a world of ubiquitous computing, with miniature data-processing devices embedded in everyday objects—"smart door locks, toothbrushes, wristwatches, fitness trackers, smoke detectors, surveillance cameras, ovens, toys and robots"—or floating through the air, surveying and shaping their environment in the form of "smart dust." Each object is to be connected to the Internet and programmed to communicate with a central server or other networked devices.

The revolution's effects extend to every level of human organization. Individuals wielding smartphones (and currently an estimated one billion people do) now possess information and analytical capabilities beyond the range of many intelligence agencies a generation ago. Corporations aggregating and monitoring the data exchanged by these individuals wield powers of influence and surveillance exceeding those of many contemporary states and of even more traditional powers. And governments, wary of ceding the new field to rivals, are propelled outward into a cyber realm with as yet few guidelines or restraints. As with any technological innovation, the temptation will be to see this new realm as a field for strategic advantage.

These changes have occurred so rapidly as to outstrip most attempts by those without technological expertise to comprehend their broader consequences. They draw humanity into regions hitherto unexplained, indeed unconceived. As a result, many of the most revolutionary technologies and techniques are currently limited in their use only by the capability and the discretion of the most technologically advanced.

No government, even the most totalitarian, has been able to arrest the flow or to resist the trend to push ever more of its operations into the digital domain. Most of the democracies have an ingrained instinct that an attempt to curtail the effects of an information revolution would be impossible and perhaps also immoral. Most of the countries outside the liberal-democratic world have set aside attempts to shut out these changes and turned instead to mastering them. Every country, company, and individual is now being enlisted in the technological

344 | World Order

revolution as either a subject or an object. What matters for the purpose of this book is the effect on prospects for international order.

The contemporary world inherits the legacy of nuclear weapons capable of destroying civilized life. But as catastrophic as their implications were, their significance and use could still be analyzed in terms of separable cycles of war and peace. The new technology of the Internet opens up entirely new vistas. Cyberspace challenges all historical experience. It is ubiquitous but not threatening in itself; its menace depends on its use. The threats emerging from cyberspace are nebulous and undefined and may be difficult to attribute. The pervasiveness of networked communications in the social, financial, industrial, and military sectors has vast beneficial aspects; it has also revolutionized vulnerabilities. Outpacing most rules and regulations (and indeed the technical comprehension of many regulators), it has, in some respects, created the state of nature about which philosophers have speculated and the escape from which, according to Hobbes, provided the motivating force for creating a political order.

Before the cyber age, nations' capabilities could still be assessed through an amalgam of manpower, equipment, geography, economics, and morale. There was a clear distinction between periods of peace and war. Hostilities were triggered by defined events and carried out with strategies for which some intelligible doctrine had been formulated. Intelligence services played a role mainly in assessing, and occasionally in disrupting, adversaries' capabilities; their activities were limited by implicit common standards of conduct or, at a minimum, by common experiences evolved over decades.

Internet technology has outstripped strategy or doctrine—at least for the time being. In the new era, capabilities exist for which there is as yet no common interpretation—or even understanding. Few if any limits exist among those wielding them to define either explicit or tacit restraints. When individuals of ambiguous affiliation are capable of undertaking actions of increasing ambition and intrusiveness, the very definition of state authority may turn ambiguous. The complexity is compounded by the fact that it is easier to mount cyberattacks than to defend against them, possibly encouraging an offensive bias in the construction of new capabilities.

The danger is compounded by the plausible deniability of those suspected of such actions and by the lack of international agreements for which, even if reached, there is no present system of enforcement. A laptop can produce global consequences. A solitary actor with enough computing power is able to access the cyber domain to disable and potentially destroy critical infrastructure from a position of near-complete anonymity. Electric grids could be surged and power plants disabled through actions undertaken exclusively outside a nation's physical territory (or at least its territory as traditionally conceived). Already, an underground hacker syndicate has proved capable of penetrating government networks and disseminating classified information on a scale sufficient to affect diplomatic conduct. Stuxnet, an example of a state-backed cyberattack, succeeded in disrupting and delaying Iranian nuclear efforts, by some accounts to an extent rivaling the effects of a limited military strike. The botnet attack from Russia on Estonia in 2007 paralyzed communications for days.

Such a state of affairs, even if temporarily advantageous to the advanced countries, cannot continue indefinitely. The road to a world order may be long and uncertain, but no meaningful progress can be made if one of the most pervasive elements of international life is excluded from serious dialogue. It is highly improbable that all parties, especially those shaped by different cultural traditions, will arrive independently at the same conclusions about the nature and permissible uses of their new intrusive capacities. Some attempt at charting a common perception of our new condition is essential. In its absence, the parties will continue to operate on the basis of separate intuitions, magnifying the prospects of a chaotic outcome. For actions undertaken in the virtual, networked world are capable of generating pressures for countermeasures in physical reality, especially when they have the potential to inflict damage of a nature previously associated with armed attack. Absent some articulation of limits and agreement on mutual rules of restraint, a crisis situation is likely to arise, even unintentionally; the very concept of international order may be subject to mounting strains.

In other categories of strategic capabilities, governments have come to recognize the self-defeating nature of unconstrained national conduct. The more sustainable course is to pursue, even among potential adversaries, a mixture of deterrence and mutual restraint, coupled with measures to prevent a crisis arising from misinterpretation or miscommunication.

Cyberspace has become strategically indispensable. At this writing, users, whether individuals, corporations, or states, rely on their own judgment in conducting their activities. The Commander of U.S. Cyber Command has predicted that "the next war will begin in cyberspace." It will not be possible to conceive of international order when the region through which states' survival and progress are taking place remains without any international standards of conduct and is left to unilateral decisions.

The history of warfare shows that every technological offensive capability will eventually be matched and offset by defensive measures, although not every country will be equally able to afford them. Does this mean that technologically less advanced countries must shelter under the protection of high-tech societies? Is the outcome to be a plethora of tense power balances? Deterrence, which, in the case of nuclear weapons, took the form of balancing destructive powers, cannot be applied by direct analogy, because the biggest danger is an attack without warning that may not reveal itself until the threat has already been implemented.

Nor is it possible to base deterrence in cyberspace on symmetrical retaliation, as is the case with nuclear weapons. If a cyberattack is limited to a particular function or extent, a "response in kind" may have totally different implications for the United States and for the aggressor. For example, if the financial architecture of a major industrialized economy is undermined, is the victim entitled only to counterattack against the potentially negligible comparable assets of its attacker? Or only against the computers engaged in the attack? Because neither of these is likely to be a sufficient deterrent, the question then turns to whether "virtual" aggression warrants "kinetic" force in response— and to what degree and by what equations of equivalence. A new world of deterrence theory and strategic doctrine now in its infancy requires urgent elaboration.

In the end, a framework for organizing the global cyber environment will be imperative. It may not keep pace with the technology itself, but the process of defining it will serve to educate leaders of its dangers and the consequences. Even if agreements carry little weight in the event of a confrontation, they may at least prevent sliding into an irretrievable conflict produced by misunderstanding.

The dilemma of such technologies is that it is impossible to establish rules of conduct unless a common understanding of at least some of the key capabilities exists. But these are precisely the capabilities the major actors will be reluctant to disclose. The United States has appealed to China for restraint in purloining trade secrets via cyber intrusions, arguing that the scale of activity is unprecedented. Yet to what extent is the United States prepared to disclose its own cyber intelligence efforts?

In this manner, asymmetry and a kind of congenital world disorder are built into relations between cyber powers both in diplomacy and in strategy. The emphasis of many strategic rivalries is shifting from the physical to the information realm, in the collection and processing of data, the penetration of networks, and the manipulation of psychology. Absent articulation of some rules of international conduct, a crisis will arise from the inner dynamics of the system.

The Human Factor

From the opening of the modern era in the sixteenth century, political philosophers have debated the issue of the relationship of the human being to the circumstances in which he finds himself. Hobbes, Locke, and Rousseau advanced a biological-psychological portrait of human consciousness and derived their political positions from this starting point. The American Founders, notably Madison in *Federalist* 10, did the same. They traced the evolution of society through factors that were "sown in the nature of man": each individual's powerful yet fallible faculty of reason and his inherent "self-love," from the interaction of which "different opinions will be formed"; and humanity's diversity of capabilities, from which "the possession of different degrees and kinds of property immediately results" and with them a "division of the society into different interests and parties." Though these thinkers differed in their analyses of specific factors and in the conclusions they drew, all framed their concepts in terms of a humanity whose inherent nature and experience of reality were timeless and unchanging.

In the contemporary world, human consciousness is shaped through an unprecedented filter. Television, computers, and smartphones compose a trifecta offering nearly constant interaction with a screen throughout the day. Human interactions in the physical world are now pushed relentlessly into the virtual world of networked devices. Recent studies suggest that adult Americans spend on average roughly half of their waking hours in front of a screen, and the figure continues to grow.

What is the impact of this cultural upheaval on relations between states? The policymaker undertakes multiple tasks, many of them shaped by his society's history and culture. He must first of all make an analysis of where his society finds itself. This is inherently where the past meets the future; therefore such a judgment cannot be made without an instinct for both of these elements. He must then try to understand where that trajectory will take him and his society. He must resist the temptation to identify policymaking with projecting the familiar into the future, for on that road lies stagnation and then decline. Increasingly in a time of technological and political upheaval, wisdom counsels that a different path must be chosen. By definition, in leading a society from where it is to where it has never been, a new course presents advantages and disadvantages that will always seem closely balanced. To undertake a journey on a road never before traveled requires character and courage: character because the choice is not obvious; courage because the road will be lonely at first. And the statesman must then inspire his people to persist in the endeavor. Great statesmen (Churchill, both Roosevelts, de Gaulle, and Adenauer) had these qualities of vision and determination; in today's society, it is increasingly difficult to develop them.

For all the great and indispensable achievements the Internet has brought to our era, its emphasis is on the actual more than the contingent, on the factual rather than the conceptual, on values shaped by consensus rather than by introspection. Knowledge of history and geography is not essential for those who can evoke their data with the touch of a button. The mindset for walking lonely political paths may not be self-evident to those who seek confirmation by hundreds, sometimes thousands of friends on Facebook.

In the Internet age, world order has often been equated with the proposition that if people have the ability to freely know and exchange the world's information, the natural human drive toward freedom will take root and fulfill itself, and history will run on autopilot, as it were. But philosophers and poets have long separated the mind's purview into three components: information, knowledge, and wisdom. The Internet focuses on the realm of information, whose spread it facilitates exponentially. Ever-more-complex functions are devised, particularly capable of responding to questions of fact, which are not themselves altered by the passage of time. Search engines are able to handle increasingly complex questions with increasing speed. Yet a surfeit of information may paradoxically inhibit the acquisition of knowledge and push wisdom even further away than it was before.

The poet T. S. Eliot captured this in his "Choruses from 'The Rock'":

> Where is the Life we have lost in living?
> Where is the wisdom we have lost in knowledge?
> Where is the knowledge we have lost in information?

Facts are rarely self-explanatory; their significance, analysis, and interpretation—at least in the foreign policy world—depend on context and relevance. As ever more issues are treated as if of a factual nature, the premise becomes established that for every question there must be a researchable answer, that problems and solutions are not so much to be thought through as to be "looked up." But in the relations between states—and in many other fields—information, to be truly useful, must be placed within a broader context of history and experience to emerge as actual knowledge. And a society is fortunate if its leaders can occasionally rise to the level of wisdom.

The acquisition of knowledge from books provides an experience different from the Internet. Reading is relatively time-consuming; to ease the process, style is important. Because it is not possible to read all books on a given subject, much less the totality of all books, or to organize easily everything one has read, learning from books places a premium on conceptual thinking—the ability to recognize comparable data and events and project patterns into the future. And style propels the reader into a relationship with the author, or with the subject matter, by fusing substance and aesthetics.

Traditionally, another way of acquiring knowledge has been through personal conversations. The discussion and exchange of ideas has for millennia provided an emotional and psychological dimension in addition to the factual content of the information exchanged. It supplies intangibles of conviction and personality. Now the culture of texting produces a curious reluctance to engage in face-to-face interaction, especially on a one-to-one basis.

The computer has, to a considerable extent, solved the problem of acquiring, preserving, and retrieving information. Data can be stored in effectively unlimited quantities and in manageable form. The computer makes available a range of data unattainable in the age of books. It packages it effectively; style is no longer needed to make it accessible, nor is memorization. In dealing with a single decision separated from its context, the computer supplies tools unimaginable even a decade ago. But it also shrinks perspective. Because information is so accessible and communication instantaneous, there is a diminution of focus on its significance, or even on the definition of what is significant. This dynamic may encourage policymakers to wait for an issue to arise rather than anticipate it, and to regard moments of decision as a series of isolated events rather than part of a historical continuum. When this happens, manipulation of information replaces reflection as the principal policy tool.

In the same way, the Internet has a tendency to diminish historical memory. The phenomenon has been described as follows: "People forget items they think will be available externally and remember items they think will not be available." By moving so many items into the realm of the available, the Internet reduces the impulse to remember them. Communications technology threatens to diminish the individual's capacity for an inward quest by increasing his reliance on technology as a facilitator and mediator of thought. Information at one's fingertips encourages the mindset of a researcher but may diminish the mindset of a leader. A shift in human consciousness may change the character of individuals and the nature of their interactions, and so begin to alter the human condition itself. Did people in the age of printing see the same world as their medieval forefathers? Is the optical perception of the world altered in the age of the computer?

Western history and psychology have heretofore treated truth as independent of the personality and prior experience of the observer. Yet our age is on the verge of a changed conception of the nature of truth. Nearly every website contains some kind of customization function based on Internet tracing codes designed to ascertain a user's background and preferences. These methods are intended to encourage users "to consume more content" and, in so doing, be exposed to more advertising, which ultimately drives the Internet economy. These subtle directions are in accordance with a broader trend to manage the traditional understanding of human choice. Goods are sorted and prioritized to present those "which you would like," and online news is presented as "news which will best suit you." Two different people appealing to a search engine with the same question do not necessarily receive the same answers. The concept of truth is being relativized and individualized—losing its universal character. Information is presented as being free. In fact, the recipient pays for it by supplying data to be exploited by persons unknown to him, in ways that further shape the information being offered to him.

Whatever the utility of this approach in the realm of consumption, its effect on policymaking may prove transformative. The difficult choices of policymaking are always close. Where, in a world of ubiquitous social networks, does the individual find the space to develop the fortitude to make decisions that, by definition, cannot be based on a consensus? The adage that prophets are not recognized in their own time is true in that they operate beyond conventional conception—that is what made them prophets. In our era, the lead time for prophets might have disappeared altogether. The pursuit of transparency and connectivity in all aspects of existence, by destroying privacy, inhibits the development of personalities with the strength to take lonely decisions.

American elections—especially presidential elections—represent another aspect of this evolution. It has been reported that in 2012 the election campaigns had files on some tens of millions of potentially independent voters. Drawn from research in social networks, open public files, and medical records, these files amounted to a profile for each, probably more precise than the target person would have been capable of doing from his own memory. This permitted the campaigns to choose the technology of their appeals—whether to rely on personal visits by committed friends (also discovered via the Internet), personalized letters (drawn from social network research), or group meetings.

Presidential campaigns are on the verge of turning into media contests between master operators of the Internet. What once had been substantive debates about the content of governance will reduce candidates to being spokesmen for a marketing effort pursued by methods whose intrusiveness would have been considered only a generation ago the stuff of science fiction. The candidates' main role may become fund-raising rather than the elaboration of issues. Is the marketing effort designed to convey the candidate's convictions, or are the convictions expressed by the candidate the reflections of a "big data" research effort into individuals' likely preferences and prejudices? Can democracy avoid an evolution toward a demagogic outcome based on emotional mass appeal rather than the reasoned process the Founding Fathers imagined? If the gap between the qualities required for election and those essential for the conduct of office becomes too wide, the conceptual grasp and sense of history that should be part of foreign policy may be lost—or else the cultivation of these qualities may take so much of a president's first term in office as to inhibit a leading role for the United States.

Foreign Policy in the Digital Era

Thoughtful observers have viewed the globalizing transformations ushered in by the rise of the Internet and advanced computing technology as the beginning of a new era of popular empowerment and progress toward peace. They hail the ability of new technologies to enable the individual and to propel transparency—whether through the publicizing of abuses by authorities or the erosion of cultural barriers of misunderstanding. Optimists point, with some justification, to the startling new powers of communication gained through instantaneous global networks. They stress the ability of computer networks and "smart" devices to create new social, economic, and environmental efficiencies. They look forward to unlocking previously insoluble technical problems by harnessing the brainpower of networked multitudes.

One line of thinking holds that similar principles of networked communication, if applied correctly to the realm of international affairs, could help solve age-old problems of violent conflict. Traditional ethnic and sectarian rivalries may be muted in the Internet age, this theory posits, because "people who try to perpetuate myths about religion, culture, ethnicity or anything else will struggle to keep their narratives afloat amid a sea of newly informed listeners. With more data, everyone gains a better frame of reference." It will be possible to temper national rivalries and resolve historical disputes because "with the technological devices, platforms and databases we have today, it will be much more difficult for governments in the future to argue over claims like these, not just because of permanent evidence but because everyone else will have access to the same source material." In this view, the spread of networked digital devices will become a positive engine of history: new networks of communication will curtail abuses, soften social and political contradictions, and help heretofore-disunited parts cohere into a more harmonious global system.

The optimism of this perspective replicates the best aspects of Woodrow Wilson's prophecy of a world united by democracy, open diplomacy, and common rules. As a blueprint for political or social order, it also raises some of the same questions as Wilson's original vision about the distinction between the practical and the aspirational.

Conflicts within and between societies have occurred since the dawn of civilization. The causes of these conflicts have not been limited to an absence of information or an insufficient ability to share it. They have arisen not only between societies that do not understand each other but between those that understand each other only too well. Even with the same source material to examine, individuals have disagreed about its meaning or the subjective value of what it depicts. Where values, ideals, or strategic objectives are in fundamental contradiction, exposure and connectivity may on occasion fuel confrontations as much as assuage them.

New social and information networks spur growth and creativity. They allow individuals to express views and report injustices that might otherwise go unheeded. In crisis situations, they offer a crucial ability to communicate quickly and to publicize events and policies reliably—potentially preventing the outbreak of a conflict through misunderstanding.

Yet they also bring conflicting, occasionally incompatible value systems into ever closer contact. The advent of Internet news and commentary and data-driven election strategies has not noticeably softened the partisan aspect of American politics; if anything, it has provided a larger audience to the extremes. Internationally, some expressions that once passed unknown and unremarked are now publicized worldwide and used as pretexts for violent agitation—as occurred in parts of the Muslim world in reaction to an inflammatory fringe cartoon in a Danish newspaper or a marginal American homemade movie. Meanwhile, in conflict situations, social networking may serve as a platform to reinforce traditional social fissures as much as it dispels them. The widespread sharing of videotaped atrocities in the Syrian civil war appears to have done more to harden the resolve of the warring parties than to stop the killing, while the notorious ISIL has used social media to declare a caliphate and exhort holy war.

Some authoritarian structures may fall as a result of information spread online or protests convened via social networking; they may in time be replaced by more open and participatory systems elaborating humane and inclusive values. Elsewhere other authorities will gain exponentially more powerful means of repression. The proliferation of ubiquitous sensors tracking and analyzing individuals, recording and transmitting their every experience (in some cases now, essentially from birth), and (at the forefront of computing) anticipating their thoughts opens up repressive as well as liberating possibilities. In this respect, among the new technology's most radical aspects may be the power it vests in small groups, at the pinnacle of political and economic structures, to process and monitor information, shape debate, and to some extent define truth.

The West lauded the "Facebook" and "Twitter" aspects of the Arab Spring revolutions. Yet where the digitally equipped crowd succeeds in its initial demonstrations, the use of new technology does not guarantee that the values that prevail will be those of the devices' inventors, or even those of the majority of the crowd. Moreover, the same technologies used to convene demonstrations can also be used to track and suppress them. Today most public squares in any major city are subject to constant video surveillance, and any smartphone owner can be tracked electronically in real time. As one recent survey concluded, "The Internet has made tracking easier, cheaper, and more useful."

The global scope and speed of communication erode the distinction between domestic and international upheavals, and between leaders and the immediate demands of the most vocal groups. Events whose effects once would have taken months to unfold ricochet globally within seconds. Policymakers are expected to have formulated a position within several hours and to interject it into the course of events—where its effects will be broadcast globally by the same instantaneous networks. The temptation to cater to the demands of the digitally reflected multitude may override the judgment required to chart a complex course in harmony with long-term purposes. The distinction between information, knowledge, and wisdom is weakened.

The new diplomacy asserts that if a sufficiently large number of people gather to publicly call for the resignation of a government and broadcast their demands digitally, they constitute a democratic expression obliging Western moral and even material support. This approach calls on Western leaders (and particularly American ones) to communicate their endorsement immediately and in unambiguous terms by the same social-networking methods so that their rejection of the government will be rebroadcast on the Internet and achieve further promulgation and affirmation.

If the old diplomacy sometimes failed to extend support to morally deserving political forces, the new diplomacy risks indiscriminate intervention disconnected from strategy. It declares moral absolutes to a global audience before it has become possible to assess the long-term intentions of the central actors, their prospects for success, or the ability to carry out a long-term policy. The motives of the principal groups, their capacity for concerted leadership, the underlying strategic and political factors in the country, and their relation to other strategic priorities are treated as secondary to the overriding imperative of endorsing a mood of the moment.

Order should not have priority over freedom. But the affirmation of freedom should be elevated from a mood to a strategy. In the quest for humane values, the expression of elevated principles is a first step; they must then be carried through the inherent ambiguities and contradictions of all human affairs, which is the task of policy. In this process, the sharing of information and the public support of free institutions are important new aspects of our era. On their own, absent attention to underlying strategic and political factors, they will have difficulty fulfilling their promise.

Great statesmen, however different as personalities, almost invariably had an instinctive feeling for the history of their societies. As Edmund Burke wrote, "People will not look forward to posterity, who never look backward to their ancestors." What will be the attitudes of those who aspire to be great statesmen in the Internet age? A combination of chronic insecurity and insistent self-assertion threatens both leaders and the public in the Internet age. Leaders, because they are less and less the originators of their programs, seek to dominate by willpower or charisma. The general public's access to the intangibles of the public debate is ever more constrained. Major pieces of legislation in the United States, Europe, and elsewhere often contain thousands of pages of text whose precise meaning is elusive even to those legislators who voted for them.

Previous generations of Western leaders performed their democratic role while recognizing that leadership did not consist of simply executing the results of public polls on a day-to-day basis. Tomorrow's generations may prove reluctant to exercise leadership independent of data-mining techniques—even as their mastery of the information environment may reward them with reelection for pursuing cleverly targeted, short-term policies.

In such an environment, the participants in the public debate risk being driven less by reasoned arguments than by what catches the mood of the moment. The immediate focus is pounded daily into the public consciousness by advocates whose status is generated by the ability to dramatize. Participants at public demonstrations are rarely assembled around a specific program. Rather, many seek the uplift of a moment of exaltation, treating their role in the event primarily as participation in an emotional experience.

These attitudes reflect in part the complexity of defining an identity in the age of social media. Hailed as a breakthrough in human relations, social media encourage the sharing of the maximum amount of information, personal or political. People are encouraged—and solicited—to post their most intimate acts and thoughts on public websites run by companies whose internal policies are, even when public, largely incomprehensible to the ordinary user. The most sensitive of this information is to be made available only to "friends" who, in practice, can run into the thousands. Approbation is the goal; were it not the objective, the sharing of personal information would not be so widespread and sometimes so jarring. Only very strong personalities are able to resist the digitally aggregated and magnified unfavorable judgments of their peers. The quest is for consensus, less by the exchange of ideas than by a sharing of emotions. Nor can participants fail to be affected by the exaltation of fulfillment by membership in a crowd of ostensibly like-minded people. And are these networks going to be the first institutions in human history liberated from occasional abuse and therefore relieved of the traditional checks and balances?

Side by side with the limitless possibilities opened up by the new technologies, reflection about international order must include the internal dangers of societies driven by mass consensus, deprived of the context and foresight needed on terms compatible with their historical character. In every other era, this has been considered the essence of leadership; in our own, it risks being reduced to a series of slogans designed to capture immediate short-term approbation. Foreign policy is in danger of turning into a subdivision of domestic politics instead of an exercise in shaping the future. If the major countries conduct their policies in this manner internally, their relations on the international stage will suffer concomitant distortions. The search for perspective may well be replaced by a hardening of differences, statesmanship by posturing. As diplomacy is transformed into gestures geared toward passions, the search for equilibrium risks giving way to a testing of limits.

Wisdom and foresight will be needed to avoid these hazards and ensure that the technological era fulfills its vast promise. It needs to deepen its preoccupation with the immediate through a better understanding of history and geography. That task is not only—or even primarily—an issue for technology. Society needs to adapt its education policy to ultimate imperatives in the long-term direction of the country and in the cultivation of its values. The inventors of the devices that have so revolutionized the collection and sharing of information can make an equal if not greater contribution by devising means to deepen its conceptual foundation. On the way to the first truly global world order, the great human achievements of technology must be fused with enhanced powers of humane, transcendent, and moral judgment.

World Order in Our Time?

I N THE DECADES FOLLOWING WORLD WAR II, a sense of world community seemed on the verge of arising. The industrially advanced regions of the world were exhausted from war; the underdeveloped parts were beginning their process of decolonization and redefining their identities. All needed cooperation rather than confrontation. And the United States, preserved from the ravages of war—indeed, strengthened by the conflict in its economy and national confidence—launched itself on implementing ideals and practices it considered applicable to the entire world.

When the United States began to take up the torch of international leadership, it added a new dimension to the quest for world order. A nation founded explicitly on an idea of free and representative governance, it identified its own rise with the spread of liberty and democracy and credited these forces with an ability to achieve the just and lasting peace that had thus far eluded the world. The traditional European approach to order had viewed peoples and states as inherently competitive; to constrain the effects of their clashing ambitions, it relied on a balance of power and a concert of enlightened statesmen.

The prevalent American view considered people inherently reasonable and inclined toward peaceful compromise, common sense, and fair dealing; the spread of democracy was therefore the overarching goal for international order. Free markets would uplift individuals, enrich societies, and substitute economic interdependence for traditional international rivalries. In this view, the Cold War was caused by the aberrations of Communism; sooner or later, the Soviet Union would return to the community of nations. Then a new world order would encompass all regions of the globe; shared values and goals would render conditions within states more humane and conflicts between states less likely.

The multigenerational enterprise of world ordering has in many ways come to fruition. Its success finds expression in the plethora of independent sovereign states governing most of the world's territory. The spread of democracy and participatory governance has become a shared aspiration, if not a universal reality; global communications and financial networks operate in real time, making possible a scale of human interactions beyond the imagination of previous generations; common efforts on environmental problems, or at least an impetus to undertake them, exist; and an international scientific, medical, and philanthropic community focuses its attention on diseases and health scourges once assumed to be the intractable ravages of fate.

The United States has made a significant contribution to this evolution. American military power provided a security shield for the rest of the world, whether its beneficiaries asked for it or not. Under the umbrella of an essentially unilateral American military guarantee, much of the developed world rallied into a system of alliances; the developing countries were protected against a threat they sometimes did not recognize, even less admit. A global economy developed to which America contributed financing, markets, and a profusion of innovations. From perhaps 1948 to the turn of the century marked a brief moment in human history when one could speak of an incipient global world order composed of an amalgam of American idealism and traditional concepts of balance of power.

Yet its very success made it inevitable that the entire enterprise would eventually be challenged, sometimes in the name of world order itself. The universal relevance of the Westphalian system derived from its procedural—that is, value-neutral—nature. Its rules were accessible to any country: noninterference in domestic affairs of other states; inviolability of borders; sovereignty of states; encouragements of international law. The weakness of the Westphalian system has been the reverse side of its strength. Designed as it was by states exhausted from their bloodletting, it did not supply a sense of direction. It dealt with methods of allocating and preserving power; it gave no answer to the problem of how to generate legitimacy.

In building a world order, a key question inevitably concerns the substance of its unifying principles—in which resides a cardinal distinction between Western and non-Western approaches to order. Since the Renaissance the West has been deeply committed to the notion that the real world is external to the observer, that knowledge consists of recording and classifying data—the more accurately the better—and that foreign policy success depends on assessing existing realities and trends. The Westphalian peace represented a judgment of reality—particularly realities of power and territory—as a temporal ordering concept over the demands of religion.

In the other great contemporary civilizations, reality was conceived as internal to the observer, defined by psychological, philosophical, or religious convictions. Confucianism ordered the world into tributaries in a hierarchy defined by approximations of Chinese culture. Islam divided the world order into a world of peace, that of Islam, and a world of war, inhabited by unbelievers. Thus China felt no need to go abroad to discover a world it considered already ordered, or best ordered by the cultivation of morality internally, while Islam could achieve the theoretical fulfillment of world order only by conquest or global proselytization, for which the objective conditions did not exist. Hinduism, which perceived cycles of history and metaphysical reality transcending temporal experience, treated its world of faith as a complete system not open to new entrants by either conquest or conversion.

That same distinction governed the attitude toward science and technology. The West, which saw fulfillment in mastering empirical reality, explored the far reaches of the world and fostered science and technology. The other traditional civilizations, each of which had considered itself the center of a world order in its own right, did not have the same impetus and fell behind technologically.

That period has now ended. The rest of the world is pursuing science and technology and, because unencumbered by established patterns, with perhaps more energy and flexibility than the West, at least in countries like China and the "Asian Tigers."

In the world of geopolitics, the order established and proclaimed as universal by the Western countries stands at a turning point. Its nostrums are understood globally, but there is no consensus about their application; indeed, concepts such as democracy, human rights, and international law are given such divergent interpretations that warring parties regularly invoke them against each other as battle cries. The system's rules have been promulgated but have proven ineffective absent active enforcement. The pledge of partnership and community has in some regions been replaced, or at least accompanied, by a harder-edged testing of limits.

A quarter century of political and economic crises perceived as produced, or at least abetted, by Western admonitions and practices—along with imploding regional orders, sectarian bloodbaths, terrorism, and wars ended on terms short of victory—has thrown into question the optimistic assumptions of the immediate post–Cold War era: that the spread of democracy and free markets would automatically create a just, peaceful, and inclusive world.

A countervailing impetus has arisen in several parts of the world to construct bulwarks against what are seen as the crisis-inducing policies of the developed West, including aspects of globalization. Security commitments that have stood as bedrock assumptions are being questioned, sometimes by the country whose defense they seek to foster. As the Western countries sharply reduce their nuclear arsenals or downgrade the role of nuclear weapons in their strategic doctrine, countries in the so-called developing world pursue them with great energy. Governments that once embraced (even while occasionally being perplexed by) the American commitment to its version of world order have begun to ask whether it leads to enterprises that the United States is in the end not sufficiently patient to see to their conclusion. In this view, acceptance of the Western "rules" of world order is laced with elements of unpredictable liability—an interpretation driving the conspicuous dissociation of some traditional allies from the United States. Indeed, in some quarters, the flouting of universal norms (such as human rights, due process, or equality for women) as distinctly North Atlantic preferences is treated as a positive virtue and the heart of alternative value systems. More elemental forms of identity are celebrated as the basis for exclusionary spheres of interest.

The result is not simply a multipolarity of power but a world of increasingly contradictory realities. It must not be assumed that, left unattended, these trends will at some point reconcile automatically to a world of balance and cooperation—or even any order at all.

The Evolution of International Order

Every international order must sooner or later face the impact of two tendencies challenging its cohesion: either a redefinition of legitimacy or a significant shift in the balance of power. The first tendency occurs when the values underlying international arrangements are fundamentally altered—abandoned by those charged with maintaining them or overturned by revolutionary imposition of an alternative concept of legitimacy. This was the impact of the ascendant West on many traditional orders in the non-Western world; of Islam in its initial wave of expansion in the seventh and eighth centuries; of the French Revolution on European diplomacy in the eighteenth century; of Communist and fascist totalitarianism in the twentieth; and of the Islamist assaults on the fragile state structure of the Middle East in our time.

The essence of such upheavals is that while they are usually underpinned by force, their overriding thrust is psychological. Those under assault are challenged to defend not only their territory but the basic assumptions of their way of life, their moral right to exist and to act in a manner that, until the challenge, had been treated as beyond question. The natural inclination, particularly of leaders from pluralistic societies, is to engage with the representatives of the revolution, expecting that what they really want is to negotiate in good faith on the premises of the existing order and arrive at a reasonable solution. The order is submerged not primarily from military defeat or an imbalance in resources (though this often follows) but from a failure to understand the nature and scope of the challenge arrayed against it. In this sense, the ultimate test of the Iranian nuclear negotiations is whether the Iranian professions of a willingness to resolve the issue through talks are a strategic shift or a tactical device—in pursuit of long-prevailing policy—and whether the West deals with the tactical as if it were a strategic change of direction.

The second cause of an international order's crisis is when it proves unable to accommodate a major change in power relations. In some cases, the order collapses because one of its major components ceases to play its role or ceases to exist—as happened to the Communist international order near the end of the twentieth century when the Soviet Union dissolved. Or else a rising power may reject the role allotted to it by a system it did not design, and the established powers may prove unable to adapt the system's equilibrium to incorporate its rise. Germany's emergence posed such a challenge to the system in the twentieth century in Europe, triggering two catastrophic wars from which Europe has never fully recovered. The emergence of China poses a comparable structural challenge in the twenty-first century. The presidents of the major twenty-first-century competitors—the United States and China—have vowed to avoid repeating Europe's tragedy through a "new type of great power relations." The concept awaits joint elaboration. It might have been put forward by either or both of these powers as a tactical maneuver. Nevertheless, it remains the only road to avoid a repetition of previous tragedies.

To strike a balance between the two aspects of order—power and legitimacy—is the essence of statesmanship. Calculations of power without a moral dimension will turn every disagreement into a test of strength; ambition will know no resting place; countries will be propelled into unsustainable tours de force of elusive calculations regarding the shifting configuration of power. Moral proscriptions without concern for equilibrium, on the other hand, tend toward either crusades or an impotent policy tempting challenges; either extreme risks endangering the coherence of the international order itself.

In our time—in part for the technological reasons discussed in Chapter 9—power is in unprecedented flux, while claims to legitimacy every decade multiply their scope in hitherto-inconceivable ways. When weapons have become capable of obliterating civilization and the interactions between value systems are rendered instantaneous and unprecedentedly intrusive, the established calculations for maintaining the balance of power or a community of values may become obsolete.

As these imbalances have grown, the structure of the twenty-first-century world order has been revealed as lacking in four important dimensions.

First, the nature of the state itself—the basic formal unit of international life—has been subjected to a multitude of pressures: attacked and dismantled by design, in some regions corroded from neglect, often submerged by the sheer rush of events. Europe has set out to transcend the state and to craft a foreign policy based principally on soft power and humanitarian values. But it is doubtful that claims to legitimacy separated from any concept of strategy can sustain a world order. And Europe has not yet given itself attributes of statehood, tempting a vacuum of authority internally and an imbalance of power along its borders. Parts of the Middle East have dissolved into sectarian and ethnic components in conflict with each other; religious militias and the powers backing them violate borders and sovereignty at will. The challenge in Asia is the opposite of Europe's. Westphalian balance-of-power principles prevail unrelated to an agreed concept of legitimacy.

And in several parts of the world we have witnessed, since the end of the Cold War, the phenomenon of "failed states," of "ungoverned spaces," or of states that hardly merit the term, having no monopoly on the use of force or effective central authority. If the major powers come to practice foreign policies of manipulating a multiplicity of subsovereign units observing ambiguous and often violent rules of conduct, many based on extreme articulations of divergent cultural experiences, anarchy is certain.

Second, the political and the economic organizations of the world are at variance with each other. The international economic system has become global, while the political structure of the world has remained based on the nation-state. The global economic impetus is on removing obstacles to the flow of goods and capital. The international political system is still largely based on contrasting ideas of world order and the reconciliation of concepts of national interest. Economic globalization, in its essence, ignores national frontiers. International policy emphasizes the importance of frontiers even as it seeks to reconcile conflicting national aims.

This dynamic has produced decades of sustained economic growth punctuated by periodic financial crises of seemingly escalating intensity: in Latin America in the 1980s; in Asia in 1997; in Russia in 1998; in the United States in 2001 and then again starting in 2007; in Europe after 2010. The winners—those who can weather the storm within a reasonable period and go forward—have few reservations about the system. But the losers—such as those stuck in structural misdesigns, as has been the case with the European Union's southern tier—seek their remedies by solutions that negate, or at least obstruct, the functioning of the global economic system.

While each of those crises has had a different cause, their common feature has been profligate speculation and systemic underappreciation of risk. Financial instruments have been invented that obscure the nature of the relevant transactions. Lenders have found it difficult to estimate the extent of their commitments and borrowers, including major nations, to understand the implications of their indebtedness.

The international order thus faces a paradox: its prosperity is dependent on the success of globalization, but the process produces a political reaction that often works counter to its aspirations. The economic managers of globalization have few occasions to engage with its political processes. The managers of the political processes have few incentives to risk their domestic support on anticipating economic or financial problems whose complexity eludes the understanding of all but experts.

In these conditions, the challenge becomes governance itself. Governments are subjected to pressures seeking to tip the process of globalization in the direction of national advantage or mercantilism. In the West, the issues of globalization thus merge with the issues of the conduct of democratic foreign policy. Harmonizing political and economic international orders challenges vested views: the quest for world order because it requires an enlargement of the national framework; the disciplining of globalization because sustainable practices imply a modification of the conventional patterns.

Third is the absence of an effective mechanism for the great powers to consult and possibly cooperate on the most consequential issues. This may seem an odd criticism in light of the plethora of multilateral forums that exist—more by far than at any other time in history. The UN Security Council—of compelling formal authority but deadlocked on the most important issues—is joined by regular summits for Atlantic leaders in NATO and the European Union, for Asia-Pacific leaders in APEC and the East Asia Summit, for developed countries in the G7 or G8, and for major economies in the G20. The United States is a key participant in all of these forums. Yet the nature and frequency of these meetings work against elaboration of long-range strategy. Discussions of schedules and negotiations over formal agendas arrogate the majority of preparation time; some forums effectively co-orbit on the calendars of leaders because of the difficulty of gathering principals in any one place on a regular basis. Participant heads of state, by the nature of their positions, focus on the public impact of their actions at the meeting; they are tempted to emphasize the tactical implications or the public relations aspect. This process permits little beyond designing a formal communiqué—at best, a discussion of pending tactical issues, and, at worst, a new form of summitry as "social media" event. A contemporary structure of international rules and norms, if it is to prove relevant, cannot merely be affirmed by joint declarations; it must be fostered as a matter of common conviction.

Throughout, American leadership has been indispensable, even when it has been exercised ambivalently. It has sought a balance between stability and advocacy of universal principles not always reconcilable with principles of sovereign noninterference or other nations' historical experience. The quest for that balance, between the uniqueness of the American experience and the idealistic confidence in its universality, between the poles of overconfidence and introspection, is inherently unending. What it does not permit is withdrawal.

Where Do We Go from Here?

A reconstruction of the international system is the ultimate challenge to statesmanship in our time. The penalty for failing will be not so much a major war between states (though in some regions this is not foreclosed) as an evolution into spheres of influence identified with particular domestic structures and forms of governance—for example, the Westphalian model as against the radical Islamist version. At its edges each sphere would be tempted to test its strength against other entities of orders deemed illegitimate. They would be networked for instantaneous communication and impinging on one another constantly. In time the tensions of this process would degenerate into maneuvers for status or advantage on a continental scale or even worldwide. A struggle between regions could be even more debilitating than the struggle between nations has been.

The contemporary quest for world order will require a coherent strategy to establish a concept of order *within* the various regions, and to relate these regional orders to one another. These goals are not necessarily identical or self-reconciling: the triumph of a radical movement might bring order to one region while setting the stage for turmoil in and with all others. The domination of a region by one country militarily, even if it brings the appearance of order, could produce a crisis for the rest of the world.

A reassessment of the concept of balance of power is in order. In theory, the balance of power should be quite calculable; in practice, it has proved extremely difficult to harmonize a country's calculations with those of other states and achieve a common recognition of limits. The conjectural element of foreign policy—the need to gear actions to an assessment that cannot be proved when it is made—is never more true than in a period of upheaval. Then, the old order is in flux while the shape of the replacement is highly uncertain. Everything depends, therefore, on some conception of the future. But varying internal structures can produce different assessments of the significance of existing trends and, more important, clashing criteria for resolving these differences. This is the dilemma of our time.

A world order of states affirming individual dignity and participatory governance, and cooperating internationally in accordance with agreed-upon rules, can be our hope and should be our inspiration. But progress toward it will need to be sustained through a series of intermediary stages. At any given interval, we will usually be better served, as Edmund Burke once wrote, "to acquiesce in some qualified plan that does not come up to the full perfection of the abstract idea, than to push for the more perfect," and risk crisis or disillusionment by insisting on the ultimate immediately. The United States needs a strategy and diplomacy that allow for the complexity of the journey—the loftiness of the goal, as well as the inherent incompleteness of the human endeavors through which it will be approached.

To play a responsible role in the evolution of a twenty-first-century world order, the United States must be prepared to answer a number of questions for itself:

What do we seek to prevent, no matter how it happens, and if necessary alone? The answer defines the minimum condition of the survival of the society.

What do we seek to achieve, even if not supported by *any* multilateral effort? These goals define the minimum objectives of the national strategy.

What do we seek to achieve, or prevent, *only* if supported by an alliance? This defines the outer limits of the country's strategic aspirations as part of a global system.

What should we *not* engage in, even if urged by a multilateral group or an alliance? This defines the limiting condition of the American participation in world order.

Above all, what is the nature of the values that we seek to advance? What applications depend in part on circumstance?

The same questions apply in principle to other societies.

For the United States, the quest for world order functions on two levels: the celebration of universal principles needs to be paired with a recognition of the reality of other regions' histories and cultures. Even as the lessons of challenging decades are examined, the affirmation of America's exceptional nature must be sustained. History offers no respite to countries that set aside their commitments or sense of identity in favor of a seemingly less arduous course. America—as the modern world's decisive articulation of the human quest for freedom, and an indispensable geopolitical force for the vindication of humane values—must retain its sense of direction.

A purposeful American role will be philosophically and geopolitically imperative for the challenges of our period. Yet world order cannot be achieved by any one country acting alone. To achieve a genuine world order, its components, while maintaining their own values, need to acquire a second culture that is global, structural, and juridical—a concept of order that transcends the perspective and ideals of any one region or nation. At this moment in history, this would be a modernization of the Westphalian system informed by contemporary realities.

Is it possible to translate divergent cultures into a common system? The Westphalian system was drafted by some two hundred delegates, none of whom has entered the annals of history as a major figure, who met in two provincial German towns forty miles apart (a significant distance in the seventeenth century) in two separate groups. They overcame their obstacles because they shared the devastating experience of the Thirty Years' War, and they were determined to prevent its recurrence. Our time, facing even graver prospects, needs to act on its necessities before it is engulfed by them.

Cryptic fragments from remote antiquity reveal a view of the human condition as irremediably marked by change and strife. "World-order" was fire-like, "kindling in measure and going out in measure," with war "the Father and King of all" creating change in the world. But "the unity of things lies beneath the surface; it depends upon a balanced reaction between opposites." The goal of our era must be to achieve that equilibrium while restraining the dogs of war. And we have to do so among the rushing stream of history. The well-known metaphor for this is in the fragment conveying that "one cannot step twice in the same river." History may be thought of as a river, but its waters will be ever changing.

Long ago, in youth, I was brash enough to think myself able to pronounce on "The Meaning of History." I now know that history's meaning is a matter to be discovered, not declared. It is a question we must attempt to answer as best we can in recognition that it will remain open to debate; that each generation will be judged by whether the greatest, most consequential issues of the human condition have been faced, and that decisions to meet these challenges must be taken by statesmen before it is possible to know what the outcome may be.

Acknowledgments

This book grew out of a dinner conversation with Charles Hill, Distinguished Fellow of the Brady-Johnson Program in Grand Strategy and senior lecturer in the Humanities Program at Yale University. Charlie was a valued member of the Policy Planning Staff when I served as Secretary of State a lifetime ago. We have been friends and occasional collaborators ever since.

At that dinner, we concluded that the crisis in the concept of world order was the ultimate international problem of our day. When I decided to write a book on the subject, Charlie offered advice and assistance. It proved invaluable. Charlie gave me the benefit of several essays he had written on various aspects of the subject, reviewed chapters in the process of drafting, was always available for discussions, and helped edit the entire manuscript upon its completion.

Schuyler Schouten was indispensable and indefatigable—adjectives I already applied to his contribution in the preparation of *On China* three years ago. Technically my research associate, he functions on my intellectual pursuits as a kind of alter ego. He undertook most of the research, collected it in thoughtful summaries, reviewed the manuscript several times, and accompanied me on many discussions on the subject. His contribution to this book was seminal; that he unfailingly maintained his composure amidst all these pressures is a tribute to his human qualities.

The editorial role of my publisher, Penguin Press, was exceptional. I have never worked with two editors simultaneously, and they complemented each other superbly. Ann Godoff added to her responsibilities as president and editor in chief by volunteering to edit this book. With penetrating intelligence and great common sense, she obliged me to elucidate obscure phrasing and historical references unfamiliar to the nonacademic reader. She also made essential structural suggestions. I do not know how she found time for her extensive and incisive comments, for which I am deeply grateful.

As a nearly obsessive history scholar, her colleague Stuart Proffitt, publisher of Penguin's U.K. imprint, volunteered to read each chapter, made meticulous and thoughtful comments, and called my attention to essential references. Working with Stuart was like a tutorial from an exceptionally learned, patient, and kind mentor at a university.

I have never written on Internet matters. I am also essentially ignorant of their technical side. But I have reflected a great deal about the impact of the new technology on policymaking. Eric Schmidt patiently and thoughtfully agreed to expose me to his world. We met many times for extensive and extremely stimulating conversations on both coasts. Jared Cohen participated in a few of the meetings and contributed significantly to this process. On two occasions, Eric invited me to visit Google to exchange ideas with a few of his fascinating and brilliant colleagues.

A number of friends and acquaintances permitted me to impose on their good nature to read and comment on sections of this manuscript. They were J. Stapleton Roy and Winston Lord (on Asia); Michael Gfoeller and Emma Sky (on the Middle East); and Professor Rana Mitter of Oxford University (on the entire manuscript). Several chapters benefited from the insight of my friends Les Gelb, Michael Korda, Peggy Noonan, and Robert Kaplan.

Collaborating with me on a sixth book, Theresa Amantea supervised the typing, fact-checking, and all other technical problems in my office with her customary organizational skill and enthusiasm. Theresa also did much of the typing, assisted by Jody Williams, who pitched in to help meet impending deadlines. Both have worked with me for many decades. I thank them for their efficiency, even more for their dedication.

Louise Kushner is a more recent addition to my staff, but she matched her colleagues' commitment. She contributed efficiently to the collation of editorial comments. At the same time firm and urbane, she kept my overall schedule under control while I concentrated on writing.

Jessee LePorin and Katherine Earle each provided valuable assistance.

Ingrid Sterner, Bruce Giffords, and Noirin Lucas of Penguin Press copyedited the manuscript and performed related tasks with great skill, bringing a special patience and attention to detail to the editorial production phase.

Andrew Wylie represented me in dealings with publishers around the world, as he had with *On China*, with his usual intelligence, tenacity, and ferocity. I am deeply grateful to him.

I have dedicated this book to my wife, Nancy, who has been my life. As always, she read the entire manuscript and made extraordinarily sensitive comments.

Needless to say, the shortcomings of this book are my own.

Notes

Introduction: The Question of
World Order

5   **"You are 20 states":** Franz Babinger,
    Mehmed the Conqueror and His Time
    (Princeton, N.J.: Princeton University
    Press, 1978), as quoted in Antony Black,
    The History of Islamic Political Thought
    (Edinburgh: Edinburgh University
    Press, 2011), 207.

Chapter 1: Europe: The Pluralistic
International Order

11 **The idea of Europe loomed:** Kevin
    Wilson and Jan van der Dussen, *The
    History of the Idea of Europe* (London:
    Routledge, 1993).

12 **In that worldview Christendom:**
    Frederick B. Artz, *The Mind of the
    Middle Ages* (Chicago: University of
    Chicago Press, 1953), 275–80.

13 **Aspirations to unity were briefly
    realized:** Heinrich Fichtenau, *The
    Carolingian Empire: The Age of
    Charlemagne,* trans. Peter Munz (New
    York: Harper & Row, 1964), 60.

15 **Charles was hailed:** Hugh Thomas,
    *The Golden Age: The Spanish Empire of
    Charles V* (London: Allen Lane, 2010),
    23.

15 **In the tradition of Charlemagne:**
    James Reston Jr., *Defenders of the Faith:
    Charles V, Suleyman the Magnificent,
    and the Battle for Europe, 1520–1536*
    (New York: Penguin Press, 2009), 40,
    294–95.

16 **The French King repudiated:** See
    Chapter 3.

16 **The universality of the Church
    Charles sought:** See Edgar Sanderson,
    J. P. Lamberton, and John McGovern,
    Six Thousand Years of History, vol. 7,

Famous Foreign Statesmen
(Philadelphia: E. R. DuMont, 1900),
246–50; Reston, *Defenders of the Faith,*
384–89. To a later Europe fractious and
skeptical of universalistic claims,
Charles's rule appeared less like a near
deliverance into desired unity than an
overbearing threat. As the Scottish
philosopher David Hume, a product of
the eighteenth-century Enlightenment,
would later write, "Mankind were
anew alarmed by the danger of
universal monarchy, from the union of
so many kingdoms and principalities in
the person of the Emperor Charles."
David Hume, "On the Balance of
Power," in *Essays, Moral, Political, and
Literary* (1742), 2.7.13.

17 **A map depicting the universe:** See
    Jerry Brotton, *A History of the World in
    Twelve Maps* (London: Penguin Books,
    2013), 82–113 (discussion of the
    Hereford Mappa Mundi, ca. 1300); 4
    Ezra 6:42; Dante Alighieri, *The Divine
    Comedy,* trans. Allen Mandelbaum
    (London: Bantam, 1982), 342; and
    Osip Mandelstam, "Conversation
    About Dante," in *The Poet's Dante,* ed.
    Peter S. Hawkins and Rachel Jacoff
    (New York: Farrar, Straus and Giroux,
    2001), 67.

21 **"red eminence":** Richelieu himself had
    a "grey eminence," his confidential
    advisor and agent François Leclerc du
    Tremblay, whose robes as Père Joseph
    of the Capuchin order led him to be
    called Richelieu's *éminence grise,* a label
    ever thereafter applied to shadowy
    figures of influence in the history of
    diplomacy. Aldous Huxley, *Grey
    Eminence: A Study in Religion and*

Politics (New York: Harper and Brothers, 1941).

21 **Machiavelli's treatises on statesmanship:** See, for example, Niccolò Machiavelli, *The Art of War* (1521), *Discourses on the First Ten Books of Titus Livy* (1531), *The Prince* (1532).

22 **To outraged complaints:** Joseph Strayer, Hans Gatzke, and E. Harris Harbison, *The Mainstream of Civilization Since 1500* (New York: Harcourt Brace Jovanovich, 1971), 420.

23 **The fragmentation of Central Europe:** Richelieu, "Advis donné au roy sur le sujet de la bataille de Nordlingen," in *The Thirty Years War: A Documentary History,* ed. and trans. Tryntje Helfferich (Indianapolis: Hackett, 2009), 151.

24 **The 235 official envoys:** Peter H. Wilson, *The Thirty Years War: Europe's Tragedy* (Cambridge, Mass.: Harvard University Press, 2009), 673.

25 **Most representatives had come with eminently practical instructions:** Ibid., 676.

25 **Both the main multilateral treaties:** *Instrumentum pacis Osnabrugensis* (1648) and *Instrumentum pacis Monsteriensis* (1648), in Helfferich, *Thirty Years War,* 255, 271.

26 **Paradoxically, this general exhaustion and cynicism:** Wilson, *Thirty Years War,* 672.

26 **novel clauses:** These formal provisions of tolerance were extended only to the three recognized Christian confessions: Catholicism, Lutheranism, and Calvinism.

27 **"We have no eternal allies":** Palmerston, Speech to the House of Commons, March 1, 1848. This spirit was also expressed by Prince William III of Orange, who fought against French hegemony for a generation (first as Dutch stadtholder and then as King of England, Ireland, and Scotland), when he confided to an aide that, had he lived in the 1550s, when the Habsburgs were on the verge of becoming dominant, he would have been "as much a Frenchman as he was

now a Spaniard" (Habsburg)—and later by Winston Churchill, replying in the 1930s to the charge that he was anti-German: "If the circumstances were reversed, we could equally be pro-German and anti-French."

30 **"When people ask me":** Palmerston to Clarendon, July 20, 1856, quoted in Harold Temperley and Lillian M. Penson, *Foundations of British Foreign Policy from Pitt (1792) to Salisbury (1902)* (Cambridge, U.K.: Cambridge University Press, 1938), 88.

31 **In his *Leviathan*:** The experience that brought Hobbes to write *Leviathan* was principally that of the English Civil Wars, whose impact on England, though less physically devastating than that of the Thirty Years' War on the Continent, was still very great.

31 **"Concerning the offices of one sovereign to another":** Thomas Hobbes, *Leviathan* (1651) (Indianapolis: Hackett, 1994), 233.

32 **There were in fact two balances of power:** It is important to keep in mind that only one major power existed in Central Europe at the time: Austria and its dominions. Prussia was still a secondary state at the eastern fringes of Germany. Germany was a geographic concept, not a state. Dozens of small, some minuscule, states made up a mosaic of governance.

33 **"He [Louis] was well aware":** Lucy Norton, ed., *Saint-Simon at Versailles* (London: Hamilton, 1958), 217–30.

35 **Split into two:** Until ruthless diplomacy led to three successive partitions of Poland, the eastern half of Frederick's territory was surrounded by Poland on three sides and the Baltic Sea on the other.

35 **When Frederick II ascended the throne in 1740:** Gerhard Ritter, *Frederick the Great: A Historical Profile,* trans. Peter Paret (Berkeley: University of California Press, 1968), 29–30.

36 **"Rulers are":** Frederick II of Prussia, *Oeuvres,* 2, XXV (1775), as quoted in Friedrich Meinecke, *Machiavellism: The Doctrine of Raison d'État and Its Place in Modern History,* trans. Douglas Scott

(New Haven, Conn.: Yale University Press, 1957) (originally published in German, 1925), 304.

36 **"Pas trop mal pour la veille d'une grande bataille":** "Not so bad for the eve of a great battle." Frederick II, as quoted in Otto von Bismarck, *Bismarck: The Man and the Statesman* (New York: Harper & Brothers, 1899), 316; and Otto von Bismarck, *The Kaiser vs. Bismarck: Suppressed Letters by the Kaiser and New Chapters from the Autobiography of the Iron Chancellor* (New York: Harper & Brothers, 1921), 144–45.

36 **Enlightment governance:** As Alexander Pope remarked in 1734, "For forms of government let fools contest; / Whatever is best administered is best." Alexander Pope, *An Essay on Man* (1734), epistle iii, lines 303–4.

36 **"The superiority of our troops":** As quoted in G. P. Gooch, *Frederick the Great* (Berkeley: University of California Press, 1947), 4–5.

37 **"lives and values were put on display":** David A. Bell, *The First Total War: Napoleon's Europe and the Birth of Warfare as We Know It* (Boston: Houghton Mifflin, 2007), 5.

37 **a single elite society:** For lively accounts of this social aspect, see Susan Mary Alsop, *The Congress Dances: Vienna, 1814–1815* (New York: Harper & Row, 1984); Adam Zamoyski, *Rites of Peace: The Fall of Napoleon and the Congress of Vienna* (London: HarperPress, 2007).

38 **"In short, from the earth to Saturn":** Jean Le Rond d'Alembert, "Éléments de Philosophie" (1759), as quoted in Ernst Cassirer, *The Philosophy of the Enlightenment,* trans. Fritz C. A. Koelln and James P. Pettegrove, (Princeton, N.J.: Princeton University Press, 1951), 3.

39 **"zeal for the best interests of the human race":** Denis Diderot, "The Encyclopedia" (1755), in *Rameau's Nephew and Other Works,* trans. Jacques Barzun and Ralph H. Bowen (Indianapolis: Hackett, 2001), 283.

39 **"solid principles [to] serve as the foundation":** Ibid., 296.

39 **"It is not fortune which rules the world":** Montesquieu, *Considérations sur les causes de la grandeur des Romains et de leur décadence* (1734), as quoted in Cassirer, *Philosophy of the Enlightenment,* 213.

40 **"*unsocial sociability*":** Immanuel Kant, "Idea for a Universal History with a Cosmopolitan Purpose" (1784), in *Kant: Political Writings,* ed. H. S. Reiss (Cambridge, U.K.: Cambridge University Press, 1991), 44.

40 **"the most difficult and the last":** Ibid., 46.

40 **"devastations, upheavals and even":** Ibid., 47.

40 **"the vast graveyard of the human race":** Immanuel Kant, "Perpetual Peace: A Philosophical Sketch (1795)," in Reiss, *Kant,* 96.

40 **The answer, Kant held, was a voluntary federation of republics:** That is, states with participatory forms of government, ruled by a system of laws applied equally to all citizens. "Perpetual Peace" has since been enlisted on behalf of the contemporary era's "democratic peace theory." Yet in the essay Kant drew a distinction between republics, which he described as representative political structures in which "the executive power (the government) is separated from the legislative power," and democracies. "Democracy, in the truest sense of the word," he argued—that is, a direct democracy such as late ancient Athens in which all matters of state are submitted to a mass vote—"is necessarily a despotism." Ibid., 101.

40 **"calling down on *themselves* all the miseries of war":** Ibid., 100. Emphasis added. Operating on the plane of abstract reason, Kant sidestepped the example of republican France, which had gone to war against all of its neighbors to great popular acclaim.

40 **"a system of united power":** Kant, "Idea for a Universal History," 49.

42 **The Revolution's intellectual godfather:** In Rousseau's famous analysis, "Man is born free, and everywhere he is in chains." The course of human development had gone wrong

with "the first person who, having enclosed a plot of land, took it into his head to say *this is mine*." Thus only when private property is abolished by being held communally and artificial gradations of social status are eliminated can justice be achieved. And because those with property or status will resist the reintroduction of absolute equality, this can only come about by violent revolution. Jean-Jacques Rousseau, *Discourse on the Origin of Inequality* and *The Social Contract,* in *The Basic Political Writings* (1755; 1762) (Indianapolis: Hackett, 1987), 61, 141.

42 **"rule of administration in the social order":** Legitimate governance, Rousseau had reasoned, would come only when "each of us puts his person and all his power in common under the supreme direction of the general will, and, in our corporate capacity, we receive each member as an indivisible part of the whole." Dissent was to be eradicated: since in a world of rational and egalitarian social structures, divergences within the popular will would reflect illegitimate opposition to the principle of popular empowerment, "whoever refuses to obey the general will shall be compelled to do so by the whole body. This means nothing less than that he will be forced to be free; for this is the condition which, by giving each citizen to his country, secures him against all personal dependence." Rousseau, *Social Contract,* in *The Basic Political Writings*, 150.

43 **"will accord fraternity and assistance":** "Declaration for Assistance and Fraternity to Foreign Peoples" (November 19, 1792), in *The Constitutions and Other Select Documents Illustrative of the History of France, 1789–1907* (London: H. W. Wilson, 1908), 130.

44 **"The French nation declares":** "Decree for Proclaiming the Liberty and Sovereignty of All Peoples" (December 15, 1792), in ibid., 132–33.

47 **"I saw the Emperor—this world-soul":** Hegel to Friedrich Niethammer,

October 13, 1806, in *Hegel: The Letters,* trans. Clark Butler and Christine Seiler with commentary by Clark Butler (Bloomington: Indiana University Press, 1985).

Chapter 2: The European Balance-of-Power System and Its End

50 **"A monstrous compound of the petty refinements":** Marquis de Custine, *Empire of the Czar: A Journey Through Eternal Russia* (1843; New York: Anchor Books, 1990), 69.

51 **"the sole Emperor of all the Christians":** Epistle of Filofei of Pskov, 1500 or 1501, as quoted in Geoffrey Hosking, *Russia: People and Empire* (Cambridge, Mass.: Harvard University Press, 1997), 5–6. Ivan's successors would give this philosophical conviction a geopolitical thrust. Catherine the Great conceived of a "Greek Project," which was to culminate in the conquest of Constantinople and the crowning of Catherine's fittingly named grandson Constantine as its ruler. Her courtier Potemkin even placed (in addition to fake villages) a sign along his patroness's Crimean route that read, "This way to Byzantium." For Russia, the reattachment of the lost capital of Orthodox Christendom became an objective of profound spiritual and (for an empire lacking warm-water ports) strategic significance. The nineteenth-century Pan-Slavist intellectual Nikolai Danilevskii summed up a long tradition of thought with his ringing assessment: "[Constantinople has been] the aim of the aspirations of the Russian people from the dawn of our statehood, the ideal of our enlightenment; the glory, splendor and greatness of our ancestors, the center of Orthodoxy, and the bone of contention between Europe and ourselves. What historical significance Constantinople would have for us if we could wrest her away from the Turks regardless of Europe! What delight would our hearts feel from the radiance of the cross that we would raise atop the dome of St.

Sophia! Add to this all the other advantages of Constantinople . . . , her world significance, her commercial significance, her exquisite location, and all the charms of the south." Nikolai Danilevskii, *Russia and Europe: A View on Cultural and Political Relations Between the Slavic and German-Roman Worlds* (St. Petersburg, 1871), as translated and excerpted in *Imperial Russia: A Source Book, 1700–1917,* ed. Basil Dmytryshyn (Gulf Breeze, Fla: Academic International Press, 1999), 373.

52 **"expanding the state in every direction":** Vasili O. Kliuchevsky, *A Course in Russian History: The Seventeenth Century* (Armonk, N.Y.: M. E. Sharpe, 1994), 366. See also Hosking, *Russia,* 4.

52 **This process developed:** John P. LeDonne, *The Russian Empire and the World, 1700–1917: The Geopolitics of Expansion and Containment* (New York: Oxford University Press, 1997), 348.

53 **"His political philosophy, like that of all Russians":** Henry Adams, *The Education of Henry Adams* (1907; New York: Modern Library, 1931), 439.

53 **It expanded each year:** Orlando Figes, *Natasha's Dance: A Cultural History of Russia* (New York: Picador, 2002), 376–77.

54 **From that perspective:** As Russian troops marched in 1864 into the territory now known as Uzbekistan, Chancellor Aleksandr Gorchakov defined Russia's expansion in terms of a permanent obligation to pacify its periphery driven forward by sheer momentum:

The state [Russia] therefore must make a choice: either to give up this continuous effort and doom its borders to constant unrest which would make prosperity, safety, and cultural progress impossible here; or else to advance farther and farther into the heart of the savage lands, where the vast distances, with every step forward, increase the difficulties and hardships it incurs . . . not so much from ambition as from dire

necessity, where the greatest difficulty lies in being able to stop. George Verdansky, ed., *A Source Book for Russian History: From Early Times to 1917* (New Haven, Conn.: Yale University Press, 1972), 3:610.

54 **Yet early European visitors:** Marquis de Custine, *Empire of the Czar,* 230. Modern scholars continued to wonder. See, for example, Charles J. Halperin, *Russia and the Golden Horde: The Mongol Impact on Medieval Russian History* (Indianapolis: Indiana University Press, 1985); Paul Harrison Silfen, *The Influence of the Mongols on Russia: A Dimensional History* (Hicksville, N.Y.: Exposition Press, 1974).

54 **Determined to explore the fruits of modernity:** With a domineering hands-on approach that prompted amazement in Western European nations, Peter enrolled as a carpenter on the docks of Holland, deconstructed and repaired watches in London, and unsettled his retinue by trying his hand at new innovations in dentistry and anatomical dissection. See Virginia Cowles, *The Romanovs* (New York: Harper & Row, 1971), 33–37; Robert K. Massie, *Peter the Great* (New York: Ballantine Books, 1980), 188–89, 208.

55 **"to sever the people from their former Asiatic customs":** B. H. Sumner, *Peter the Great and the Emergence of Russia* (New York: Collier Books, 1962), 45.

55 **A series of ukases issued forth:** Cowles, *Romanovs,* 26–28; Sumner, *Peter the Great and the Emergence of Russia,* 27; Figes, *Natasha's Dance,* 4–6.

55 **"Russia is a European State":** Catherine II, *Nakaz* (Instruction) to the Legislative Commission of 1767–68, in Dmytryshyn, *Imperial Russia,* 80.

55 **Stalin too has acquired:** Maria Lipman, Lev Gudkov, Lasha Bakradze, and Thomas de Waal, *The Stalin Puzzle: Deciphering Post-Soviet Public Opinion* (Washington, D.C.: Carnegie Endowment for International Peace, 2013) (reporting polls of contemporary Russians showing 47 percent agreement with the statement "Stalin was a wise

leader who brought the Soviet Union to might and prosperity" and 30 percent agreement with the statement "Our people will always have need of a leader like Stalin, who will come and restore order").

56 **"The Extent of the Dominion requires":** Catherine II, *Nakaz* (Instruction) to the Legislative Commission of 1767–68, 80.

57 **"In Russia, the sovereign is the living law":** Nikolai Karamzin on Czar Alexander I, as quoted in W. Bruce Lincoln, *The Romanovs: Autocrats of All the Russias* (New York: Anchor Books, 1981), 489.

57 **"at the interface of two vast and irreconcilable worlds":** Halperin, *Russia and the Golden Horde,* 126.

57 **"this ceaseless longing":** Fyodor Dostoevsky, *A Writer's Diary* (1881), as quoted in Figes, *Natasha's Dance,* 308.

57 **"orphan cut off from the human family":** Pyotr Chaadaev, "Philosophical Letter" (1829, published 1836), as quoted in Figes, *Natasha's Dance,* 132, and Dmytryshyn, *Imperial Russia,* 251. Chaadaev's commentary struck a nerve and circulated widely, even though the publication was immediately suppressed and the author was declared insane and placed under police supervision.

57 **"Third Rome":** Mikhail Nikiforovich Katkov, May 24, 1882, editorial in *Moskovskie vedomosti (Moscow News),* as excerpted in Verdansky, *A Source Book for Russian History,* 3:676.

58 **"What a people! They are Scythians!":** Figes, *Natasha's Dance,* 150.

58 **"It is to the cause of hastening the true reign":** Lincoln, *The Romanovs,* 404–5.

59 **"There no longer exists an English policy":** Ibid., 405.

59 **"the course, formerly adopted by the powers":** Wilhelm Schwarz, *Die Heilige Allianz* (Stuttgart, 1935), 52.

60 **The vanquished enemy would become:** It was analogous to the decision in 1954 of (West) Germany to join the Atlantic Alliance, less than a decade after its

unconditional surrender at the end of a murderous war against its newfound partners.

63 **"too weak for true ambition":** Klemens von Metternich, *Aus Metternich's nachgelassenen Papieren,* ed. Alfons v. Klinkowstroem (Vienna, 1881), 1:316.

67 **"the contingency of an attack by France":** Palmerston's dispatch no. 6 to the Marquess of Clanricarde (ambassador in St. Petersburg), January 11, 1841, in *The Foreign Policy of Victorian England,* ed. Kenneth Bourne (Oxford: Clarendon Press, 1970), 252–53.

68 **The German philosopher Johann Gottfried von Herder:** See Isaiah Berlin, *Vico and Herder: Two Studies in the History of Ideas* (New York: Viking, 1976), 158, 204.

68 **"Underlying the theory was fact":** Jacques Barzun, *From Dawn to Decadence: 500 Years of Western Cultural Life* (New York: Perennial, 2000), 482.

68 **Linguistic nationalisms made traditional empires:** Sir Lewis Namier, *Vanished Supremacies: Essays on European History, 1812–1918* (New York: Penguin Books, 1958), 203.

69 **"powerful, decisive and wise regents":** Otto von Bismarck, *Die gesammelten Werke,* 3rd ed. (Berlin, 1924), 1: 375.

73 **The war received its name:** The battle was memorialized in classic literature on both sides, including Alfred Tennyson's "Charge of the Light Brigade" and Leo Tolstoy's *Tales of Sevastopol.* See Nicholas V. Riasanovsky, *A History of Russia* (Oxford: Oxford University Press, 2000), 336–39.

73 **"We will astonish the world by the magnitude of our ingratitude":** *Allgemeine deutsche Biographie 33* (Leipzig: Duncker & Humblot, 1891), 266. Metternich left office in 1848.

74 **"Where everything is tottering":** Heinrich Sbrik, *Metternich, der Staatsmann und der Mensch,* 2 vols. (Munich, 1925), 1:354, as cited in Henry A. Kissinger, "The Conservative Dilemma: Reflections on the Political

Thought of Metternich," *American Political Science Review* 48, no. 4 (December 1954): 1027.

75 **"invention is the enemy of history"**: Metternich, *Aus Metternich's nachgelassenen Papieren,* 1:33, 8:184.

75 **For Metternich, the national interest of Austria:** Algernon Cecil, *Metternich, 1773–1859* (London: Eyre and Spottiswood, 1947), 52.

75 **"The great axioms of political science"**: Metternich, *Aus Metternich's nachgelassenen Papieren,* 1:334.

76 **"A sentimental policy knows no reciprocity"**: *Briefwechsel des Generals Leopold von Gerlach mit dem Bundestags-Gesandten Otto von Bismarck* (Berlin, 1893), 334.

76 **"For heaven's sake no sentimental alliances"**: Ibid. (February 20, 1854), 130.

76 **"The only healthy basis of policy"**: Horst Kohl, *Die politischen Reden des Fursten Bismarck* (Stuttgart, 1892), 264.

76 **"Gratitude and confidence will not bring"**: Bismarck, *Die gesammelten Werke* (November 14, 1833), vol. 14, nos. 1, 3.

76 **"Policy is the art of the possible"**: Ibid. (September 29, 1851), 1:62.

77 **"a greater political event than the French Revolution"**: Speech of February 9, 1871, in Hansard, *Parliamentary Debates,* ser. 3, vol. 204 (February–March 1871), 82.

79 **German strategy:** By contrast, Moltke, the architect of Prussian victories in the wars that led to unification, had in his day planned a defense on both fronts.

80 **World War I broke out:** For stimulating accounts of these developments, see Christopher Clark, *The Sleepwalkers: How Europe Went to War in 1914* (New York: HarperCollins, 2013) and Margaret MacMillan, *The War That Ended Peace: The Road to 1914* (New York: Random House, 2013).

85 **In the 1920s, the Germany of the Weimar Republic:** See John Maynard Keynes, *The Economic Consequences of*

the Peace (New York: Macmillan, 1920), Chapter 5.

87 **Their residue would continue:** See Chapters 6 and 7.

Chapter 3: Islamism and the Middle East

97 **"the first deliberate attempt":** Adda B. Bozeman, "Iran: U.S. Foreign Policy and the Tradition of Persian Statecraft," *Orbis* 23, no. 2 (Summer 1979): 397.

98 **That a small group of Arab confederates:** See Hugh Kennedy, *The Great Arab Conquests: How the Spread of Islam Changed the World We Live In* (London: Weidenfeld & Nicholson, 2007), 34–40.

99 **"If you embrace Islam":** Kennedy, *Great Arab Conquests,* 113.

99 **Islam's rapid advance:** See generally Marshall G. S. Hodgson, *The Venture of Islam: Conscience and History in a World Civilization,* vol. 1, *The Classical Age of Islam* (Chicago: University of Chicago Press, 1974).

102 **"The dar al-Islam":** Majid Khadduri, *The Islamic Law of Nations: Shaybani's Siyar* (Baltimore: Johns Hopkins University Press, 1966), 13.

102 **"by his heart; his tongue":** Majid Khadduri, *War and Peace in the Law of Islam* (Baltimore: Johns Hopkins University Press, 1955), 56. See also Kennedy, *Great Arab Conquests,* 48–51; Bernard Lewis, *The Middle East: A Brief History of the Last 2,000 Years* (New York: Touchstone, 1997), 233–38.

103 **Other religions—especially Christianity:** To the extent that democracy and human rights now serve to inspire actions in the service of global transformation, their content and applicability have proven far more flexible than the previous dictates of scripture proselytized in the wake of advancing armies. After all, the democratic will of different peoples can call forth vastly different outcomes.

104 **"Islamic legal rulings stipulate":** Labeeb Ahmed Bsoul, *International*

Treaties (Muʿāhadāt) *in Islam: Theory and Practice in the Light of Islamic International Law* (Siyar) *According to Orthodox Schools* (Lanham, Md.: University Press of America, 2008), 117.

104 **"The communities of the dar al-harb":** Khadduri, *Islamic Law of Nations,* 12. See also Bsoul, *International Treaties,* 108–9.

105 **In the idealized version of this worldview:** See James Piscatori, "Islam in the International Order," in *The Expansion of International Society,* ed. Hedley Bull and Adam Watson (New York: Oxford University Press, 1985), 318–19; Lewis, *Middle East,* 305; Olivier Roy, *Globalized Islam: The Search for a New Ummah* (New York: Columbia University Press, 2004), 112 (on contemporary Islamist views); Efraim Karsh, *Islamic Imperialism: A History* (New Haven, Conn.: Yale University Press, 2006), 230–31. But see Khadduri, *War and Peace in the Law of Islam,* 156–57 (on the traditional conditions under which territory captured by non-Muslims might revert to being part of *dar al-harb*).

106 **These factions eventually formed:** An analysis of this schism and its modern implications may be found in Vali Nasr, *The Shia Revival: How Conflicts Within Islam Will Shape the Future* (New York: W. W. Norton, 2006).

108 **"the order of the world":** Brendan Simms, *Europe: The Struggle for Supremacy from 1453 to the Present* (New York: Basic Books, 2013), 9–10; Black, *History of Islamic Political Thought,* 206–7.

108 **In this context, formal Ottoman documents:** These were called, misleadingly in English, "capitulations"—not because the Ottoman Empire had "capitulated" on any point, but because they were divided into chapters or articles (*capitula* in Latin).

109 **"I who am the Sultan of Sultans":** Answer from Suleiman I to Francis I of France, February 1526, as quoted in Roger Bigelow Merriman, *Suleiman the Magnificent, 1520–1566* (Cambridge, Mass.: Harvard University Press, 1944), 130. See also Halil Inalcik, "The Turkish Impact on the Development of Modern Europe," in *The Ottoman State and Its Place in World History,* ed. Kemal H. Karpat (Leiden: E. J. Brill, 1974), 51–53; Garrett Mattingly, *Renaissance Diplomacy* (New York: Penguin Books, 1955), 152. Roughly five hundred years later, during a period of strained bilateral relations, Turkey's Prime Minister Recep Tayyip Erdogan presented a ceremonial copy of the letter to French President Nicolas Sarkozy but complained, "I think he did not read it." "Turkey's Erdoğan: French Vote Reveals Gravity of Hostility Towards Muslims," *Today's Zaman,* December 23, 2011.

110 **"the Sick Man of Europe":** In 1853, Czar Nicholas I of Russia was reputed to have told the British ambassador, "We have a sick man on our hands, a man gravely ill, it will be a great misfortune if one of these days he slips through our hands, especially before the necessary arrangements are made." Harold Temperley, *England and the Near East* (London: Longmans, Green, 1936), 272.

111 **"attacks dealt against the Caliphate":** Sultan Mehmed-Rashad, "Proclamation," and Sheik-ul-Islam, "Fetva," in *Source Records of the Great War,* ed. Charles F. Horne and Walter F. Austin (Indianapolis: American Legion, 1930), 2:398–401. See also Hew Strachan, *The First World War* (New York: Viking, 2003), 100–101.

112 **"the establishment in Palestine":** Arthur James Balfour to Walter Rothschild, November 2, 1917, in Malcolm Yapp, *The Making of the Modern Near East, 1792–1923* (Harlow: Longmans, Green), 290.

113 **Two opposing trends appeared:** See Erez Manela, *The Wilsonian Moment: Self-Determination and the International*

Origins of Anticolonial Nationalism, 1917–1920 (Oxford: Oxford University Press, 2007).

118 **From its early days as an informal gathering:** See Roxanne L. Euben and Muhammad Qasim Zaman, eds., *Princeton Readings in Islamist Thought: Texts and Contexts from al-Banna to Bin Laden* (Princeton, N.J.: Princeton University Press, 2009), 49–53.

119 **"which was brilliant":** Hassan al-Banna, "Toward the Light," in ibid., 58–59.

119 **"Then the fatherland of the Muslim expands":** Ibid., 61–62.

120 **Where possible, this fight would be gradualist:** Ibid., 68–70.

120 **"low associations based on race":** Sayyid Qutb, *Milestones,* 2nd rev. English ed. (Damascus, Syria: Dar al-Ilm, n.d.), 49–51.

121 **"the achievement of the freedom of man":** Ibid., 59–60, 72, 84, 137.

121 **core of committed followers:** For a discussion of the evolution from Qutb to bin Laden, see Lawrence Wright, *The Looming Tower: Al-Qaeda and the Road to 9/11* (New York: Random House, 2006).

122 **"freedom":** Barack Obama, Remarks by the President in Joint Press Conference with Prime Minister Harper of Canada, February 4, 2011; interview with Fox News, February 6, 2011; Statement by President Barack Obama on Egypt; February 10, 2011; "Remarks by the President on Egypt" February 11, 2011.

126 **"The future of Syria":** Statement by the President on the Situation in Syria, August 18, 2011, http://www.whitehouse.gov/the-press-office/2011/08/18/statement-president-obama-situation-syria.

128 **The main parties thought themselves:** Mariam Karouny, "Apocalyptic Prophecies Drive Both Sides to Syrian Battle for End of Time," Reuters, April 1, 2014.

138 **deploying military personnel to Saudi Arabia:** On Riyadh's request, to deter

any attempt by Saddam Hussein to seize Saudi oil fields.

138 **Osama bin Laden had preceded the attack:** See "Message from Usama Bin-Muhammad Bin Ladin to His Muslim Brothers in the Whole World and Especially in the Arabian Peninsula: Declaration of Jihad Against the Americans Occupying the Land of the Two Holy Mosques; Expel the Heretics from the Arabian Peninsula," in FBIS Report, "Compilation of Usama bin Ladin Statements, 1994–January 2004," 13; Piscatori, "Order, Justice, and Global Islam," 279–80.

143 **When states are not governed:** For an exposition of this phenomenon, see David Danelo, "Anarchy Is the New Normal: Unconventional Governance and 21st Century Statecraft" (Foreign Policy Research Institute, October 2013).

Chapter 4: The United States and Iran

146 **"Today what lies in front of our eyes":** Ali Khamenei, "Leader's Speech at Inauguration of Islamic Awakening and Ulama Conference" (April 29, 2013), *Islamic Awakening* 1, no. 7 (Spring 2013).

147 **"This final goal cannot be anything":** Ibid.

148 **"The developments in the U.S.":** Islamic Invitation Turkey, "The Leader of Islamic Ummah and Oppressed People Imam Sayyed Ali Khamenei: Islamic Awakening Inspires Intl. Events," November 27, 2011.

149 **The Persian ideal of monarchy:** Among the most famous instances of this tradition was the sixth-century B.C. liberation of captive peoples, including the Jews, from Babylon by the Persian Emperor Cyrus, founder of the Achaemenid Empire. After entering Babylon and displacing its ruler, the self-proclaimed "king of the four quarters of the world" decreed that all Babylonian captives would be free to return home and that all religions

would be tolerated. With his pioneering embrace of religious pluralism, Cyrus is believed to have been an inspiration over two millennia later for Thomas Jefferson, who read an account in Xenophon's *Cyropedia* and commented favorably. See "The Cyrus Cylinder: Diplomatic Whirl," *Economist,* March 23, 2013.

150 **"Most of all they hold in honor":** Herodotus, *The History,* trans. David Grene (Chicago: University of Chicago Press, 1987), 1.131–135, pp. 95–97.

150 **"The President of the United States":** Kenneth M. Pollack, *The Persian Puzzle: The Conflict Between Iran and America* (New York: Random House, 2004), 18–19. See also John Garver, *China and Iran: Ancient Partners in a Post-imperial World* (Seattle: University of Washington Press, 2006).

151 **"great interior spaces":** See Roy Mottahedeh, *The Mantle of the Prophet: Religion and Politics in Iran* (Oxford: Oneworld, 2002), 144; Reza Aslan, "The Epic of Iran," *New York Times,* April 30, 2006. Abolqasem Ferdowsi's epic *Book of Kings,* composed two centuries after the arrival of Islam in Persia, recounted the legendary glories of Persia's pre-Muslim past. Ferdowsi, a Shia Muslim, captured the complex Persian attitude by penning a lament spoken by one of his characters at the end of an era: "Damn this world, damn this time, damn this fate, / That uncivilized Arabs have come to make me Muslim."

152 **"prudential dissimulation":** See Sandra Mackey, *The Iranians: Persia, Islam, and the Soul of a Nation* (New York: Plume, 1998), 109n1.

153 **"imperialists":** Ruhollah Khomeini, "Islamic Government," in *Islam and Revolution: Writings and Declarations of Imam Khomeini (1941–1980),* trans. Hamid Algar (North Haledon, N.J.: Mizan Press, 1981), 48–49.

153 **"the relations between nations":** As quoted in David Armstrong, *Revolution and World Order: The Revolutionary*

State in International Society (New York: Oxford University Press, 1993), 192.

153 **"an Islamic government":** Khomeini, "Islamic Government," "The First Day of God's Government," and "The Religious Scholars Led the Revolt," in *Islam and Revolution,* 147, 265, 330–31.

153 **"What was wanted":** R. W. Apple Jr., "Will Khomeini Turn Iran's Clock Back 1,300 Years?," *New York Times,* February 4, 1979.

153 **Amidst these upheavals a new paradox:** See Charles Hill, *Trial of a Thousand Years: World Order and Islamism* (Stanford, Calif.: Hoover Institution Press, 2011), 89–91.

155 **Tehran's imperative:** Accounts of this phenomenon, carried out largely covertly, are necessarily incomplete. Some have suggested limited cooperation, or at least tacit accommodations, between Tehran and the Taliban and al-Qaeda. See, for example, Thomas Kean, Lee Hamilton, et al., *The 9/11 Commission Report* (New York: W. W. Norton, 2004), 61, 128, 240–41, 468, 529; Seth G. Jones, "Al Qaeda in Iran," *Foreign Affairs,* January 29, 2012, http://www .foreignaffairs.com/articles/137061/ seth-g-jones/al-qaeda-in-iran.

155 **"This lofty and great author":** Akbar Ganji, "Who Is Ali Khamenei: The Worldview of Iran's Supreme Leader," *Foreign Affairs,* September/October 2013. See also Thomas Joscelyn, "Iran, the Muslim Brotherhood, and Revolution," Longwarjournal.org, January 28, 2011.

156 **"In accordance with the sacred verse":** Constitution of the Islamic Republic of Iran (October 24, 1979), as amended, Section I, Article 11.

156 **"We must strive to export our Revolution":** Khomeini, "New Year's Message" (March 21, 1980), in *Islam and Revolution,* 286.

156 **temporarily exercises:** This status is set out in Iran's constitution: "During the occultation of the Wali al-'Asr [the

Guardian of the Era, the Hidden Imam] (may God hasten his reappearance), the leadership of the Ummah [Muslim community] devolves upon the just and pious person, who is fully aware of the circumstances of his age, courageous, resourceful, and possessed of administrative ability, will assume the responsibilities of this office in accordance with Article 107." Constitution of the Islamic Republic of Iran (October 24, 1979), as amended, Section I, Article 5. In the Iranian revolution's climactic phases, Khomeini did not discourage suggestions that he was the Mahdi returned from occultation, or at least the forerunner of this phenomenon. See Milton Viorst, *In the Shadow of the Prophet: The Struggle for the Soul of Islam* (Boulder, Colo.: Westview Press, 2001), 192.

156 **"Without any doubt":** "Address by H.E. Dr. Mahmoud Ahmadinejad, President of the Islamic Republic of Iran, Before the Sixty-second Session of the United Nations General Assembly" (New York: Permanent Mission of the Islamic Republic of Iran to the United Nations, September 25, 2007), 10.

157 **"Vasalam Ala Man Ataba'al hoda":** Mahmoud Ahmadinejad to George W. Bush, May 7, 2006, Council on Foreign Relations online library; "Iran Declares War," *New York Sun,* May 11, 2006.

158 **"By dressing up America's face":** As quoted in Arash Karami, "Ayatollah Khamenei: Nuclear Negotiations Won't Resolve US-Iran Differences," Al-Monitor.com Iran Pulse, February 17, 2014, http://iranpulse.al-monitor.com/index.php/2014/02/3917/ayatollah -khamenei-nuclear-negotiations-wont -resolve-us-iran-differences/.

158 **"When a wrestler is wrestling":** As quoted in Akbar Ganji, "Frenemies Forever: The Real Meaning of Iran's 'Heroic Flexibility,'" *Foreign Affairs,* September 24, 2013, http://www .foreignaffairs.com/articles/139953/ akbar-ganji/frenemies-forever.

161 **Plutonium enrichment:** Two types of material have been used to drive nuclear explosions—enriched uranium and plutonium. Because the control of a plutonium reaction is generally seen as a technically more complex task than the equivalent work required to produce an explosion using enriched uranium, most attempts to prevent a breakout capability have focused on closing the route to uranium enrichment. (Plutonium reactors are also fueled by uranium, requiring some access to uranium and familiarity with uranium-processing technology.) Iran has moved toward both a uranium-enrichment and a plutonium-production capability, both of which have been the subject of negotiations.

163 **The process resulted in the November 2013:** This account of the negotiating record makes reference to events and proposals described in a number of sources, including the Arms Control Association, "History of Official Proposals on the Iranian Nuclear Issue," January 2013; Lyse Doucet, "Nuclear Talks: New Approach for Iran at Almaty," BBC.co.uk, February 28, 2013; David Feith, "How Iran Went Nuclear," *Wall Street Journal,* March 2, 2013; Lara Jakes and Peter Leonard, "World Powers Coax Iran into Saving Nuclear Talks," *Miami Herald,* February 27, 2013; Semira N. Nikou, "Timeline of Iran's Nuclear Activities" (United States Institute of Peace, 2014); "Timeline: Iranian Nuclear Dispute," Reuters, June 17, 2012; Hassan Rohani, "Beyond the Challenges Facing Iran and the IAEA Concerning the Nuclear Dossier" (speech to the Supreme Cultural Revolution Council), *Rahbord,* September 30, 2005, 7–38, FBIS-IAP20060113336001; Steve Rosen, "Did Iran Offer a 'Grand Bargain' in 2003?," *American Thinker,* November 16, 2008; and Joby Warrick and Jason Rezaian, "Iran Nuclear Talks End on Upbeat Note," *Washington Post,* February 27, 2013.

166 **"The reason for the emphasis":**
Ayatollah Ali Khamenei, remarks to
members of the Iranian Majles
(Parliament), Fars News Agency, as
translated and excerpted in KGS
NightWatch news report, May 26, 2014.

169 **Administration spokesmen:** David
Remnick, "Going the Distance," *New
Yorker,* January 27, 2014.

170 **"Today we are embarking":** Address
by Yitzhak Rabin to a joint session of
the U.S. Congress, July 26, 1994, online
archive of the Yitzhak Rabin Center.

Chapter 5: The Multiplicity of Asia

172 **Until the arrival:** Philip Bowring,
"What Is 'Asia'?," *Far Eastern Economic
Review,* February 12, 1987.

178 **"the basic principle of modern
international relations":** Qi Jianguo,
"An Unprecedented Great Changing
Situation: Understanding and Thoughts
on the Global Strategic Situation and
Our Country's National Security
Environment," *Xuexi shibao [Study
Times],* January 21, 2013, trans. James A.
Bellacqua and Daniel M. Hartnett
(Washington, D.C.: CNA, April 2013).

179 **In Asia's historical diplomatic systems:**
See Immanuel C. Y. Hsu, *The Rise of
Modern China* (New York: Oxford
University Press, 2000), 315–17; Thant
Myint-U, *Where China Meets India*
(New York: Farrar, Straus and Giroux,
2011), 77–78; John W. Garver,
*Protracted Contest: Sino-Indian Rivalry
in the Twentieth Century* (Seattle:
University of Washington Press, 2001),
138–40; Lucian W. Pye, *Asian Power
and Politics* (Cambridge, Mass.:
Harvard University Press, 1985), 95–99;
Brotton, *History of the World in Twelve
Maps,* chap. 4.

181 **Yet in a region:** See, for example, David
C. Kang, *East Asia Before the West: Five
Centuries of Trade and Tribute* (New
York: Columbia University Press, 2010),
77–81.

182 **At the apex of Japan's society:** Kenneth
B. Pyle, *Japan Rising* (New York: Public
Affairs, 2007), 37.

182 **"Japan is the divine country":** John W.
Dower, *War Without Mercy: Race and

Power in the Pacific War (New York:
Pantheon, 1986), 222.

183 **In 1590, the warrior Toyotomi
Hideyoshi:** See Samuel Hawley, *The
Imjin War: Japan's Sixteenth-Century
Invasion of Korea and Attempt to
Conquer China* (Seoul: Royal Asiatic
Society, Korea Branch, 2005).

183 **After five years of inconclusive
negotiations:** Kang, *East Asia Before the
West,* 1–2, 93–97.

184 **strict diplomatic equality:** Hidemi
Suganami, "Japan's Entry into
International Society," in Bull and
Watson, *Expansion of International
Society,* 187.

184 **Chinese traders were permitted to
operate:** Marius Jansen, *The Making
of Modern Japan* (Cambridge, Mass.:
Belknap Press of Harvard University
Press, 2002), 87.

184 **"edict to expel foreigners":** Suganami,
"Japan's Entry into International
Society," 186–89.

185 **"If your imperial majesty":** President
Millard Fillmore to the Emperor of
Japan (presented by Commodore Perry
on July 14, 1853), in Francis Hawks and
Matthew Perry, *Narrative of the
Expedition of an American Squadron to
the China Seas and Japan, Performed in
the Years 1852, 1853, and 1854, Under the
Command of Commodore M. C. Perry,
United States Navy, by Order of the
Government of the United States*
(Washington, D.C.: A. O. P. Nicholson,
1856), 256–57.

185 **"most positively forbidden by the
laws":** Translation of the Japanese reply
to President Fillmore's letter, in ibid.,
349–50.

186 **"1. By this oath":** Meiji Charter Oath,
in *Japanese Government Documents,* ed.
W. W. McLaren (Bethesda, Md.:
University Publications of America,
1979), 8.

188 **"New Order in Asia":** Japanese
memorandum delivered to the
American Secretary of State Cordell
Hull, December 7, 1941, as quoted in
Pyle, *Japan Rising,* 207.

190 **Having established:** See, for example,
Yasuhiro Nakasone, "A Critical View of

the Postwar Constitution" (1953), in
Sources of Japanese Tradition, ed. Wm.
Theodore de Bary, Carol Gluck, and
Arthur E. Tiedemann (New York:
Columbia University Press, 2005),
2:1088–89. Nakasone delivered the
speech while sojourning at Harvard as a
member of the International Seminar, a
program for young leaders seeking
exposure to an American academic
environment. He argued that in the
interest of "accelerating permanent
friendship between Japan and the
United States," Japan's independent
defense capability should be
strengthened and its relations with its
American partner put on a more equal
footing. When Nakasone became Prime
Minister three decades later, he pursued
these policies to great effect with his
counterpart Ronald Reagan.

191 "as Japan's security environment":
National Security Strategy (Provisional
Translation) (Tokyo: Ministry of
Foreign Affairs, December 17, 2013),
1–3. The document, adopted by Japan's
Cabinet, stated that its principles "will
guide Japan's national security policy
over the next decade."

192 "the long and diversified history":
S. Radhakrishnan, "Hinduism," in *A
Cultural History of India,* ed. A. L.
Basham (New Delhi: Oxford
University Press, 1997), 60–82.

192 "in search of Christians and spices":
Such was the Portuguese explorer
Vasco da Gama's explanation to the
King of Calicut (the present-day
Kozhikode, India, then a center of the
global spice trade). Da Gama and his
crew rejoiced at the opportunity to
profit from the thriving Indian trade in
spices and precious stones. They were
also influenced by the legend of the lost
realm of "Prester John," a powerful
Christian king believed by many
medieval and early-modern Europeans
to reside somewhere in Africa or Asia.
See Daniel Boorstin, *The Discoverers*
(New York: Vintage Books, 1985),
104–6, 176–77.

193 The Hindu classic: *The Bhagavad Gita,*
trans. Eknath Easwaran (Tomales,

Calif.: Nilgiri Press, 2007), 82–91;
Amartya Sen, *The Argumentative
Indian: Writings on Indian History,
Culture, and Identity* (New York:
Picador, 2005), 3–6.

194 Against the background of the eternal:
See Pye, *Asian Power and Politics,*
137–41.

195 "The conqueror shall [always]":
Kautilya, *Arthashastra,* trans. L. N.
Rangarajan (New Delhi: Penguin
Books India, 1992), 6.2.35–37, p. 525.

196 "If . . . the conqueror is superior":
Ibid., 9.1.1, p. 588. Prussia's Frederick
the Great, on the eve of his seizure of
the wealthy Austrian province of
Silesia roughly two thousand years
later, made a similar assessment. See
Chapter 1.

196 "The Conqueror shall think of the
circle": Ibid., 6.2.39–40, p. 526.

196 "undertake such works as would":
Ibid., 9.1.21, p. 589.

196 "make one neighboring king fight":
Ibid., 7.6.14, 15, p. 544.

197 "all states of the circle": See Roger
Boesche, *The First Great Political
Realist: Kautilya and His "Arthashastra"*
(Lanham, Md.: Lexington Books,
2002), 46; Kautilya, *Arthashastra,*
7.13.43, 7.2.16, 9.1.1–16, pp. 526, 538,
588–89.

197 To be sure, Kautilya insisted: In
Kautilya's concept, the realm of a
universal conqueror was "the area
extending from the Himalayas in the
north to the sea in the south and a
thousand *yojanas* wide from east to
west"—effectively modern-day
Pakistan, India, and Bangladesh.
Kautilya, *Arthashastra,* 9.1.17, p. 589.

197 The *Arthashastra* advised: See
Boesche, *First Great Political Realist,*
38–42, 51–54, 88–89.

197 "truly radical 'Machiavellianism'":
Max Weber, "Politics as a Vocation," as
quoted in ibid., 7.

197 Whether following the *Arthashastra's*
prescriptions: Asoka is today revered
for his preaching of Buddhism and
nonviolence; he adopted these only after
his conquests were complete, and they
served to buttress his rule.

198 "grafted to the Greater Middle East": Robert Kaplan, *The Revenge of Geography: What the Map Tells Us About Coming Conflicts and the Battle Against Fate* (New York: Random House, 2012), 237.

198 "We seem, as it were, to have conquered": John Robert Seeley, *The Expansion of England: Two Courses of Lectures* (London: Macmillan, 1891), 8.

200 "There is not, and never was an India": Sir John Strachey, *India* (London: Kegan, Paul, Trench, 1888), as quoted in Ramachandra Guha, *India After Gandhi: The History of the World's Largest Democracy* (New York: Ecco, 2007), 3.

201 "Whatever policy you may lay down": Jawaharlal Nehru, "India's Foreign Policy" (speech delivered at the Constituent Assembly, New Delhi, December 4, 1947), in *Independence and After: A Collection of Speeches, 1946–1949* (New York: John Day, 1950), 204–5.

202 "We propose to avoid entanglement": As quoted in Baldev Raj Nayar and T. V. Paul, *India in the World Order: Searching for Major-Power Status* (New York: Cambridge University Press, 2003), 124–25.

203 "It would have been absurd": As quoted in ibid., 125.

203 "Are we, the countries of Asia and Africa": Jawaharlal Nehru, "Speech to the Bandung Conference Political Committee" (1955), as printed in G. M. Kahin, *The Asian-African Conference* (Ithaca, N.Y.: Cornell University Press, 1956), 70.

205 "(1) mutual respect": "Agreement (with Exchange of Notes) on Trade and Intercourse Between Tibet Region of China and India, Signed at Peking, on 29 April 1954," United Nations Treaty Series, vol. 299 (1958), 70.

206 Treated as provisional: As of this writing, Afghanistan does not officially recognize any territorial border with Pakistan; India and Pakistan dispute the Kashmir region; India and China dispute Aksai Chin and Arunachal

Pradesh and fought a war over these territories in 1962; India and Bangladesh have expressed a commitment to negotiate a resolution of the dozens of exclaves in each other's territory but have not ratified an agreement resolving the issue and have clashed over the patrol of these territories.

206 the larger Muslim world: See Pew Research Center Forum on Religion and Public Life, *The Global Religious Landscape: A Report on the Size and Distribution of the World's Major Religious Groups as of 2010* (Washington, D.C.: Pew Research Center, 2012), 22.

209 geographically an Asian power: "European Russia," or Russia west of the Ural Mountains, constitutes roughly the westernmost quarter of Russia's landmass.

Chapter 6: Toward an Asian Order

213 "Sinocentric": See Mark Mancall, "The Ch'ing Tribute System: An Interpretive Essay," in *The Chinese World Order,* ed. John K. Fairbank (Cambridge, Mass.: Harvard University Press, 1968), 63.

214 A Chinese foreign ministry: See Mark Mancall, *China at the Center: 300 Years of Foreign Policy* (New York: Free Press, 1984), 16–20; Jonathan Spence, *The Search for Modern China,* 2nd ed. (New York: W. W. Norton, 1999), 197–202.

215 "To give them . . . elaborate clothes": Ying-shih Yü, *Trade and Expansion in Han China: A Study in the Structure of Sino-Barbarian Economic Relations* (Berkeley: University of California Press, 1967), 37.

217 "Swaying the wide world": Qianlong's First Edict to King George III (September 1793), in *The Search for Modern China: A Documentary Collection,* ed. Pei-kai Cheng, Michael Lestz, and Jonathan Spence (New York: W. W. Norton, 1999), 105.

217 England's Prince Regent: Governing in the place of King George III,

whose mental faculties had deteriorated.

218 **"henceforward no more envoys":** "The Emperor of China," *Chinese Recorder* 29, no. 10 (1898): 471–73.

219 **"Having, with reverence, received":** *Papers Relating to Foreign Affairs Accompanying the Annual Message of the President to the First Session of the Thirty-eighth Congress* (Washington, D.C.: U.S. Government Printing Office, 1864), Document No. 33 ("Mr. Burlingame to Mr. Seward, Peking, January 29, 1863"), 2:846–48.

219 **"During the past forty years":** James Legge, *The Chinese Classics; with a Translation, Critical and Exegetical Notes, Prolegomena, and Copious Indexes,* vol. 5, pt. 1 (Hong Kong: Lane, Crawford, 1872), 52–53.

221 **Though emerging as one of the victorious:** See Rana Mitter, *Forgotten Ally: China's World War II, 1937–1945* (Boston: Houghton Mifflin Harcourt, 2013).

222 **"The cycle, which is endless":** "Sixty Points on Working Methods—a Draft Resolution from the Office of the Centre of the CPC: 19.2.1958," in *Mao Papers: Anthology and Bibliography,* ed. Jerome Ch'en (London: Oxford University Press, 1970), 63–66.

224 **Interestingly, a CIA analysis:** "National Intelligence Estimate 13-7-70: Communist China's International Posture" (November 12, 1970), in *Tracking the Dragon: National Intelligence Estimates on China During the Era of Mao, 1948–1976,* ed. John Allen, John Carver, and Tom Elmore (Pittsburgh: Government Printing Office, 2004), 593–94.

228 **A Harvard study:** See Graham Allison, "Obama and Xi Must Think Broadly to Avoid a Classic Trap," *New York Times,* June 6, 2013; Richard Rosecrance, *The Resurgence of the West: How a Transatlantic Union Can Prevent War and Restore the United States and Europe* (New Haven, Conn.: Yale University Press, 2013).

229 **America's so-called pivot policy:** In a speech of February 13, 2009, Secretary of State Hillary Clinton announced the Obama administration's "Pivot to East Asia" regional strategy, the extent of which has yet to be fully elaborated.

230 **"Actually, national sovereignty":** As quoted in Zhu Majie, "Deng Xiaoping's Human Rights Theory," in *Cultural Impact on International Relations,* ed. Yu Xintian, Chinese Philosophical Studies (Washington, D.C.: Council for Research in Values and Philosophy, 2002), 81.

232 **number of players is small:** Europe before World War I was reduced to five players by the unification of Germany; see Chapter 2.

Chapter 7: "Acting for All Mankind"

235 **"liberty according to English ideas":** "Speech on Conciliation with America" (1775), in Edmund Burke, *On Empire, Liberty, and Reform: Speeches and Letters,* ed. David Bromwich (New Haven, Conn.: Yale University Press, 2000), 81–83. Burke sympathized with the American Revolution because he considered it a natural evolution of English liberties. He opposed the French Revolution, which he believed wrecked what generations had wrought and, with it, the prospect of organic growth.

235 **In New England:** Alexis de Tocqueville, "Concerning Their Point of Departure," in *Democracy in America,* trans. George Lawrence (New York: Harper & Row, 1969), 46–47.

236 **"We feel that we are acting":** Paul Leicester Ford, ed., *The Writings of Thomas Jefferson* (New York: G. P. Putnam's Sons, 1892–99), 8:158–59, quoted in Robert W. Tucker and David C. Hendrickson, *Empire of Liberty: The Statecraft of Thomas Jefferson* (New York: Oxford University Press, 1990), 11.

236 **"candidly confess[ed]:** Jefferson to Monroe, October 24, 1823, as excerpted in "Continental Policy of the United

States: The Acquisition of Cuba," *United States Magazine and Democratic Review,* April 1859, 23.

236 **"We should then have only to include the North":** Jefferson to Madison, April 27, 1809, in ibid.

238 **For the early settlers:** This was largely true for settlers from England and Northern Europe. Those from Spain largely saw it as a territory to be exploited and inhabited by natives to be converted to Christianity.

238 **"We shall find that the God of Israel":** John Winthrop, "A Model of Christian Charity" (1630). See Brendan Simms, *Europe,* 36.

239 **"an empire in many respects":** Publius [Alexander Hamilton], *The Federalist* 1, in Alexander Hamilton, James Madison, and John Jay, *The Federalist Papers* (New York: Mentor, 1961), 1–2. The use of "empire" here denoted a totally sovereign independent entity.

240 **"our manifest destiny":** John O'Sullivan, "Annexation," *United States Magazine and Democratic Review,* July–August 1845, 5.

241 **"America, in the assembly of nations":** John Quincy Adams, "An Address Delivered at the Request of the Committee of Citizens of Washington, 4 July 1821" (Washington, D.C.: Davis and Force, 1821), 28–29.

242 **"[America] goes not abroad":** Ibid.

242 **"Besides, it is well known":** Jedidiah Morse, *The American Geography; or, A View of the Present Situation of the United States of America,* 2nd ed. (London: John Stockdale, 1792), 468–69, as excerpted in *Manifest Destiny and American Territorial Expansion: A Brief History with Documents,* ed. Amy S. Greenberg (Boston: Bedford/St. Martin's, 2012), 53.

242 **"travelling from east to west":** That is, the "translatio imperii mundi"—transfer of the rule of the world—that had theoretically seen the seat of paramount political power travel across time and space: from Babylon and Persia, to Greece, to Rome, to France or

Germany, thence to Britain, and, Morse supposed, to America. Also the famous line of George Berkeley in his "Verses on the Prospect of Planting Arts and Learning in America":

> *Westward the course of empire takes its way;*
> *The four first Acts already past,*
> *A fifth shall close the Drama with the day;*
> *Time's noblest offspring is the last.*

243 **"The American people having derived":** John O'Sullivan, "The Great Nation of Futurity," *United States Magazine and Democratic Review,* November 1839, 426–27.

244 **"Though they should cast into the opposite":** O'Sullivan, "Annexation," 9–10.

244 **As the United States experienced total war:** See Amanda Foreman, *A World on Fire: Britain's Crucial Role in the American Civil War* (New York: Random House, 2011); Howard Jones, *Blue and Gray Diplomacy: A History of Union and Confederate Foreign Relations* (Chapel Hill: University of North Carolina Press, 2009).

245 **all but disbanded it:** Foreman, *World on Fire,* 784. The U.S. Army went from 1,034,064 men at arms at the close of the Civil War to 54,302 regular troops and 11,000 volunteers eighteen months later.

245 **In 1890, the American army ranked:** Fareed Zakaria, *From Wealth to Power: The Unusual Origins of America's World Role* (Princeton, N.J.: Princeton University Press, 1998), 47.

245 **"any departure from that foreign policy":** Grover Cleveland, First Inaugural Address, March 4, 1885, in *The Public Papers of Grover Cleveland* (Washington, D.C.: Government Printing Office, 1889), 8.

245 **"To-day the United States is practically":** Thomas G. Paterson, J. Garry Clifford, and Kenneth J. Hagan, *American Foreign Policy: A History* (Lexington, Mass.: D. C. Heath, 1977), 189.

247 **"To us as a people":** Theodore
Roosevelt, Inaugural Address, March 4,
1905, in *United States Congressional
Serial Set* 484 (Washington, D.C.:
Government Printing Office,
1905), 559.

248 **"In new and wild communities":**
Theodore Roosevelt, "International
Peace," Nobel lecture, May 5, 1910, in
Peace: 1901–1925: Nobel Lectures
(Singapore: World Scientific Publishing
Co., 1999), 106.

249 **"As yet there is no likelihood":**
Roosevelt's statement to Congress, 1902,
quoted in John Morton Blum, *The
Republican Roosevelt* (Cambridge,
Mass.: Harvard University Press,
1967), 137.

249 **"It is . . . a melancholy fact":** Roosevelt
to Spring Rice, December 21, 1907, in
*The Selected Letters of Theodore
Roosevelt,* ed. H. W. Brands (Lanham,
Md.: Rowman & Littlefield, 2001), 465.

249 **"we need a large navy":** Theodore
Roosevelt, review of *The Influence of
Sea Power upon History,* by Alfred
Thayer Mahan, *Atlantic Monthly,*
October 1890.

250 **"grasp the points of vantage":**
Theodore Roosevelt, "The Strenuous
Life," in *The Strenuous Life: Essays and
Addresses* (New York: Century, 1905), 9.

250 **This was an astonishingly ambitious:**
When German and British warships
cruised toward chronically indebted
Venezuela in 1902 to enforce a long-
overdue loan, Roosevelt demanded
assurances that they would seek no
territorial or political aggrandizement
by way of repayment. When the
German representative promised only
to forgo "permanent" territorial
acquisitions (leaving open the
possibility of a ninety-nine-year
concession, as Britain had achieved
under similar circumstances in Egypt,
and Britain and Germany had in
China), Roosevelt threatened war.
Thereupon he ordered an American
fleet south and distributed maps of the
Venezuelan harbor to the media. The
gambit worked. While Roosevelt
remained silent to allow Kaiser
Wilhelm a face-saving way out of the
crisis, imperial Germany's ambitions in
Venezuela were given a decisive rebuke.
See Edmund Morris, *Theodore Rex*
(New York: Random House, 2001),
176–82.

250 **"wrongdoing or impotence":** Theodore
Roosevelt's Annual Message to
Congress for 1904, HR 58A-K2,
Records of the U.S. House of
Representatives, RG 233, Center for
Legislative Archives, National
Archives.

250 **"All that this country desires":** Ibid.

251 **Backing up this ambitious concept:** To
demonstrate the strength of the
American commitment, Roosevelt
personally visited the Canal Zone
construction project, the first time a
sitting president had left the continental
United States.

252 **"pursued a policy of consistent
opposition":** Morris, *Theodore Rex,* 389.

252 **"make demands on [the] Hawaiian
Islands":** Ibid., 397.

252 **"should be left face to face with
Japan":** Roosevelt's statement to
Congress, 1904, quoted in Blum,
Republican Roosevelt, 134.

252 **"practice cruise around the world":**
Morris, *Theodore Rex,* 495.

253 **"I do not believe there will be war
with Japan":** Letter to Kermit
Roosevelt, April 19, 1908, in Brands,
Selected Letters, 482–83.

253 **"I wish to impress upon you":**
Roosevelt to Admiral Charles S. Sperry,
March 21, 1908, in ibid., 479.

254 **"Do you not believe that if Germany":**
Roosevelt to Hugo Munsterberg,
October 3, 1914, in ibid., 823.

254 **civilization would spread:** See James R.
Holmes, *Theodore Roosevelt and World
Order: Police Power in International
Relations* (Washington, D.C.: Potomac
Books, 2007), 10–13, 68–74.

254 **"Our words must be judged by our
deeds":** Roosevelt, "International
Peace," 103.

254 "We must always remember":
Roosevelt to Carnegie, August 6, 1906,
in Brands, *Selected Letters,* 423.

257 "It was as if": Woodrow Wilson,
Commencement Address at the U.S.
Military Academy at West Point (June
13, 1916), in *Papers of Woodrow Wilson,*
ed. Arthur S. Link (Princeton, N.J.:
Princeton University Press, 1982),
37:212.

257 "the culminating and final war":
Woodrow Wilson, Address to a Joint
Session of Congress on the Conditions
of Peace (January 8, 1918) ("Fourteen
Points"), as quoted in A. Scott Berg,
Wilson (New York: G. P. Putnam's
Sons, 2013), 471.

258 "cooling off": In all, the United States
entered such arbitration compacts with
Bolivia, Brazil, Chile, China, Costa
Rica, Denmark, Ecuador, France,
Great Britain, Guatemala, Honduras,
Italy, Norway, Paraguay, Peru,
Portugal, Russia, and Spain. It began
negotiations with Sweden, Uruguay,
the Argentine Republic, the Dominican
Republic, Greece, the Netherlands,
Nicaragua, Panama, Persia, Salvador,
Switzerland, and Venezuela. *Treaties for
the Advancement of Peace Between the
United States and Other Powers
Negotiated by the Honorable William J.
Bryan, Secretary of State of the United
States, with an Introduction by James
Brown Scott* (New York: Oxford
University Press, 1920).

258 "We have no selfish ends": Woodrow
Wilson, Message to Congress, April 2,
1917, in *U.S. Presidents and Foreign
Policy from 1789 to the Present,* ed.
Carl C. Hodge and Cathal J. Nolan
(Santa Barbara, Calif.: ABC-CLIO,
2007), 396.

258 "These are American principles":
"Peace Without Victory," January 22,
1917, in supplement to *American Journal
of International Law* 11 (1917): 323.

259 "Self-governed nations do not":
Wilson, Message to Congress, April 2,
1917, in *President Wilson's Great
Speeches, and Other History Making
Documents* (Chicago: Stanton and Van
Vliet, 1917), 17–18.

259 "The worst that can happen":
Woodrow Wilson, Fifth Annual
Message, December 4, 1917, in *United
States Congressional Serial Set* 7443
(Washington, D.C.: Government
Printing Office, 1917), 41.

260 "the destruction of every arbitrary
power": Woodrow Wilson, "An
Address at Mount Vernon," July 4,
1918, in Link, *Papers,* 48:516.

260 "no autocratic government could be
trusted": Wilson, Message to Congress,
April 2, 1917, *President Wilson's Great
Speeches,* 18.

260 "that autocracy must first be shown":
Wilson, Fifth Annual Message,
December 4, 1917, in *The Foreign Policy
of President Woodrow Wilson: Messages,
Addresses and Papers,* ed. James Brown
Scott (New York: Oxford University
Press, 1918), 306.

260 "dare . . . attempting any such
covenants": Ibid. See also Berg, *Wilson,*
472–73.

260 "an age . . . which rejects": Woodrow
Wilson, Remarks at Suresnes Cemetery
on Memorial Day, May 30, 1919, in
Link, *Papers,* 59:608–9.

262 "a number of small states": Lloyd
George, Wilson memorandum, March
25, 1919, in Ray Stannard Baker, ed.,
Woodrow Wilson and World Settlement
(New York: Doubleday, Page, 1922),
2:450. For a conference participant's
account of the sometimes less than
idealistic process by which the new
national borders were drawn, see
Harold Nicolson, *Peacemaking, 1919*
(1933; London: Faber & Faber, 2009).
For a contemporary analysis, see
Margaret MacMillan, *Paris 1919: Six
Months That Changed the World* (New
York: Random House, 2002).

262 "not a balance of power, but a
community of power": Address,
January 22, 1917, in Link, *Papers,*
40:536–37.

263 All states, in the League of Nations
concept: Wilson, Message to Congress,
April 2, 1917, *President Wilson's Great
Speeches,* 18.

263 "open covenants of peace": Wilson,
Address to a Joint Session of Congress

on the Conditions of Peace (January 8, 1918) ("Fourteen Points"), in *President Wilson's Great Speeches*, 18. See also Berg, *Wilson*, 469–72.

264 **Rather than inspire:** The United Nations has provided useful mechanisms for peacekeeping operations—generally when the major powers have already agreed on the need to monitor an agreement between them in regions where their own forces are not directly involved. The UN—much more than the League—has performed important functions: as a forum for otherwise difficult diplomatic encounters; several peacekeeping functions of consequence; and a host of humanitarian initiatives. What these international institutions have failed to do—and were incapable of accomplishing—was to sit in judgment of what specific acts constituted aggression or prescribe the means to resist when the major powers disagreed.

265 **They submitted an analysis:** "Differences Between the North Atlantic Treaty and Traditional Military Alliances," appendix to the testimony of Ambassador Warren Austin, April 28, 1949, in U.S. Senate, Committee on Foreign Relations, *The North Atlantic Treaty*, hearings, 81st Cong., 1st sess. (Washington, D.C.: Government Printing Office, 1949), pt. I.

265 **"I am for such a League provided":** Roosevelt to James Bryce, November 19, 1918, in *The Letters of Theodore Roosevelt*, ed. Elting E. Morrison (Cambridge, Mass.: Harvard University Press, 1954), 8:1400.

266 **what if an aggressor:** Seeking to crush resistance to Italy's colonial expansion, Mussolini ordered Italian troops to invade what is today's Ethiopia in 1935. Despite international condemnation, the League of Nations took no collective security counteractions. Using indiscriminate bombing and poison gas, Italy took occupation of Abyssinia. The nascent international community's failure to act, coming after a similar failure to confront imperial Japan's

invasion of China's Manchuria, led to the collapse of the League of Nations.

268 **"an instrument of national policy":** Treaty between the United States and other powers providing for the renunciation of war as an instrument of national policy. Signed at Paris, August 27, 1928; ratification advised by the Senate, January 16, 1929; ratified by the President, January 17, 1929; instruments of ratification deposited at Washington by the United States of America, Australia, Dominion of Canada, Czechoslovakia, Germany, Great Britain, India, Irish Free State, Italy, New Zealand, and Union of South Africa, March 2, 1929; by Poland, March 26, 1929; by Belgium, March 27, 1929; by France, April 22, 1929; by Japan, July 24, 1929; proclaimed, July 24, 1929.

270 **Not all of this—especially the point on decolonization:** See Peter Clarke, *The Last Thousand Days of the British Empire: Churchill, Roosevelt, and the Birth of the Pax Americana* (New York: Bloomsbury Press, 2009).

270 **"The kind of world order":** Radio Address at Dinner of Foreign Policy Association, New York, October 21, 1944, in *Presidential Profiles: The FDR Years*, ed. William D. Peterson (New York: Facts on File, 2006), 429.

270 **"We have learned the simple truth":** Fourth Inaugural Address, January 20, 1945, in *My Fellow Americans: Presidential Inaugural Addresses from George Washington to Barack Obama* (St. Petersburg, Fla.: Red and Black Publishers, 2009).

271 **"Bill, I don't dispute your facts":** William C. Bullitt, "How We Won the War and Lost the Peace," *Life,* August 30, 1948, as quoted in Arnold Beichman, "Roosevelt's Failure at Yalta," *Humanitas* 16, no. 1 (2003): 104.

271 **During the first encounter of the two leaders:** On Roosevelt's arrival in Tehran, Stalin claimed that Soviet intelligence had identified a Nazi plot, Operation Long Jump, to assassinate Churchill, Roosevelt, and Stalin together at the summit. Members of the

American delegation harbored serious doubts about the Soviet report. Keith Eubank, *Summit at Teheran: The Untold Story* (New York: William Morrow, 1985), 188–96.

273 **"They talk about pacifism":** As quoted in T. A. Taracouzio, *War and Peace in Soviet Diplomacy* (New York: Macmillan, 1940), 139–40.

274 **"He [Roosevelt] felt that Stalin":** Charles Bohlen, *Witness to History, 1929–1969* (New York: W. W. Norton, 1973), 211. See also Beichman, "Roosevelt's Failure at Yalta," 210–11.

274 **Another view holds that Roosevelt:** Conrad Black, *Franklin Delano Roosevelt: Champion of Freedom* (New York: PublicAffairs, 2003). Roosevelt was enough of a sphinx to prevent an unambiguous answer, though I lean toward the Black interpretation. Winston Churchill is easier to sum up. During the war, he mused that all would be well if he could have a weekly dinner at the Kremlin. As the end of the war was approaching, he ordered his chief of staff to prepare for war with the Soviet Union.

Chapter 8: The United States

276 **All twelve postwar presidents:** As Truman, the first postwar President, explained it, "The foreign policy of the United States is based firmly on fundamental principles of righteousness and justice" and "our efforts to bring the Golden Rule into the international affairs of this world." Eisenhower, tough soldier that he was, as President described the objective in almost identical terms: "We seek peace . . . rooted in the lives of nations. There must be justice, sensed and shared by all peoples . . . There must be law, steadily invoked and respected by all nations." Thus, as Gerald Ford stated in a 1974 joint session of Congress, "Successful foreign policy is an extension of the hopes of the whole American people for a world of peace and orderly reform and orderly

freedom." Harry S. Truman, Address on Foreign Policy at the Navy Day Celebration in New York City, October 27, 1945; Dwight D. Eisenhower, Second Inaugural Address ("The Price of Peace"), January 21, 1957, in *Public Papers of the Presidents: Dwight D. Eisenhower, 1957–1961,* 62–63. Gerald Ford, Address to a Joint Session of Congress, August 12, 1974, in *Public Papers of the Presidents: Gerald R. Ford (1974–1977),* 6.

277 **"Any man and any nation":** Lyndon B. Johnson, Address to the United Nations General Assembly, December 17, 1963.

277 **a new international order:** For an eloquent exposition, see Robert Kagan, *The World America Made* (New York: Alfred A. Knopf, 2012).

281 **"Whoever occupies a territory also imposes":** Milovan Djilas, *Conversations with Stalin,* trans. Michael B. Petrovich (New York: Harcourt Brace & Company, 1962), 114.

284 **"A basic conflict is thus arising":** Kennan to Charles Bohlen, January 26, 1945, as quoted in John Lewis Gaddis, *George Kennan: An American Life* (New York: Penguin Books, 2011), 188.

284 **"foreign policy of that kind":** Bohlen, *Witness to History,* 176.

284 **without requiring ambassadorial approval:** The American Embassy was then, briefly, without an ambassador: W. Averell Harriman had left the post while Walter Bedell Smith had yet to arrive.

285 **"contained by the adroit and vigilant application":** "X" [George F. Kennan], "The Sources of Soviet Conduct," *Foreign Affairs* 25, no. 4 (July 1947).

285 **"the unity and efficacy of the Party":** Ibid.

286 **"The question is asked":** Robert Rhodes James, ed., *Winston S. Churchill: His Complete Speeches, 1897–1963* (New York: Chelsea House, 1974), 7:7710.

287 **"freedom under a government of laws":** A Report to the National Security Council by the Executive

Secretary on United States Objectives and Programs for National Security, NSC-68 (April 14, 1950), 7.

288 **"difficult for many to understand":** John Foster Dulles, "Foundations of Peace" (address to the Veterans of Foreign Wars, New York, August 18, 1958).

290 **Should the victorious army cross:** George H. W. Bush faced a similar issue after Saddam Hussein's forces had been expelled from Kuwait in 1991.

291 **"If the American imperialists are victorious":** Shen Zhihua, *Mao, Stalin, and the Korean War: Trilateral Communist Relations in the 1950s,* trans. Neil Silver (London: Routledge, 2012), 140.

292 **"indeed the focus of the struggles in the world":** Chen Jian, *China's Road to the Korean War: The Making of the Sino-American Confrontation* (New York: Columbia University Press, 1994), 149–50. On the Chinese leadership's analysis of the war and its regional implications, see also Sergei N. Goncharov, John W. Lewis, and Xue Litai, *Uncertain Partners: Stalin, Mao, and the Korean War* (Stanford, Calif.: Stanford University Press, 1993); Henry Kissinger, *On China* (New York: Penguin Press, 2011), chap. 5; Shen, *Mao, Stalin, and the Korean War;* and Shu Guang Zhang, *Mao's Military Romanticism: China and the Korean War, 1950–1953* (Lawrence: University Press of Kansas, 1995).

292 **Considerations such as these induced Mao:** See Chapter 5.

293 **"the wrong war, at the wrong place":** General Omar N. Bradley, Chairman of the Joint Chiefs of Staff, testimony before the Senate Committees on Armed Services and Foreign Relations, May 15, 1951, in *Military Situation in the Far East,* hearings, 82nd Cong., 1st sess., pt. 2, 732 (1951).

298 **Charges of immorality:** See Peter Braestrup, *Big Story: How the American Press and Television Reported and Interpreted the Crisis of Tet 1968 in Vietnam and Washington* (Boulder, Colo.: Westview Press, 1977); Robert Elegant, "How to Lose a War: The Press and Viet Nam," *Encounter* (London), August 1981, 73–90; Guenter Lewy, *America in Vietnam* (New York: Oxford University Press, 1978), 272–79, 311–24.

303 **"We must remember the only time":** "An Interview with the President: The Jury Is Out," *Time,* January 3, 1972.

304 **"prepared to establish a dialogue with Peking":** Richard Nixon, *U.S. Foreign Policy for the 1970's: Building for Peace: A Report to the Congress, by Richard Nixon, President of the United States,* February 25, 1971, 107. To this point, American government documents had referred to "Communist China" or had spoken generally of authorities in Beijing or (the Nationalist name for the city) Beiping.

304 **"any sense of satisfaction":** Richard Nixon, Remarks to Midwestern News Media Executives Attending a Briefing on Domestic Policy in Kansas City, Missouri, July 6, 1971, in *Public Papers of the Presidents,* 805–6.

305 **These phrases, commonplace today:** See Kissinger, *On China,* chap. 9.

305 **"only if we act greatly":** Richard Nixon, Second Inaugural Address, January 20, 1973, in *My Fellow Americans,* 333.

305 **"our instinct that we knew what was best for others":** Richard Nixon, *U.S. Foreign Policy for the 1970's: Building for Peace,* 10.

306 **"The second element of a durable peace":** Richard Nixon, *U.S. Foreign Policy for the 1970's: A New Strategy for Peace,* February 18, 1970, 9.

306 **"All nations, adversaries and friends":** Richard Nixon, *U.S. Foreign Policy for the 1970's: Shaping a Durable Peace,* May 3, 1973, 232–33.

311 **"I've spoken of the shining city":** Ronald Reagan, Farewell Address to the American People, January 11, 1989, in *In the Words of Ronald Reagan: The*

Wit, Wisdom, and Eternal Optimism of America's 40th President, ed. Michael Reagan (Nashville: Thomas Nelson, 2004), 34.

312 **"I have a gut feeling I'd like to talk":** Ronald Reagan, *An American Life* (New York: Simon & Schuster, 1990), 592.

312 **"the helicopter would descend":** Lou Cannon, *President Reagan: The Role of a Lifetime* (New York: Simon & Schuster, 1990), 792.

312 **"governments which rest upon the consent":** Ronald Reagan, Address Before a Joint Session of Congress on the State of the Union, January 25, 1984, in *The Public Papers of President Ronald W. Reagan*, Ronald Reagan Presidential Library.

315 **"commonwealth of freedom":** George H. W. Bush, Remarks to the Federal Assembly in Prague, Czechoslovakia, November 17, 1990, accessed online at Gerhard Peters and John T. Woolley, eds., *The American Presidency Project*.

315 **"great and growing strength":** Ibid.

316 **"beyond containment and to a policy":** George H. W. Bush, Remarks at Maxwell Air Force Base War College, Montgomery, Alabama, April 13, 1991, in Michael D. Gambone, *Small Wars: Low-Intensity Threats and the American Response Since Vietnam* (Knoxville: University of Tennessee Press, 2012), 121.

316 **"enlargement":** "Confronting the Challenges of a Broader World," President Clinton Address to the UN General Assembly, New York City, September 27, 1993, in *Department of State Dispatch* 4, no. 39 (September 27, 1993).

316 **"a world of thriving democracies":** Ibid.

318 **"Deliver to United States authorities":** George W. Bush, Presidential Address to a Joint Session of Congress, September 20, 2001, in *We Will Prevail: President George W. Bush on War, Terrorism, and Freedom* (New York: Continuum, 2003), 13.

318 **"These carefully targeted actions":** George W. Bush, Presidential Address

to the Nation, October 7, 2001, in ibid., 33.

318 **"the establishment of a broad-based":** "Agreement on Provisional Arrangements in Afghanistan Pending the Re-establishment of Permanent Government Institutions," December 5, 2001, UN Peacemaker online archive.

318 **"to support the Afghan Transitional Authority":** UN Security Council Resolution 1510 (October 2003).

319 **No institutions in the history:** Surely it was telling that even while calling for gender sensitivity in the new regime, the drafters at Bonn felt obliged to praise the "Afghan mujahidin . . . heroes of jihad."

319 **"Except at harvest-time":** Winston Churchill, *My Early Life* (New York: Charles Scribner's Sons, 1930), 134.

322 **Belgian neutrality:** See Chapter 2.

322 **"on the same side—united by common dangers":** *The National Security Strategy of the United States of America* (2002).

322 **"Iraqi democracy will succeed":** George W. Bush, Remarks by the President at the 20th Anniversary of the National Endowment for Democracy, United States Chamber of Commerce, Washington, D.C. (November 6, 2003).

323 **UN Security Council Resolution 687 of 1991:** UN Security Council Resolution 687 of 1991 made the end of hostilities in the first Gulf War conditional on the immediate destruction by Iraq of its stock of weapons of mass destruction and a commitment never to develop such weapons again. Iraq did not comply with Resolution 687. As early as August 1991, the Security Council declared Iraq in "material breach" of its obligations. In the years following the Gulf War, ten more Security Council resolutions would attempt to bring Iraq into compliance with the cease-fire terms. The Security Council found in later resolutions that Saddam Hussein "ultimately ceased all cooperation with UNSCOM [the UN Special Commission charged with weapons

inspections] and the IAEA [International Atomic Energy Agency] in 1998," expelling the UN inspectors the cease-fire had obliged him to accept.

In November 2002, the Security Council passed Resolution 1441, "deploring" Iraq's decade of noncompliance, deciding that "Iraq has been and remains in material breach of its obligations under relevant resolutions." Chief inspector Hans Blix, not an advocate for war, reported to the Security Council in January 2003 that Baghdad had failed to resolve outstanding questions and inconsistencies.

The world will long debate the implications of this military action and the strategy pursued in the subsequent effort to bring about democratic governance in Iraq. Yet this debate, and its implications for future violations of international nonproliferation principles, will remain distorted so long as the multilateral background is omitted.

324 **"The United States wants Iraq":** William J. Clinton, Statement on Signing the Iraq Liberation Act of 1998, October 31, 1998.

324 **"a forward strategy of freedom":** Remarks by the President at the 20th Anniversary of the National Endowment for Democracy, Washington, D.C., November 6, 2003.

326 **"this war is lost and the surge":** Peter Baker, *Days of Fire: Bush and Cheney in the White House* (New York: Doubleday, 2013), 542.

326 **"If we're not there to win":** Ibid., 523.

329 **"Americans, being a moral people":** George Shultz, "Power and Diplomacy in the 1980s," Washington, D.C., April 3, 1984, *Department of State Bulletin*, vol. 84, no. 2086 (May 1984), 13.

Chapter 9: Technology, Equilibrium, and Human Consciousness

332 **Strategic stability was defined:** For a review of these theoretical explorations, see Michael Gerson, "The Origins of

Strategic Stability: The United States and the Threat of Surprise Attack," in *Strategic Stability: Contending Interpretations,* ed. Elbridge Colby and Michael Gerson (Carlisle, Pa: Strategic Studies Institute and U.S. Army War College Press, 2013); Michael Quinlan, *Thinking About Nuclear Weapons: Principles, Problems, Prospects* (Oxford: Oxford University Press, 2009).

333 **When, in the 1950s, Mao spoke:** See Chapter 6.

334 **But neither side:** Much has since been written about the U.S. "nuclear alert" during the 1973 Middle East crisis. In fact, its principal purpose was to alert conventional forces—the Sixth Fleet and an airborne division—to deter a Brezhnev threat in a letter to Nixon that he might send Soviet divisions to the Middle East. The increase in the readiness of strategic forces was marginal and probably not noticed in Moscow.

342 **Reflecting in the 1960s:** C. A. Mack, "Fifty Years of Moore's Law," *IEEE Transactions on Semiconductor Manufacturing* 24, no. 2 (May 2011): 202–7.

342 **The revolution in computing:** For mostly optimistic reviews of these developments, see Rick Smolan and Jennifer Erwitt, eds., *The Human Face of Big Data* (Sausalito, Calif.: Against All Odds, 2013); and Eric Schmidt and Jared Cohen, *The New Digital Age: Reshaping the Future of People, Nations and Business* (New York: Alfred A. Knopf, 2013). For more critical perspectives, see Jaron Lanier, *Who Owns the Future?* (New York: Simon & Schuster, 2013); Evgeny Morozov, *The Net Delusion: The Dark Side of Internet Freedom* (New York: PublicAffairs, 2011); and *To Save Everything, Click Here: The Folly of Technological Solutionism* (New York: PublicAffairs, 2013).

342 **Cyberspace—a word coined:** Norbert Wiener introduced the term "cyber" in his 1948 book, *Cybernetics,* though in reference to human beings rather than computers as nodes of communication.

The word "cyberspace" in something approaching its current usage came about in the work of several science fiction authors in the 1980s.

342 **As tasks that were primarily manual:** Viktor Mayer-Schönberger and Kenneth Cukier, *Big Data: A Revolution That Will Transform How We Live, Work, and Think* (Boston: Houghton Mifflin Harcourt, 2013), 73–97.

343 **"smart door locks, toothbrushes":** Don Clark, "'Internet of Things' in Reach," *Wall Street Journal,* January 5, 2014.

343 **(and currently an estimated one billion people do):** Smolan and Erwitt, *Human Face of Big Data,* 135.

345 **The complexity is compounded:** See David C. Gompert and Phillip Saunders, *The Paradox of Power: Sino-American Strategic Relations in an Age of Vulnerability* (Washington, D.C.: National Defense University, 2011).

345 **Stuxnet:** Ralph Langer, "Stuxnet: Dissecting a Cyberwarfare Weapon," *IEEE Security and Privacy* 9, no. 3 (2011): 49–52.

346 **"the next war will begin":** Rex Hughes, quoting General Keith Alexander, in "A Treaty for Cyberspace," *International Affairs* 86, no. 2 (2010): 523–41.

348 **"sown in the nature of man":** Publius [James Madison], *The Federalist* 10, in Hamilton, Madison, and Jay, *Federalist Papers,* 46–47.

348 **Recent studies suggest:** See "Digital Set to Surpass TV in Time Spent with US Media: Mobile Helps Propel Digital Time Spent," eMarketer.com, August 1, 2013 (reporting that the average American adult spends "5 hours per day online, on nonvoice mobile activities or with other digital media" and 4.5 hours per day watching television); Brian Stelter, "8 Hours a Day Spent on Screens, Study Finds," *New York Times,* March 26, 2009 (reporting that "adults are exposed to screens . . . for about 8.5 hours on any given day").

350 **"Where is the Life":** T. S. Eliot, *Collected Poems, 1909–1962* (Boston: Harcourt Brace Jovanovich, 1991), 147.

351 **"People forget items they think":** Betsy Sparrow, Jenny Liu, and Daniel M. Wegner, "Google Effects on Memory: Cognitive Consequences of Having Information at Our Fingertips," *Science* 333, no. 6043 (2011): 776–78.

351 **Information at one's fingertips:** See Nicholas Carr, *The Shallows: What the Internet Is Doing to Our Brains* (New York: W. W. Norton, 2010).

352 **"to consume more content":** Erik Brynjolfsson and Michael D. Smith, "The Great Equalizer? Consumer Choice Behavior at Internet Shopbots" (Cambridge, Mass.: MIT Sloan School of Management, 2001).

352 **"which you would like":** Neal Leavitt, "Recommendation Technology: Will It Boost E-commerce?," *Computer* 39, no. 5 (2006): 13–16.

354 **They look forward:** See Clive Thompson, *Smarter Than You Think: How Technology Is Changing Our Minds for the Better* (New York: Penguin Press, 2013).

354 **"people who try to perpetuate myths":** Schmidt and Cohen, *New Digital Age,* 35, 198–99.

355 **Yet they also bring conflicting:** See, for example, Ofeibea Quist-Arcton, "Text Messages Used to Incite Violence in Kenya," National Public Radio, February 20, 2008, and "When SMS Messages Incite Violence in Kenya," *Harvard Law School Internet & Democracy Blog,* February 21, 2008. For a discussion of this and other examples, see Morozov, *Net Delusion,* 256–61.

356 **anticipating their thoughts:** That is, the burgeoning field of "predictive analytics," with uses expanding in both commercial and governmental spheres to anticipate thoughts and actions at both the societal and the individual level. See Eric Siegel, *Predictive Analytics: The Power to Predict Who Will Click, Buy, Lie, or Die* (Hoboken, N.J.: John Wiley & Sons, 2013).

356 **In this respect, among the new technology's:** For an exploration of this concept, particularly as applied to the

commercial realm, see Lanier, *Who Owns the Future?*

356 **The West lauded the "Facebook":** See Chapter 3.

356 **"The Internet has made tracking":** Mayer-Schönberger and Cukier, *Big Data,* 150.

358 **"People will not look forward":** Edmund Burke, *Reflections on the Revolution in France* (1790; Indianapolis: Hackett, 1987), 29.

Conclusion: World Order in Our Time?

364 **In the world of geopolitics:** For a compelling exploration of this shift and its possible implications, see Charles Kupchan, *No One's World: The West, the Rising Rest, and the Coming Global Turn* (New York: Oxford University Press, 2012).

365 **More elemental forms of identity:** The seminal work about prospects for a world ordered on such a basis is Samuel Huntington, *The Clash of Civilizations and the Remaking of World Order* (New York: Simon & Schuster, 1996).

371 **particular domestic structures:** On the evolution and appeal of different models, see John Micklethwait and Adrian Wooldridge, *The Fourth Revolution: The Global Race to Reinvent the State* (New York: Penguin Press, 2014).

372 **"to acquiesce in some qualified plan":** Edmund Burke to Charles-Jean-François Depont, November 1789, in *On Empire, Liberty, and Reform,* 412–13.

374 **Cryptic fragments from remote antiquity:** G. S. Kirk and J. E. Raven, *The Presocratic Philosophers: A Critical History with a Selection of Texts* (Cambridge, U.K.: Cambridge University Press, 1957), 193, 195, 199 (on Heraclitus); Friedrich Nietzsche, *The Pre-Platonic Philosophers,* trans. with commentary by Greg Whitlock (Urbana: University of Illinois Press, 2001).

374 **"The Meaning of History":** Henry A. Kissinger, "The Meaning of History: Reflections on Spengler, Toynbee and Kant" (undergraduate thesis, Department of Government, Harvard University, 1950).

Index

Page numbers in *italics* refer to maps.